AUTHOR	CLASS
ANDERSON, B.W.	553·8
TITLE Gemstones for everyman.	**No.** 440275032

GEMSTONES FOR EVERYMAN

by the same author

GEM TESTING

*(8th revised edition
published in 1971
by Butterworth and Co.)*

GEMSTONES FOR EVERYMAN

by

B. W. ANDERSON

FABER AND FABER
3 Queen Square
London

First published in 1976
by Faber and Faber Limited
3 Queen Square London WC1
Printed in Great Britain by
W. & J. Mackay Limited, Chatham
All rights reserved

ISBN 0 571 10527 0

To BARBARA,
to whom this book owes so much

CONTENTS

9

CONTENTS

ILLUSTRATIONS

———— ◁▷ ————

FIGURES

ACKNOWLEDGEMENTS

———— ◊ ————

IT HAS BEEN my endeavour in choosing or commissioning the illustrations for this book to ensure that each one should throw light on some part of the text and bring it to life for the reader. In order to provide more detailed information than is possible in the conventional caption, a numbered 'key' to the coloured illustrations of stones from the Museum of the Institute of Geological Sciences has been given, and extended notes added to the short titles of the black and white plates.

I have to thank the several friends who have so willingly helped me in this difficult and important matter. Firstly, I should like to record my sincere appreciation of the advice, care and skill put at my disposal by Mr. E. A. Jobbins and his colleague Mr. J. Martin Pulsford, of the Institute of Geological Sciences in South Kensington, who were responsible for the preparation of the superb colour transparencies from which the plates C to N were prepared. I have also to thank the Director of the Institute for permitting the use of fine specimens from their Museum, and for granting copyright facilities.

For the picture of Ceylon gem gravel I have to thank my old friend Mr. R. K. Mitchell, and also Mr. C. R. Mathews who provided the sample. The photograph showing ruby boules in process of growth was kindly loaned by the firm of Djevahirdjian which manufactures synthetic corundum on a vast scale in Monthey, Switzerland.

As for the black and white illustrations, the twelve plates dealing with different aspects of diamond were made available through the kind offices of the giant De Beers organisation. The crystals shown in plates 9, 12, 13a, 13b and 14 are from the Mineral Gallery of the

British Museum (Natural History) in South Kensington—a collection which is reputed to be the finest in the world. The photographs were prepared and made available through the kindness of my friend Sir Frank Claringbull, former Keeper of Minerals and now Director of the Museum, to whom I am very grateful.

The photographs of the zoisite mine and the crystals therefrom were kindly sent to me by Mr. Rudolf Thurm.

Finally, I should put on record that all the diagrams in the book were drawn, with professional skill, by the Rev. John F. Mosey, who, fortunately for me, lives in the nearby town of Barnstaple.

——————— ⟨◊⟩ ———————

CHAPTER ONE

WHAT EXACTLY *IS* A GEMSTONE?

THE WORLD IS full of a vast variety of beautiful things, but most of them are ephemeral. The dewdrop and the daffodil, the rainbow and butterfly, last for a few moments or a few days and are gone; preserved only in memory or in lines written by a great poet. Precious stones, more than any other things which are lovely to the eye, endure, in terms of human measurement, eternally.

This is a book about precious stones, written by one who loves them, not only for their appearance but for their wonderful properties, and who has studied them in depth for nearly half a century. It is written for all those who are attracted by the beauty of gems and would like to know more about them rather than for those whose interest is purely commercial or professional. It is a personal and unconventional book, written as far as possible from the author's own experience, which should make it authentic and (I sincerely hope) easy to read.

Although it assumes no previous knowledge of the subject and starts from the very beginning, there will be found, during the course of the book, a great deal of information not generally available in a popular text, which may make it worth reading by those who consider themselves to be quite knowledgeable in this field.

Anyone writing a book about birds, butterflies or flowers is not expected to begin by explaining what it is that he is talking about. But in attempting a book about gemstones for the general reader one starts with the uneasy suspicion that the majority of people, even tolerably well-educated people, have only the vaguest conception of what a gemstone really is. So, at the risk of boring the better informed, I am going to begin this book by getting the fundamentals straight before proceeding to the more entertaining aspects of the subject. Gemstones can fairly easily be defined as those varieties of minerals which are sufficiently attractive (or which can be made sufficiently attractive by cutting and polishing) to be used for human adornment. But this definition assumes that the reader understands what is meant by the word 'mineral'. I can remember my mother, who inherited a keen interest in minerals from her father, telling me of her bitter disappointment as a child when, following a sign marked MINERALS, she was offered the choice of ginger beer or fizzy lemonade!

In explaining the word 'mineral' as used in this book I think it best to start with something that most people have often seen, or can, if they are city workers, see almost daily as the material of a kerbstone, tombstone, bridge or public building—I refer to the rock we call *granite*.

Granite is one of the fundamental materials of the earth's rocky crust, and was formed by the slow crystallisation of the molten magma which contained most of the raw materials for the building of our globe. What magma looks like can be seen by careful approach to any active volcano, or more comfortably and safely, from a film of volcanic activity in the cinema or on television. It pours out from the throat of the volcano as a red- or white-hot fluid stream, the exterior of which quickly cools and darkens, and descends at a steady rate (being tolerably viscous) down the sides of the mountain, sometimes with tragic destruction of local fields and villages.

The molten fluid cools quickly to form a black glassy rock such as obsidian, or a grey mass full of vesicles (a sort of solidified froth) known as pumice. Under such conditions cooling was too rapid for individual crystals to form, but where a great mass of magma has cooled very slowly under pressure below the already solid surface of the earth, a number of compounds began to crystallise out in accordance with their stability and their melting-points, at long intervals of time, until the whole mass was solidified.

The solid mass as a whole we know as a *rock*: the individual crystals are the *minerals* that go to form that rock. To take a homely analogy, if one takes a fruit cake to represent a rock, then the individual constituents, such as the sultanas or peel, would represent the 'minerals' of which the rock was made. A mineral is homogeneous, has a definite crystal form, definite chemical composition, and properties which are constant within narrow limits, while a rock, as a rule, consists of an aggregate of individual minerals.

To many, the term 'crystallising out' may be a stumbling block to understanding; but this is easily remedied by dissolving a spoonful of table salt or of alum in hot water and allowing a drop of the solution to evaporate on a glass slide. In each case the solid will 'crystallise out' and a magnifying glass will reveal the salt crystals as little cubes and the alum in the form of tiny octahedral pyramids.

In the case of our starting-point, granite, quite casual inspection (especially of a polished surface) reveals the presence of large, more or less rectangular pieces, which may be off-white or reddish-brown, according to locality, as a main constituent. These crystals are forms of the mineral *feldspar*, which crystallise early and thus have time to grow and assume their own individual crystal shapes without interference. On average, the feldspar crystals constitute about two-thirds of the rock: they are silicates of aluminium and potash. The remainder of the rock consists chiefly of translucent, nearly white quartz grains, together with dark grains of minerals containing iron, of which the glistening flakes of mica are most easily recognised. These can be dug out with the point of a penknife and will be found to separate into thin leaflets—a property particularly characteristic of this mineral.

The colour and texture of granite from different localities vary quite widely—the chief differences being in the colour and size of the feldspar crystals. The choice of granite as a material for building rests upon its hardness, its resistance to weathering, and its availability. Its usefulness as a building-stone for this book depends also upon several factors. In the first place, it is almost universally known and recognised: secondly, it can quite clearly be seen to consist of two or more different kinds of materials which, as explained above, we know as minerals, and thirdly, the two main constituents, quartz and feldspar, are, in certain of their varieties, quite important as gem materials.

This may well astonish an innocent reader, but it serves to illustrate another important point about gemstones—that the minerals of which they are specially favoured varieties are often of quite common occurrence. Ruby and sapphire, for instance—two of the most justly prized and rarest of precious stones—are both transparent and superbly coloured varieties of *corundum*, the aluminium oxide mineral of which common emery is an impure example.

Of the two main granite minerals, quartz, though extremely common in nature, is hard enough and beautiful enough in many of its forms to be a very popular gemstone. The magnificent violet or purple amethyst, the fine clear yellow citrine, the cloudy pink rose quartz, and the limpid purity of rock crystal all have their place in jewellery, while agate, chrysoprase, bloodstone and onyx all consist of tiny quartz grains or fibres differently arranged or coloured to give each its special attraction.

The feldspar gems are not quite so highly valued or popular, but the bluish or silvery sheen of moonstone, and the turquoise tint of amazon stone, are undoubtedly very pleasing to the eye, while the rainbow tints reflected from labradorite feldspar make it a most handsome decorative material.

It is true that fine gemstones, even of these two species, are never extracted from granite itself. But much more coarsely crystallised veins of *pegmatite*, in which water vapour and other gases were present which were particularly favourable to the growth of large, clear mineral specimens, are often associated with granite, and from these, or from gravels derived from these, come fine specimens of a whole range of gem materials, including beryl, tourmaline, topaz and kunzite, which grace our museums and provide important material for the lapidary.

CHAPTER TWO

—— ◊ ——

NAMES AND RELATIONSHIPS

IN FORMER TIMES, the name given to a precious stone was based almost solely on its colour and appearance: thus the term 'diamond' could be used (though usually with some geographical prefix) for transparent crystals of quartz—'topaz' for any yellow gemstone, and so on. It was not until the beginnings of systematic mineralogy started to emerge at the end of the eighteenth and early in the nineteenth centuries that it became obvious that stones of very different appearance could be fundamentally the same, while conversely, stones which resembled each other very closely could be entirely different in every other particular.

It is very important to realise that each mineral species has a composition, crystal structure, hardness, density and optical properties which in pure specimens vary only within narrow limits and which are unique for that mineral. Thus by 'fundamentally the same' I mean 'belonging to the same mineral species'.

The difference in appearance in varieties of the same mineral is often merely a matter of colour, which may have a very important influence on its value as a gemstone, but in fact depends on the presence or absence of small and inessential traces of certain elements such as chromium or iron—a matter we must go into more deeply later in the book. Perhaps the most striking examples of this are ruby and sapphire, which I referred to in Chapter 1. Or, it may be a matter of texture as well as colour which makes the essential sameness of, say, the agate and rock-crystal forms of quartz so hard to believe.

This sort of thing is a great stumbling-block to the layman who appreciates the beauty of precious stones but does not understand their nature. And the best thing to do with a stumbling-block is not to pretend it isn't there, or go a long way round to avoid it, but to find a way to climb over it. If you take the trouble to do that you may find that what seemed a stumbling-block was really a stepping-stone.

While it would be simpler in some ways if special variety names were abolished and were replaced with merely the species name with colour description added—as indeed happens with most of the less important gems—using 'red corundum' and 'blue corundum' in place of ruby and sapphire, we would not only destroy the poetry, romance and sense of history wrapped up in such names, but also fail to provide an adequate description—at least without an intolerable degree of circumlocution. To substitute 'green beryl' for 'emerald' for instance would not be enough to define it, since there are plenty of green beryls which lack the touch of chromium which alone can provide the rare, rich and coveted green of true emerald, which makes it perhaps the most valuable of all precious stones. And to describe agate in any other terms would require a whole sentence. One has to strike some sort of balance between overloading the language with excess baggage in the shape of variety names which are so little known as to be useless as descriptions without having a glossary handy, and, at the other extreme, trying to ban names which are apt and euphonious and therefore popular both with the trade and the public in general. Red spinel and blue spinel, for instance, would probably be more in popular demand had they been provided with attractive special names. Such names as 'rubicelle' and 'balas ruby' which have been used in the past for spinel varieties are obviously *not* acceptable since they are clearly designed to imply an affinity with ruby which doesn't exist.

One of the aims in any modern nomenclature of precious stones is to avoid using any name which has been extensively employed for more than one gem species. The ancient name 'chrysolite' for instance (which simply means 'golden-coloured stone') is certainly attractive to the ear, but has had to be abandoned as it was used as a name for olivine or peridot in America, but in Britain as a variety name for chrysoberyl.

The whole question of the nomenclature of precious stones has been the subject of earnest discussion for many years at an international level and agreement is now virtually complete. The nomenclature recommended by the Gemmological Association of Great Britain in this country is a safe one to follow, and will be found at the end of this book.

The descriptive names given to the colour-varieties of some of the main gem species are given here to help the reader thus early in the book, followed by a list, in alphabetical order, of all the variety names likely to be encountered, giving in each case the mineral group to which they belong. Names which are definitely wrong or misleading are *not* given in this list, as it has been found that their unwanted perpetuity has been largely fostered by their continued appearance in books on precious stones: it is, however, hoped that the Trade Descriptions Act will before long succeed in ousting them altogether.

The CORUNDUM gemstones include *ruby*—red; *sapphire*—blue, and a variety of other colours which are referred to as forms of sapphire thus, white sapphire, pink sapphire, yellow sapphire, green sapphire, violet sapphire. There are also star-rubies and star-sapphires in a domed (*cabochon*) form which show a six-rayed star by reflected light.

The BERYL gemstones include *emerald*—rich grass-green; *aquamarine* —pale blue to bluish-green; *morganite* or pink beryl—pale rose-pink; *heliodor* or golden beryl—yellow. Morganite and heliodor are somewhat unnecessary names and the descriptions pink and yellow or golden beryl are to be preferred.

The QUARTZ gemstones include *rock-crystal*—colourless; *amethyst*— violet or purple; *citrine*—yellow; *cairngorm*—brown; *morion*—smoky; *rose-quartz*—pink, cloudy. These might be described as crystallised quartz varieties. There are also quartz with inclusions which give them special characters such as *quartz cat's-eye*, a pale brown milky type containing parallel asbestos fibres giving a cat's-eye effect when *cabochon*-cut; *tiger's-eye* or *crocidolite*—a handsome fibrous, golden-brown banded quartz which shows a spectacular cat's-eye ray when fashioned *en cabochon* or as beads, and *aventurine quartz*, which is a granular jade-like quartz coloured green by flakes of chrome-rich mica, which give it a spangled effect. There is also an impure massive quartz found in mottled browns and other colours, and well known as a decorative material under the name of *jasper*.

Then come the CHALCEDONY or AGATE group of minerals, which are made up of microscopic needles of quartz and throughout history have been given different names according to their patterning and colours. Here are the main ones: *agate*, concentric or irregular parallel bands of various colours; *moss agate* or *mocha stone*, milky agate showing little banding, but containing mossy or tree-like inclusions; *cornelian*, flesh-red or orange-brown chalcedony with subdued banding. *Sard* is much the same material. Agate with straight bands of red and white is known as *sardonyx*; if the bands are black and white the term *onyx* is used, and *black onyx* is the description for completely black material (which is always due to artificial impregnation with carbon).

The most valued form of this group is the pale green translucent *chrysoprase*, while the list can be ended with the deep green *plasma*, which, when bright red spots of iron oxide are present is known as *heliotrope*, or more commonly, *bloodstone*.

Here then is an alphabetical list of all the variety names of gemstones that the non-specialist needs to know.

Variety Name	Mineral	Description
Agate	Quartz	Cryptocrystalline, banded, various colours
Alexandrite	Chrysoberyl	Green, appearing red in tungsten light, rare
Almandine	Garnet	Commonest purplish-red variety
Amazon Stone	Feldspar	Blue-green opaque variety of microcline
Amethyst	Quartz	Pale violet to deep purple-blue, transparent
Aquamarine	Beryl	Clear pale blue to bluish-green, transparent
Aventurine	Quartz	Spangled with dark green flakes of mica
Blue-john	Fluorspar	Dark to pale purple banded variety, Derbyshire
Bonamite	Smithsonite	Green, jade-like translucent variety
Bowenite	Serpentine	Pale green, translucent, jade-like
Cairngorm	Quartz	Transparent brown; originally local to Scotland
Californite	Idocrase	Massive green, jade-like variety
Cat's-eye	Chrysoberyl	Name reserved for chrysoberyl unless other species stated
Ceylonite	Spinel	Dark blue to black, iron-rich variety

Variety Name	Mineral	Description
Chalcedony	Quartz	General name for cryptocrystalline quartz
Chinese jade	Jadeite	Jade from Upper Burma; see Nephrite
Chrysoprase	Quartz	Pale green translucent chalcedony
Cinnamon stone	Garnet	Orange-brown grossular or hessonite garnet
Cornelian	Quartz	Reddish or orange-brown chalcedony
Crocidolite	Quartz	Fibrous golden-brown quartz
Demantoid	Garnet	Bright green variety of andradite garnet
Dichroite	Iolite	Alternative name for iolite or cordierite
Eilat Stone	Mixture	Mixture of blue and green copper minerals
Emerald	Beryl	Rich grass-green variety; rare and costly
Flèches d'amour	Quartz	Rutilated rock-crystal
Grossular	Garnet	Orange-brown hessonite, or jade-like massive green
Hessonite	Garnet	Calcium aluminium garnet, orange-brown
Hiddenite	Spodumene	Pale green to emerald-green, rare variety
Iceland Spar	Calcite	Clear, optically pure, cleavage pieces
Indicolite	Tourmaline	Dark greenish-blue; term seldom used
Jade	Jadeite/ Nephrite	'Umbrella' term covering two similar minerals
Jargoon	Zircon	Old name for pale forms of zircon
Jasper	Quartz	Impure form of quartz, usually brown
Kauri gum	Natural resin	Fossil resin more recent than real amber
Kunzite	Spodumene	Accepted name for lilac spodumene

Variety Name	Mineral	Description
Labradorite	Feldspar	Usually massive showing iridescence
Marcasite	Pyrite	'Marcasite' in jewellery is usually pyrite
Moonstone	Feldspar	Intergrowth of orthoclase and albite, showing sheen
Morganite	Beryl	Pink beryl (name not often used)
Morion	Quartz	Brown smoky quartz
Moss Agate	Quartz	Off-white chalcedony with fern-like inclusions
Olivine	Peridot	Used by mineralogists for peridot group
Onyx	Quartz	Black, white, or banded black and white chalcedony
Onyx Marble	Calcite	Disputed term for decorative banded marble
Padparadsha	Corundum	Fancy name for pinkish-orange sapphire
Paste	Glass	Jewellers' name for glass imitation gems
Pleonaste	Spinel	Black, iron-rich spinel
Prasiolite	Quartz	Pale green transparent quartz
Pyrope	Garnet	Bright red magnesium garnet, associated with diamond
Rhodolite	Garnet	Rhododendron-coloured almandine-pyrope
Rock-Crystal	Quartz	Pure, colourless quartz used for carvings, etc.
Rose-Quartz	Quartz	Cloudy pink quartz seldom found as crystals
Rubellite	Tourmaline	Pink to red; can resemble ruby
Ruby	Corundum	Blood-red to garnet-red
Sapphire	Corundum	Pale to dark blue
Sard	Quartz	Brownish-red chalcedony
Sardonyx	Quartz	Banded brown and white chalcedony
Saussurite	Zoisite, etc.	Jade-like rock derived from decomposed feldspar

Variety Name	Mineral	Description
Schorl	Tourmaline	Black opaque
Spectrolite	Feldspar	Fancy name for Labradorite found in Finland
Spessartite	Garnet	(More properly Spessartine); orange manganese garnet
Sphalerite	Blende	Alternative species name for zinc blende
Succinite	Amber	Baltic amber (containing succinic acid)
Tanzanite	Zoisite	Name coined by Tiffany for purplish-blue zoisite

CHAPTER THREE

————— ◊ —————

OCCURRENCE AND RECOVERY
OF GEMSTONES

THERE ARE THREE main classes of rocks, known as igneous, metamorphic and sedimentary, names which give a pretty clear clue as to the manner in which they were formed. Igneous rocks form the primary material of the earth's outer crust and consist of minerals which have crystallised out from the molten state, either quickly on the surface, or much more slowly under rocks which have already solidified. As a laboratory experiment will show, rapid crystallisation yields small crystals and slow crystallisation yields large ones. Surface-cooled rocks are either glassy, like obsidian, or very finely-grained. Only the originally deep-seated 'Plutonic' rocks yield crystals large enough to be distinguished by the naked eye and only in the most coarsely crystallised rocks of all, the 'Pegmatites', are large clear individual crystals found which can be used as gems. These represent the last stages of crystallisation round the margins of a block of cooling magma which may be of immense size, and crystallisation has been aided by the presence of mineralising vapours containing water, fluorine, boron compounds, etc. Sedimentary rocks are formed by deposits of sand, grit, clay and so on, derived from older rocks by weathering and the action of streams, which in the course of thousands, or even a million or so years, have become hardened and consolidated. Or they may consist of calcareous material which has been slowly deposited on the beds of large lakes or seas, to form limestone or chalk. Sedimentary rocks contain no primary gem material, except such materials as jet or amber of organic origin. But important gem minerals may form later in crevices of sedimentary rocks—opal and turquoise being good examples.

Metamorphic rocks, as their name suggests, are derived from older igneous or sedimentary rocks which have been altered under the influence of enormous pressures and temperatures below the earth's surface. Some of the most important gem minerals such as corundum and garnet have been formed in this way.

The recovery of gems from such primary sources is seldom a paying proposition. Even if rich veins of crystals can be uncovered, these have to be removed laboriously with hammer and chisel, and the majority of crystals, though forming attractive mineral specimens, are not worth cutting as gems. Fortunately nature has done much of the breaking-down of rocks through the action of weathering whereby the harder minerals (which of course includes the gem minerals) are transported by streams and rivers and eventually form deposits of gravel which in a few favoured localities are rich in gem minerals. The rough treatment the crystals have undergone during their age-long transport from their hillside home to a valley gravel-bed has ensured that all the flawed material has been broken away and pulverised to sand, the softer minerals pulverised to particles of clay and the lighter minerals carried further afield, thus acting as a rough and infinitely slow sorting mechanism.

In the favoured few cases, the ancient streams concerned in depositing the gravel-beds have originated in or cut through rocks in which gem minerals abound. The most famous of such gem-bearing gravels are found in the East, and the adjective 'Oriental' was applied to many gems in earlier days as it added a sort of *cachet* to the goods.

Gems in Ceylon[1]

The famous gem gravels of Ceylon cover a large area of the country, with Ratnapura ('City of Gems') as the centre. The minerals originally derived from very ancient metamorphic and pegmatitic rocks and include an astonishing variety of gems, including ruby, sapphire, zircon, spinel, chrysoberyl, moonstone, tourmaline, topaz, almandine, pyrope, hessonite and spessartite garnets, as well as such rarities as kornerupine, sinhalite, fibrolite and ekanite.

The gem-mining industry in Ceylon goes back through many centuries, some of the earliest foreign merchants visiting the island being the Chinese, to whom it was known as Pa-ou-tchow or 'Isle of Gems'.

[1] The official name for Ceylon is now Sri Lanka, but the older and more familiar title is retained throughout this text.

The actual mining is still carried on in the traditional manner, by peasants and small-time speculators while the profit goes chiefly to those who market the goods.

Pits are sunk (often in the middle of a paddy-field) some ten to twenty feet square, with their sides contained by bamboo poles and canes to prevent their caving in. The overburden is removed in small baskets and the water, which is usually present, in buckets by the operation of a primitive crane which is balanced by stones at the other end to reduce the effort of lifting. When the gem gravel or 'illam' is reached this is raised and washed in shallow conical baskets in a nearby pool or stream. This washing is a skilful manipulation and is carried out (though in slightly different types of container) throughout the world where prospecting in streams whether for gold, diamonds, or other gem minerals is practised.

In Ceylon the meshes of the basket allow the fine silt to filter through, while a swirling motion ensures that the lighter pebbles are ejected from the rim of the water-laden container. Thus the heavy minerals which include the gems are concentrated at the bottom of the basket, which is then inverted with a quick turn of the wrists on to a heap or a large sorting table for subsequent careful visual inspection.

The other really important gem deposit of the East is in Upper Burma and is centred in Mogok, a township situated about 4,000 feet above sea level and lying about ninety miles to the east-north-east of Mandalay. The 'stone tract' covers an area of at least 45 square miles, and the ruby-bearing mines, mostly long disused, cover a far wider area than this. The district is heavily forested and notoriously unhealthy both for Europeans and natives.

As with the Ceylon deposits the history of the ruby mines of Mogok goes back through the centuries to times when the country was part of China. The methods of mining have altered very little and resemble those used in the gem gravels of Ceylon, though for some thirty years after the annexation of Burma by the British in 1886 large-scale production was attempted by the Burma Ruby Mines Company, using heavy machinery and power pumps which first had to be transported along specially built roads for sixty miles through jungle which was fever-ridden and infested with wild beasts. The Company also constructed a 400 kw electric power-station and large washing mills. But the annual rental demanded by the Indian Government and the impossibility of controlling thefts of all the major stones by the native workers resulted in the gradual failure of the Company to operate at a profit—a fate which has been shared by almost all who have attempted to mine gemstones on a large scale by sophisticated methods in the wild and inaccessible regions where they seem always to be located.

The original matrix of the magnificent rubies from Upper Burma is a metamorphic rock; a white recrystallised limestone or marble in which the original clay impurities, rich in alumina, have been crystallised as ruby and as a red spinel somewhat similar in colour and sometimes also in shape. Both ruby and spinel, however, are for the most part recovered from the gem-bearing alluvial gravel (known as 'byon') of the valley floor. In favourable places which have little overburden, small untimbered pits are sunk and the gravel from these raised in baskets and subsequently washed and sorted. Larger pits with timbered sides are sunk to depths of 200 feet or more. Usually in the deeper pits water has to be removed by means of ingenious bamboo pumps and bailing with oildrums or cans.

These pits can only be operated in the dry season. When the rains come the pits are abandoned and work is carried out on hillside deposits which are opened with pick and crowbar and then attacked by jets of water falling from bamboo pipes which wash away the light soil while the heavier portions containing the gems are washed down a series of narrow water courses in which there are holes where the gems are trapped and sorted by hand.

In accordance with tradition the women are allowed freedom of access to the tailings, and succeed in collecting quite a fair haul of small stones which they store first in their mouths and then in little leather bags.

As with the Ceylon deposits, while the corundum gems are the most sought-after of the mineral products, other gem minerals in large variety are found in the neighbourhood. The world's finest peridots come from there, moonstones of rare beauty, chrysoberyls, tourmalines, scapolite cat's-eyes, iolite and even amber of distinctive dark golden-brown colour.

Emeralds in Colombia

Quite another kind of mining is carried out in Colombia where, in the eastern system of the Andes, the world's finest emeralds are found. There are five operating emerald mines in Colombia: Muzo, Chivor, Gachala, Buena Vista and Cosquez. Of these Muzo is the largest, and has the reputation of producing the finest emeralds, but the Chivor mine (previously known as the Somondoco mine, after the nearest town) is the oldest and the one whose chequered history has been most clearly recorded. It is situated some 100 miles to the east of Bogota where all the initial trading is carried out.

In the Inca days, long before the Spanish Conquest, Chivor was worked by the Chibcha Indians and was probably the only source for the fabulously large and beautiful stones plundered by Cortez in his conquest of Mexico, and by Pizarro the *conquistador* of Peru. In 1537 the Spaniards succeeded in finding the Chivor mine, and subsequently worked it by forced labour, whereby 1,200 of the local Indians were caged in the tunnels and made to earn their rations by producing the coveted green crystals.

This inhuman treatment of the natives was later condemned by more enlightened rulers of Spain. The Spanish finally abandoned the mine, which quickly became overgrown with tropical trees and vegetation, the growth of which is phenomenally rapid, aided as it is by a rainfall of over 150 inches a year, and a temperature range of $7°-18°C$.

For two centuries El Chivor was lost to the world, until it was rediscovered by Don Francisco Restrepo, a Colombian mining engineer, after a seemingly hopeless search. Restrepo had as his main clue from an old Spanish report on the mine the fact that the Chivor mine was the only spot in the Andean hills from which the plains of the Orinoco were visible. One day he and his companions stumbled across an old reservoir used by the Spaniards. He thereupon sent a man up a tree, who saw from his look-out post a gap in the range through which the llanos were visible—a supremely romantic moment comparable, one feels, with that depicted by Keats when stout Cortez, with eagle eyes

> ... star'd at the Pacific—and all his men
> Look'd at each other with a wild surmise—
> Silent, upon a peak in Darien.

Since that date the famous mine has had a chequered history, being run by a German syndicate just before the First World War and subsequently by various American companies. One of the American managers, Peter W. Rainier, wrote a highly coloured account of his experiences in his best-selling book *Green Fire* (1943). The romantic story of this famous mine (for which I have chiefly to thank a remarkable article by Paul W. Johnson) has delayed the intended account of the mining methods.

The emeralds are found in veins or occasionally in pockets in thick beds of shale of Cretaceous age which form a sharp ridge running north and south. As already mentioned, the Spaniards used tunnelling methods to win their emeralds, but step-cutting the hillside in a series of terraces has been found to be both cheaper and more efficient, as a tunnel is working 'blind' and may be just missing a valuable pocket of emeralds which, on the open rock-face, must become visible. The terraces are worked from side to side by miners in line using strong hoes and special crowbars wedge-shaped at one end, and pointed at the other. Occasionally mild blasting has to be used to remove an exceptionally hard bed of shale. When there is any sign of emeralds the work is halted and the stones carefully removed with the aid of sheath-knives carried by all the workers, and placed in a leather bag by the inspector.

When a terrace has been completed a flood of water is released from one of a series of strategically placed reservoirs, which has the effect of washing all the loose rocky debris into the valley below. The process is then repeated.

Despite the high price obtainable for the finest-quality crystals, when one realises that the proportion of emeralds to overburden has been estimated to be about one to ninety million, and that less than 1 per cent of the production is of the best cutting quality, it is not so surprising to find that over long periods the mine has actually run at a loss.

Profits might be considerable were it not again for the near impossibility of preventing thefts by the mine workers. Only the finest stones, of course, are stolen by such drastic methods as swallowing them, feeding them to chickens (to be recovered by slaughtering later), and a whole range of other ingenious tricks. Professor Bank records that in the Muzo mine, despite a heavy guard by police and regular thorough searching of everyone who comes and goes, it is reckoned that 30 per cent of the production is illicitly exported.

DIAMONDS

For many centuries the only sources of diamond were alluvial fields in India and Brazil, and here recovery of the stones was by the traditional panning, washing, and hand-picking as carried out in other gem deposits.

With the discovery of the famous diamond 'pipes' in South Africa descending to thousands of feet below the earth's surface, an entirely new kind of mining came into existence developing into a highly complicated engineering operation, which had also to be extremely efficient if the recovery of one part of diamond in some twenty million was to be possible as a paying proposition. The extraction of diamonds is so much a story on its own that I feel it needs to be told in a separate chapter.

CHAPTER FOUR

---◇---

OCCURRENCE AND RECOVERY
OF DIAMONDS

As INDICATED IN the last chapter, for centuries India was the only source of diamonds known to man. The 'mines' were a series of alluvial fields extending from the Pinner river in the Madras Presidency northwards to the friendly-sounding rivers Son and Ken in Bundelkhand. These were usually referred to collectively as the 'Golconda' mines, as the fortress of Golconda served as the market centre for the stones.

From the most famous of the mines, the Kollur mine near the Kistna river came the great Koh-i-Nur diamond which already had a long history before it was cut into a multifaceted irregular form weighing 190 carats. After changing hands several times as conqueror succeeded conqueror it 'came into the possession', as the phrase goes, of the East India Company, who presented it to Queen Victoria in time for it to be shown at the Great Exhibition of 1851, when, it may be remembered, the Crystal Palace was erected in Hyde Park. Shortly afterwards by an incredible act of vandalism it was re-cut in the form of a shallow brilliant losing 90 carats and most of its historic significance. The Koh-i-Nur is now set in the Crown made by Garrard & Co. for the Coronation of Queen Elizabeth the Queen Mother.

The mines were visited by Jean-Baptiste Tavernier, a leading French jeweller, in the mid-seventeenth century, and he claimed that as many as 60,000 men, women and children were working in the mines centred on Kollur. The men dug away the surface deposits to a depth of some 12 feet to expose the diamond-bearing gravels, which were then removed piecemeal in buckets by the women and children to be puddled and washed and finally hand-picked. An interpolation here: people who don't really know diamonds are apt to say that in the rough they look like washing-soda. But, while of course they don't show the fire and glitter of the polished stone, they have an entirely characteristic greasy gleam which is very distinctive to the experienced eye. And in the bright sunshine of India the sharp eyes of the women and children will have missed very little, so that this crude method of recovery was not so haphazard and inefficient as it sounds.

It must not be thought that the vast work-force reported by Tavernier was swarming uncontrolledly over the whole area. The process was, in fact, quite orderly because the field was divided into small claims some 200 paces in compass owned by an individual merchant who paid duty to the local ruler and employed perhaps 100 workers to operate his claim.

Tavernier must have seen the 'Golconda' mines at about their peak. The output of diamonds began to dwindle soon afterwards, and by the early eighteenth century when the first diamonds were discovered in Brazil, the output from India was inadequate to supply the increasing world demand.

The old mines have long ago been abandoned, and the only diamonds produced in India now are farther to the north, centred on the town of Panna in the State of Madhya. The output of these mines so far amounts to only a few thousand carats in a year.

It is a curious fact of diamond history that as the yield from one source of supply dwindles another and quite unexpected source is discovered. This is fortunate, because the world demand, especially for industrial diamonds on which the steel and engineering industries now depend very heavily, grows year by year.

The date 1725 is usually given for the first discovery of diamonds in Brazil, but probably crystals of diamond had been recovered earlier than this from washings in river gravels while prospecting for gold near Tepico in Minas Gerais. The pebbles were at first unrecognised and were being used as counters in card-games, when they were noticed by an official who had seen service in India and was struck by their lustre, their crystal form, and their high density compared with quartz. A sample was sent to Lisbon and identified as diamond. Moreover, some were sent to Holland by the Dutch Consul and after cutting were pronounced equal in quality to stones from Golconda.

Further discoveries were made, not only in Minas Gerais but in Bahia, and there was for a time something of a glut, which caused the Portuguese Government (Brazil was a Portuguese colony) to impose restrictions on diamond mining. Brazil became independent in 1822, and mining was continued, important new fields being discovered in Bahia in 1844. It was in this region that the tough black granular form of diamond known as carbonado came to light and proved of very great value in rock-drilling crowns and for similar 'heavy duty' industrial purposes. Brazil was the world's chief source of supply for some 140 years, though towards the end of this period the output was slowly diminishing.

Then, again unexpectedly, a new and enormously important chapter in diamond history opened when, in 1867, the first authenticated find of diamond was made near Hopetown in Cape Colony, South Africa. The precise details of any major discovery are always full of interest, and often reveal how much accident or chance enters into the matter. In a very different field, Fleming's discovery of penicillin is a case in point.

Here then, is the story. Schalk van Niekerk, a farmer who also traded for a living, had become interested in collecting attractive pebbles from his own and neighbouring farms, and had been given a book on precious stones to help him in his hobby. One day, when visiting the Jacobs family who had a small house on the farm where he worked, van Niekerk was told by Mrs. Jacobs of a shining pebble which her son Erasmus had found near the banks of the Orange river and which the children had been using when playing the game of five-stones. After a search, the stone was found in the yard under one of the windows.

Looking carefully at the stone, van Niekerk was reminded of drawings of diamond in his book, and this encouraged him to test its hardness on one of the window panes in the Jacobs' house. He found that it scratched the glass deeply. He offered to buy the crystal from Mrs. Jacobs, but she told him to keep it. Van Niekerk showed the stone to several people, and eventually gave it to a travelling hunter and trader, J. O'Reilly, who undertook to take it to Lorenzo Boyes, who was then the Assistant Commissioner at Colesberg. Boyes thought the stone might be diamond and it was agreed that it be sent by post cart to Dr. Atherstone, a mineralogist, in Grahamstown. Dr. Atherstone, who was the first man to test it properly, reported to Mr. Boyes that the stone was undoubtedly a diamond, the weight being $21\frac{1}{4}$ carats, and he valued it at £500.

It was then purchased for this sum by Sir Philip Wodehouse, the Governor of Cape Colony, and van Niekerk was given £350 for his share. Despite the lack of any agreement, written or verbal, he gave half this amount to Mrs. Jacobs: thus everyone was satisfied.

It is good to know that the Jacobs' window-pane with van Niekerk's diamond scratch upon it is now preserved in the Colesberg Museum, and that the 'Eureka' diamond, as it is now called as a cut stone weighing 10·73 carats, is still occasionally on show.

News of this first authentic diamond 'find' caused a number of the local Boers to try their luck in digging out gravels from the banks of the Vaal and Orange rivers in search of diamonds, including, it is amusing to relate, the Assistant Commissioner, Lorenzo Boyes mentioned above, who obtained special leave of absence for the purpose.

Disappointingly little success was reported until two years later when, in March 1869, a shepherd boy called Booi, who was trekking with a few sheep in search of a job, picked up a magnificent crystal weighing 83½ carats (later to be known as the 'Star of South Africa') on Zandfontein Farm.

After vainly trying to barter the stone in exchange for a night's lodging Booi was sent to see van Niekerk, who promptly backed his judgement by offering the lad all the goods he possessed—ten oxen, a wagon, 500 fat-tailed sheep and the horse he was riding—in exchange for the stone. Another example of fair dealing with a simple boy who would have been happy with far less, even though the £11,300 that van Niekerk eventually received for the stone represented a very handsome profit.

This second find was far away from the rivers, and in the rush of largely amateur miners and speculators which inevitably followed there were mixed opinions as to whether the 'river diggings' or 'dry diggings' offered the better prospects of a fortune.

The discovery of diamonds at Jagersfontein Farm in August 1870 was quickly followed by similar finds in the nearby farms of Dutoitspan and Bultfontein, while in 1871 rich finds were made at De Beers farm at a spot which later became famous as Kimberley. A large town—at first of sheds and shanties—sprang up there, and the town has ever since remained the diamond-mining centre.

In each of these new deposits the diamonds were found to occupy roughly circular areas of yellowish decomposed rock, 'yellow ground' which was easily worked and extended to a depth of some fifty feet. At this level the 'yellow ground' passed into a more compact bluish rock, 'blue ground', which, surprisingly, also contained diamonds. The yellow ground was in fact only blue ground in which the iron content had become hydrated and oxidised by weathering. Years later, when mining had continued to many thousands of feet in each of these extraordinary mines it was found that they all had the form of rock-filled volcanic 'pipes' shaped rather like a gigantic carrot. Some two hundred of such pipes have subsequently been found in South Africa, but only very few have yielded an appreciable supply of diamonds.

Mining diamonds from these newly discovered 'pipe' sources raised problems never before encountered. Digging began in a fairly orderly fashion in which each 31 foot square claim was bordered by a 15 foot roadway to allow access to the plot. But inevitably some claims were worked more rapidly than others, while greed gave rise to undercutting of the roadways. There were accidents, some of them fatal, as claims collapsed. By 1876 the 'Big Hole' at Kimberley presented an extraordinary sight, the floor of the mine being chequered with crumbling blocks of various heights representing the remains of the first claims, while from each a system of cables extended to the rim of the mine where there were pulleys fixed to a staging in several tiers. Up and down these cables ran buckets and later trolleys carrying the diamond-bearing earth. The cables were operated by winding round a large drum or 'whim' originally worked by gangs of labourers or by horses, but later by steam engines.

Much though one may favour the idea of the individual miner or small group as opposed to organised 'big business', unified control and vast financial resources were clearly needed if mining were to continue successfully to even greater depths—and there was no sign of a diminishing yield of the coveted diamonds. In some of the neighbouring open-cast mines flooding added problems of its own.

There was a titanic financial battle for the Kimberley mine between the only two men with resources of the order called for. These were Barnett Isaacs, 'Barney Barnato', and Cecil James Rhodes, who was later famous as an empire-builder. Rhodes was backed by the Rothschilds, and in 1888 eventually gained control on handing over a famous cheque for £5,338,650, whereby he was able to absorb the Kimberley mine into his own De Beers Company, forming a new company known as De Beers Consolidated Mines. Other mines came later under the same control and in most of these the open-cast system became unworkable at depths of 400 or 500 feet and was abandoned in favour of a far more elaborate system which allowed working to continue in a controlled and orderly manner to very great depths.

This system involved the sinking of a large main rock-shaft vertically into the country rocks some 1,000 feet from the pipe and tunnelling horizontally from this into the diamond-bearing material of the pipe, which was removed systematically either by 'chambering' or 'block-caving' methods, loaded into trolleys, and sent to the surface for treatment.

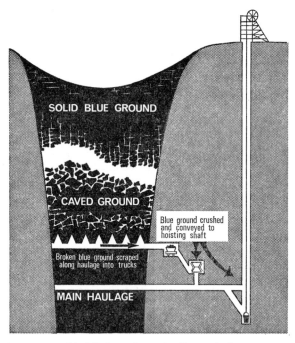

SOLID BLUE GROUND

CAVED GROUND

Blue ground crushed and conveyed to hoisting shaft

Broken blue ground scraped along haulage into trucks

MAIN HAULAGE

4 (1). Mining scheme in diamond pipe

In the vast Premier mine far away near Pretoria in Transvaal, which was first discovered in 1902, the diamonds are still recovered partly by open-cast mining but also by underground working.

Having mined and hauled the diamond-bearing blue ground to the surface, the battle begins to extract the one part of diamond from the twenty million parts of worthless rock in which it is contained. That this can be done at a profit speaks volumes for the design of the machinery, the efficiency of the organisation, and the control of the whole process. One needs only a very general knowledge of what a chain of processes goes on between the stage when a diamond crystal lies hidden in its blue-ground matrix and the day when it can appear as a mounted gem in a jeweller's window to realise how foolish is the notion that were it not for the fact that De Beers controlled the prices diamonds could be bought quite cheaply!

Putting it as briefly as possible, the blue ground is first crushed to six-inch lumps and then to one-inch pieces before being passed to two sets of washing-pans filled with a paste of mud and water called 'puddle' in which revolving arms fitted with teeth keep the lighter minerals in suspension while the heavier minerals (including diamond) settle to the bottom and are gradually moved to the perimeter of the pan, where they are continuously extracted. The process is repeated in secondary pans, leaving a relatively small concentrate.

As an alternative, heavy media separation plants are used in which ferrosilicon and water form a mixture of density 3·0 in a conical tank, from the rim of which the lighter material flows. Treatment of the heavy mineral concentrate in a further tank in which the mixture has density 3·25 further reduces the concentrate before passing to the final stages.

These final stages usually involve the famous 'grease tables' invented by F. Kirsten (a De Beers employee) in 1897. Diamond, unlike most minerals, has a great affinity to grease and will cling to it even in the presence of water.

The heavy-mineral concentrate is accordingly made to pass over cast-aluminium decks, four feet wide by two and a half long, which are formed into three steps and sloped at an angle of 15°. These are coated with pure petroleum jelly to a depth of a quarter of an inch and caused to vibrate by electromagnetic means. When the tables are in action there is a steady flow of water passing with the concentrate, previously classified into four or more sizes, over the entire width of the tables. The top film of grease, which contains the diamonds, is scraped off with a blunt knife every hour or so (or automatically removed by electrically heated scrapers) and put into a pot for removal of the grease by means of boiling water. The grease is recovered and used again, usually with a topping of fresh petroleum jelly spread on it with a trowel.

For many years the output of diamonds from the giant pipe mines of South Africa dominated the market. These were made up of the Kimberley group of Cape Colony which included the Bultfontein, Dutoitspan, Wesselton and De Beers mines; with the Jagersfontein and Koffiefontein mines seventy miles away in the Orange Free State. It has been estimated that during the period 1889 to 1914 some 38 million carats were produced by the De Beers and Kimberley mines, a total which probably about equalled the entire production from Brazil since diamonds were first found there nearly 200 years earlier.

But richer sources than the pipe mines were soon to be discovered —so rich indeed that the Government had to assume control of the mining to avoid upsetting the whole carefully built-up structure of the diamond industry.

These new deposits were on the beaches near the mouth of the Orange river, and it can be assumed that the diamonds had been transported there by the river from weathered pipes far away in the interior. Recently, geologists have found reasons to believe that land in the area of the Kimberley pipes was originally 5000 feet higher than now, which might well account for the 3000 million carats of diamonds estimated to have been transported to the coasts near the mouth of the Orange river. The mysterious fact that no diamonds have been found in the river-bed between Kimberley and the sea may be explained by a recent discovery of 'fossil' river-beds at a lower level than the present bed of the Orange river, and these *did* contain diamonds.

The first discovery was made in 1908 near Luderitz in what was then German South West Africa. A coloured worker who had previously been employed by De Beers at Kimberley was shovelling sand-drifts which threatened to block the railway which the Germans had built there, when he recognised crystals of diamond in the sand. The news got around, and soon there was the usual mad rush to stake claims.

Shortly afterwards it was discovered that diamonds were to be found over a stretch of coast 300 miles long and from one to twelve miles wide. In some parts the stones were actually exposed on the surface in such profusion that the Germans employed African workers to crawl in line abreast across the coastal sands picking up crystals as they went.

The First World War largely put a stop to German activity in the area. After the war the deposits were surveyed and worked under the direction of a geologist named Dr. Hans Merensky, who in 1928 was persuaded to sell his holding to Ernest Oppenheimer, representing the Anglo-American Corporation, and formed the Consolidated Diamond Mines of South West Africa.

In these coastal deposits the availability of the diamond-bearing levels varies considerably; in some places quite a large amount of overburden has to be removed by huge machines of the bulldozer type before the open-cast mining can begin. The deposits were also found to extend beyond low-water mark on to the ocean floor, and special dredging vessels were employed in an attempt to recover these stones, and met with partial success. A curious feature of these coastal crystals is that their surface has been so affected by the scouring in salt water that they do not adhere to the grease tables unless they have undergone previous chemical treatment.

The largest producer of all in terms of quantity proved to be what was then the Belgian Congo, where the first diamonds were discovered in the basin of the Kasai river in 1910. The Congo fields were found to extend southward into Portuguese-owned Angola and to cover a vast area. The Congo provides most of the world's industrial diamonds, only some 3 per cent of the output being of gem quality. There are also large alluvial fields in Ghana and in Sierra Leone.

Although these alluvial sources were so productive as to alter the 'balance of power' in the diamond world and even threatened to upset the carefully built equilibrium of the diamond market—an equilibrium, it should be said, which is beneficial to all parties, including the man in the street—the day of the large pipe-mines was not over.

Dr. John T. Williamson, a Canadian geologist, had a hunch about there being a pipe source for alluvial diamonds which had been found in Tanganyika (now Tanzania) and after long and persistent search he did indeed discover a large diamond pipe at Mwadui near Lake Victoria, which was eventually proved to be even bigger than the Premier. The annual production is now about 500,000 carats, of which about half are of gem quality. A beautiful pink diamond from this mine was presented to the Queen before her accession to the throne, as a wedding gift in 1947. This weighed 54 carats in the rough and 26·60 carats after cutting as a round brilliant. It is mounted as the centre of an 'alpine rose' brooch with five colourless diamonds as petals. This beautiful stone has been valued at £500,000.

The discovery of a still larger pipe mine was made by A. F. Fincham in 1960 when prospecting for asbestos near Postmasburg 100 miles north-west of Kimberley. It is known as the Finsch mine after Fincham and his partner, E. Schwabel, and was sold to De Beers in 1963 for £2¼ million. Fincham's discovery was largely a matter of chance, but it was far otherwise with the last of the South African diamond pipes that I shall describe.

This, the Orapa mine, is in the province of Botswana and in desert country 176 miles from the nearest railhead. Its discovery by a geologist, Dr. Gavin Lamont, and his team was due largely to patient sampling of the quantity of pyrope garnets on the desert surface, these garnets

4 (2). Location of diamond mines in Southern Africa

being commonly associated with kimberlite diamond-bearing rock. The ants which thrive in the Kalahari desert build huge ant-hills, in the making of which they bring to the surface mineral fragments from quite considerable depths. These ant-hills eventually crumble and weather away leaving the mineral samples on the surface.

This new mine is certainly a vast one, its area being five times even that of the Finsch pipe where, by the way, open-cast mining will rule the day for several years to come. Though only recently opened, the Orapa mine has already produced 800,000 carats in the year.

The locations of the main African mines are shown in Fig. 4(2).

RUSSIAN DIAMONDS

For years geologists held the view that diamond was a mineral peculiar to 'Gondwanaland', the name given to an ancient continent which existed before the present continents of Africa and South America and the subcontinent of India were torn apart by the so-called 'continental drift'.

This theory was rudely shattered by the discovery of diamonds in considerable quantity in the frozen wastes of Siberia.

The Soviet Union's growing need for industrial diamonds caused them to set on foot orderly and intensive searches for diamonds within their own territory. Here again pyrope garnet was used as a clue to follow, together with other minerals associated with diamond. The concentration of these tell-tale minerals in different parts of chosen streams was plotted, and after patient searching the first primary source was found in 1954 by a team led by a young woman geologist. This was on the Daldyn river and was nearly on the Arctic Circle.

Within two years more than forty kimberlite pipes were found clustered near the Circle, in a land of permanent frost, frozen swamps, frozen rivers and vast stretches of forest. The richest of the mines so far seems to be the Mir (Peace) mine in the basin of the Batuobiya, 150 miles from the port of Kukhtuya on the river Lena, which has become an important supply base.

The largest diamond recovered to date from the Mir pipe weighed 54·14 carats which is, of course, an important size for a gem diamond. The fact that the majority of the stones are extremely small does not worry the Russians, since such crystals are extremely suitable for industrial use, and this is their chief concern. Special methods of recovery, however, had to be developed and here again the Soviet scientists must be given credit for succeeding in 1958 with a method which was later adopted by the Diamond Research Laboratory in Johannesburg. This depends upon the fact that practically all diamonds show a blue fluorescence when exposed to X-rays. The diamond-bearing gravel is caused to travel (one pebble or crystal at a time) under an X-ray beam. The feeble light emitted by a diamond under the rays is picked up by a photomultiplier tube which immediately activates an electronic circuit which triggers an air ejector which puffs the diamond particle out of the main stream of the tailings.

Although such an apparatus might seem like something contrived by Heath Robinson or Rowland Emmett, it is in fact extremely efficient, and the feed capacity of one machine is as much as 300 pounds of gravel of under a quarter of an inch diameter. This form of final separation is actually now being used in the Finsch mine.

Another successful means of separation which has been used to replace the traditional grease tables is the electrostatic separator in which the gravels are given an electric charge and deflected towards positively charged rollers while the diamonds, being electrical insulators, fall straight down and are collected in a separate container.

It will have been gathered even from the very condensed account I have given of the main sources of diamond in the world today that the total annual production is exceedingly large. According to the latest figures given by Harry Oppenheimer, the Chairman of De Beers, world production for 1971 amounted to 49½ million carats, of which rather more than 11½ million were classed as gemstones. In addition, some 40 million carats of man-made diamond grit were produced to add to the stock available for use in industry.

It is impossible to visualise what 49 million carats of diamond would look like if piled in a heap. But since there are 141·7 carats in an ounce avoirdupois, calculation indicates that a year's world production weighs approximately 9 tons, and could presumably be loaded onto a large and sturdy lorry. For me, at any rate, that seems to cut these huge figures down to comprehensible proportions.

The reader may be surprised at so much space being taken up by even this shortened and incomplete account of diamond sources and recovery, especially when compared with the meagre treatment accorded to all the other forms of gem mining.

There are several reasons for this. Firstly, the overwhelming importance of diamond, not only as a gemstone, in which field it accounts for some 95 per cent in value of all stones used in jewellery, but also as an industrial mineral. Secondly, the story of diamond discovery and the methods of diamond mining in the 100 years since the first finds in South Africa (which has taken most of my space) has been fully recorded and documented, and can thus be given in authentic detail, whereas to find a coherent account of discoveries and procedures in other gem fields is very rare. They are sporadic, haphazard, and local. And thirdly, the techniques used in diamond recovery (except in small alluvial deposits) are unique to that mineral.

But the disappointed reader can rest assured that I shall deal with the special localities for the other gemstones as I come to describe each of them later in the book.

CHAPTER FIVE

CUTTING AND POLISHING

It is very seldom that a gemstone as found in nature is in a condition to show its full beauty of colour, transparency and lustre which the lapidary is able to develop by his skilled treatment. Admittedly some gemstones are found in crystals which have well-developed smooth faces and these have their own special beauty, but attempts to mount these as such in jewellery have seldom been really effective. Either the crystals are so heavy as to be unwearable, or so small as to need close examination for their appreciation. One of the many advantages of cut gemstones, particularly diamonds, is that even if quite small they can signal something of their beauty at a distance by their sparkle and fire.

It is significant that in some of the gem materials which were valued by the earliest men (though probably more as charms and amulets than for personal adornment) were those like amber and pearl, which reveal their attraction without artificial treatment, and stones like turquoise and lapis lazuli where the colour can be enjoyed very effectively after the simplest type of polishing.

As anyone knows who has picked up pebbles on a beach these look far prettier when wet from the waves than they do when taken home and re-examined in the dry state. So it is, of course, with pebbles in a gem gravel, which appear at their best when wet from their washing and can be best sorted in a tray of water or kerosene.

For opaque or translucent materials a simple shaping and polishing operation is really all that is required. And in the earliest beginnings of jewellery-making the shape of the stone clearly did not matter very much to the artificer, as we can see in such historic gems as the Black Prince's Ruby and the Timur Ruby (both of them, incidentally, not ruby but red spinel) in the Crown Jewels, which have clearly retained very much their original irregular shape. The setting, in fact, had to be adapted to fit the jewel, and symmetry had little importance. Even in comparatively recent times it was the practice of lapidaries in the East to retain the shape of the original crystal or pebble so far as possible, as cutting or grinding to any appreciable extent would involve a loss of weight. Facets were chiefly applied to remove or disguise flaws in the stone, and the majority of such old stones would have to be re-cut symmetrically before finding favour amongst European jewellers.

The earliest form of cutting which is still in use at the present time is the domed form often without any flat facets, which is known as *cabochon*, a French word derived from the Latin *cabo*, or head. The basic feature is the rounded top, but otherwise there can be a good deal of variation according to the nature of the stone. The simple *cabochon* form has a flat base, but the perimeter can vary from round to oval, and the height of the *cabochon* is influenced by the nature of the stone. In the case of opal, the nearly flat or 'tallow-topped' shape is preferred to display the iridescent colours of the stone. In star-stones or cat's-eyes, for which this cut is essential, the dome must be fairly steep to give sharpness to the reflected rays of the star or chatoyant 'eye'. The base is left rough in these cases. Where the stone is an almandine garnet the colour is often so deep that the base may be hollowed out to form a 'concave-convex' double *cabochon*. Further brightness can be gained by placing a layer of foil under the hollowed surface. At one time red garnets, or 'carbuncles' as they were called, were cut in *cabochon* style, and gave a wonderful air of richness when mounted on the covers of a church bible or on gold-plated chalices and the like. Various *cabochon*-cuts are shown in Fig. 5(1). Occasionally a double *cabochon* form would be cut with a rim of facets on the shallow side. This curious style was at one time fashionable for chrysoprase, and I have seen it used in amethyst on occasion.

Moonstone, turquoise and jade are universally *cabochon* cut to show their schiller, colour, and texture respectively. Where an emerald, ruby or sapphire is seen in this form it is usually a sign that they are too full of flaws to be suitable for display as a faceted stone, but occasionally they may be found worth re-cutting in faceted form.

In the East, whence came practically all the precious stones in early times, there seemed to be no desire to produce faceted stones of regular shape. Small triangular facets were distributed all over the stone, apparently at random, but usually shrewdly placed to disguise any

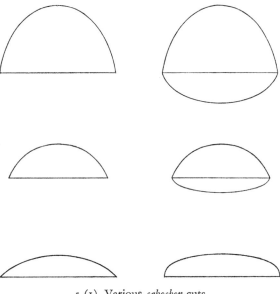

5 (1). Various *cabochon*-cuts

flaws. The lapidary had the good sense to make the best use of colour in the stone, but one of his main concerns always was to lose as little weight as possible, so that if the original pebble was of awkward and lumpy shape it remained awkward and lumpy when he had completed his task of polishing the stone. In later centuries much of the time of European lapidaries was spent in drastically re-shaping sapphires and rubies imported from India or Ceylon, it being realised that the increased value per carat of the now much more attractive stone more than compensated for the inevitable loss in weight.

It seems quite possible that the preference for strict symmetry of outline shown by European lapidaries was due, not to an innate sense of balance or good form, but to the regular shape of the octahedral crystal of diamond, since the styles developed in the West for faceted stones were largely dictated by those suitable for diamond. It was in the mid-fourteenth century that the art of grinding one diamond into shape with another and polishing it on a wheel coated with diamond dust was developed, and once that shape had been reached there was no intrinsic reason why a variety of styles should not have been attempted. But the fact remains that cutters adhered pretty closely to the form shown by the original crystal. Of these the simplest was the *table-cut*, which was merely an octahedron with a rather large portion ground away from one apex to form the table and a smaller facet parallel to this acting as a culet (Fig. 5(2)).

5 (2). Table-cut

The actual octahedron faces could not be polished as this is a direction of cleavage and practically impossible to work. But polishing at a slight angle was accomplished and the effect was most attractive, with the back facets acting as mirrors to reflect all the light entering the front of the stone. The table-cut is really the simplest form of a *step-cut* or trap-cut stone, which is the most rewarding style of cutting for most of those stones in which colour and transparency are the main features which the lapidary wishes to display. As the name suggests the facets are disposed in a series of parallel steps. This cut is used very generally for aquamarine, emerald, tourmaline, topaz, etc. There are certain essentials if it is to be really effective: the parallel facets must be truly parallel to each other and to the perimeter of the stone and the surface of each face must be truly flat. Absolute flatness of faces in a faceted stone gives it a crispness and snap: any perceptible curvature at once gives the impression that the stone is moulded and not lapidary cut—and therefore probably a paste.

A step-cut stone in which the outline is a simple rectangle has rather a bare and over-simplified look, except in the case of quite small stones. Important specimens are more usually given an octagonal outline and the edges of the stepped facets run in four different directions (Fig. 5(3)). This style is so favoured for emerald that it is commonly referred to as the 'emerald-cut'.

Rather surprisingly the emerald-cut is very suitable for diamond provided great care is taken with the proportions of the stone.

Another simple style of cutting for diamond which is quite effective is the *rose-cut* (Fig. 5(4)) in which the diamond has a flat base from which a series of triangular facets rise to a pointed apex. There are different styles of rose known to specialists as the 'Dutch rose', the 'Antwerp rose' and so on, but they are all alike in having triangular facets, a flat base and hexagonal symmetry. The style is only justified for fairly small stones since for a diamond of any size the brilliant-cut would give a very much better display of fire.

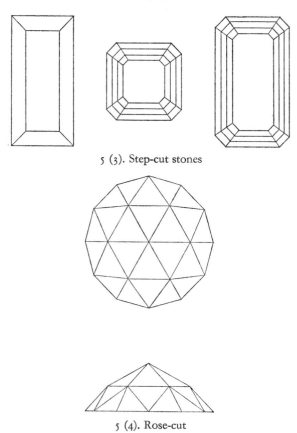

5 (3). Step-cut stones

5 (4). Rose-cut

Examination with a lens will show that many of the tiny diamonds used as a frame to enhance the setting of a coloured stone in a ring or other piece of jewellery, though by courtesy described as 'roses' are little more than diamond chips with a flat base on which perhaps not more than three triangular facets have been polished. It speaks well for the reflecting power of diamond that even in this form it has the effect of enhancing the jewel.

All the styles of cutting so far described are unimportant, at least so far as diamond is concerned, compared to the *brilliant-cut*. So tailor-made to display both the brilliance and fire of diamond is this style of cutting, and so customarily used for the stone that the term 'brilliant' has come to be synonymous with diamond in common parlance.

The invention of the brilliant form of cutting has almost universally been ascribed in books to a seventeenth-century lapidary called Vincenzio Peruzzi, but careful research by H. Tillander, the Finnish gemmologist who has studied for years the history of diamond design, has resulted in the firm conclusion that no such person as Peruzzi ever existed. He was reputed to have been a Venetian lapidary, whereas the Peruzzi family came from Florence, and there is no record of any member named Vincenzio.

It seems more likely that there was no single inventor of the brilliant-cut, but that it was gradually evolved during the seventeenth century from the traditional table-cut, first by adding additional facets to the corners, and finally ending with a form having eight-fold symmetry, in which there were thirty-two facets in the crown and twenty-four facets in the base or 'pavilion' of the stone, in addition to the small culet face parallel to the table facet.

These extra facets resulted in a great increase in the display of 'fire' in diamond, but by modern standards the proportions were wrong, the main angles of the pavilion and crown facets to the plane of the girdle were too steep, adhering more closely to the angles of the original octahedral crystal. The table facet was too small, the culet too large— appearing as a black 'hole' in the base of the stone when viewed from the front (Fig. 5(5)).

A great change in the design of the brilliant followed the publication of a treatise by Marcel Tolkowsky in London and New York in 1919. It is doubtful whether recommendations based on mathematical calculations would have had much influence on the age-old practices of the skilled workers in diamond-cutting workshops, had these been made say, fifty years earlier. In 1919, with the war over, the air was full of new ideas; the entrenched diamond industry of Belgium and the Netherlands had suffered a bad shake-up during four years of war, and was ripe for fresh techniques.

The basic principles on which Tolkowsky worked (also Rosch and Eppler who later suggested modifications of his design) are not very difficult to understand and perhaps should be given here. Some of the optical terms used may be strange and therefore frightening to the

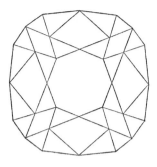

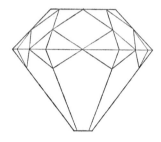

5 (5). Early brilliant-cut

layman, but reading through the next chapter should help to explain matters.

In every transparent solid, light travels more slowly than it does in air and, as a result of this, a ray of light travelling into air from that solid is refracted away from the 'normal' or perpendicular to the surface of the solid. In each case a point is reached where the emergent ray only just grazes the surface between the two media. Any rays which reach the intersurface at angles greater than this *critical angle* are totally reflected back into the solid. The higher the refractive index of the solid, the smaller will be this critical angle. In quartz with a refractive index of 1·55, the critical angle is 40° 15′; in sapphire with R.I. 1·77 the critical angle is 34° 25′; and in diamond with the high R.I. of 2·417 the critical angle is only 24° 26′.

Now the object in the design of a perfect brilliant-cut for diamond is that virtually all the light passing into the stone through the table facet should be *totally reflected* by the pavilion facets and emerge through the crown facets, where the effect of *dispersion* will have broken up the white light into its spectrum colours giving the beautiful 'fire' which is one of the main attractions in a cut diamond (see Fig. 5(6)). Since a ray of light must always follow the same path, if its direction is reversed it follows that light falling on the crown facets is totally reflected by the pavilion facets and emerges through the table. Thus in such a stone all the light perpendicularly incident on the table will be returned to the eye of the viewer.

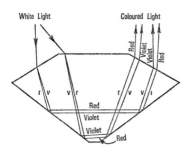

5 (6). Total reflection and dispersion of rays entering brilliant

One can easily test whether this is true by holding a *clean* unmounted brilliant with its table facet facing a window or other light source, and viewing it from the back. The only light passing through the stone should be a tiny spot representing the culet. I stressed that the stone should be *clean*, because diamonds readily pick up a film of grease from the fingers and this would have the effect of lowering the critical angle and destroying the 'total reflection' effect. This is the main reason why it is of prime importance to keep diamonds mounted in jewellery as clean as possible since only then can they give of their full beauty.

I have said that the diamond design was profoundly influenced by the suggestions of Tolkowsky and later scientists; but there were other factors which had to be considered, such as the angles fixed by nature in the original octahedron (in which the angle between the 'girdle' and an octahedron face is 54° 44′) and the commercial need to conserve as much weight as possible.

All the modern brilliants show the following major differences from the brilliants of sixty plus years ago:

(a) a larger table facet in proportion to the girdle width giving a larger 'spread';

(b) a much smaller culet;

(c) a circular girdle;

(d) an eight-fold symmetry.

In the older brilliants which had a cushion-shaped outline the main facets in the crown were subdivided into two groups of four known as bezels and quoins, while in the base of the stone the main facets were in two groups of four quoins and four pavilion facets, and this differentiation was retained even in stones with a circular girdle. In the modern brilliant these groups are identical; hence the eight-fold symmetry referred to in (d) above.

Of the several models of standard round brilliant now recommended by interested authorities in the different countries most concerned with diamond design, I have chosen the Scandinavian standard to serve as an illustration and it is shown in profile in Fig. 5(7).

The names given to the various facets of a brilliant used to be rather confusing as there were variants of each. Above the girdle, the table facet (eight-sided) was surrounded by eight triangular star facets; next

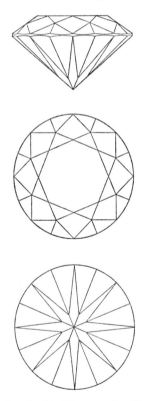

5 (7). Standard brilliant-cut for diamond

came four quadrilateral bezel or templet facets alternating with four quadrilateral quoins or lozenges, while the upper edge of the girdle showed eight triangular cross or skew facets and eight skill facets. Below the girdle were eight triangular cross and eight triangular skill facets below which were the large four five-sided pavilions and four five-sided quoins with, finally, the small eight-sided culet.

In the modern brilliant the names have been simplified (except perhaps by some old-timers) to the following: above the girdle, the tablet facet (eight-sided) and eight triangular stars (as before) surrounded by eight four-sided kite facets and sixteen triangular upper-girdle facets. Below the girdle come sixteen triangular lower-girdle facets, eight four-sided pavilions, and the tiny culet.

In each case the total number of facets remains at fifty-eight: thirty-three above and twenty-five below the girdle. In former times the girdle of a brilliant was left unpolished, but the best cutters now seem to prefer to polish or even to facet the perimeter.

There are a number of variations on both the step-cut and brilliant-cut styles which are fairly frequently used in diamond and the names of these should perhaps be given at this point. The step-cut variations include:

square-cut — square with pointed corners
emerald-cut — square or oblong with truncated corners
baguette — elongated oblong with pointed corners (usually small stones)
keystone — four-sided tapered
kite — four-sided kite-shaped
triangle, hexagon, etc.

The variations in the brilliant are chiefly the navette or marquise, in which the fifty-eight facets of the standard brilliant are distorted to fit a boat-shaped outline; and the pendeloque, also of fifty-eight facets adapted to a drop-shaped outline (Fig. 5(8)). The marquise is an elegant shape for a single-stone up-the-finger ring, but tends to 'leak' light near the centre, giving it a blank look in this region, while the pendeloque shape is admirably adapted for drop ear-rings, or as a pendant to a brooch, etc.

For small diamonds the expense of producing a full brilliant-cut is not worth while, and 'single-cut' or 'eight-cut' forms are used with eight facets below and above the girdle plus table and culet. 'Swiss-cut' diamonds having $16 + 16 + 2 = 34$ facets are also used for small diamonds (Fig. 5(9)). At the other end of the scale, a standard brilliant of over ten carats looks intolerably bare, and in all larger diamonds extra facets are added. In the 'Jubilee-cut', for instance, there are eighty facets, and the famous 'Tiffany yellow' diamond weighing 128·51 carats, is a cushion-shaped brilliant having ninety facets. Any marked departure from an angle of 41° between the plane of the girdle and the pavilion facets in a brilliant is at once noticeable. Too great an angle gives the stone a dark centre when viewed from the front, while a shallow pavilion gives a washed-out or 'fish-eye' appearance.

5 (8). Pendeloque and marquise brilliants

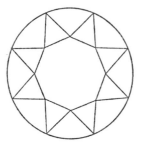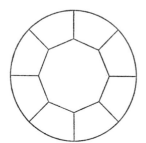

5 (9). Single-cut and Swiss-cut diamonds

Diamonds sometimes occur in very flat crystals and these are occasionally utilised with simply the top and bottom surfaces polished in Indian jewellery. They are known as 'lasque' stones. More finished and symmetrical polished diamond plates with faceted edges have been used in rings to cover a miniature portrait or lock of hair or even as a very expensive 'watch-glass'. These are called 'portrait stones'. I have managed to acquire four of these attractive stones, each of a different optical type, weighing about a carat apiece with a spread of 6 mm or

7 mm. The largest portrait stone I have seen was a giant of nearly an inch in diameter, weighing 10½ carats.

So far, the brilliant-cut has been described as though it were used exclusively for diamond, whereas it is a very popular cut with other gemstones, in particular those which show a certain degree of 'fire', such as zircon and demantoid garnet. Mixed cuts in which the front of the stone is faceted more or less in the brilliant fashion and the back is roughly step-cut are also often found in coloured stones. The close attention to angles and proportions necessary in diamond is not needed with other gems. Here there are other important considerations. If possible the direction of best colour has to be that at right angles to the table facet; pale coloured stones must have their colour enhanced by making the stone as deep as possible; ugly flaws or inclusions must be so placed in the stone as to be as little noticeable as possible; planes of easy cleavage must be avoided as polished surfaces, and symmetry maintained.

In stones such as ruby, sapphire and emerald 'calibré' stones are provided by the lapidary—that is, small step-cut stones made to fixed dimensions. These are necessary where 'eternity' rings or line bracelets, etc., are to be manufactured.

Cutting Methods

When it comes to cutting methods there is complete dichotomy between the diamond cutter and the lapidary who deals with what are usually referred to as 'coloured stones', a term which includes all other gems. Both are craftsmen; but in diamond cutting there are rigid guide-lines which must be followed and a good deal of rather elaborate machinery, so that the whole operation savours rather of the engineer, whereas the lapidary has greater freedom of choice and is able to show more individuality and artistry in his work.

In each case probably the most important task of all, the one calling for judgement, experience and responsibility above all others belongs to the expert who inspects the stone before any work is done, and determines, after prolonged study of the rough material, how best it shall be treated, and what loss of weight may be involved if cut as one stone or two; in the case of diamond whether to begin the operation by cleaving or sawing; in the case of a coloured stone, in which direction the table facet must be cut to produce the best colour effect without too much loss of weight; what flaws or unsightly inclusions there are, and whether these can be removed or must be incorporated in the way least damaging to the appearance. Let us now deal with the typical procedures in the two cases.

DIAMOND CUTTING

The first stage, as indicated above, is the vitally important one as to how the rough crystal may best be exploited. In the case of stones classified as 'shapes', i.e. regular octahedra, by the sorters, there is probably little argument—the stone will be sawn in halves and fashioned into two brilliants. But where the stone is irregular in shape or unusually large, much more deliberation will be necessary.

There are two alternative methods of reducing the original crystal into a form suitable for the grinding and polishing processes to begin. One is cleaving—that is, splitting the stone along one of its four directions of perfect cleavage; the other is sawing by means of a rapidly rotating diamond-charged slitting wheel. Once the point and direction of the desired cleaving has been decided upon the operation itself need take little time, and there is virtually no loss in weight as a result of the operation. But clearly only one stone can be worked on at a time. With sawing the operation may take several days to complete, but once the stones are set up one operator may control a bank of a dozen or more sawing machines. There is a loss in weight of about 3 per cent. Some diamond crystals known as 'makeables' may be ground straight away without sawing or cleaving.

CLEAVING

This must always be 'with the grain', that is, parallel to any one of the faces of the octahedron. This means there are four directions in which a diamond can be split. The position where the cleavage is planned has been marked by the operator or by the 'designer', and a nick or kerf is made with the cleavage edge of another diamond mounted in a stock. The diamond to be cleaved will have been cemented to the end of a stick about eight inches long with a cement which usually consists of a mixture of shellac and resin with some 'filler' such as brick dust or powdered glass. The cleavage stick is then fixed upright in a tapered hole in the cleaver's bench or in his sturdily made wooden cleavers' box. Then comes the crucial moment when the cleaver rests the thick steel blade of the cleaving knife on the notch or kerf and gives it a sharp tap with a stick or short iron bar, when, if all goes well, the stone will part cleanly along the cleavage plane, both parts remaining embedded in the slightly elastic cement.

That tap on the cleaving knife is a 'moment of truth' which needs a man not only of skill but of steady nerves to undertake at all calmly. The most skilled cleaver in the world in the year 1907 was reputed to be Joseph Asscher of the firm of Asscher in Amsterdam. This was the year when consideration was being given to the cutting of the Cullinan, that 3106-carat monster diamond which had been found in the Premier mine and presented to King Edward VII. So Joseph Asscher was entrusted with the preliminary cleaving operations. He studied the stone again and again over a period of two months before essaying his first cleavage. That first attempt failed, and Asscher must have felt rather as the public executioner felt when his axe failed to make a neat job of decapitation. The second attempt succeeded, however, and the present generation of Asschers hotly deny the popular story that Joseph fainted and had to have attention from a doctor. And as they had the story from their father, who was present, one should take their word for it.

SAWING

While cleaving must obviously be 'with the grain' sawing must be across it; parallel, that is, to a cube face and dividing the original octahedron into two equal or unequal portions. For sawing, the diamond is mounted in a clamp or dop and made to rest on a vertical sawing-disc rotating at 5000 r.p.m., made of paper-thin phosphor bronze, the edge of which is slightly thickened to prevent jamming, and charged with diamond dust and olive oil. Heavier metal flanges support the disc to within half an inch from the cutting edge. Once mounted in position a number of diamonds can be sawn simultaneously under the vigilant eye of one man. A one-carat crystal can usually be sawn through in a working day.

BRUTING

Bruting is a word which conveys the feeling that the diamond is being rough-handled into shape. And this is true, though more so in early days when the diamond to be shaped was rubbed powerfully against another by hand, each being cemented at the end of a wooden holder.

After years of this unpleasant work the bruter's hands, particularly the thumbs, were grossly distorted.

For many years now the much more rapid and less damaging method is to have the diamond to be shaped mounted in a lathe and ground into a peg-top shape by pressing another diamond (mounted at the end of a long wooden holder held under the arm) against it. After the diamond being operated upon has attained the required shape the stone used as a grinding tool is usually mounted in its place, ready to receive attention in its turn.

GRINDING AND POLISHING

In the next and final operations the diamond is transformed from its rough grey-finished state in the shape of a truncated double cone into a finished brilliant, and this calls for the highest skills of the diamond cutter who is expected to produce perfect symmetry and correct angular relationships between the fifty-eight facets he applies.

The diamonds to be cut used to be cemented into an acorn-shaped cup at the end of a thick copper stalk called a 'dop', but a mechanical dop or holder is now preferred which allows more control over angular tilts and less frequent resetting of the stone. The grinding and polishing surface is a cast-iron disc known as a scaife (a great many of the diamond terms are derived from the Dutch, who for centuries have specialised in diamond work and trade). The scaife is about half an inch thick and twelve inches in diameter and is cast round a spindle about one and a half inches thick. It rotates anti-clockwise and is driven at a speed of from 2000 to 2500 r.p.m. It is so perfectly balanced that an observer finds it difficult to be sure whether or not it is in motion.

The surface of the scaife is carefully prepared by 'truing', and about 2 carats of diamond dust mixed with a little olive oil is finally rubbed into the wheel. The dop is clamped in a wooden vice or tang which forms a long low tripod, two legs of which rest on the bench and the third (which consists of the diamond in its dop) rests on the rotating scaife. By placing a weight on the tang, which can be moved nearer or farther away from the diamond, varying degrees of pressure can be applied to the stone being worked. A peg on the bench serves to prevent the tang from being swept on one side by the motion of the wheel. There are usually four dops accommodated on the one scaife, and there is one area reserved for the final polishing of each facet, to remove the fine grooves caused by the initial grinding. The cutter or 'cross-cutter' who puts on the first eighteen facets can tell the direction of the grain by the sawing lines and by the marking of any natural crystal surfaces which have been left by the bruter. A trial run is made to ensure the work is going sweetly. A special part of the wheel is reserved for this try-out.

The table facet is ground first and then the first facet—a corner at the top of the stone. There follows the opposite corner facet and the third and fourth top facets before tackling the first four bottom facets, which must meet the girdle at an angle of between 41° and 40° and converge to a point dead in the centre of the base of the stone, where the culet (if any) will be. Four more facets are then added to the top and to the bottom before returning the stone to the bruter for 'rondisting', that is, truing the girdle into a perfect circle.

The remaining twenty-four facets are added by another specialist, the operation being known as 'brillianteering'. The finished stone is then carefully inspected and, if all is well, given an acid bath in order to clean away any traces of oil or dirt. It will never again look quite so good as it does now, because it will never again be quite so clean.

Cutting and Polishing Other Gemstones

In considering the work of the lapidary we enter a far more haphazard and in some ways more romantic world than that of the diamond cutter. The latter is dealing always with the same material and uses the same tools and machines for each stone; he has a regular routine which can be described in detail, as we have just seen. The lapidary on the other hand has to deal with stones of very different degrees of hardness, with different degrees and directions of cleavage, with stones in which flaws and inclusions are the rule rather than the exception, and with the all important aspect of colour—which he may be able to enhance, but equally may mar or ruin by faulty judgement.

The lapidary has to face a wide variety of problems: stones are sent to him to be reshaped after accidental damage, he may be asked to 'heal' a flaw in an emerald which has reached the surface and become visible and which, by skilful over-polishing, may disappear or become less evident: he may be asked to supply and fit a rock-crystal watch-glass, a replacement for a snuff-box lid, a calibré stone missing from a line bracelet, or any other of a dozen types of aid to the manufacturing or retail jeweller. Whereas the diamond cutter is cloistered in his workshop and can concentrate solely on his delicate task, the lapidary is a friend and consultant to all the trade and has to be constantly accessible.

He also has to be something of a practical gemmologist as, if a stone sent to him to cut or repair turns out to be synthetic and he has failed to spot this, there may be trouble such as hints of substitution—if not from those who know and trust him, then from the ever-suspicious private customer who does not understand the high degree of integrity that is an essential factor in the jewellery trade. In fact, before the advent of specialised laboratories where scientific tests enable proved statements to be written rather than verbal opinions offered on any doubtful stone, the lapidary was the best man in the trade to consult. Not only did he have an intimate knowledge both of the external and the internal features of a wide variety of stones, but long experience taught him the 'feel' of each stone when being polished on the wheel.

But occasionally even an experienced lapidary, by relying too heavily on such empirical criteria, could make serious mistakes and would hold to his opinion even when scientific evidence proved him wrong.

One particular instance of this still rankles in my mind because of its absurdity. A well-known dealer submitted a handsome step-cut yellow stone for test in our laboratory in Hatton Garden. Density and refractive-index tests coupled with a study of its inclusions enabled us to pronounce the stone to be a natural yellow sapphire. No trouble and no doubt. The dealer's trusted lapidary, however, would not have it as a sapphire—to him the 'feel on the wheel' was that of topaz, and he would not budge from his opinion. So accustomed throughout the years had the dealer become to relying on his lapidary's judgement, that the stone was sliced in halves and one half sent for chemical analysis! The result, 'aluminium oxide', proved to his satisfaction that we were right; but he still was not convinced that the non-destructive tests which we employed were actually more conclusive than the analysis, which had ruined the value of his stone. A synthetic sapphire, for instance, would also have shown the same analysis.

In cutting and polishing gemstones other than diamond the first stage may be to slit the stone to remove any unwanted material, and the relative softness of coloured stones makes this a fairly rapid operation, in which the stone is held by hand or in a mechanical holder and pressed against a vertical bronze or soft iron disc, charged with diamond powder and olive oil, which has been worked into the edge, and rotating at 1000–4000 r.p.m.

As with diamond, a very important factor in the success of the whole operation lies in the careful study given by the master lapidary to the stone to decide in which direction lies the best colour (since the table facet must be ground at right angles to this direction), the style of cutting to be adopted which will be suitable to the shape of the rough, whether the stone must be shallow or deeply cut to diminish or increase the depth of the colour, whether any large inclusions can be concealed to some extent by the faceting, and, if the stone has a pronounced cleavage, whether all the facets to be polished are safe not to be in a cleavage direction, which would make it impossible to achieve a good finish.

The stone is then cemented to a short wooden holder with a tapered end, in such a way that the proposed table facet is at right angles to the length of the holder. The grinding laps are made of copper, gun-metal or lead according to the type of stone to be cut and the individual preference of the lapidary, and the grinding material may be carborundum (the artificially manufactured silicon carbide which is far harder than emery and can be obtained in all degrees of fineness), or for softer stones it may be emery, a naturally occurring impure form of sapphire. For the more costly hard stones diamond powder may be used. With carborundum or emery the only lubricant used is water.

The table facet having been completed, the remaining facets are ground on until the entire crown of the stone has been given its shape. It is then carefully cleaned to rid it of any coarse abrasive particles and passed to the polisher to finish, in this case usually on pewter or wooden laps which may be faced with cloth or leather. Polishing agents are not necessarily very hard, but should have a high melting-point, as the local temperatures produced by friction on the irregularities of the surface which it is the aim of polishing to reduce to the common level are extremely high.

When the upper part of the stone has been completely faceted and polished, the gemstone is reset and the base facets applied and polished in their turn. For the stone to present a really fine appearance each facet must be truly flat and show no scratches or polishing marks. In a step-cut stone each facet must be truly parallel to the adjoining 'step', and must be exactly superimposed to the facets in the base of the stone. In brilliant-cut forms the triangular facets should meet its neighbours exactly in a point.

Until some fifty years ago everyone thought, with Newton, that the process of polishing minerals was merely one of finer and finer abrasion until a completely flat surface was attained, any scratch-marks remaining being so fine as to be invisible. A series of researches by Sir George Beilby indicated that the matter was not so simple. Beilby found, for instance, that having obtained a fine polish on the surface of the rather soft mineral calcite, if he then lightly etched the surface with acid, the scratches caused in the preliminary grinding operation re-appeared, indicating that they had not been removed by the polishing surface, but smeared over by locally fused material which had then recrystallised. In the nineteen thirties Professor G. I. Finch of Imperial College, London, furthered our knowledge of the nature of the polished surfaces in gemstones through examining their structure by an electron diffraction technique at grazing incidence. Finch found that minerals did not all behave alike when polished. There were those, like diamond, in which the melting-point was so high that polishing was indeed merely ultra-fine abrasion. In others such as quartz and corundum, local fusion took place with formation of a liquid Beilby layer, which, however, recrystallised immediately, congruently with the underlying crystal. In others again recrystallisation of the Beilby layer only took place parallel to important crystal planes where the underlying atomic layers exerted sufficient influence to cause this to happen, though the amorphous layer in less favoured directions eventually crystallised if the mineral were heated. And finally, a few minerals, of which zircon and spinel are examples, permanently retained their liquid-like Beilby layer after being polished.

These researches by Professor Finch, which might be thought to have little practical value, did in fact enable him to solve a vexing problem as to why aluminium pistons working in steel cylinders caused such excessive wear, though aluminium was the softer metal. The damage was in fact caused, not by the aluminium itself but by tiny spicules of aluminium oxide, that is, of sapphire, which formed on the surface of the cylinder. By alloying the aluminium with magnesium a spinel layer was formed, which in its polished surface remained smooth thus reducing wear on the enclosing cylinder.

CUTTING CENTRES

The art of diamond cutting seems to have originated in Venice in the fourteenth century. Later, it spread to Bruges, Flanders and Paris; and it was not until the end of the fifteenth century that Antwerp came into prominence as a diamond-finishing centre, which, with ups and downs, it has remained ever since, with Amsterdam being its closest rival. The change began when the Portuguese navigators discovered the direct sea route to India via the Cape, and thereby were able to supplant the Doges of Venice as Europe's chief traders with India. From Lisbon the diamonds from India were sent to the Flemish guild near Antwerp for finishing. The centuries-old rivalry with Amsterdam began when the Dutch East India Company became the dominant trading organisation with India, which gave Amsterdam a virtual monopoly, so that Antwerp's cutters had to go cap in hand to the Dutch city for diamonds to cut. The discovery of diamonds in South Africa swung the balance in favour of Antwerp again, and the huge diamond fields of the Belgian Congo, and trading agreements with London, further increased its prosperity.

At the present time Antwerp with the very high wage structure enjoyed by their cutters, including fringe benefits, and at the same time a shortage of skilled men when trade is brisk, is finding it difficult to cope with Indian competition in cutting small diamonds, where labour costs are so very much lower. There is also strong competition by the Soviet Union; and the Israeli diamond cutters, too, are gaining in importance. There are in addition quite important cutting centres in Johannesburg, New York, Idar-Oberstein and Puerto Rico. While London remains the main centre of supply for rough diamonds, there are now relatively few diamond cutters in the city. The largest British diamond cutting concern, in fact, has its factory in Brighton.

With regard to other gemstones, the lapidaries of London have also almost disappeared from the scene, those remaining being chiefly employed (on account of their high degree of skill) on important stones when quality of finish is more important than low cost, and on repair and re-cutting jobs. Mass production of the less valuable gemstones was never attempted in London: this has for long been the prerogative of Idar-Oberstein in West Germany, where the industry began as a cutting centre for their local agates which were ground and polished by the crudest means on huge sandstone wheels driven by water-power, against which the operator, lying on his stomach on a low bench with his feet braced on a wooden sill, pressed the stones with considerable force, an occupation, as one can imagine, leading inevitably to diseases of the lungs.

When the local agate supply ran low German pioneers, who had settled in Brazil, were able to send to their home town huge supplies not only of fine agates, but of amethysts, aquamarines and tourmalines. The old sandstone wheels were superseded (except as a tourist attraction) by modern power-driven lapidary equipment, and Idar grew to be the centre for all the lesser gemstones. And in a township where everyone works with gemstones in some capacity, and works hard and skilfully, the output is vast and unbeatably low in price. In Idar there are all the skills. Such things as bead necklaces of amethyst, citrine and rock-crystal are produced in vast quantity and can hardly be manufactured elsewhere at an economic price. And not only cutting goes on in Idar: staining of agate, onyx and chalcedony was an art initiated here, and almost all the stones they receive in the rough are heat-treated in some way to improve their colour. This may worry the purist, who would like to think that the stone he buys bears the colour given it by nature, but the fact remains that the stones they treat in Idar are undoubtedly made more saleable in the process and that, after all, is the merchant's main concern.

We have so far considered only the professional lapidary. In the United States where there are numerous localities where gem minerals abound, there is an ever-growing body of enthusiasts who combine the open-air hobby of mineral collecting with the indoor craft of gem cutting. These 'rock-hounds' and amateur lapidaries are well catered for by suppliers of cuttable minerals, cutting and polishing apparatus, books of instruction, and a lavish monthly magazine, the *Lapidary Journal* where, in between columns of advertisements, valuable articles can often be discerned.

Great Britain, though it has produced some of the world's finest crystals of fluorspar, calcite, etc., is poor in stones really suitable to be cut as gems. But a remarkable awakening to the beauty of mineral crystals, and an attendant interest in polishing stones, has taken place here during the past decade, and specimens, books of instruction, and apparatus for lapidary work are now made available on a fairly large scale. And even the humble 'tumbling machine' which requires no skill in use, should not be despised, as it can give an admirable gloss to those attractive pebbles picked up on the beach, and perhaps provide a 'way in' for more ambitious collecting and study.

CHAPTER SIX

———————— ◊ ————————

CRYSTALS AND CUBES

IF ONE WANTS to have more than a purely superficial idea of the nature of precious stones and the minerals from which they are derived, it is necessary to understand what the term 'crystal' entails in terms of science, since the properties of any mineral depend far more upon its crystal structure than upon its chemical composition. One example only need be given here to drive that point home, as it could hardly be more dramatic as an instance: it is that *diamond and graphite are chemically identical*, each consisting of the one element: carbon. Thus, all the vast differences in appearance and properties between the clear, transparent, intensely hard king of gemstones, and the black opaque material graphite, so soft that it forms the 'lead' of lead pencils and is used as a lubricant, must depend upon the way in which the atoms are arranged —that is, upon their crystal structure.

In this and the following chapter I am going to describe the nature and classification of crystals as simply as possible. But I know from experience that the reader who has had no scientific education may still find the subject hard to assimilate. If this is the case, I suggest that he skims and skips his way through these two chapters and returns to them later for reference, or after the handling of actual crystal specimens has awakened his interest in a way that no written words or diagrams can do.

The term 'crystal' is used loosely for clear transparent forms of glass and (more excusably) for clear rock-crystal quartz, but mineralogists and other scientists (and while reading this book you are invited to think in their way) have a more fundamental use for the word. The definition of a crystal could read: 'A body whose atoms are arranged in a definite pattern, outwardly expressed, under favourable circumstances, by a geometrical form bounded by plane faces.' Twenty-three words, which some modern physicists would reduce to merely five: 'matter in the solid state', but not be so helpful, I feel, to the nonscientific reader.

The name is derived from a Greek word meaning 'ice', since the ancient Greeks conceived the notion that the clear prisms of quartz which they found in cavities in the mountains were simply ice which had been congealed so thoroughly by intense cold as to have become permanently frozen into that form. Other transparent minerals were thought to be of like origin and so the word came to be used in its more general sense.

Let us now begin with the basic building-blocks of our material world, the atoms. Ever since the days of Rutherford and Bohr we picture these in terms of a tiny, heavy nucleus, positively charged, surrounded by even tinier negatively charged particles known as electrons. These electrons (don't ask me why—don't ask *anyone* why) travel round and round the nucleus in fixed elliptical orbits. According to the charge on the nucleus there are ninety-two chemically different kinds of atom found in nature, which are known as the elements. These range from the simplest and lightest atom, hydrogen, which has only one positively charged proton as nucleus, round which a solitary electron wings its way, to the heaviest and most complicated atom, that of uranium, which has a charge of ninety-two on its nucleus, compensated by the equivalent number of electrons travelling in no fewer than seventeen different 'shells' or orbits.

Now, though the closest conception of the actual structure of any atom is of a central, hardly visible speck in a space as big as the Albert Hall, around the periphery of which midge-like electrons continuously whizz in fixed orbits, in practice each atom can be considered as a sphere to which (for each element) a fairly precise radius can be given. These spheres are the building-blocks from which all the thousands of different crystals are constructed, and the three-dimensional pattern in which they are packed is the crystal structure on which their external form and all their physical properties depend.

In any crystal the atoms are packed together in the closest possible formation consistent with their size and electrical nature. If experiments are carried out with spheres of equal size, such as ping-pong balls, it will be found that there are two ways of packing them closely together in layers. After the first three or four layers it can be seen that the arrangement is repeating itself and could go on *ad infinitum* to build a crystal of any size. Packing of equal-sized atoms like this can produce crystals having either cubic or hexagonal symmetry. Where the crystal is composed of several sorts of atoms each with different radii it may not be possible for the packing to be so symmetrical.

In theory, the 'faces' forming the external shape of a crystal might correspond with any of the layers of atoms from which it is built. In practice, the faces most commonly developed are those most thickly studded with atoms: these are the 'strongest' faces—that is, the least vulnerable to abrasion or chemical corrosion. Thus in the one-dimensional diagram shown as Fig. 6(1), the possible planes represented by

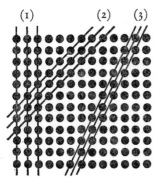

6 (1). Network of atoms showing possible crystal planes

the lines (1) and (2) are more likely than those shown as (3) to form stable crystal faces. Interatomic electrical forces and external physical and chemical factors determine which of the possible forms predominate in any given mineral specimen. Since the conditions under which a mineral grows vary in each locality, it often happens that crystals of the same mineral vary in 'habit' (the word used to describe the typical form of a mineral) according to their origin. One of the most protean of the common minerals is calcite, beautiful clear crystals of which examples, varying greatly in shape, can be seen in any museum or private collection of minerals.

Most of us are accustomed to the device of plotting the position of a point, or points, on a plane by measuring its distance from two axes at right angles to each other. This is usually done on squared paper and is known as a graph. See Fig. 6(2) where the point shown is fixed at 9X, 5Y. Where we wish to fix the position in space of a plane bounding a solid such as a crystal, we need to refer to at least three axes, as in the drawing shown as Fig. 6(3). In crystallography these axes of reference are known as crystal axes. Crystal axes are, of course, a mathematical device and purely imaginary.

Both from mathematical theory and from a study of well-formed crystals of all kinds it is known that all crystals can be grouped in

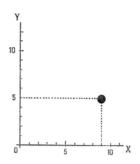

6 (2). Fixing position of point in one plane

terms of their symmetry into thirty-two 'classes' and more broadly into seven 'systems'. In each of these a set of three (or in one case, four) axes of reference can be chosen which bear an equal relationship with all crystal faces of the same kind. In order to simplify things and yet

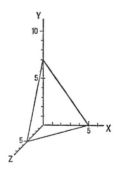

6 (3). Fixing position of a plane in space

ram home some important points, I shall deal in this chapter with only one of these systems—the cubic system.

The cubic system is one to which a number of important gem minerals belong, including diamond, spinel, the garnets and fluorspar. The symmetry of these crystals, as the name suggests, is that of the cube itself, which can easily be visualised from a three-dimensional drawing, or constructed from wood, cardboard, or Plasticine. Plasticine is best, because one can carve crystal faces on the basic cube form and see quite clearly how the other crystal shapes, such as the octahedron, are derived from it.

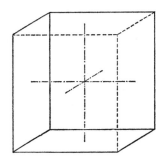

6 (4). Cube showing 3 crystal axes

Now let's get to work. First of all, here is a drawing (Fig. 6(4)) showing a cube, with the three crystal axes in position. It can be seen that the cube consists of six equal square faces and that each cuts one of the axes of reference and is parallel to the other two. It can also be

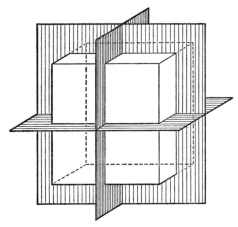

6 (5). Cube showing 3 planes of symmetry (diagonal planes not shown)

seen that each of these crystal axes is also an *axis of four-fold symmetry*, i.e. that the cube can be turned around any of them and present the same appearance four times in a complete revolution. In Fig. 6(5) is another drawing showing how a cube can be cut into equal halves in three directions—each half being the mirror image of the other. These dividing planes are called *planes of symmetry*. It is hoped that the reader, having got the general idea, can see from a study of his cube that in addition to the three axes of four-fold symmetry coincident with the crystal axes, there are, in a perfect cube, *four axes of three-fold or 'trigonal' symmetry*, which can be pictured as running from one corner of the cube to the corner diagonally opposite. There are also six two-fold axes of symmetry which run from the centre of each edge to the centre of the diagonally opposite edge of the crystal. And finally it can, I hope, be visualised (or proved by slicing a Plasticine model) that there are *six diagonal planes of symmetry* running from the edge of the cube to the diagonally opposite edge.

The foregoing passage may have seemed to be just solid geometry of no practical interest, but if he now will read a little further, the reader may see how a grasp of symmetry will 'make sense' of the crystal shapes found in nature, and why, for instance, the octahedron and dodecahedron which I am just about to describe, can be clearly considered as belonging to the cubic system.

Let us first look at a truncation of one of the corners of the cube. Because of the requirements of symmetry, the truncation would have to be an even one—that is, the intercepts of the new triangular face on the three adjacent cube faces would have to be equal. Then, because of the two-fold planes of symmetry, an equal triangular face would have to be developed on *each* of the eight corners of the cube. These triangular faces are the faces of the octahedron, which when fully developed, is an eight-sided figure, as its name denotes, the edges of each side forming an equilateral triangle and the whole solid looking like a double pyramid, with a shared square base (Fig. 6(6)). One could reverse the process and truncate the corners of an octahedron evenly, to arrive at the cube. In natural crystals, actually, a combination of the

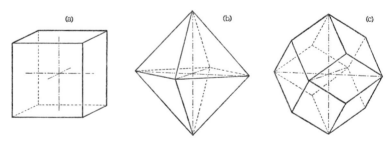

6 (6). (a) cube (b) octahedron (c) rhombic dodecahedron

two forms is quite often seen. The octahedron is famous for being the usual shape for diamond crystals.

Now let us consider a further process of truncation this time of the twelve *edges* of the cube. This eventually provides a twelve-faced form, each face being rhombic (lozenge-shaped) in outline. The complete solid is thus known as a rhombic dodecahedron, dodecahedron being the Greek word for a twelve-sided solid, and is the most usual form adopted by garnet crystals (Fig. 6(6)).

And yet another 'bevelling', this time of the edges of the dodecahedron, produces the trapezohedron shown in Fig. 6(7), which is another favoured form for garnet. This has twenty-four faces and is thus often known as the icositetrahedron from the Greek word for twenty-four.

(a)   (b)

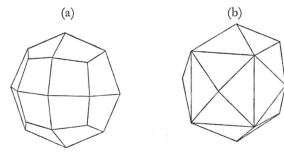

6 (7). (a) icositetrahedron (b) four-faced cube

In nature most crystals grow outwards from the walls of a vein or cavity, so that the attached end is lacking in the faces which would complete the crystal. In several of the minerals which crystallise in the cubic system we have been discussing, however, the crystals have grown under the influence of pressure and were completely surrounded by the matrix in which they formed, so that they show their complete geometric form very little distorted. This is another good reason why cubic crystals are the best starting-point for the beginner.

Crystals of other systems often grow in very elongated or flattened forms which differ very much from the idealised drawings seen in textbooks. However, their very distortions may be characteristic of the mineral and thus an aid to its recognition by an experienced 'rockhound'.

There are still several important things to say before we leave these cubic crystals. First, that all faces belonging to the same 'form' in a crystal are identical in their hardness and other physical properties—

and this includes any characteristic growth or etch-marks on the faces such as the well-known 'trigons' on an octahedron of diamond. Their interfacial angles are also always the same. In the cubic system these angles are largely fixed by geometrical considerations: in other systems the angles between faces may be unique to that mineral.

It should also be understood that the axes and planes of symmetry ascribed above to the perfect cube apply only to the highest class of symmetry in this system. There are crystals, such as those of iron pyrites, which are often met with in the form of cubes which have a lower degree of symmetry, though they are still grouped in the cubic system since their faces can all be referred to the framework of three equal crystal axes intersecting at right angles to each other.

A study of brassy iron pyrite crystals (which are readily obtainable from mineral dealers) will reveal that the majority of the cube faces show heavy striations in one direction only. This means that the diagonal planes of symmetry must be missing.

Crystals, as recovered by miners from stream beds, or the dry gravels derived from former streams, are often considerably water-worn, sometimes to the shape of rounded pebbles showing no crystal form. Often, however, the process may not have proceeded so far as this, and enough of the original shape can be seen to aid in recognising the mineral. Examples of this are seen in worn octahedral crystals of spinel and elongated crystals of white topaz which show the remnants of a prismatic crystal terminated by pyramids.

A mineral which, though too soft and lacking in lustre and fire to be used successfully as a cut gemstone, crystallises in transparent cubes of violet, green, pink, or yellow colours which make supremely beautiful mineral specimens, is fluorspar, and the reader is strongly advised to purchase some good specimens of this mineral. An inspection of fluorspar crystals will reveal several interesting features. In the first place the cubes frequently interpenetrate and the point where each emerges will be at the apex of a very low pyramid formed from what are known as 'vicinal' faces; in the second place fluorspar cleaves very readily parallel to the octahedral planes, and cracks of incipient cleavage can usually be clearly seen: often they spoil the appearance of the specimen. Thirdly, it can often be seen that the surface of the cube consists of a mosaic of nearly parallel cubes of smaller size. This means that a cleavage surface of fluorspar is never quite perfect, but characteristically uneven. To notice such small details is one of the important skills of the gemmologist.

———————— ✧ ————————

CHAPTER SEVEN

MORE ABOUT CRYSTALS

IN THE PRECEDING chapter the general nature of crystals was explained and the fact that all crystals can be classified according to their symmetry into one of seven crystal 'systems' according to the axes of reference needed to establish the spatial relationships of their faces.

The most symmetrical system, the cubic, has been dealt with in enough detail, I hope, to enable the reader to understand how such different shapes as the cube, the octahedron and dodecahedron are related, and display the same essential symmetry.

In a quick review of the remaining six systems in which crystals are grouped, it may be helpful to describe a basic form for each from which more complicated crystals can be 'derived' by truncating edges or corners as we pictured happening in the case of the cube.

THE TETRAGONAL SYSTEM

If a cube can be visualised as being slightly elongated so as to form a four-sided block with a square top and bottom then we have the simplest basic form of a tetragonal crystal. The four 'sides' are all identical, but the top and bottom pair of faces are different from these. There are still three crystal axes intersecting at right angles, but the vertical axis in this case is different from the other two which are horizontal and equal. The vertical axis is an axis of four-fold symmetry but the other two are axes of two-fold symmetry only. This simple tetragonal form is shown in Fig. 7(1).

In all crystal systems except the cubic there are special names to describe the crystal faces, the most important of which are pyramid, prism, pinacoid and dome. The following brief definitions may help to make sense of the descriptions of crystals to be found in this and almost any other book on minerals or gemstones:

A pyramid is a form each of whose faces cuts all three crystal axes. A crystal consisting only of pyramid faces can be seen to form two conventional 'pyramid' shapes on opposite sides of the same base. Such a form is thus referred to as a bipyramid.

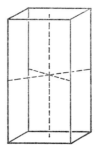

7 (1). Tetragonal prism and basal plane

A prism is a form each of whose faces cuts two lateral axes and is parallel to the vertical axis.

A pinacoid is one of two parallel faces which intersect one crystal axis and are parallel to the other two. The word is derived from a Greek word meaning 'slat' or 'board' and it is helpful, perhaps, when visualising a pinacoid to think of the two parallel advertisement boards on a sandwich-man.

A dome is the name given to a form any face of which cuts the vertical axis of a crystal and one horizontal axis. In the simple shape shown in Fig. 7(1) the four vertical faces are prism faces, and a crystal in which these faces are prominently developed is referred to as a 'prismatic' crystal. The square faces forming the top and bottom of the form are pinacoids, and because of their position are usually referred to as 'basal pinacoids' or 'basal planes'.

There are only three gemstones which crystallise in the tetragonal system: zircon, idocrase and cassiterite, and each of these is often found as well-developed crystals. Zircon, the only commercially important one of the three, commonly occurs in square prisms terminated by a pyramid at either end.

THE HEXAGONAL SYSTEM

Minerals belonging to the hexagonal system and the closely associated trigonal system include some of the most important gemstones. They are often well developed in nature and can be seen even by the layman to justify the name 'hexagonal' since a hexagonal prism is usually the most prominent form.

The crystallographer finds it convenient to refer the forms found in this system to four axes, three of which are horizontal, equal in length and intersect each other at angles of 60°. The fourth and principal axis is vertical and thus intersects the other three at right angles.

The commonest forms are hexagonal prisms (six faces) parallel to the principal axis, basal pinacoids (two faces) and hexagonal bipyramids (twelve faces). Fig. 7(2) shows a hexagonal prism with basal pinacoids

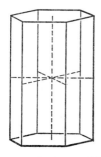

7 (2). Hexagonal prism and basal plane

and the four crystal axes. Only beryl (emerald, aquamarine) and apatite amongst the gemstones have the full hexagonal symmetry in which the principal axis (known as the c axis) is also an axis of six-fold symmetry. But there are many more gem minerals crystallising in the closely allied trigonal system described below, in which the c axis has only three-fold symmetry, and these often show hexagonal forms.

THE TRIGONAL SYSTEM

Crystals in this system have forms which can be referred to three equal horizontal axes and the fourth (c) axis at right angles to these, has only three-fold symmetry. This is often considered as a subdivision of the hexagonal system, but most modern crystallographers prefer to treat it separately. Trigonal crystals such as those of quartz and corundum (ruby and sapphire) appear to the uncritical eye to show full hexagonal symmetry, but others, particularly tourmaline, quite clearly reveal the trigonal symmetry of the c axis, since a cross-section or end-on view of a prismatic crystal shows a distinctly triangular outline and pyramids showing three faces instead of six. The beautiful mineral calcite, important for its optical properties but too soft for use for ornament except in its massive forms as marble, crystallises in the trigonal system. This mineral, crystals of which superficially resemble those of quartz, have a strong tendency to break or split (known as 'cleavage') parallel to the faces of a form known as the rhombohedron. This cleavage is in fact so readily developed that if calcite is broken by a tap with a hammer the broken fragments will be found to be rhombohedral in shape. The rhombohedron can be visualised as a cube which has been slightly compressed along one of the three-fold symmetry axes which run from corner to opposite corner (Fig. 7(3)). The six faces are rhomb-shaped,

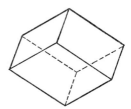

7 (3). The rhombohedron

hence the name 'rhombohedron'. The rhombohedron is so typical and important a form in the trigonal system that the name rhombohedral system has often been used as an alternative. Rhombohedra can be either positive or negative according to their relationship with the crystal axes. When the two combine, a form closely resembling a hexagonal bipyramid results and this development is almost universally seen in crystals of quartz, as will be mentioned when we are describing that important mineral.

THE ORTHORHOMBIC, MONOCLINIC AND TRICLINIC SYSTEMS

Crystals belonging to the remaining three systems, the orthorhombic, monoclinic and triclinic, show a progressive lessening in symmetry. We have seen that a cube is a solid bounded by six equal square faces which can be referred to three equal axes at right angles to each other. Also that the corresponding tetragonal form is bounded by four oblong prism faces terminated by a pair of square pinacoid faces, and how in this system the two lateral axes are equal while the vertical (c) axis is either longer or shorter than these. Now in the orthorhombic system the axes of reference, though still at right angles, are all unequal in length, the primary shape being that of a matchbox. In monoclinic crystals not only are all the axes unequal, but one is now inclined to the other two (hence the name) and the matchbox shape has had a 'push' from one end; while in the triclinic system, least symmetrical of all, all of the axes are unequal, and all are inclined.

The important gem minerals chrysoberyl, peridot and topaz crystallise in the orthorhombic system: they tend to have a lozenge-shaped cross-section. Sphene, spodumene and orthoclase feldspar are among the monoclinic minerals—but the mineral which most clearly shows the monoclinic symmetry is gypsum of which crystals are readily obtainable and worth studying for this reason. Amongst triclinic minerals, axinite, kyanite, and many of the feldspars can be counted as gems.

Crystal Habit

Minerals which crystallise in the same system do not by any means exhibit the same crystal shapes. Every mineral has what might be called its favourite form or combination of forms, which, as mentioned earlier in this chapter, is known as its 'habit' and helps a great deal in enabling it to be recognised. The habit of a mineral is not necessarily the same in different localities, which is hardly surprising, since we know from experiment that the form shown by a crystal when grown from solution can be altered by adding traces of different chemicals to the solution, and that the shape of synthetic diamond crystals can be controlled by altering the temperatures and pressures, cubes being formed at the lower range and octahedra at higher pressures and temperatures.

The habit of a crystal is sometimes described by reference to a particular crystal form: thus, diamond in general has an octahedral habit, garnet a dodecahedral or icositetrahedral habit, fluorspar a cubic habit, and so on—it will be noted that these are cubic forms and thus can form the complete crystal without accessory faces of another form. Or the term can be used more generally to give an idea of its shape without going into crystallographic detail. Thus, when a mineral is said to have a 'prismatic' habit this means that the vertical prism faces are well developed, which will give the crystal a slender appearance. Where the crystals are small in cross-section and very elongated, the term 'acicular' (needle-like) is used. A 'tabular' crystal is one in which the basal planes are prominent and the prism zone insignificant.

In general it may be said that crystals growing from the walls of cavities or veins in the rocks tend to be long in relation to their girth, e.g. quartz, aquamarine, tourmaline, while crystals growing within a rock under pressure tend to be more compact, e.g. garnet, diamond, spinel.

Apart from the system and habit of a crystal there are many other signs which help to identify specimens of a given species. Colour may have a bearing on it as in the case of ruby, emerald, iolite: lustre also, as in diamond and demantoid garnet. Cleavage is another important factor as in topaz, euclase and blende, while perhaps most useful of all are striations or angular etch-marks on the faces of a crystal. Striations are usually considered as oscillations between the choice of one face or another in the growing crystal. In the case of the brassy cubes of iron pyrites, for instance, the faces are heavily striated with incipient faces of the pyritohedron or pentagonal dodecahedron. In quartz crystals, which are frequently distorted and thus difficult to interpret, horizontal striations on the prism faces which are typical of the mineral, may prove very helpful.

Etch- or growth-patterns on a crystal face are most revealing, since they give a clue to the symmetry in a direction at right angles to the face on which these occur. For instance, triangular pits or 'trigons' so typically seen on the octahedral faces of diamond indicate that there is an axis of three-fold symmetry perpendicular to that face. The same is true of the triangular marks commonly seen on the basal plane of the trigonal crystals of ruby and sapphire.

Another point to note in studying crystals is that any markings or patterns on one face of a given 'form' should be repeated on similar faces of the form on other parts of the crystal, as having the same substratum of atoms they are physically identical. A striking example of this can be seen in crystals of apophyllite, hardly a gem mineral, but one which occurs in beautiful large transparent crystals in the Deccan trap of India and elsewhere. The crystals are tetragonal, but when they consist of four tetragonal prisms enclosed at either end by basal pinacoids they might easily be mistaken for cubes, were it not that the four prism faces are lustrous and vertically striated while the basal planes have a rough surface and pearly lustre.

The very low pyramids (formed of what are known as 'vicinal' faces) so often seen on the cube faces of fluorspar are a ready means of identifying this lovely mineral, especially when the ready but uneven octahedral cleavage is also visible. More will be said about such identifying features under the descriptions of each gem mineral later in the book.

What I particularly wish to emphasise is that the close and intelligent observation of crystals is not only of great interest but of real practical value in identification.

TWINNING

Very often two or more individual crystals grow together or inter-penetrate in symmetrical fashion. One crystal may be the reflection of the other across a common plane known as the 'twinning plane', or it may be brought into parallelism with it by rotation through 180° around a 'twinning axis'.

In some twins the two individuals are in contact. The well-known 'spinel twins' or 'macles' seen so often in spinel and diamond are examples of such contact twins. In others the two individuals inter-penetrate: this is commonly seen in cubes of fluorspar.

In certain orthorhombic minerals triple twins are very common and these present a convincingly hexagonal appearance. Aragonite crystals show this triple twinning admirably and in fact it is quite rare to find an untwinned aragonite specimen. More important to the gemmologist are the triple twins of chrysoberyl which are often seen both in the yellow-green variety and in the valued alexandrite chrysoberyls.

PARALLEL GROWTH

Not to be confused with twin crystals are those in parallel growth. Here all like faces are similarly oriented while in twins they are in reversed or mirror-image positions. Some apparently single crystals are really composed of many individuals in nearly but not quite parallel alignment. Some synthetic emerald crystals show this habit, and in fluorspar the cube faces often show a mosaic structure while the octa-hedral cleavage though easy seldom presents a smooth surface because of this slight lack of alignment.

CRYSTALS AND OPTICAL PROPERTIES

Although to most non-scientists approaching the subject for the first time what may be termed mathematical crystallography is difficult to apprehend, tedious and even unnecessary—rather like the finer points of grammar may seem when attempting a quick grasp of colloquial French—there can be no doubt about the beauty and many fascinating aspects of crystals. But in so far as crystallography helps one to recognise and classify them by their symmetry and the interrelationship of their faces, some knowledge of the subject is worth acquiring.

Quite apart from their external shapes, their internal structure determines the properties of the minerals concerned, as we have already mentioned in the case of diamond and graphite. In particular the type of optical properties shown by gemstones depends upon the crystal system to which they belong (see Chapter 8). In cubic crystals a beam of light travels in all directions at the same speed, which means that all cubic minerals are singly refractive or 'isotropic'. In hexagonal, trigonal and tetragonal crystals, there is one direction (the optic axis, parallel to the c axis) in which they are singly refractive. In all other directions light is split into two polarised rays which travel at different speeds and thus have two different indices of refraction, one of which (the 'ordinary' ray) is invariable while the other (the 'extraordinary' ray) varies according to direction. Such crystals are called uniaxial.

In the three least symmetrical systems there are two directions of single refraction, i.e. two optic axes, and they are known as biaxial. In all other directions light is split into two polarised rays which vary in speed according to direction. There are thus, so to speak, two 'extraordinary' rays.

I have been talking at some length about crystals, and the reader may be wondering 'What about stones or other things which don't form crystals?'

Amongst inorganic solids the great antithesis to a crystal is glass—which is a mixture of various silicates in which the atoms are in random orientation, as in a liquid. Amongst scientists, in fact, glass, despite its apparent rigidity, is simply a supercooled liquid. When heated it has no sharp melting-point as a crystal has, but softens and becomes plastic long before it becomes truly fluid.

In mineral nature the only glasses are those igneous rocks in which the molten magma has cooled quickly at the earth's surface, of which obsidian is the best-known example. Amongst gemstones, only opal is non-crystalline, being a solidified form of a silica jelly containing water. And even in opal there is a good deal of regular structure, as we shall see later.

Jet and amber are non-crystalline, but these are organic in origin—

that is, they are derived from living substances. Amber indeed is a fossil resin, exuded by ancient pine-trees, and the man-made resins or 'plastics' are only too much part of our daily lives.

To anyone new to the subject, this chapter will have seemed hard going. But it contains some essential ideas and information and will seem less formidable when referred to later.

CHAPTER EIGHT

———— ⟨◊⟩ ————

HOW LIGHT BEHAVES IN
GEMSTONES

THERE IS A great deal to be said for the simple enjoyment of a beautiful object without bothering to ask 'why?'. And devoted though I am to scientific gemmology I like to think that my own first reaction to a fine crystal or cut gemstone will always be one of sheer uncritical pleasure. So I should hate to feel that this book will do anything to spoil that 'first fine careless rapture'. Rather do I hope that after the first impact is over, it will add further dimensions of interest by taking a closer look and trying to understand better the individual phenomena which contribute to the attraction and character of each variety of precious stone.

If one were thinking of buying the stone concerned a closer scrutiny with a lens would, of course, be necessary to see that it contained no flaws or ugly inclusions, that it was well cut, and so on. But for the moment I am thinking in more general terms of the reaction of light with a gemstone.

To start with, let us make a list of the factors which play their part in making precious stones attractive. Firstly in the case of transparent stones, the perfection of *transparency* is exceedingly important in giving brightness to the specimen—any trace of cloudiness or milkiness is to be deplored. Next there are the surface reflections which give rise to the *lustre* of the stone; then, from the light which has been refracted into the stone, there are the internal reflections from the back facets which give it *brilliance*; the dispersion of the light into its spectrum colours, which gives it '*fire*', and the *body colour* of the specimen, or complete lack of colour, which depends upon selective absorption of the incident light. In translucent or opaque stones sheer colour is often

the most important attraction, but surface texture or patterning, iridescence, sheen, chatoyancy (cat's-eye effect), or asterism (star-stone effect)
may play their part.

Each of these effects is of course due to the action of light on or in
the stone, but what sort of action?

First, let me say a few words about light itself. It is a form of
electromagnetic energy transmitted in waves of very short but measur-
able length, which hurtle through space at a speed of 186,000 miles per
second—a speed which enables it, for instance, to bring signals across
the 93 million miles which separates us from the sun in a matter of
eight minutes flat. Radio waves, which are more demonstrably electromagnetic in origin, travel at the same speed and are essentially of the
same nature, though their wavelengths are measured in metres while
the waves of visible light are less than a thousandth part of a millimetre
in length, that is, there are about forty thousand waves to the inch.
X-rays, incidentally, belong to the same category and have wavelengths
some thousand times shorter still.

The wavelengths of visible light are conveniently given in Ångström
units ($1 \text{ Å} = 0 \cdot 0000001$ mm), or in nanometres which are ten times
as long. The colour of light depends upon its wavelength, red light
having the longest waves (approximately 7000–6400 Å), followed by
orange (6400–5950), yellow (5950–5750), green (5700–5000), blue
(5000–4400), and violet (4400–4000). There are no sharp divisions
between the colours so that the figures given must be considered as
only approximate. Beyond the red end of the spectrum are invisible
infra-red rays which have a strong heating effect, while beyond the
violet lie the ultra-violet rays which tan our skin and can produce the
curious coloured glow called fluorescence in many gemstones and
minerals.

Though it is convenient to talk and think of a 'ray' of light and
represent it by a straight line it is well to remember that this merely
represents the direction in which a front or train of light waves is
moving. When such a train of waves meets the surface of a transparent
substance such as a gemstone, what happens? Two things: *reflection* of
some of the rays (in a proportion determined by the optical density of
the stone and the angle at which the rays meet the surface) and *refraction*
of those rays which penetrate into the denser medium—that is, a change
of direction which is a natural consequence of the sudden slowing down
of the end of the wave front to enter the stone first while the other end
is still travelling at full speed. By the time the whole group is inside the

stone it will be advancing in a new direction, with the waves more nearly parallel to the surface and the direction of the rays nearer the perpendicular (Fig. 8 (1)).

One can see much the same thing happening if one looks down from a cliff at sea-waves as they approach the shore. These always break parallel or nearly parallel to the beach, though they may have been

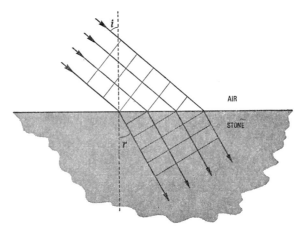

8 (1). Refraction of light waves on entering a denser medium i = angle of incidence, r = angle of refraction

advancing quite obliquely to the shore before the slowing down effect of the land made itself felt in shallow water. The refracting power of a substance is conveniently and universally expressed by its 'refractive index'; an optical constant of great importance in gemmology. In its most understandable form the refractive index of a stone can be defined as the ratio of the velocity of light in air to its velocity in the stone. This is expressed mathematically as the ratio of the sine of the angle of incidence to the sine of the angle of refraction. Since the velocity varies with the colour (wavelength) of the light, yellow sodium light is fixed as the standard. The refractive index of a faceted gemstone as well as the extent of its double refraction, if any, can be quickly measured on an instrument known as a refractometer.

In what has been said we have been assuming that the light rays are striking the surface of the stone obliquely, whereas most of the light when we look down on a faceted stone will have struck the table facet perpendicularly. With such rays reflection still takes place, but the rays entering the stone are not refracted, although of course they are slowed down as before. Refraction obviously will take place, however, at the other facets of the crown.

SURFACE LUSTRE

The surface lustre of a stone depends partly on the perfection of its polish, and the harder the stone the better polish it will take. But mainly it depends upon its refractive index. To give some idea of the effect of this index on the brightness of lustre, quartz with an index of 1·55 reflects only 4 per cent of the light incident upon it perpendicularly; sapphire, index 1·77, reflects 8 per cent; while diamond, with its index of 2·42, reflects no less than 17 per cent of the incident light. Metals, of course, and minerals with a metallic lustre, reflect much more light than this. Pyrite, for instance, which jewellers know better under the name of marcasite reflects 54·5 per cent of incident light and does it so constantly that it is used as a standard for reflectivity measurements.

While the brightest reflections come from opaque minerals with a *metallic lustre*, the most brilliant lustre seen in transparent minerals is that of diamond, and is thus termed an *adamantine lustre*. Amongst gemstones diamond is really almost alone in possessing this degree of lustre. Though zinc blende or sphalerite reflects almost the same amount of light it is so soft that the polish can't quite achieve the distinctive look of a diamond surface. The nearest candidates amongst gemstones used in jewellery are sphene, zircon and demantoid garnet which reflect little more than half the light that diamond does. In the case of zircon some peculiarity in the polish gives a curious greasy or resinous undertone to its otherwise near-adamantine lustre.

Since the majority of gemstones have refractive indices similar to those of glass (1·5–1·7) it is natural that they should have a glassy or *vitreous lustre*. Since amber is a fossil resin it is natural that it should have a *resinous lustre*; likewise that pearl should have a *pearly lustre*.

BRILLIANCE

So much for surface lustre, but what happens to the greater proportion of the light which has entered the stone? In the case of diamond, as I have described in Chapter 5, the proportions of the brilliant-cut are carefully chosen so as to ensure that all the light falling on the front of the stone is totally reflected by the facets as though they were a series of mirrors; and it is this reflected light combined with the surface reflections which gives the diamond its exceptional brilliance.

A skilled lapidary, by using suitably modified cuts, can ensure that in other colourless stones practically all the light is reflected back to the observer, and in the case of the glass imitations commonly known as 'pastes' the brilliance is sometimes artifically enhanced by having a metallic backing to the rear facets.

FIRE

But sheer brilliance is only part of the particular beauty of diamond, which can also be relied upon to show 'fire', the name given to the sparkle of spectrum colours due to dispersion of the refracted rays in their passage in and out of the brilliant. The dispersion is caused by the greater degree of refraction undergone by violet rays compared with rays at the red end of the spectrum when they enter the stone. This can be measured and numerically stated as the difference between the refractive index of the stone for red light and its refractive index for violet light. Only zircon of the colourless natural stones can show a similar dispersion to diamond. Demantoid garnet and sphene have a dispersion higher than diamond (which, considering its high refractive index, is *not* a very dispersive mineral), but in these, where the stone is coloured green or yellow the play of spectrum colours is not so obvious to the eye, and it is also unlikely that the lapidary has made any attempt to cut the stones in the best proportions for showing the effect.

COLOUR IN GEMSTONES

So far in this chapter I have used a great many words (perhaps too many) in explaining the nature and reasons for lustre, brilliance and fire in faceted precious stones. These effects are all-important in the case of diamond, a singly refracting stone in which complete absence of colour is considered perfection, but have far less significance in the realm of coloured stones, which we are about to enter.

From now on the plot thickens and unsuspected tricks of behaviour begin to show themselves. Colour in itself is a pretty complicated subject, but its proper understanding in the case of minerals must embrace the effects not only of absorption but also of double refraction, dichroism and fluorescence to make the story at all complete. To study all this thoroughly needs expensive apparatus and some scientific training, but the simple bits and pieces described in the next chapter will provide keys for anyone who is sufficiently interested to open most of the essential doors to understanding those effects which I have called the 'further dimensions of interest' at the beginning of the chapter. 'Further dimensions of interest' are dull and donnish words for the world of magic behaviour which is part and parcel of every gemstone and serves to build its character.

The true nature of colour was first revealed by Isaac Newton in 1666. He was then twenty-four years old and had just taken his degree at Trinity College, Cambridge. At Stourbridge Fair (which was then a famous market off the Newmarket Road and the origin of Bunyan's 'Vanity Fair') he had purchased a prism of glass, intending 'to try therewith the celebrated phenomena of colours', and later carried out simple but fundamental experiments, the first of which was to place the prism in the path of a thin shaft of sunlight entering through a quarter-inch hole in the shutter of his darkened room. This produced an oblong spectrum thirteen inches long on the opposite wall, consisting of all the colours of the rainbow from red, the least refracted rays, to violet, the most refracted. Further experiments convinced him that the origin of all colours was in what we call 'white' light from the sun or any other incandescent source, and that these were separated by the prism on account of their different 'refrangibility'. Objects appear 'coloured' to us because they absorb most of the colours of the spectrum but reflect or transmit freely the colour that they appear to be. This is known as 'selective absorption'.

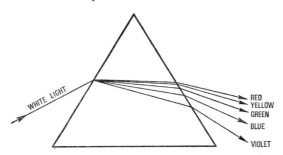

8 (2). Dispersion of white light into spectrum colours on passing through a prism

The prism Newton used was rather crudely made and the slit in his shutter rather wide. Had the conditions of his experiment been more refined he must have noticed that the projection of the sun's spectrum on his wall showed a number of narrow dark lines crossing the strip of colours. It would be fascinating to know how his giant mind would have interpreted this quite unexpected complication. Newton would indeed probably have carried on with his researches into colour, but his ideas were bitterly assailed by Hooke and other contemporaries. Hating controversy, Newton preferred to turn to the many other problems in mathematics and physics which engaged his attention.

Thus it was not until 150 years later (1817) that the detailed examination of the sun's spectrum began, and from this, by rapid stages, the study of spectra of all kinds, and the invention of the *spectroscope* which made such advances possible.

It was the German optician Fraunhofer (who lived only thirty-nine years) who made the key discoveries. For his observations he used a narrow slit to admit sunlight which was 24 feet away from a fine prism of his own making, which he mounted on a theodolite, through the telescope of which he viewed the spectrum of the sun. Under these conditions he could see hundreds of dark lines crossing the spectrum, and he made a map of these on which he named the most prominent lines A, B, C, etc. A was in the very deep red and his last prominent line, H, was in the very deep violet. Fraunhofer also made the first diffraction grating (an alternative means of splitting light into its component wavelengths) and with its aid calculated with surprising accuracy the wavelengths of some of the main lines in the sun's spectrum. He was also the first to observe the spectrum of a star. But it was not until some thirty years later that scientists hit on the simple device of interposing a lens between slit and prism, thus giving a parallel beam and a pure spectrum without the necessity of having the slit many feet distant.

The main Fraunhofer lines are still used by opticians as markers for various parts of the spectrum. We now know their exact wavelengths and the reason for their existence. Each of the thousands of lines in the sun's spectrum is due to absorption of light by a particular element in the vapours surrounding the sun's incandescent body. They are the exact reversal of the bright lines emitted by these elements when vaporised in a hot flame or an arc lamp in the laboratory. The dark D lines in the yellow part of the sun's spectrum are due to sodium, and can be seen through a small spectroscope as a bright yellow line in any luminous flame, so ubiquitous are traces of sodium compounds and so sensitive is the test; but more powerfully, of course, in light from sodium vapour lamps such as those used for street lighting. This light is virtually 'monochromatic' consisting of two yellow lines very close together and known as the sodium 'doublet': their wavelengths are 5896 and 5890 Ångströms. Sodium light is very important as being the standard light for refractive index measurements. All the R.I. figures given for gemstones in this or any other book are understood as being for sodium light.

The spectroscope, which in its essentials consists of a narrow slit to admit the light, a collimating lens to make the rays parallel and a train of prisms, may be considered the most simple in construction of all scientific instruments, and yet it has revealed to us more information about the universe than any other, from the structure of the atom to the composition and movements of the stars. With its aid new elements have been discovered (caesium, rubidium, thallium, indium) each named after the colour of its most tell-tale spectrum line, and with its help—to come down with a bump to the subject of this book—the majority of gemstones can be identified with speed and certainty.

As already stated, stones appear 'coloured' to us because they absorb preferentially many of the colours of the spectrum and transmit or reflect rays of the colour that the stone appears to be. The spectroscope enables us to see just which colours have been absorbed by the stone in the shape of dark 'absorption bands' which cross the continuous background of rainbow colours provided by a beam of white light passing through the specimen. This is known as the absorption spectrum of the stone. Some specimens of zircon are well-known for showing a striking absorption spectrum, as shown in Fig. 8 (3).

What causes the 'selective absorption' of light which gives rise to colour in minerals? Of the ninety-two elements of which this world is built, there are eight which are known to produce colour in their salts or compounds. These, the so-called 'transition elements' can be listed as titanium, vanadium, chromium, manganese, iron, cobalt, nickel and copper. Of these iron and chromium are by far the most important. Iron is the almost universal colouring agent in nature, the tints it produces of green, brown and red being, however, somewhat sad and sombre when compared with those of chromium which is the aristocrat of colour-makers in gemstones, producing as it does the rich red of ruby and the glorious green of emerald.

As I pointed out in Chapter 2, colour in gemstones is curiously more often an 'accidental' quality than an intrinsic one. By which I mean that the mineral concerned is usually fundamentally colourless, there being nothing in its chemical composition to cause colour. The mere fact that a gem species has a wide colour-range must always point

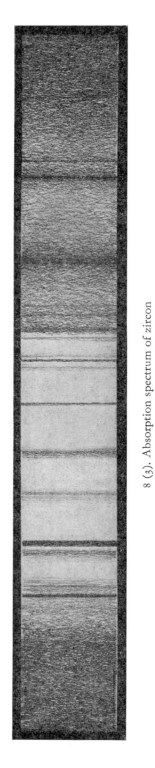

8 (3). Absorption spectrum of zircon

to this fact. Corundum, beryl, quartz, tourmaline, spinel, chrysoberyl, are all important examples of these so-called 'allochromatic', that is 'other-coloured' stones, whereas peridot and almandine garnet with their essential iron content, and the copper mineral malachite, are amongst the few 'idiochromatic' or self-coloured gem minerals.

DOUBLE REFRACTION AND DICHROISM

When dealing with crystals in Chapter 7 I explained that in crystals belonging to all the systems of symmetry other than cubic a ray of light on entering the crystal was split into two polarised rays each vibrating in one direction only and at right angles to the other. These rays have different velocities in the stone, which means that the mineral has a different refractive index for each. In the tetragonal, hexagonal and trigonal systems there is one direction of single refraction or 'optic axis', which is coincident with the vertical 'c' crystal axis and axis of maximum symmetry. In minerals crystallising in the orthorhombic, monoclinic and triclinic systems there are two optic axes. In the uniaxial stones one of the two polarised rays is always vibrating at right angles to the optic axis and this has a constant refractive index and colour attached to it and is known as the 'ordinary' ray. The other varies in its refractive index and colour from coincidence with the ordinary ray in the direction of the optic axis, to maximum divergence at right angles to this. Hence it is dubbed the 'extraordinary' ray. The detection of double refraction in a cut stone simply by careful scrutiny with a lens is a very valuable trick to learn, and this will be dealt with fully in the next chapter.

Where the two rays have markedly different colours the stone itself will appear differently coloured when viewed from different directions. This important effect is known as *dichroism*. A little instrument called a dichroscope separates the colours, and enables them to be compared side by side when looking through its eyepiece, but one can view one colour at a time simply by turning a piece of polaroid film in front of the eye, when first one of the polarised colours and then the other will appear. If the polaroid is not marked to show the vibration direction of light passing through it, this can be easily determined by looking through it at light reflected from the polished surface of a desk or a plain sheet of glass (not a mirror or a metal). We know that reflected light is largely polarised parallel to the reflecting surface, hence the anti-glare effect of polaroid spectacles, in which the film is so oriented that it only passes light vibrating vertically and thus effectively nullifies the glare caused by reflection. So we only need to turn our polaroid until the reflection from desk or glass is at its minimum to know that the vibration direction of our polaroid is vertical.

Now for a practical application of all this curious behaviour: if a crystal of ruby can be held with its optic axis (main axis of symmetry) vertical and viewed through a 'marked' polaroid it will be found that the best carmine colour is seen when the vibration direction of the polaroid is horizontal, this corresponds to the *ordinary* ray; the extra-ordinary ray will be seen to have a rather unpleasant yellowish red. This is fortunate for the lapidary and the gem-lover; for if the table facet be cut at right angles to the optic axis it means that the rich colour of the ordinary ray will be virtually the only one seen on looking down on the stone. The reverse is true unfortunately in the case of aqua-marine, for the best colour is seen when the polaroid vibration direction is parallel to the axis of the crystal, which is the vibration-direction of the extraordinary ray. Now, though the ordinary ray can be more or less isolated the extraordinary ray cannot. The best one can do in the case of aquamarine is to cut the stone with the table facet parallel to the optic axis when, at any rate, 50 per cent of the better-coloured ray will be seen on looking down at the cut stone. The lapidary seldom thinks in scientific terms and to him all this talk of ordinary and extra-ordinary rays would seem highbrow nonsense. What he does know, however, from experience is that the best colour in ruby is looking down the crystal, and the best colour in aquamarine when looking across it. And most fortunately the 'habit' of the Burma ruby crystals makes it easy and natural for the basal plane to become the plane of the table facet, while the prismatic (columnar) habit of aquamarine crystals would in any case mean that the largest step-cut stones can only be obtained when the table facet is parallel to the axis.

Before leaving this discussion of the causes and effects of colour in gemstones, I must say a few words on the effect of fluorescence on the colour in certain gems, though it is seldom recognised by the writers of textbooks. Fluorescence is the name given to the emission of visible light by a substance when it is illuminated by light of shorter wavelength. It is usually thought of in connection with the attractive coloured glows shown by certain minerals when exposed to invisible ultra-violet rays from a mercury lamp fitted with a suitable filter. But such fluorescent glows, particularly if they are at the red end of the spectrum, can also be powerfully stimulated by visible blue and violet light. Now this is especially so in the case of ruby, and more still with synthetic ruby. One of the most spectacular yet simple experiments I know will demonstrate this, and the effect is so beautiful that I urge the enterprising reader to try it, particularly if he has access to chemical supplies and glassware in a school or university laboratory. All that are needed is a 750 ml or 600 ml spherical flat-bottomed glass flask filled with concentrated copper sulphate solution, filtered so as to make it free from any trace of milkiness, and a good red gelatine filter such as Ilford's 'spectrum red'. Next a really powerful light-source, most readily provided perhaps by a slide-projector which sends out a strong beam from its quartz-iodine bulb without dazzling all around. And finally, of course, the ruby or synthetic ruby to be examined. Light from the projector is made to pass through the copper sulphate flask on to the stone in a darkened room, a drape of black cloth being arranged if necessary round the projector lens and flask to ensure that the only light visible is that shining on the specimen. Then, holding the red filter close to the eye look at the ruby, which should be seen to glow like a red-hot coal. I have shown this experiment many hundreds of times to people visiting our laboratory, and the effect never failed to elicit a gasp of surprise and admiration.

The function of the copper sulphate solution is to absorb every vestige of red light from the white beam passed through it. This can be proved by looking at the pool of blue light transmitted by the flask through the red filter with no ruby present. The result should be complete blackness. Thus the ruby has been stimulated by the blue and violet rays and caused to emit the red rays which we see through the filter (against a black background which makes the effect more spectacular). A similar effect is seen with red spinel, though the spectroscope can easily analyse the light and shows them to be different, and thus a sensitive test for each species.

Clearly, since ruby is stimulated to this extent by blue and violet light it will also be emitting fluorescent red light when exposed to sunlight or strong electric light, and this undoubtedly adds a richness to the colour we see, while red garnet for instance, which has no fluorescence, looks dull by comparison. The fluorescent glow is due to the trace of chromium which also gives rise to the colour. And since emerald and alexandrite also owe their colour principally to chromium, it is hardly surprising that the 'crossed filter' technique described above will cause these stones to glow red also, though not so brightly as ruby does. It should perhaps be added that certain diamonds fluoresce bright blue in sunlight, and this may enhance their apparent colour by helping to disguise a hint of unwanted yellow in their body-colour.

Not all colour is due to absorption: it can be due to effects known as interference or diffraction, where light waves of most of the colours get 'out of step' and destroy one another, while those of another colour are in step and reinforce one another, giving brilliant flashes of almost monochromatic colour. The brilliant colours due to interference are familiar to anyone who has blown soap-bubbles or seen light reflected from a thin film of oil floating on a puddle in the road. The supreme example amongst gemstones is in precious opal, particularly the so-called 'black opal' from Australia, a fine specimen of which is arguably the most beautiful of all gemstones. Quite recently the electron micro-scope has revealed that the opal which shows these colours contains areas of closely packed spheres of silica which are of just the right dimensions to act as a diffraction grating, giving rise to the vivid interference colours. More will be said about this when we come to deal with opal.

Beautiful iridescent colours are also seen at certain angles when light is reflected from a cleavage surface of the feldspar mineral labradorite. The 'interference' colours in this case are due to the lamellar structure of the mineral produced by repeated twinning.

I hope I have succeeded in this long chapter in describing and explaining the main optical effects seen in gemstones.

— ◦ ◊ ◦ —

CHAPTER NINE

THE POCKET LENS AND OTHER ACCESSORIES

THE POCKET LENS

IT IS NOT my intention in this simple introduction to the study of gemstones to suggest the purchase of expensive instruments or to explain their use. This has been done in many general texts such as Webster's *Gems* and in my own book *Gem Testing*. But an interest in gemstones can be so much widened by having a few simple accessories available and knowing what to do with them that I thought it worth while describing some of these and giving some practical hints on their use, beginning with that indispensable instrument, the pocket lens.

A good lens is as essential to the gemmologist as are a good pair of binoculars to the ornithologist, and should be his constant companion. There are many magnifiers available from opticians, but most of these, such as the ordinary reading-glass, are too low powered to be of use in examining gemstones, though they may be of some value in looking at crystal groups. The watchmaker's glass or loupe which one can fix in the eye, leaving the hands free, is much favoured by jewellers, as it not only enables them to study the delicate mechanism of a watch, but also to examine hallmarks, the 'make' of jewellery, and the more obvious features of a gemstone. There is also an element of showmanship in using such a lens: it makes one *look* like an expert, and this is very popular, for instance, on TV programmes. But the magnification is usually too low (perhaps four diameters) to satisfy the keen gemmologist, who prefers an 8 or 10 × lens corrected for chromatic and spherical aberration, giving a flat field with no colour fringes. Such lenses are usually triplets and can be quite inexpensive.

The higher the power of a lens the more difficult it is to use, as the focal length is shorter and the position of exact focusing critical. The field of view is also more restricted in high-power lenses, so that a 20 × instrument is really very little use for the most commonly needed types of observation.

While the 8 or 10 × lenses made by Zeiss are probably the best on the market, and being housed in plastic are pleasantly light-weight for the pocket, cheaper lenses in a chrome-steel or aluminium mount such as those made by Gowllands can hardly be faulted. For general sorting purposes where low power and binocular vision are advantages, a 'head loupe' is very useful, in which there is a lens for each eye and an adjustable band to suit each wearer. This also, of course, leaves the hands free.

There is quite an art in using a 10 × lens to best advantage. There is a tendency to get in one's own light, and some difficulty in obtaining the position of sharp focus (which is only about one inch from the object) and in maintaining this steadily without wobble. An expert does all this as a matter of course, and so unconsciously that he finds it as difficult to put his actions into words as he would in explaining how to ride a bicycle. The lens must always be held as close to the eye as possible, and steadiness of focus is ensured by a light contact of the hand holding the lens with that holding the specimen. The photograph will show the position adopted better than words (see Plate 10a).

Holding an unmounted gem for lens examination is a problem in itself, and the beginner would do well to practise first with something easily held in the hand, like a gem-set ring. Otherwise (unless the stone be very large) some form of tongs or tweezers will be necessary. The diamond or stone expert is thoroughly accustomed to picking up a stone in 'corn-tongs' and tilting it here and there while he scrutinises it with his lens. But the beginner finds it very difficult to avoid gripping the tongs too tightly and so suffers the annoyance of seeing or hearing the stone spring away into some inaccessible corner of the room. If it is of any comfort to the reader, I am one of those who finds handling stones in tongs a difficult matter. Choice of tongs is very important. These should be fairly large in size, blunt ended, and of *mild spring*. For some reason the tips of such tongs are internally serrated crosswise, presumably to afford a better grip—which may work with such things as stamps, but is of little help with gemstones. These can more safely be handled if a longitudinal groove be made with a file into which the girdle of the stone can fit, thus giving less tendency to skid away.

The stone to be examined is first cleaned with a handkerchief and placed table facet down on a flat surface. It should then be possible to pick it up with the table facet dead parallel to the length of the tongs, using just sufficient pressure to hold it. Easier forms of holder are spring tongs with deeply grooved tips: these are universally used in the U.S.A., Switzerland and Germany for holding stones which are to be examined under the microscope. Easiest of all in some ways are spring tongs in which three wire prongs project and retract in a pencil-like holder. These are better for round than for step-cut specimens, and will not accommodate large stones.

Having learned to obtain a clear view of a gemstone with his lens, the beginner may wonder what features in a stone he is supposed to look for—what advantage has he gained? The full answer to such an understandable question can only be given piecemeal in the descriptive part of this book, where the features in every gem variety which can be seen with a lens will be given priority over those which require more elaborate instruments for their observation. In experienced hands, diamond, zircon, peridot, demantoid, amethyst, hessonite, lapis lazuli, aventurine quartz, ivory, pearl and cultured pearl, as well as pastes, doublets, and many synthetics, should be identified with certainty by using a lens only.

But there is one particular skill with a lens that is the most important of all in the study and recognition of gemstones, and that is the detection of double refraction, and a rough estimate of its strength, by observation of the 'doubling' of the back facet edges, and I strongly recommend the reader to practise this art with all the sizable cut gems he can lay hands on.

A zircon is undoubtedly the best stone to experiment with: preferably a brilliant-cut white zircon of one carat or more in weight. If such a stone is held in the tongs and the lens focused sharply on the rear facets as seen through the table, it should be noticeable that the image of each edge marking the junction of the facets is not a single line but two parallel lines close together. The effect can be seen in the drawing taken from a photograph reproduced in Fig. 9 (1). The extent of the doubling will be plainly more on some facet edges than on others, because the difference in refractive index between the rays varies from zero in the direction of the optic axis (see Chapter 8) to its maximum at right angles to this.

The maximum difference between the least and greatest refractive index of a stone is known as its 'birefringence' or its 'double refraction' (D.R.), and is a very important number to remember when distinguishing one stone from another. In the case of white zircon it is 0·059, which may seem a small amount, but represents a quite strong degree of D.R. for a gemstone. In peridot (0·036), tourmaline (0·020) and kunzite (0·015), the effect is still quite easily seen with a lens, as it is with quartz (0·009) in stones of 5 carats and over. Going upwards from zircon we have the rare and beautiful gemstone, sphene, with a birefringence of 0·12, in which the 'doubling' is noticeably more than in zircon, and synthetic rutile in which the D.R. is 0·287 and the separation between the two images so great that one can easily miss it!

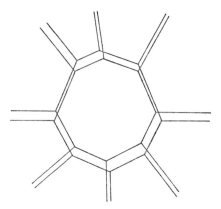

9 (1). Double refraction in cut zircon (from a photograph)

An admirable example of double refraction visible to the naked eye is given by clear cleavage pieces of calcite in the form known as Iceland spar, and it is well worth purchasing a specimen of this to observe without any trouble this very curious phenomenon. Large clear pieces of Iceland spar of fine quality are in demand for optical instruments and therefore rather expensive, but quite a smallish piece (say half an inch thick or so) will serve for the purpose in hand.

Calcite (like most other carbonates) has a very large double refraction—0·172 to be exact—and if the clear block of Iceland spar is placed over a black spot on a sheet of white paper, the spot will appear to be 'doubled'. If the spar is rotated, one image of the dot will remain stationary: this is due to the 'ordinary' ray. The other image will circle round the stationary one, and this belongs to the 'extraordinary' ray. In a block of Iceland spar one inch thick the apparent displacement measures nearly three millimetres.

The mere fact that a stone exhibits double refraction is enough to show that it must be a crystal and not glass, though it must be remembered that cubic crystals such as diamond and the garnets are singly refractive. An amusing example of the practical value of a test for double refraction which does not involve the use of any apparatus at all can be given here. It concerns the distinction between spheres of rock-crystal and glass. In these days when horoscopes, fortune-telling and the like are both popular and fashionable, the 'crystal ball' should be a fairly familiar object. Properly speaking these should be carved from 'rock-crystal', that is from a transparent crystal of quartz. The cost of such true crystal balls is quite considerable, however, and increases rapidly with the diameter of the sphere, so that most of these objects are actually made of glass. Should the reader see a reasonably priced 'crystal ball' offered for sale in a second-hand shop, and wish to ensure that it really is made from rock-crystal, there are two simple tests he can apply.

After cleaning the sphere with a handkerchief without warming it in the hands, the first test is to apply the tip of the tongue to its surface. If crystal, it should feel decidedly cold to the touch. The second is to test for double refraction. This can be done very simply. The sphere will act as a giant magnifying glass, and looking through it at the corner of a card or piece of notepaper placed against its opposite surface, a magnified image of this should be visible. If the sphere is made from crystal then one or both edges of the card or paper will appear to be 'doubled' and variations in the doubling will be seen as the sphere is turned. Only in one direction (the optic axis) will there be no visible double refraction. A glass sphere will of course show no doubling effects in any direction, be notably less cold to the touch of the tongue, and quite likely include some spherical bubbles. As to what may be considered 'reasonably priced', I should say that £20 for a two-inch flawless crystal ball, £40 for a three-inch, and £80 for a four-inch ball might be considered good value. An ebony stand for the sphere is usually provided as a matter of course.

POLAROID

Another inexpensive and simple accessory which will provide the gem-lover with a much more sensitive test for double refraction (though not a quantitative one) is the remarkable material known as 'polaroid'. This consists of a plastic sheet containing a compound so strongly dichroic that one of the two polarised rays which pass through it is completely absorbed. Light passing through a sheet of polaroid is thus completely polarised—that is, it is vibrating in one direction only. If two sheets of polaroid are superimposed in parallel positions light can pass quite freely, but if they are in the 'crossed' position there is virtual extinction of light. It is when they are in the crossed position that two sheets of polaroid form such a sensitive test for double refraction, and will show, for instance, the traces of birefringence, due to strain, to be found in almost all diamonds, garnets, synthetic spinels, and many pastes. In the case of a truly birefringent crystal which is rotated between crossed polaroids or 'polars', the effect to be looked for is that in four positions during a complete rotation of 360° by the specimen there will be no light transmitted. These are known as 'extinction' positions and occur when the polarised rays passing through the crystal are vibrating parallel to the light passing through the polaroid sheets. In all other positions the polarised ray from the first polaroid is split up on entering the crystal into two polarised rays, vibrating mutually at right angles, but now obliquely to the vibration direction of the second polaroid, so that some light is able to pass through.

Though it is possible to apply this sensitive test for birefringence with two unmounted one-inch squares of polaroid film, it is better to mount these in glass, as one would a lantern slide, to prevent their being scratched by contact with gemstones tested, and since the test requires that the stone examined be rotated in the plane of the polarisers, it is best to have these mounted in the 'crossed' position at either end of a short tube, with a slot between them through which the specimen can be accommodated. Unless one has a passion for making one's own gadgets it is best to purchase some form of commercially made polariscope. These are not expensive, and of course are designed to be easy to use. Two types can be recommended—the Rutland polariscope, which is a pocket instrument, and the Rayner polariscope, which is designed to be used on the bench or table and has built-in lighting. In the latter there is ample room between the polars to accommodate quite large specimens or an immersion cell containing liquid. Both these instruments can be obtained from Gemmological Instruments Ltd., Saint Dunstan's House, Carey Lane, London EC2V 8AB, while polaroid film, mounted or unmounted, can be purchased from H. B. S. Meakin Ltd., 9 Tredown Road, London SE26 5QQ.

Apart from being used as a sensitive test for birefringence, polaroid can be used to detect dichroism, as already explained in the last chapter.

This can be done either by rotating a single sheet of polaroid while viewing light transmitted by the stone or crystal, or by mounting two polars with their vibration directions mutually at right angles in a pair of old spectacle frames; then by closing first one eye and then the other the two different tints shown by the specimen can each be seen in rapid succession. In the conventional 'dichroscope' a rhomb of calcite is incorporated in a tube at one end of which is a small square aperture, and at the other a lens. The strong double refraction of the calcite presents the observer with two continuous images of the square 'window' and each image is polarised at right angles to the other. If a dichroic stone is examined through such an instrument the two colours transmitted can be seen side by side, an arrangement which enables even slight differences in tint to be observed.

The Chelsea Colour Filter

The last simple accessory I want to recommend in this chapter is a colour filter which has been found to be a useful means of distinguishing between stones in which the colour looks to be much the same to the naked eye. This was devised in 1934 by the author and his colleague, C. J. Payne, and was received with such enthusiasm by the students of gemmology at Chelsea Polytechnic that it was decided to make it generally available through the Gemmological Association and to name it the 'Chelsea' colour filter. There are actually two filters incorporated, the combined effect being that only two narrow bands of colour are transmitted—one in the deep red, the other in the yellow-green part of the spectrum. This means that any coloured object viewed through the filter must appear either red or green or a curious intermediate shade which it is difficult to name. It so happens that stones which owe their colour to chromium, whether they be red as in ruby and spinel, or green as in emerald and alexandrite chrysoberyl, transmit freely in the deep red and absorb a good deal of the yellow-green light which the filter transmits. The result is that such stones appear red through the filter. In the case of ruby there is the added effect of fluorescence, so that a ruby has a distinctive glow through the filter which a red glass, for instance, would not display. Much more important is the case of emerald, for the distinction of which from most of its imitations the filter was originally designed. The finest emeralds, i.e. those from Colombia and from the Ural Mountains, appear quite decidedly red through the filter, and this at least tends to confirm their authenticity, as green glass and the so-called '*Soudé* emerald' imitations appear green. But since the filter was first prepared synthetic emeralds have arrived on the market, and these show even more glowingly red through the filter than natural stones, as they are exhibiting something of the fluorescent effect which has been described in ruby. As a further warning it should be said that emeralds from India and South Africa show little change of colour through the filter, while demantoid garnet, green fluorspar and green zircons show a pinkish effect. Chalcedony stained green with chromium salts to represent the more valuable chrysoprase (which owes its colour to nickel) can be distinguished by its pink appearance through the filter.

The above summary may well have proved more confusing than helpful. However, I can assure the reader despite all the ifs and buts, that the Chelsea filter can be of real assistance when used with common sense and discretion.

More simple to describe are the effects seen with certain blue stones coloured by cobalt, all of which show strongly red through the Chelsea filter. It so happens that no natural gemstone owes its colour to cobalt, thus 'red through the filter' is a useful danger sign, signifying either cobalt glass, synthetic blue spinel or possibly synthetic blue quartz. Synthetic spinel of pale blue colour resembles aquamarine very closely, and here the filter affords a definite and rapid test. True aquamarine assumes a distinctly green appearance, while the synthetic spinel has a very characteristic chestnut red. Even with blue stones, unfortunately, a warning must be given that natural blue spinels have a rather reddish appearance through the filter, and so do natural mauve sapphires from Ceylon which contain a trace of chromium.

In the descriptions of gemstones which form the later part of this book, reference will be made to effects seen through the Chelsea filter where these seem significant, and it is hoped that the information so given may prove more helpful than the above paragraphs might lead one to believe.

To obtain the best effects with the Chelsea filter the stone to be examined should be placed under a strong tungsten light and the filter held close to the eye. For spectacular results I can recommend cobalt-coloured synthetic spinel, and Chatham synthetic emerald, both of which show a most satisfying red reaction.

————— ◊ —————

CHAPTER TEN

HARDNESS, CLEAVAGE AND DENSITY

HARDNESS

SECOND ONLY TO beauty, hardness is an essential feature of a precious stone, since it must be capable of taking a high polish and of retaining that polish in the face of daily wear in a piece of jewellery.

Unfortunately, the definition and the measurement of hardness, unlike that of refractive index and density, is not a simple matter. Moreover a test for hardness is likely to be to some extent a destructive test, and is thus considered tabu in gemmological circles except in certain specific cases which will be described in due course.

The type of hardness which we consider and use in gemmology can be defined as 'the degree of resistance to scratching' and a scale of scratch-hardness using well-known minerals, which was devised as long ago as 1816 by the mineralogist Friedrich Mohs is still in use at the present time and the hardness 'numbers' quoted in this or any other book are Mohs hardness numbers.

To have lasted for more than a century and a half Mohs's classification must have great practical value, but its one great defect is that though it gives a true *order* of scratch-hardness, the numbers have no quantitative significance. In particular, the gap between hardness of sapphire, given as 9, and diamond, listed as 10, is enormously greater than the hardness difference between any of the other minerals.

Here is Mohs's scale:

1	Talc	6	Orthoclase
2	Gypsum	7	Quartz
3	Calcite	8	Topaz
4	Fluorspar	9	Sapphire
5	Apatite	10	Diamond

In the old days, before synthetic stones of hardness equal to natural gems became a commonplace, the jeweller's chief concern was to distinguish between real stones and 'pastes', that is, glass imitations, and to do this he used a hardened steel file which had a hardness on Mohs's scale of between 6 and 7. This would make a nasty mark on a soft glass imitation gem but leave most natural gems unscathed. The test was thus effective in a brutal way, but tended to spoil much beautiful paste jewellery. Moreover there are a few natural gems, such as opal and sphene, which can be marked by a file, as well as many harder stones which are brittle enough to crumble at the girdle or on facet edges if a file is roughly used.

The number 7 (quartz) on Mohs's scale is particularly important, since the gritty particles in ordinary dust consist mainly of quartz and are thus likely to cause scratches on gemstones which have a lower hardness value. Ordinary window-glass ranks about $5\frac{1}{2}$ on the scale, that is it can be faintly marked by feldspar, and quite easily by quartz, topaz and a whole host of gem minerals. Thus to reckon the ability to scratch glass as a prerogative of diamond is pretty good nonsense.

Hardness in minerals is very much a directional property, that is, a crystal is scratched much more readily on some faces than on others; and on any one face more readily in some directions than in others. This effect is most strikingly shown by the beautiful blue mineral, kyanite, sometimes cut as a collector's stone. Crystals of kyanite can readily be scratched by the point of a needle drawn down the length of a prism face, but resist scratching at right angles to this. The Mohs hardness in this extreme case varies between 4 and 7.

The fact that diamond can be abraded and polished by means of its own powder depends upon the considerable variations in hardness it displays on different crystal planes and in different directions on each plane. The cube face is the softest plane and the octahedron the hardest. In the plane of the cube the easiest directions for abrasion are those parallel to the crystal axes, perhaps 100 times more easy than at $45°$ to the axes. On planes parallel to the octahedron all directions are hard, but the most favourable directions for polishing are towards the corners of the triangular face. Diamond powder can abrade or polish diamond surfaces because an appreciable proportion of the millions of grains in the powder will be presenting their hardest directions against the softer directions of the surface to be polished.

Many attempts have been made to measure the hardness of minerals quantitatively, and the results obtained vary, as might be expected, with the method used. Rosiwal used as his criterion the loss in weight in the specimen on grinding the surface under controlled conditions. Eppler used a sand-blast abrasion method, while Knoop and O'Neill used the depth of indentation of a lozenge-shaped pyramid of diamond under standard pressures. This last method is obviously measuring a different quality from those using abrasion, but is very successful in gauging the hardness of metals. Here, as a matter of interest, are the figures. To make comparison easier, all results have been scaled so that corundum (sapphire) = 1000.

Mineral	Mohs	Rosiwal	Eppler	Knoop	O'Neill
Diamond	10	90,000	18,530	5,180	6,350
Sapphire	9	1,000	1,000	1,000	1,000
Topaz	8	194	154	766	625
Quartz	7	175	170	483	567
Feldspar	6	59	85	300	458

In the abrasion methods, at least, it can be seen from these figures that diamond is enormously harder than the next hardest mineral, corundum. Into the gap between them come several man-made abrasives not found in nature, including silicon carbide, better known under its trade name of carborundum, and the carbides of boron and tungsten.

The fact that diamond is harder than any other mineral does make a careful hardness test both conclusive and feasible. Should a stone under test appear to be a diamond, an edge of the stone can be carefully rubbed against a polished surface of sapphire (either low quality natural or synthetic). If the stone is a diamond it will be felt to 'grip' on the sapphire surface, and make a distinct mark which will not disappear when rubbed with a moistened finger. If it is not, it will 'skid' on the sapphire surface and leave no mark.

It is perhaps justifiable in the case of one of the most deceptive of diamond simulants, strontium titanate, to pass over to the attack, so to speak, and give its surface (near the girdle where it will show least) a gentle prod with the point of a needle. Strontium titanate has a hardness of only $5\frac{1}{2}$ Mohs, and thus can be marked by a needle point.

Other cases where hardness tests can be justified—always if used with caution on inconspicuous parts of the specimen—are the many translucent stones which resemble the two minerals nephrite and jadeite, the only ones to which the name jade can properly be given. Jadeite, the more brightly coloured and more highly prized form of jade, has a hardness just under that of quartz (say $6\frac{3}{4}$), while nephrite is just a little softer than this. Neither stone, then, should be vulnerable to the point of a needle or the steel blade of a penknife. Bowenite, however, which closely resembles jade, though harder than most serpentines will show a scratch when a needle point is applied, and as this admittedly beautiful material is often sold as 'new jade' so simple a test may be quite useful.

In later chapters there will be a number of other instances where a careful hardness test will be suggested. Always, however, use other means of testing where possible and avoid damaging even an imitation material more than is absolutely necessary.

'Hardness points' consisting of sharp fragments of the harder minerals in Mohs's scale mounted in holders can be purchased, but are not greatly to be recommended as they are rather clumsy for carrying out so delicate an operation as a hardness test. The point of a needle, on the other hand, provides a delicate and precise probe, and polished pieces of low-quality sapphire or of synthetic sapphire are most useful in testing diamond as indicated above. Always rub any possible scratch mark with a moistened finger and examine with a lens, and take a pride in leaving no easily seen trace of damage done.

Before leaving this discussion on hardness a word should be said on the effect that hardness in a gemstone has upon its appearance. One often hears people saying, of a stone whose nature is unknown or under question, that it 'looks hard' or 'looks soft' and one may tend to laugh at such a statement as an absurdity. But it is a fact that hard materials take a brighter polish than soft ones, and this gives a cleanness and 'snap' to the specimen. The worst effects are noticeable where the facets are not truly flat and the edges where they meet not sharp. This inevitably gives the stone a moulded look which one associates with glass imitations.

The type of jewellery for which a gemstone is suitable must depend a good deal on its hardness. Only the hardest stones can stand up to the wear and tear which a stone mounted as a ring is bound to suffer. Stones in brooches or pendants are usually worn less constantly and in less exposed positions, while for necklaces such soft materials as pearl, coral and amber can be used with perfect propriety.

CLEAVAGE

The tendency for crystals to split or break along definite planes has already been mentioned in Chapters 5 and 6. Cleavage planes are always thickly studded with atoms and have a comparatively weak attachment to the adjoining layers. They are always parallel to some important crystal face in the mineral concerned, and of course the number of directions the cleavage follows depends upon the type of face to which it is parallel. Thus a *basal* cleavage, such as that so perfectly developed in topaz, and even more perfectly in mica, will be parallel to one direction only. *Prismatic* cleavage, such as that in diopside, will be parallel to two directions and the angle between these may form a useful feature for identification. *Cubic* or *rhombohedral* cleavage must follow three directions. Calcite has the most perfect rhombohedral cleavage of any mineral, while galena, a well-known ore of lead, splits very readily parallel to the three directions of the cube faces. Diamond and fluorspar both have *octahedral* cleavage, which is thus parallel to four directions, while finally in zinc blende (or sphalerite) there is a perfect cleavage parallel to the rhombic dodecahedron, which means there are no less than six cleavage directions.

The terms used to describe the ease and quality of cleavage in minerals are commonly 'perfect' where it is easily induced and yields smooth lustrous surfaces; 'distinct', and 'indistinct' or 'imperfect' where the cleavage is less easily induced and the resulting surfaces not quite so smooth. It seems to me a pity that the two factors, 'ease of production' or 'readiness to cleave' and the perfection of the resulting surface, are not described separately. Thus cleavage in mica, topaz and calcite could be described as both 'perfect' and 'easy', but the effect in fluorspar I should describe as 'easy' but 'imperfect' because though readily induced the resulting surfaces are never truly smooth and lustrous, and the same might be said of the prismatic cleavages in barytes.

Too ready a cleavability is a distinct disadvantage in gemstones for the lapidary, since it is impossible to polish a stone along a cleavage plane, and moreover the vibration during cutting the stone may induce cleavage flaws not originally present or increase an incipient flaw till it reaches the surface, air enters and at once it becomes an unsightly blemish. Some stones indeed are notoriously risky to cut and polish because of their ready cleavage. Kunzite and euclase are examples of this: the lapidary may have finished the cutting and polishing without apparent mishap and be proudly contemplating the resulting gemstone, when, with a gentle 'ping' the stone falls into two pieces along a cleavage plane.

In diamond the octahedral cleavage must be considered a fortunate attribute since it is not so readily induced as to provide risks during cutting, such as those just described: yet a skilled worker can divide his rough diamond in any one of the four cleavage directions by tapping a blunt blade in the desired direction, as described in Chapter 5, and thus save much time and material. And the value of diamond grit and dust as an abrasive or polishing material is enormously enhanced by the 'self-sharpening' action of the cleavage whereby fresh sharp angular pieces are constantly being produced as the grit breaks up into fine particles.

One of the factors in the weathering away of rocks exposed to the air is known to geologists as insolation, or exposure to the heat of the sun's rays. This causes expansion of the surface layers followed by contraction during the chill of night, which tends to loosen the surface layers and allow them to be blown away as dust by a strong wind or washed away by torrential rain. In minerals with an easy cleavage collectors of fine crystals may find to their cost that something of the kind can happen when a specimen is on show in a window or near an electric light in a showcase. On several occasions I have realised sadly that my former clear crystals of fluorspar or barytes have become riddled with unsightly cleavage cracks.

A keen mineralogist or gemmologist should be able to distinguish between a natural crystal surface, a cleavage surface and a polished plane. Crystal surfaces, however perfect they may appear, will always show some faint striations or other markings which can be explained either as growth lines or etch markings. Cleavage planes can be more perfectly smooth and flat than the growth plane of a crystal, but are seldom without slight ridges or 'steps' where another level of cleavage begins. Another common feature of a cleavage surface is iridescence where a film of air has entered along an incipient cleavage plane giving 'interference colours' like those on a soap bubble or oil film on water. Artificially polished surfaces are, by contrast with the natural surfaces, completely featureless and seldom quite flat unless they are produced by a skilled optician.

The surfaces of cut diamonds are exceptions to the general rule, being almost optically flat as can be proved by observing reflections, shall we say, of a light bulb from a polished facet, when a perfect image can be seen with the name Osram (or whatever it may be) clearly legible. Modern zircons, which are cut in Bangkok by methods similar to those used for diamond, also have exceptionally flat surfaces.

The observation of actual cleavage planes on the surface of a cut gemstone, or flaws representing incipient cleavage within a stone may often help to identify it. By using a lens tiny 'nicks' in the girdle of a brilliant-cut diamond can often be spotted, which show the flat surfaces enclosing the typical cleavage angle of the mineral. When a gem mineral has an easy cleavage it behoves one to be especially careful in handling specimens mounted in jewellery. Any sharp jar is particularly dangerous. I have known several cases where drop ear-rings of topaz have 'snapped' along a cleavage plane simply by falling a few inches on to the plate-glass top of a dressing-table!

FRACTURE

Where a stone breaks other than along a cleavage plane the resultant surface, which is technically known as its 'fracture', may show characteristic features. The most commonly seen fracture has a curved, shell-like surface, for which reason it is known as a 'conchoidal fracture'. Conchoidal fracture is particularly typical of glass, but is also common in quartz and other minerals in which there is no pronounced cleavage.

DENSITY

It is a matter of common experience that some substances feel 'heavy' and others 'light', no matter what their actual weight may be. Thus iron we should reckon as 'heavy' while wood, which floats on water, we might rank as 'light', though an attempt to carry a wooden railway sleeper might alter our estimate of the latter.

For any true comparison of this important quality of matter we must obviously compare the weights of equal volumes of the substances concerned, or else use some agreed substance as a standard of comparison. Scientists have made both these approaches and, as a result, two different terms are used, which are practically synonymous— density and specific gravity. The *density* of a substance is defined as being its weight in grams per cubic centimetre, while its *specific gravity* is its weight compared with that of an equal volume of pure water at 4°C. But since the weight of 1 cc of water is 1 g the two quantities are numerically the same. The term density will be preferred here as being the simpler, but if an odd reference or two to the S.G. of a gemstone should slip through, the reader will, I hope, understand what is meant. I should perhaps mention here that scientists nowadays have decided to use the term millilitre in preference to the cubic centimetre of a fluid—but as a litre has a volume of 1000 cc it makes no real difference.

Having defined the term 'density', now let us consider its importance in connection with precious stones. So far as appearance is concerned, it has no influence at all. While there are psychological reasons which make us feel that a weighty substance is more authentic and important than one less ponderous, the advantage (other things being equal) in gemstones lies with stones of lighter density, as at a given price per carat you get more for your money.

The range in density for gemstones lies between amber, 1·08, and zircon, 4·68, and the densities of the great majority of gem species lie between 2·5 and 4·0. There are a few seldom-used stones with a density higher than zircon: hematite for one, a black and metallic-looking oxide of iron, has a density of 5·1; pyrites, with density a little lower; scheelite, a calcium tungstate mineral, which can resemble diamond (6·1); and highest of all, the important ore of tin, cassiterite, of which clear pieces are collectors' items. This has a density of 6·9, which makes it feel startlingly 'heavy' when held in the hand.

This effect of heaviness in the hand, which the Americans (making use of an old English word) denote as 'heft', is one which is well worth noting and constantly trying to use as a rough means of estimating the density of a loose stone. With a little practice, it should be possible to differentiate between a necklace of true amber (1·08) and the transparent brown bakelite beads which so commonly imitate it, even though the density of this plastic is only 1·26, which is low in any comparison except with the natural resins. The difference between the rare and valuable yellow topaz from Brazil, density 3·53, and the citrine or yellow quartz, density 2·65, which is, or was so commonly and wrongly sold under the better selling name of 'topaz', 'quartz topaz' or 'topaz quartz' should be discernible in the hand, assisted here by the notably slippery feel of true topaz when polished.

But quite clearly these estimates of density by 'heft' are little more than informed guesses, and since the density of a gemstone is a very constant and diagnostic feature and its measurement involves no risk of damage to the stone, it is worth taking a little trouble to ascertain it. The one great limitation to the practical value of the method is pretty obvious—that the density of a stone cannot be measured unless it is free from its setting, though stone necklaces can be measured complete unless there is a heavy clasp. Size and shape may pose problems but these are not insuperable.

Using a Balance

If the reader has access to an accurate jeweller's or chemical balance he is in a position to undertake a fairly exact density determination by the so-called hydrostatic method. A few simple arrangements must first be made. A bridge should be purchased or constructed to straddle the left-hand pan of the balance, leaving it free to swing. Two matchboxes (preferably loaded with tin-tacks or other small heavy objects to make them stand firmly) and a six-inch ruler-protractor will serve the purpose. A piece of stiff copper wire is then made into a spiral coil, large enough to act as a cage to hold any normal-sized gemstone, and this is connected by a short length of very fine thread or wire to a wire loop which enables the cage to be suspended from the hook at the top of the balance-pan. A glass beaker or small straight-sided tumbler, nearly filled with distilled or previously boiled water is then placed on the bridge over the balance-pan, and a small drop of liquid detergent stirred in to improve its 'wetting' powers. The length of the hook, wire and coil should be such that the coil is totally immersed in the water, but does not touch the bottom of the beaker, even when the balance is swinging. The only tricky and time-consuming operation in the above is the preparation of the suspending wire and coil—but once this has been made it will, of course, serve for an unlimited number of experiments. The drawing in Fig. 10(1) and the photograph in 10b will serve to make the arrangements clear.

The stone to be measured is first weighed in air in the ordinary way, as accurately as the balance and weights will allow. The units of weight do not greatly matter, but grams or metric carats (200 mg) are the most convenient, as decimals are so much more easy to use than fractions for the simple calculations that follow.

Make a note of this weight. Next, rig up the bridge, the beaker and the wire coil so that the latter is suspended in the water. Now weigh the empty coil while in the water. Make a note of this weight and carefully insert the stone to be tested (using tongs) into the wire coil, then weigh the suspended coil plus stone. If the weight of the coil in water now be subtracted from the weight of the coil and stone in water, we clearly have a figure for the apparent weight of the stone while it is suspended in water, and subtracting this from the weight of the stone in air gives one a figure for the 'loss of weight in water'. Now, as Archimedes was the first to realise, the loss in weight sustained by a body when suspended in water is equal to the weight of the water displaced. And the water displaced by the stone is obviously equivalent to the volume of the stone.

$$\text{Thus we have density of stone} = \frac{\text{weight of stone in air}}{\text{loss of weight in water}}$$

The method outlined above is described in all textbooks of gemmology, and is capable of giving results accurate to two places of decimals provided the stone is not too small (say, over 5 carats), the

10 (1). Left-hand pan of balance arranged for hydrostatic weighing

balance a good one, and great care taken. The stipulation for boiled water and a trace of liquid detergent is to avoid the formation of air bubbles which otherwise can cling tenaciously to the wire cage or surface of the specimen greatly falsifying the result. The suspending wire or nylon thread needs to be very fine to avoid the clinging effect of the surface tension of the water having too marked an influence. Though the method is fundamentally simple, density measurements recorded in the literature have often been inaccurate, as a rule being too high.

HEAVY LIQUIDS

An easier method of assessing density and one which requires no balance and no calculation, makes use of the very few liquids which are heavy enough to allow some gems at least to float on their surface. For the most part these are smelly, poisonous, and expensive, but two at least can be recommended which are not excessively unpleasant on any of these counts, and though their cost may seem high their useful life as a quick check on identity can extend over a number of years.

The two liquids concerned are bromoform, density 2·86, and methylene iodide, density 3·33. Bromoform is virtually colourless when fresh, and being a near relation to chloroform has a similar rather heady ethereal smell. Methylene iodide is pale yellow when fresh but darkens when exposed to light owing to separation of iodine. This can be avoided by putting some copper filings or strips of copper in the phial or bottle which contains the fluid. Methylene iodide has rather a pungent disinfectant smell and is a most useful liquid to gemmologists as besides having so high a density it also has the high refractive index of 1·742.

An ounce of each of these fluids can usefully be purchased as a beginning and placed in small wide-mouthed bottles, preferably with ground-glass stoppers such as the so-called 'weighing bottles' used by chemists.

The methylene iodide should be used undiluted; its density is very similar to that of several quite important gemstones such as peridot and jadeite which will rise or fall very slowly in the fluid as a consequence of this. It will separate with ease and certainty topaz (3·53) which will sink, and citrine which will bob briskly to the surface, and so on.

The density of bromoform, on the other hand, comes at a rather non-crucial point in the scale for gemstones, and it may more usefully be carefully diluted with benzene (lighter-fuel will do) stirring the while with tongs or a glass rod, to a point at which a clear piece of cut or crystal quartz suspends in the fluid. Some pure bromoform should always be held in reserve for topping up should one overshoot the mark while diluting, a thing which often happens to the best of us.

The quartz specimen used as an 'indicator' should be left in the liquid as evaporation of the benzene may be more rapid than that of the bromoform, and the fluid increase slightly in density on keeping, even in a stoppered bottle. With quartz in suspension we know that the density of the fluid is exactly 2·651, so constant is the density of any pure quartz. The fluid as it stands can thus act as a check for the identity of any unmounted specimen of rock-crystal, citrine, amethyst or rose-quartz one may wish to check, as these will float alongside the indicator. It so happens that synthetic emeralds made by Chatham in the U.S.A. and Gilson in France have a density distinctly lower than that of any natural emeralds and almost exactly matching quartz. The liquid will thus provide useful confirmation of any emerald suspected (perhaps because of its very red colour under the Chelsea filter) of being one of these synthetics. In the same fluid all aquamarines and natural emeralds will sink fairly slowly, thus confirming their nature.

This limited use of the heavy liquid method goes as far as one can safely recommend for the non-technical gem-lover, who will at least gain some amusement from seeing stones which look alike revealing their differences in density by so simple a means. The necessary liquids and containers can be obtained from Gemmological Instruments Ltd., and even in these expensive days, £5 should cover the entire outlay on fluids and wide-necked containers.

Density measurements can be highly important in distinguishing the two jade minerals jadeite and nephrite from each other and from the numerous minerals which resemble them, and aspire to their best-selling name.

Here we may have to deal with sizable vases or carved ornaments, so that neither the use of a balance nor of small bottles of heavy liquids will be at all feasible. Much can be done with improvisation in such cases, if one is fortunate enough to procure good-quality spring balances with a ring at one end and a hook at the other. Useful ranges are from 0–500 g and 0–50 Troy oz. With such balances and great care in taking readings (using a lens and the eye on a level with the 'pointer') the ornaments (suspended by strong thread or thin string), can be first weighed in air and then immersed in a bucket of water containing some detergent. A paint-brush may be necessary to remove bubbles from nooks and crannies when immersed. The formula weight in air/loss of weight in water, can then be applied. A balance in which almost the whole scale is extended in taking the 'weight in air' is the one most likely to be accurate.

Jadeite has a fairly constant density of just over 3·3, while nephrite jade has a wider range of 2·93–3·03. The values for possible substitutes will be found in the chapter dealing with jade.

The density of minerals which have a simple chemical composition and occur in clear pieces is usually extremely constant—examples being quartz, 2·65; calcite, 2·71; fluorspar, 3·18; diamond, 3·52; corundum, 3·99. Though more complex gems may show density variations these variations may have significance and assist the keen worker to distinguish between stones of the same species but from different localities, and more importantly, between natural and synthetic gems.

A list of the density values for all important gemstones will be found in the tables at the end of the book, and these important figures will also naturally be included in the description of individual gemstones which forms the latter half of this book.

———————— ◁▷ ————————

CHAPTER ELEVEN

DIAMOND, THE INCOMPARABLE MINERAL

DIAMOND HOLDS, and always must hold, an unassailable position as the most popular and most important of all the precious stones. It has *par excellence* the essential attributes of durability and of beauty in terms of lustre, brilliance and fire; and though it can hardly be described as rare, the cost of recovery from rocks in which it forms only one part in twenty million, buried thousands of feet below the surface, and of processing and presenting the stone as a perfectly fashioned gemstone will always ensure that its value will be high, and will even compare with that of the much rarer ruby and emerald. The name diamond came to us through the old French *diamant* from the late Latin *adamant* and the earlier Greek *adamas* meaning unconquerable, in recognition of its extreme hardness. However, the name adamas in ancient texts must be accepted with caution since it was also applied to hard steel, while adamant refers not only to diamond but to magnetic iron ore or lodestone.

In jewellery diamond is virtually ubiquitous. In almost every fine jewel it plays either the principal or a prominent supporting role. There is perhaps a danger here: its very omnipresence may cause it to be taken rather for granted. In a ruby ring with a surround of diamonds to enhance it, the ruby will be praised and admired and scrutinised, the quality of the diamonds disregarded, and even in a diamond solitaire ring, though the size and value of the stone may be expected to impress a friend, the beauty of the diamond itself is so little understood or regarded that the pavilion facets will too often be fouled by the film of grease and dirt so quickly acquired in daily wear, when it only needs a gentle brushing in warm detergent water to restore the power of total reflection to the facets and thus enormously increase its sparkle and fire.

Diamond, as remarked in the opening chapter, is one of the two forms of crystallised carbon. Graphite is the other, and is a far commoner mineral as it is the stable form under ordinary terrestrial conditions. Charcoal is often quoted as an amorphous form of carbon, being the residue when wood, bone, or other organic material is submitted to 'destructive distillation' during which the water, oxides of carbon, naphtha, etc., are expelled. But the resulting charcoal is only some 93 per cent carbon, containing approximately 3 per cent of ash, as well as oxygen and hydrogen.

One thing that charcoal, graphite and diamond have in common is their faculty for burning in air when heated to bright redness, but with no flame. Flame can only be produced when the burning object is emitting an inflammable gas, whereas the combustion of carbon in air produces the non-inflammable carbon dioxide.

Scientists have learned, after a century of vain endeavour, the conditions under which diamond can be made artificially. The failure of all previous workers, until pioneers in Sweden and the U.S.A. independently broke through the barrier, was largely due to the seeming impossiblity of achieving the pressures of 100,000 atmospheres and simultaneously temperatures above 2775°C which the researches of P. W. Bridgman showed to be necessary if carbon were to assume the diamond rather than the graphite formation. Details of the first and subsequent successes in manufacturing diamond will be found in the chapter on synthetic gemstones later in the book, but the figures are mentioned here as indicating the conditions under which diamond must have been formed in nature. The pressures and temperatures needed can only obtain at depths of fifty or a hundred miles below the earth's surface, and for diamonds to form there must have been sources rich in carbon, presumably organic residues such as petroleum or coal. And even supposing that diamond crystals can be formed under these special conditions, there remains the problem of how they were transported to the earth's surface without being burned or converted to graphite. The latter stages of the journey at least must have been carried out at explosive speeds—probably through enormous steam pressure which forced the diamond-bearing rock through the rocky crust, forming the roughly circular vents we know as diamond 'pipes'. It seems probable that all the world's diamonds were originally 'delivered' to the surface through such vents, though in the millions of years which have passed the precious cargo has often spread across vast areas by the processes of weathering and water transport, to form the alluvial diamond fields from which they are now recovered.

The curious blue ground in which the diamonds are found in these pipes (known as 'kimberlite', at least in its South African form) is not thought to be the actual mother-rock of diamond. It is a form of igneous rock originally rich in olivine (peridot) which has been altered extensively by hydrothermal action, so that the olivine has largely been changed to serpentine. It has also been broken up extensively by mechanical stresses produced by earth movements. When exposed to the surface the oxidation of the iron content causes a change in colour to yellow, the 'yellow ground' encountered in the first 'dry diggings'.

Among the minerals associated with diamond in the kimberlite are blood-red pyrope garnet and green enstatite, as well as chrome spinel, iron-rich peridot, and magnetite; and as these are also found as inclusions in diamond crystals their association must be real and not accidental. A type of rock in which this assemblage of minerals is found is known as 'eclogite', and it is a fact that detached boulders of eclogite have been found embedded in the kimberlite, and that a few of these have contained diamond crystals.

Though the octahedron is undoubtedly the most common form assumed by diamond in nature, octahedra with flat faces and sharp edges are not common. These are known in the trade as 'glassies' and though their clarity is good, they are seldom free from traces of the unwanted yellowish colour. Uneven development of the faces may disguise the fundamental symmetry of these crystals, producing flattened forms. Far more frequent are octahedra with rounded or grooved edges. The faces are often domed, and formed from stacks of triangles, and there are also traces of other possible crystal forms. The term 'octahedroid' seems to cover these imperfectly shaped crystals more aptly than describing them as octahedra. One universal feature of octahedral faces in diamond is the presence of numerous triangular markings known as 'trigons'. These triangles, which mark the outlines of shallow pits, are strictly oriented in reverse direction to the octahedral face on which they appear. It is interesting to note that similar pits can be produced by etching a diamond with hot oxidising agents, but that the edges of these etched triangles are *parallel* to those of the faces on which they occur. Trigons are rarely seen on man-made crystals of diamond, and when seen these too are parallel to the underlying face.

Another very common habit in diamond is the rhombic dodecahedron, or rather intermediate forms with curved faces which show basically a dodecahedral shape. Very frequently indeed the dodecahedron faces show a 'seam' across their shorter diagonal and these are properly faces of the 'hexakis hexahedron', or to use a more homely name, the four-faced cube Fig. 6(7b). The cube itself is fairly often found in certain localities such as the Congo, but almost invariably these are diamonds of industrial quality only. The cube faces are never smooth, but roughened by growth or etch marks: sometimes the faces are hollowed to form what is known as a 'hopper' crystal, after the inverted pyramid known as a hopper through which grain passes into a mill.

In addition to the three basic forms just briefly described, twin crystals are very common, particularly the flattened triangular 'macle' as it is called by the diamond fraternity. This is a 'contact' twin, in which one half of an octahedron can be considered as having rotated through 180° on an octahedral plane. A diagram, Fig. 11(1), will help the reader to visualise this, or better still, a Plasticine model of an octahedron sliced with a knife and suitably rotated. It should of course be realised that no such rotation actually takes place, the crystal (for some mysterious reason) having assumed the reversed position during growth. These flattened triangular twins have a tell-tale re-entrant angle at the tips of each triangle. In a single crystal a re-entrant angle is not possible.

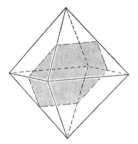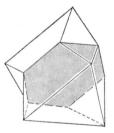

11 (1). Derivation of 'spinel' contact twin ('macle') in diamond

Other types of twin are not uncommon, including 'interpenetrant' twins in which two crystals appear to have grown within the same space but with different orientations which, none the less, have a symmetry relationship with one another. Interpenetrant cubes produce an attractive star-like form.

The immense hardness of diamond ensures that some traces of crystal form can be seen even in samples which have been transported for hundreds of miles and milled around with hard minerals and even other diamonds in the beds and pot-holes of turbulent streams. Even those recovered from the sea-bed off South West Africa are surprisingly uninjured by the battering of the waves. Occasionally, however, completely rounded pebbles of diamond are encountered. One such which was recently met with in a parcel of industrial diamonds was so smoothly rounded and so deprived of the characteristic subdued glitter that marks rough diamonds that I must confess that I needed to carry out a density test before being sure of its identity.

Both the crystal habit and the quality of diamonds vary greatly in different mines even when these are quite close together.

The diamonds recovered from the old 'wet diggings' by the Vaal river were finer and whiter than those from the group of mines round Kimberley, which tended to have a yellowish cast. The yield from the De Beers mine comprises mostly yellow and brown stones: sometimes 'Silver Capes' which to the layman would show hardly any colour at all. The Dutoitspan has produced a number of large yellow diamonds; Bultfontein on the whole yields small and spotted stones; Wesselton is noted for flawless octahedra and diamonds of deep orange tint, while of all the mines, Jaggersfontein in the Orange Free State has the highest reputation for so-called 'blue-white' crystals.

The giant Premier mine, made immortal by the discovery there in 1905 of the world's finest and largest diamond, the Cullinan, is also famous, amongst scientists at least, for being the only present-day source of type IIb diamonds, which are generally bluish in tint and conduct electricity, whereas most diamonds are non-conductive.

A rough idea of the quality of diamonds produced by a mine is given by the proportion of the output which is classed as 'gem' diamond to that classed as 'industrial', though it must be understood that there is no sharp distinction between the lowest gem grades and the highest industrials and the quality level at which the division takes place can be varied to suit the particular supply and demand in any one year.

At the present time the highest average quality of diamonds come from the alluvial fields of South West Africa, some 95 per cent of which are classed as being of gem quality. Stones produced in the vast Congo fields are classified as being practically the reverse of this, with 95 per cent of the diamonds being destined for industry. As for diamonds outside Africa, a student recently stated (in an examination answer) that 'most Russian diamonds are industrious diamonds'—which somehow seems appropriate in the case of people so hard-working and practical in their outlook.

Some clues as to the factors which influence the habit of diamond crystals are given by varying the conditions during their synthetic production. At the lowest feasible temperatures and pressures the cube is the commonest form and the crystals are black in colour. At higher temperatures the habit changes to cubo-octahedra or to dodecahedra, and the colour progresses through dark to light green. Finally, at the highest temperatures attained the crystals take the form of octahedra and are white in colour. By analogy with these experimental results it is not surprising that amongst the worst quality of natural diamonds in the Congo there are more diamonds showing a cubic habit than in any other locality.

Before leaving this matter of quality and habit in diamond one very curious fact should be noted, that virtually all the largest gem diamonds belong to the rare class known to physicists as type II, which are characterised by their chemical purity, transparency to ultra-violet rays, and their lack of crystal form. That largest and finest diamond of them all, the Cullinan, belongs to this select class.

THE CHEMICAL AND PHYSICAL PROPERTIES OF DIAMOND

Let us now look at the chemical, and more importantly, the physical properties of this astonishing mineral. We have already seen that diamond consists of crystallised carbon in a very pure form. Spectrographic analysis of large numbers of stones has usually shown the presence of minute quantities of silicon, aluminium, magnesium, and iron. What for diamond must class as a major impurity was quite unsuspected until 1959 when Kaiser and Bond found that *nitrogen* was present —some specimens containing as much as 0·23 per cent. This may not seem a lot, but in fact the presence or absence of nitrogen and the distribution of the element in the lattice has very marked effects on its properties: not, admittedly, properties which would affect its beauty or value, but peculiarities of behaviour towards light in the infra-red and ultra-violet regions which had puzzled physicists for several decades. So delicate is the response of diamond to traces of impurities or minute changes in structure of the lattice that even the presence or absence of aluminium, measured though it is in parts per million, is thought to affect the fluorescent properties of the mineral.

In common with the other forms of carbon, diamond is chemically inert, being unattacked by the most powerful acids. Being combustible it is, however, vulnerable to oxidation and it can be etched and finally vaporised away by, for instance, potassium nitrate at a dull red heat. At the higher temperature of 800°C, corresponding to a bright red heat, diamond begins to burn in air, and much more vigorously in oxygen. The burning process proceeds more rapidly with diamond powder or grit than with sizable stones whether cut or uncut. Workers in gem-testing laboratories become familiar with the ruined appearance of diamonds mounted in a ring or other piece of jewellery which has accidentally fallen in the fire. There is a general milkiness, which for-tunately being only on the surface can often be polished away, and the burning process may have produced artificial 'trigons', which at least prove that the stone was indeed a diamond.

Robert Boyle, in 1664, was the first to prove that when a diamond was exposed to extreme heat it was dissipated in 'acrid vapours', and thirty years later this was put to public proof in Florence when in the presence of the Grand Duke of Tuscany a diamond was burned by concentrating on it the rays of the sun with a glass lens. This must have been quite an occasion. The melting point of diamond is very high. When heated in the absence of air it will begin to blacken and eventually will become entirely converted into the more stable form of graphite. Graphite is said to melt at about 3500°C, and if the pressure were high enough to make diamond the stable form, it might be expected to melt at some point above this temperature.

Turning now to the physical properties of the mineral—we have already said a good deal in the last chapter about its supreme quality of *hardness*, for which it has been famous throughout history and which is still its most valuable attribute. The hardness of diamond can only be measured by using diamond itself, which cannot lead to a very satis-factory comparison with other substances. Leaving aside the estimates given in the previous chapter it may interest the reader to be given some figures from the late Professor Tolansky's readable book *The History and Use of Diamond* (1962). These relate to Vickers hardness numbers, which are derived from the amount of penetration by a shaped diamond point when pressed on the surface of a substance under a given applied load. Some of these Vickers numbers are brass, 100; steel, 500; topaz, 1300; sapphire, 2000; boron carbide, 2800; tantalum nitride, 3200; and silicon carbide (carborundum), 3500. When we come to diamond itself a hard-ness figure of 10,000 is estimated even for the softest directions!

Next, the *density*. For a mineral which is composed of pure carbon which has the low atomic weight of 12, diamond has the remarkably high density of 3·52. The fact that the other crystallised form of carbon, graphite, has the much lower value of 2·26 gives an idea of the more compact packing of the atoms in the diamond crystal. Precision determinations on thirty-five gem-quality diamonds showed their densities averaged 3·515, and varied hardly at all to three places of decimals.

Another physical property of diamond which is far less known than it should be is its remarkably *high conductivity* for heat. This is in fact of great importance in practical terms since it enables the rapid removal of heat by conduction when a diamond-set tool is grinding a material at high speed. The extreme 'coldness' when a diamond is touched with the tongue is a homely indication of this property. Another exceptional quality is its low linear expansion when heated and its low compressibility.

OPTICAL PROPERTIES

But it is of course the optical properties of the mineral which qualify it so superbly for use in jewellery. At its best it is wonderfully transparent. Because of this a far higher premium is placed on purity in diamond than in any other gemstone. Its hardness and the techniques used in cutting and polishing the stone ensure truly flat, bright surfaces, while the high refractive index (2·417) gives rise to a bright surface lustre and enables the properly proportioned brilliant to reflect back to the eye all the light falling on the front of the stone, while its power of dispersion provides the coloured flashes of fire which are its crowning beauty.

As mentioned in Chapter 8, in relation to its refractive index diamond has in fact a decidedly low dispersion: strontium titanate, for instance, which has the same index of refraction, has five times its dispersive power—and this can be accounted as normal. There are some who think that this fact must give strontium titanate the edge over diamond in this particular; but, in common with other diamond lovers, I disagree. Too great a play of colour makes a stone appear almost opalescent and one misses that sense of a pure white simplicity underlying all, which one can see in diamond. Shall we say that one prefers fire as an extra rather than as the most obtrusive optical quality in a precious stone which has so much else to offer.

Diamond crystals or cut diamonds when viewed between 'crossed polaroids' display a lively pattern of light and dark usually accompanied by patches of vivid interference colours. Such effects are typical of an isotropic mineral under strain, and are unlikely to be confused with true birefringence which gives rise to four sharp extinction positions when the stone is rotated through 360°. Each tiny inclusion in the stone has a little strain pattern round it which makes it easier to detect than it would be merely by inspection with a lens. Often the birefringence pattern shows zones marked by straight lines which may intersect to form a triangular outline. Probably no two diamonds have quite the same interference pattern and Professor Cavenago-Bignami of Milan has suggested that this provides a means of identification for individual diamonds, which might be valuable in case of theft. Even recutting the stone should not sensibly alter the character of its appearance in the polariscope.

The Carat Weight

The universal unit of weight for diamond and other precious stones is known as the carat, and is now fixed, by international agreement, at 200 mg or 0·200 g. It was not always thus. In past ages it was found convenient to use large seeds as units of weight for precious stones, pearls, or other small objects. In England the natural choice was a *grain* of wheat, 'drie and gathered out of the middle eare' as the old prescription gave it—and eventually it was agreed that there were 7000 such grains to the pound avoirdupois.

In the East the most favoured seeds were those found in the horn-shaped pods of the carob or locust tree (*ceratina siliqua*) which abounds in Mediterranean countries and extends to the Far East. These seeds are remarkably uniform, and average fractionally above 200 mg in weight. The name carat comes from the Greek *keration* which means 'little horn' and refers to the shape of the pods. Until the present century there was no exact agreement between the main trading cities of Europe as to the exact value of the carat weight. For example, in Florence it was 0·1972 g; in Venice, 0·2070; Amsterdam, 0·2057; and London, 0·2053.

A proposal to adopt a 'metric carat' of 0·200 g or 200 mg was accepted at an International Conference of Weights and Measures in Paris in 1907, but was slow in being officially adopted by the countries concerned, as it entailed provision of new weights, alterations of weights in stock books, etc. Remembering our own recent reluctant change to decimal coinage one can sympathise with the conservative desire to leave things as they were. Reminders of the old carat variations are still sometimes met with: in two recent books, for instance, the weight of the giant Cullinan crystal is given as 3025 carats, whereas we know the true weight to have been 3106 metric carats. The lower figure was

A.   Granite with topaz crystal

B.   Ceylon gem gravel

C. Corundum group

D. Chrysoberyl and Spinel

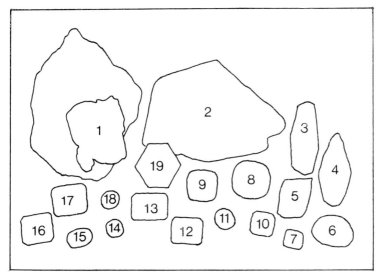

Key to C. CORUNDUM: **1.** Ruby crystal, Burma **2.** Zoned rough sapphire, Thailand **3-4.** Corundum crystals, Ceylon **5.** Corundum crystal, Burma **6.** 19.07ct **7.** 5.10ct **8.** 36.41ct **9.** 20.90ct **10.** 9.0ct, Burma **11.** 4.90ct, Burma **12.** 15.80ct, Burma **13.** 21.50ct, Burma **14.** 2.84ct, Burma **15.** 6.71ct, Burma **16.** 17.95ct **17.** 19.67ct, Burma **18.** 2.60ct **19.** 57.26ct, Ceylon

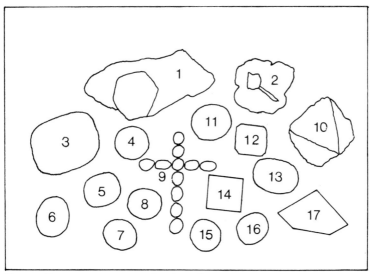

Key to D. CHRYSOBERYL (1–9) and SPINEL (10–17): **1.** Twinned alexandrite crystal in mica-schist, Fort Victoria, Rhodesia **2.** Twinned crystal, Brazil **3.** 57.10ct **4.** 7.89ct, Brazil **5.** 7.66ct **6.** Cat's eye 11.15ct **7.** 4.92ct, Tiofilo Otoni, Minas Gerais, Brazil **8.** 5.68ct **9.** Cat's eye cross **10.** Crystal, Burma **11.** 11.82ct, Burma **12.** 9.75ct, Burma **13.** 9.84ct, Burma **14.** 10.96ct, Burma **15.** 3.89ct **16.** 3.88ct, Burma **17.** 11.69ct, Burma

E. Beryl group

F. Garnet group

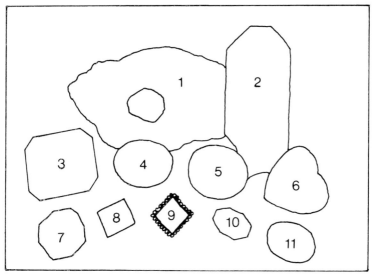

Key to E. BERYL: **1.** Emerald crystal in calcite, Muzo, Colombia **2.** Aquamarine crystal, Ouro Preto, Brazil **3.** Beryl 135.93ct **4.** Morganite 55.68ct, Tiofilo Otoni, Brazil **5.** Aquamarine 67.38ct **6.** Heliodor 82.24ct **7.** Goshenite 26.54ct **8.** Beryl 9.09ct, Malagasy **9.** Emerald, about 6ct, Colombia, Townsend Collection, Victoria and Albert Museum **10.** Heliodor 9.45ct **11.** Orange-pink beryl 22.90ct, Minas Gerais, Brazil

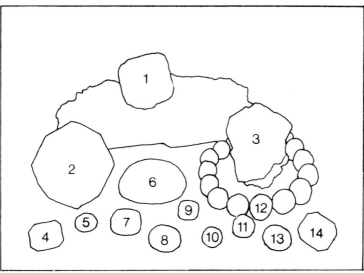

Key to F. GARNETS: **1.** Almandine, modified rhombdodecahedron on mica-schist, Fort Wrangel, Alaska **2.** Almandine icositetrahedron, Rhodesia **3.** Hessonite crystals, Jeffrey Mine, Asbestos, Quebec, Canada **4.** Spessartine 12.00ct **5.** Spessartine 3.35ct, Malagasy **6.** Almandine carbuncle **7.** Pyrope-almandine 10.07ct, Tanzania **8.** Almandine 10.14ct, Tanzania **9.** Demantoid 3.37ct **10.** Demantoid 3.79ct **11.** Hessonite 5.28ct **12.** Hydrogrossular beads, Transvaal **13.** Grossular 7.06ct, Tanzania **14.** Hessonite 15.43ct

G. Topaz and Tourmaline

H. Zircon

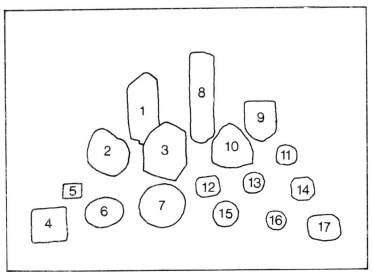

Key to G. TOPAZ (1–7) and TOURMALINE (8–17): **1.** Crystal, Brazil **2.** Rolled pebble (cleaved) **3.** Crystal, Mursinsk, U.S.S.R. **4.** 58.47ct, Mogok, Burma **5.** 7.48ct, Morambaia, Minas Gerais, Brazil **6.** 33.45ct **7.** 72.12ct, Brazil **8.** Crystal, Mesa Grande, San Diego, California, U.S.A. **9.** Crystal, variety schorl **10.** Sectioned crystal **11.** 12.38ct **12.** Variety rubellite, 17.39ct, Brazil **13.** 7.13ct, Brazil **14.** 20.45ct **15.** 17.26ct **16.** 6.25ct, Brazil **17.** 22.91ct

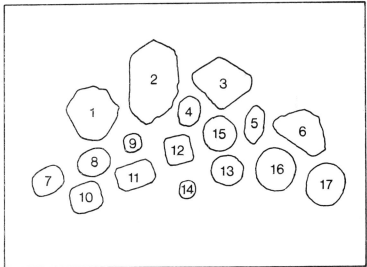

Key to H. ZIRCON: **1.** Crystal, Kenya **2.** Crystal, Renfrew, Ontario, Canada **3.** Crystal, Kenya **4–5.** Crystals, Indo-China **6.** Rolled fragment, Rakwana, Ceylon **7.** 12.34ct **8.** 14.27ct, Burma **9.** 4.15ct **10.** 9.85ct **11.** 16.52ct, Ceylon **12.** 18.76ct, Ceylon **13.** 15.55ct, Burma **14.** 3.19ct, Mogok, Burma **15–17.** Heat treated, Indo-China **15.** 21.32ct **16.** 33.34ct **17.** 27.58ct

I. Quartz group

J. Opal

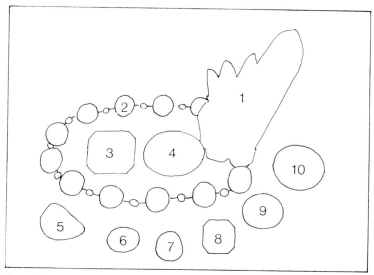

Key to I. QUARTZ varieties: **1.** Rock crystal group, Dauphiné, France **2.** Necklace of gold-mounted rock crystal spheres **3.** Rock crystal 91.54ct **4.** Brown quartz 114.44ct **5.** Tiger's Eye, Griqualand West, Africa **6.** Green quartz 11.64ct **7.** Rose quartz 13.24ct, Lac Aloatra, Malagasy **8.** Citrine 29.95ct **9.** Brown quartz 24.86ct **10.** Amethyst 97.58ct

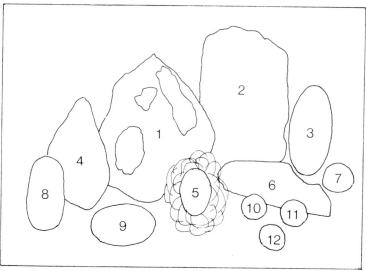

Key to J. OPAL: **1.** Opal in matrix, Queensland, Australia **2.** Banded opal in matrix, Australia **3.** Flat doublet, Australia **4.** Opal, Virgin Valley, Nevada, U.S.A. **5.** Brooch, water opal **6.** Opal, Boi Monto Mine, Piauí, Brazil **7.** Water opal cabochon 12.76ct, Queretaro, Mexico **8.** Bird cameo, Queensland, Australia **9.** Flat doublet 15.96ct, Australia **10–12.** Fire opals 3.47, 3.82 and 3.21ct, Mexico

K. Chalcedony group

L. Jade minerals

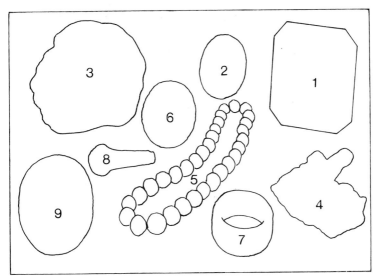

Key to K. CHALCEDONY varieties: **1.** Bloodstone **2.** Mocha stone **3.** Agate **4.** Chalcedony, botryoidal, Faroe Islands **5.** Carnelian necklace **6.** Moss agate **7.** Onyx ring **8.** Chrysoprase handle **9.** Plasma cameo

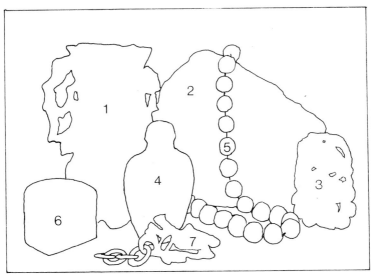

Key to L. JADE, JADEITE and NEPHRITE: **1.** Nephrite Chinese vase **2.** Jadeite boulder, Taw Maw, Burma **3.** Nephrite Chinese carving **4.** Nephrite Chinese snuff bottle, rose quartz stopper **5.** Jadeite necklace, Burma **6.** Jadeite archer's ring, Burma **7.** Jadeite, Imperial Jade praying mantis, Burma

M.   Lapis Lazuli, Turquoise and Feldspars

N.   Spodumene, Peridot, Sinhalite and Zoisite

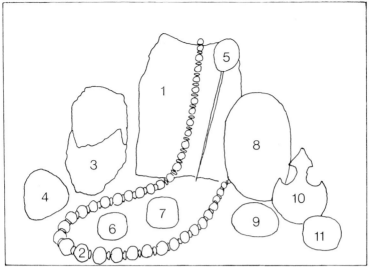

Key to M. LAPIS LAZULI (1–2), FELDSPARS (3–8) and TURQUOISE
(9–11): **1.** Polished slab, Badakshan, Afghanistan **2.** Necklace with
rock crystal **3.** Microcline variety amazonstone crystal, Pike's Peak,
Colorado, U.S.A. **4.** Amazonstone, tumbled, South Africa **5.** Oligoclase
variety sunstone tiepin **6.** Moonstone 33.70ct **7.** Orthoclase 29.95ct,
Malagasy **8.** Labradorite cameo, Labrador, Canada **9.** Turquoise matrix
bead **10.** Carved and engraved amulet, Persia **11.** Cabochon 34.80ct,
Nishapur, Province of Khorassan, Persia

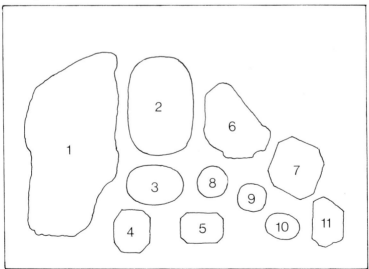

Key to N. SPODUMENE (1–5), OLIVINE (PERIDOT) (6–7), SINHALITE
(8–9) and ZOISITE (10–11): **1.** Kunzite crystal, Pala, San Diego,
California, U.S.A. **2.** Kunzite 424.59ct, Mine de Urupuca, Itambacuri,
Minas Gerais, Brazil **3.** 78.25ct, Governador Valadares, Minas Gerais,
Brazil **4.** 36.21ct, Brazil **5.** 29.77ct, Pala Chief Mine, San Diego,
California, U.S.A. **6.** Olivine crystal, St. John's Island, Red Sea
7. 146.17ct, St. John's Island, Red Sea **8.** 15.53ct **9.** 14.85ct **10.** 14.07ct,
Tanzania **11.** Crystal, Gerevi Hills, Tanzania

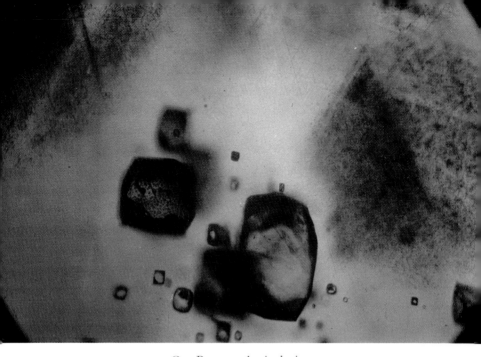

O.   Burma ruby inclusions

P.   Siam ruby inclusions

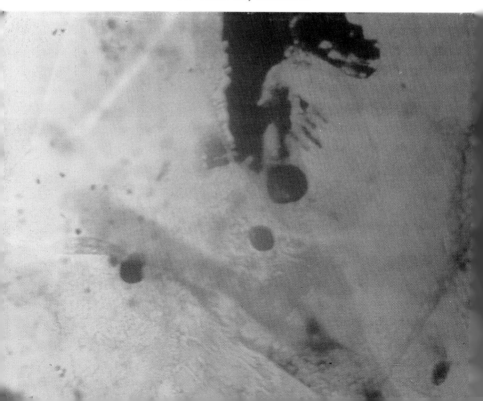

Q. Ruby boules in Verneuil furnace

clearly not a mistake in these reputable books, but a hangover from the time when the Cullinan was sent to Amsterdam (where the carat weighed 0·2057 g) for cleaving and cutting.

There is a natural enough confusion between the word carat as used as a unit of weight and the same word denoting the quality of gold. In this latter context it simply refers to the quantity of gold present in twenty-four parts of alloy. Pure gold, which is a lovely-looking metal, but too soft to find general use in jewellery, would be reckoned as 24 carat. The gold used in our long-lost sovereigns was 22 carat, and this has a fairly common use in wedding rings. But for jewellery 18 carat (that is 18 parts gold, 6 of alloy) is the highest grade one meets with.

Returning to the carat weight—where formerly it was subdivided into fractions $\frac{1}{2}$, $\frac{1}{4}$, $\frac{1}{8}$, with $\frac{1}{64}$ as the smallest recognised weight, the metric carat is divided into hundredths, which in the trade are referred to as 'points'. Thus a diamond weighing 3·98 carats might be alluded to as 'two points short of 4 carats', and one dealer might say to another 'my balance reads a point higher than yours' when disputing the weight of a valuable stone.

Weights are quoted to two places of decimals only. The average jeweller's balance is not in fact capable of greater accuracy than this. The grain is not an official weight for diamonds or precious stones, but the term is often used in talk between dealers and refers to a quarter of a carat or 50 mg—quite different from the grain of the Troy and avoirdupois systems. The grain will be referred to again when we come to the chapter on pearls, since the grain is traditionally the unit on which the value of pearls is calculated and, in consequence, is often known as the 'pearl grain' which at least avoids possible confusion.

Diamond Sorting and Grading

One of the many ways in which diamond is treated differently from other precious stones is the degree to which it is sorted and graded. One can see the rationale of this even if one thinks the passion for classification is carried too far at the present time.

It begins at the mine itself. For the rough diamonds to be sold they must first be valued, and this means in the first place sorting the industrial goats from the sheep which are considered as potential gems, and these are again subdivided according to size and quality, the best crystals being known as 'close goods'. In South Africa there is a Central

Sorting Office at Kimberley which deals with parcels containing two months' production from each of the mines. The stones are sorted again at the offices of the Diamond Trading Company when they reach London. A team of trained men and women wearing head-loupes are seated at long benches covered with white paper under a north-facing window. First, stones which weigh more than a standard figure (about 1·2 carat) are known as 'sizes' and are separated and accorded more detailed treatment than the smaller sizes which are collectively known as *mêlée*. The 'sizes' are separated into groups according to their shape, their quality and finally their colour.

The selling of gem-quality rough diamonds is primarily in the hands of the Central Selling Organisation which handles 80 per cent of the world production and is able to control and keep steady the level of prices. There are some two hundred accredited dealers and cutters from this and other countries who are knowledgeable and important enough financially to be invited to view large parcels of rough diamonds at the 'sights' arranged ten times a year by the Diamond Trading Company at their premises at 2 Charterhouse Street, London EC1. The parcels of rough which are offered to each customer are arranged to satisfy as far as possible his known requirements, but he must accept or refuse the whole consignment, and there is no bargaining as to price. Arrangements are made for buyers to be able to study the stones in a good light and at their leisure before coming to a decision. As some £100,000 is involved in the transaction this is certainly not to be taken lightly, though purchasers have the reassuring knowledge that the prices have been set at what is considered the true market level obtaining at that time. Though the merchant is at liberty to refuse the entire parcel there is a certain unspoken pressure at work in favour of acceptance, as too many refusals may result in his no longer being granted the privilege and prestige of attending the 'sights'.

Eventually, of course, the rough stones go through the cutting and polishing processes described in Chapter 5, and are purchased by dealers in cut diamonds, who in turn supply the manufacturing jewellers who mount them in rings, clips, brooches, ear-rings, pendants or necklaces for sale to jewellers and finally the public. When one considers the long chain of specialists which lies between the unmined stone and its sale as a diamond engagement ring, and that at each stage a reasonable profit must be made, the cost of the finished article no longer seems surprisingly high.

'The Four Cs'

When it comes to the evaluation of cut diamonds the same sort of orderliness and standardisation persists which has been evident throughout the whole diamond story. The elements which form the basis for grading a cut diamond have been popularised by De Beers, though they do not deal themselves with cut goods, under the catch title of 'The Four Cs', which refers to the qualities of *clarity*, *colour* and *cut*, together with *carat*, which recognises the weight factor.

Since there is quite a vogue for buying diamonds for investment, selling important stones with some sort of 'certificate of purity' attached, and so on, it may be useful for the reader to have some explanation as to how these qualities are assessed and how they affect the value of the stone.

Clarity first. A flawless or 'clean' diamond is one which is completely transparent and free from inclusions when viewed by a skilled observer with a 10× lens. Such stones are extremely rare and the urge to possess them has unfortunately become something of a fetish with the public, an urge stimulated and fostered by a type of advertising not favoured by the better class of jeweller. The accepted shorthand for the next category is VVS, which stands for very very slightly imperfect. This applies to a stone containing a very small inclusion difficult to find with a 10× lens and not seen through the table facet. Or it may apply to an otherwise perfect stone which shows minor 'naturals' or other blemishes on the girdle—but all still quite difficult to distinguish with a 10× lens.

We then enter the SI or 'slightly imperfect' class where similar defects can just be seen by a watchmaker's low-power lens, and only after this to the various grades of 'piqué' diamonds in which defects gradually become more and more visible to the naked eye.

Next comes colour. Diamonds of decided brown or yellow colour are acceptable as 'fancy' stones, but as a standard rule the top 'colour' in diamond is a complete absence of colour. The commonest and least favoured are those in the lower ranges of the 'Cape' series. Names vary in different countries for the various colour grades, but in Britain the top grade is traditionally known as Jager which is a very rare type which has a bluish cast due to fluorescence, but properly starts with River, followed by Top Wesselton, Wesselton, Top Crystal, Crystal, Top Silver Cape, Silver Cape, Cape, and so on through deeper shades of yellow or brown. To see any hint of colour in the top three or four grades the stones need to be unmounted and viewed edgeways in a groove in a piece of pure white paper in a white light. Diamonds viewed face-up, that is as seen when the stones are mounted in jewellery, will not show colour down to the Silver Cape grade, except to a trained eye. So it is fair to say that so straining for perfection is the diamond trade that it degrades stones which have tiny inclusions or faint tinges of colour, neither of which can be detected by those who wear them in jewellery; surely a rather strange proceeding.

The third 'C' which refers to perfection in cutting, or what is known as the 'make' of a stone again does not usually involve defects which would be noticeable to the layman, such as lop-sidedness, unsymmetrical facets, the table or culet out of true centre, etc. The ideal proportions for a round brilliant have been shown in Fig. 5(7). In the rare cases where there is a serious departure from the ideal the eye quickly learns to recognise the 'fish-eye' effect of a stone with too shallow a pavilion, and the dark-centred appearance or 'lumpy' look of one which is too deeply cut. The girdle of the stone should be examined to see that it is neither too thin and thereby liable to chipping, nor too thick, which makes for a clumsy stone and increases the weight. A polished or faceted girdle whether or not it seriously adds to the appearance of the stone is to be welcomed as a sign that it has been in the hands of a cutter who prides himself on giving the stone a fine finish.

In antique or Victorian jewellery the modern ideals of proportion have no place. The outlines of the brilliants were nearly square instead of round, the crowns higher, the table smaller and the culet much bigger, giving the effect of a 'hole' at the bottom of the stone. To compensate for some leakage of light through the stone there is a wonderful display of fire, and such stones in a cluster ring or brooch can be very beautiful. Their value per carat, however, must be reckoned a good deal lower than that for a stone of the same quality in modern cut. For small diamonds the full fifty-eight facets of a brilliant are not considered necessary, and single-cut or eight-cut stones with eight facets above and below the girdle (in addition to the table and culet) are commonly used, or the rather more elaborate Swiss-cut stones with thirty-four facets. Where it is desired to keep the cost of a jewel as low as possible, rose-cut diamonds (often little more than chips with a flat base and three triangular upper facets) are used as a surround to the main stone in a ring or brooch, and unless critically examined make quite an effective show.

With exceptionally large stones a number of extra facets are added to avoid the stark appearance that the standard brilliant-cut would give. With such stones a cushion-shaped outline often results in a more pleasing stone than one with a perfectly circular girdle. Emerald-cut diamonds are also nowadays often favoured for stones of important size. These have great dignity and lend themselves to modern designs when flanked with baguettes. Though the fire is less evident in emerald-cut stones, the astonishing optical perfection of the diamond substance itself is well displayed. Personally I find this quality of the 'flesh' of diamond one of its most impressive attributes, but experience some difficulty in explaining to others what I mean by such a term as 'optical perfection'.

The effect of the weight of a diamond on its value which is represented by the last of 'The Four Cs' is not so simple as might be supposed. The value per carat for a given quality of clarity, colour and cut tends to rise quite steeply from sizes of about $\frac{1}{2}$ carat to 3 carats, the proportional increase being very near to the *square* of their weight, which was a rule promulgated by David Jeffries 250 years ago. For stones above 3 carats the increase in the rate per carat begins to slow down as the prices become prohibitive and the demand lessens.

At the other end of the scale, the cost per carat of cutting is relatively high and the price thus increases somewhat. There is a curious prestige about a diamond which just weighs, or slightly exceeds, a carat, compared with one which looks identical but weighs rather less than the coveted mark, and the same effect is seen at 2 and at 3 carats. Thus there is an illogical surge in value at these particular points. Absurd maybe, but there can be no doubt that every cricketer would prefer his innings to close at 101 rather than at what should be an equally reputable 99.

The reader may be curious to know to what extent the value of a diamond is reduced when it is judged to fall a little below perfection standard in one or more of the 'Cs'. To give some idea of this I have compiled the small table shown below on the basis of figures published some years ago in America, showing the price for a 1 carat cut stone of different qualities.

		River	Top Crystal
Flawless	Fine cut	£800	£680
	Fair	600	550
VSI	Fine cut	540	470
		430	360

One of my reasons for showing this table is that the layman would be unable to distinguish between diamonds of River and Top Crystal in colour, of fine or fair cut, and flawless and VSI. Yet these invisible differences have tumbled the asking price from a hypothetical £800 per carat to £360, which serves to indicate how much we are in the hands of experts in this field. This leads logically to the question of diamonds as an investment, which is very much talked about today.

To begin with, in the natural order of things, a member of the public is buying at the wrong end of the market and the producer, the cutter, the manufacturer and the retail jeweller (to name but a few) have each made enough profit from it to earn their living. When it comes to selling the stone, however, the case is different: the owner may be able to sell to a retailer but he certainly can't expect to get a better price for it than the dealer or manufacturing jeweller can obtain from the retailer concerned: no enhancement in *value* then for the stone invested in for quite a number of years.

On the other hand the purchaser, if he has been honestly served, has acquired a uniquely stable and disposable asset, portable and durable. As the cost of living rises, so will the price of diamonds, owing to the wise administration of the whole diamond organisation. Diamonds are internationally acceptable currency and many thousands of refugees have been able to start life again in a new country thanks to this portable form of wealth. Against all this, of course, diamonds or diamond jewellery will always be a target for the thief. If used and shown as they should be, the owner runs a considerable risk of loss, and insurance premiums are high. If shut away in a bank the pleasure of ownership is locked away with them.

Coloured Diamonds

Alone amongst the gemstones perfection colour in diamond is traditionally pure white—in other words, complete absence of colour. As we have just seen, there is a definite scale of depreciation when shades of yellow and (less commonly) brown can be seen in the finished gem. On the other hand diamonds of a definite colour are very beautiful objects and fetch good prices as 'fancy' diamonds. The commonest of these are stones of golden- or canary-yellow or cinnamon-brown. The point at which a 'deep Cape' becomes interesting as a 'fancy' stone is a somewhat moot one. The rarer colours such as blue, pink, red or green fetch very high prices if a wealthy enough bidder can be found.

The most famous blue diamond is undoubtedly the 'Hope', which was derived from rough brought back from the Kollur mines of India in 1642. The 'Hope' in its present form is a cushion-shaped brilliant weighing 44·4 metric carats and has a fine violet-blue colour. After a long history during which ill luck was said to attend each successive owner, it was purchased by the well-known dealer in big diamonds, Harry Winston, and later presented by him to the Smithsonian Institution in Washington. There is rather a nice story of a man who, finding that a fellow passenger on his plane to New York was destined to be Mrs. Harry Winston, managed at the last moment to excuse himself and change onto another plane. It was not until he was half-way across the Atlantic that he became aware to his dismay that the passenger sitting next to him on this second flight was none other than Harry Winston himself!

Practically all the blue diamonds mined in recent years come from the Premier mine in Pretoria. These were found to belong to a special category which was labelled Type IIb, which are distinguished principally for conducting electricity, whereas diamond normally is a good insulator.

As for pink diamonds, these seem to be rather a speciality of the Williamson mine in Tanzania. A crystal weighing $54\frac{1}{2}$ carats was presented to Queen Elizabeth as a wedding gift, and was cut in Clerkenwell, London, into a magnificent brilliant of 23·6 carats. In her Coronation year the Queen had this stone set in the centre of a flower-spray brooch with curved petals of navette-cut diamonds, a flower stalk fashioned from baguettes and two large navette diamonds to represent leaves—a superb piece of jewellery. Red diamonds are so scarce in nature that not much can be said about them, while green stones are also very seldom seen, though a beautiful apple-green diamond, weighing 41 carats, which is known as the Dresden Green is one of the famous diamonds of history.

ARTIFICIAL COLORATION

During the last twenty years or so methods have been developed for producing coloured diamonds from natural off-coloured stones by bombardment with sub-atomic particles. A pioneer in this kind of treatment was Sir William Crookes, who found that contact with radium salts caused diamonds to turn green, the colour being apparently permanent. The effect was later proved to be due to the alpha-particles (helium nuclei) emitted by radium or its salts and these had little penetrating power, thus recutting the stone would remove the colour, as would prolonged heating at 450°C. Such stones were not very attractive and remained strongly radioactive for fifty years or more, which enabled them to be easily recognised in the Laboratory when unscrupulous dealers attempted to sell them as rare natural green diamonds.

In the late forties bombardment by charged particles such as deuterons, accelerated in a cyclotron, was found to have a similar effect. In this process the stone became strongly radioactive but the effect wore off in a matter of hours and proof that the stone had been treated rested on a curious 'umbrella' pattern to be seen round the culet when viewed through the table, if the stone had been bombarded from the back; or zones of colour parallel to the facets if bombardment of the crown had been carried out. As with radium treatment the colour effect produced in a cyclotron is only skin deep, and so is the green or pale blue colour induced by electrons. On the other hand neutrons produced in an atomic pile, which also induce a green tint in diamond, are uncharged particles and thus able to penetrate right through the stone. The green colour produced by any of these treatments is not very attractive: it is only the extreme rarity of green diamonds in nature which tempts dealers or collectors to buy them if they are thought to be natural. Richard T. Liddicoat, in his excellent *Handbook of Gem Identification* states that all natural cut green diamonds show green-coloured 'naturals' on their girdles and in the absence of these the stone can be assumed to have been treated. This statement is based on the very wide experience of the Gemological Institute of America laboratories in New York and Los Angeles.

When these green bombarded stones are carefully annealed (for example by heating at 900°C in argon) the colour is found to change first to brown and then to golden-yellow: even prolonged heating never quite restores the diamond to its original colour. The brown and yellow shades are undoubtedly attractive and a great improvement on the indifferently coloured stones of the 'Cape' series, which are naturally those chosen for treatment. Such bombarded stones are sold extensively in the U.S.A. and have opened up new possibilities by enabling coloured diamonds to be used in jewellery far more freely than was formerly possible. It is necessary, however, in the interests of fair trading, that such stones should be sold as 'treated diamonds' and not passed off as rare natural gems.

Fortunately for the gem-testing laboratories of the world there are detectable differences between the absorption bands to be seen in natural and in treated yellow and brown diamonds which can be detected by experienced workers using a hand spectroscope. In the case of brown diamonds the natural stones show a characteristic zoning or banding of colour which is absent in treated brown diamonds. This forms a useful additional clue.

ABSORPTION AND FLUORESCENCE

In a book intended for the general reader it is not desirable to go into great technical detail on such subjects as absorption and fluorescence, but so much that is important and interesting in diamond is bound up with these two interrelated properties that the picture of this amazing mineral would be missing in some of its main ingredients if something were not said about them. Those allergic to science can quite easily switch off at this point and resume the narrative later.

All colourless transparent substances transmit light of all wavelengths (colours) in the visible spectrum and most of them continue to pass light of shorter wavelengths in the ultra-violet region. This is true of diamond, but whereas most diamonds absorb virtually all light beyond a wavelength of 3300 Å, some were found to transmit waves down to 2200 Å, and these were naturally accepted as purer stones. The common form, called Type I, was later found to contain nitrogen and perhaps much smaller traces of other elements such as aluminium. These impurities seem to assist crystallisation into regular forms such as the octahedron. The pure type, known as Type II, which includes most of the large diamonds, do not show good crystal form. There have been further subdivisions, of which Type IIb has already been mentioned, consisting of blue or bluish diamonds which show 'semi-conducting' properties. There is usually a certain admixture between Type I and Type II diamonds. In fact one of the amazing aspects of the mineral is that though it provides millions of gemstones which have an almost precisely similar appearance, the exact behaviour of each stone is an individual matter and unpredictable. And least predictable of all is the strength and colour of its fluorescence.

In Chapter 8 a means of observing the strong red fluorescence of ruby was suggested to the reader by means of a simple 'crossed-filter' arrangement. In diamond the fluorescence is mainly in the blue, and can best be observed under a mercury discharge lamp in which the visible rays have been absorbed by means of a Wood's glass filter. This is in fact the type of apparatus most favoured for showing off a display of fluorescent minerals in mineral galleries, etc. The main stimulating radiation is a powerful mercury emission line at 3650 Å which the Wood's glass luckily transmits pretty freely.

The majority of diamonds show a blue fluorescence, with a very brief phosphorescence or afterglow. These belong to the 'Cape' series and have also a characteristic absorption spectrum with the 'key' band at 4155 Å in the deep violet. When this is strongly developed it is invariably accompanied by a broader band at 4780 Å in the blue and by other weaker bands. It is absorption in this series of bands which causes the yellowish cast associated with 'Cape' stones. Stones of the 'Brown' series on the other hand have a green or greenish-yellow fluorescence, and the key absorption band is seen as a rather weak line at 5040 Å between the green and the blue, accompanied by an even weaker line at 4980 Å. A third and very rare category are the true 'canary'-yellow diamonds which have a yellow fluorescence and show no absorption bands.

The above sounds reasonably straightforward, but the strange thing is the enormous variation shown in the strength of the fluorescent effects which vary in a ratio of something like 10,000 to 1, so that in the majority of diamonds it is too feeble to be seen under ultra-violet light, though much more constant under X-rays.

In diamonds which have a strong blue fluorescence the yellow after-glow can be easily seen by dark-adapted eyes if the stone be closely observed when taken out quickly from under the rays. A point I wish to emphasise is that since the fluorescence is so variable in the mineral the absence of fluorescence in a colourless stone or even a number of such stones is no indication that they are not diamonds. In a ruby-set ornament we should at once be suspicious if any of the red stones failed to fluoresce like the rest. In the case of a diamond ornament we should be deeply suspicious if the stones *did* show an even glow. This variability led my colleague Robert Webster to suggest that the pattern formed by strongly and weakly fluorescent stones seen in, shall we say, a diamond brooch could, if photographed, serve as a means of identification, as it would be unique to that piece of jewellery.

In past years the 'trace' elements to be found in diamond have been checked carefully by spectrographic analysis, and tiny quantities of aluminium, silicon, calcium, magnesium and copper are always to be found; but no correlation of these elements with the colour or strength of the fluorescence could be found. The discovery of free nitrogen in diamond has altered the picture drastically and given a plausible basis for variations both in absorption and fluorescence. It seems likely that nitrogen and aluminium together can account for most of the fluorescent phenomena. But the mysteries of diamond behaviour are not explained or solved simply by naming an element or two responsible. It is the effect of the impurity on the diamond lattice itself causing distortions, vacancies, electron traps, and the like which give rise to absorption and fluorescence. That is how it is possible to alter the colour, the absorption and the fluorescence of an irradiated diamond by subsequent heat-treatment.

The initial effect of bombardment (leading, as explained above, to a green colour) is to douse any fluorescent properties the stone may have had before treatment. But after annealing, the stone becomes fluorescent, even if it was scarcely so to begin with. And the interesting thing is that there is a shift in the 'Cape' stones usually treated towards the absorption and fluorescence features of the 'Brown diamond' series. The original 'Cape' absorption bands at 4155 and 4780 Å are very strongly entrenched and remain visible, but the absorption system at 5040 and 4980 Å becomes markedly visible, with 4980 more prominent than in untreated diamonds, while the fluorescence tends towards green as against the blue typical of the 'Cape' series. A faint line in the yellow at 5940 Å also makes its appearance and is important as indicating clearly that the stone has been treated. A few natural diamond crystals show this line, presumably because they have suffered bombardment with particles from radioactive minerals and later undergone a natural 'heat-treatment'. But the charged particles in nature penetrate less than a millimetre below the surface of the stone and the colour and the characteristic lines disappear when the stone is cut.

Before passing on to a final section in which the simplest means of identifying diamond are considered, a few words on diamonds for industrial purposes should be said. It has already been indicated that there is no sharp line of demarcation between gem quality and industrial diamonds and there are large numbers of stones which could be included in either category depending upon the laws of supply and demand. For many industrial purposes freedom from flaws or other imperfections are as important as they are in gems—but there is one property, *colour*, which has little influence on the working properties, but can make a stone virtually unacceptable as a gem. The general name for industrial diamonds especially of the lower qualities, is 'bort' or 'boart'. But there are two special forms in which diamond occurs, especially in Brazil, which are valuable industrially but out of court for jewellery. One of these is a completely rounded form known as 'short bort' or ballas, in which little crystals of diamond are in radial formation, producing a very tough stone for rock-drills and the like, since the cleavage weaknesses cancel out in such an aggregation.

The other form is an unattractive coke-like black material known as 'carbonado' or sometimes just 'carbon' which is apparently only found in the State of Bahia in Brazil. This is granular in structure and contains a considerable amount of impurities. Its quality, i.e. its diamond content, can be gauged fairly conveniently by measuring its density which varies from about 3·15 to as high as 3·45, the higher figures representing the purer material.

At one time, before the manufacturers of diamond rock-drills became so cunning in the best use of ordinary bort in their drilling crowns, carbonado was much sought after for the job because of its toughness, and was very costly. A crown set with carbons might easily cost £500. By using modern sintering methods it is now common to arm diamond crowns with pieces of bort as small as 200 to the carat, firmly held in matrices of tungsten or copper, thus saving greatly on the cost of the tool.

IDENTIFICATION OF DIAMOND

From what has been said in the foregoing pages it should be clear that diamond is a peculiarly distinctive mineral. Moreover of all gemstones it is the most familiar to every jeweller and indeed to the public, so that one would expect any *diamond* dealer at any rate to have no difficulty in recognising a brilliant at sight, or at least on lens inspection, and to remain undeceived by the cleverest of substitutes. But I have known quite a few undoubted diamonds go the rounds of the trade gathering conflicting opinions until their authenticity has been proved by a laboratory test, and contrariwise, dealers have also been known to offer high prices for specimens of the synthetic material strontium titanate, when cunningly presented to them. The reasons for such fallibility are in the first case suspicion roused by scare stories in the press about 'undetectable' new substitutes for diamond which unsettles their confidence when there is any small deviation from normal cutting or colour in the stone, or the fact that it is offered by someone of dubious reputation: and in the second case, lack of suspicion because, in the ordinary run of trade, dealers are handling goods from known sources and doing business with men of known integrity, so that their examination of a plausible 'fake' will not be directed towards proving it to be a diamond, but purely as to its quality and value as a diamond. And in both cases the rule-of-thumb methods by which they operate let them down when there is no vestige of scientific knowledge with which to back their purely visual impression.

I became aware of these weaknesses in experts quite early in my career in the Hatton Garden gem-testing laboratory, and as the story illustrates very cogently what I have been saying I may as well give a short version of it here. It culminated in a case known as *Rex* v. *Rice*; Rice being a tall, distinguished-looking elderly rogue with a mane of white hair and a black eye-shade, who had successfully defrauded quite a number of pawnbrokers by pawning zircon rings as diamonds by means of a clever technique and an imposing personality. His method in each case was the same. First he would establish a relationship with the pawnbroker by pawning a gold watch, using a very respectable but (as afterwards discovered) fictitious address. In redeeming it some two weeks later (always late in the afternoon when the light was poor) he would produce what was ostensibly a five-stone diamond ring of some importance in which one stone was missing, and ask how much it would cost to replace the missing stone. This was a cunning move, as Rice would never mention the word diamond, leaving it to the shop-keeper to assume it and base his estimate accordingly. If the pawnbroker had spotted that they were in fact white zircons Rice could either have said that he knew that of course, but liked the ring and would wear it if its complement of five zircons were complete, or he could express dismay and say that he must have been defrauded when he bought it some years previously. In fact on each occasion (until the last fatal day) the pawnbroker under the influence of that impressive figure, that grand manner, and that respectable address, accepted them as diamonds, and had no hesitation in advancing a fair sum on the security of the ring until Rice 'could afford to have the stone replaced'.

Next morning, in good light and away from the Rice aura the unfortunate man was aware at once that the stones, whatever they were, were *not* diamonds, and on checking found the address given him to be a false one. This routine succeeded for quite a while, Rice having found that these ex-diamond rings were available in good supply from a certain 'red-faced' Roy Plumley—a setter working in Clerkenwell who replaced the diamonds from stolen rings with white zircons or jargoons, as they were then called in the trade. The eventual disaster came when Rice tried the usual game on a pawnbroker who had been warned of these goings-on by a victim in another shop with which he was in business partnership but under another name. Thus when Mr. Rice came to redeem his watch and produced one of his zircon rings, he held him in conversation while a colleague quietly rang up the police.

The rings were brought by the police to our laboratory and all the stones were found to be zircons. I was asked to act as an expert witness in the case and, knowing the difficulty in explaining to laymen on the jury and the bench how exactly did one distinguish between diamond and zircon, I thought it wise to prepare X-ray photographs in which the transparency of diamond to the rays compared to the opacity of zircons was clearly displayed. Since then this method of demonstration has been found convincing in many Courts of Law. One of the original *Rex* v. *Rice* photographs is shown on Plate 11a.

This narrative serves to show how failure to recognise the difference between diamond and white zircon is as much a matter of the mood in which the inspection is made as it is a test of the perspicacity and eye-knowledge of the expert concerned.

Another thing which impressed me in this case, while chatting with a long line of sheepish, cheated pawnbrokers waiting to give evidence, was that though all had been convinced on re-inspecting the rings that the stones were not diamonds, some thought they were pastes, some thought synthetic white sapphires, and even those who plumped for jargoons had no basis for their guess apart from sheer appearance. I have explained in Chapter 9 how easy it is to see the 'doubling' of the back facets of zircon by means of a pocket lens. It seemed to me extraordinary that not one of these men, whose livelihood depended upon correct assessments, should be aware of this simple aid to identification.

In the trial Rice protested that he had never claimed his stones to be diamonds, but all those rings, all those substantial unredeemed pledges, and all those false addresses were too much for the jury. He was convicted and sent to prison for quite a while.

From the above true story I hope the reader will have gathered not only the morals it serves to illustrate, but also that white zircon is a plausible substitute for diamond so far as appearance goes, especially in artificial light, but that it is easily identified by means of a pocket lens. White zircon is in fact the only natural gemstone which has the general 'look' of a diamond, having high refractive indices and enough dispersion to show considerable fire. In Victorian days these stones (their colour probably removed by heat treatment) were obtainable in quantity from the gem-rich island of Ceylon, where they were known as 'Matura diamonds'. Lens examination not only reveals the strong D.R.

in zircon but also its peculiar brittleness which usually gives the facet edges a rubbed or worn appearance quite foreign, of course, to the supremely hard diamond. In the laboratory another quick test for white zircon is provided by characteristic fine lines in the red end of its absorption spectrum when light reflected from the stone is examined with a hand spectroscope. Zircon is seldom chosen nowadays where fraud is intended, since any of at least three synthetic stones will prove more effective, but small white zircons in eternity rings, or small rose-cut zircons, may sometimes be mistaken for diamonds, and in such cases the spectrum test can be very useful.

Before proceeding to describe the most effective diamond substitutes now in use, it should be of benefit to summarise some of the distinctive features of diamonds themselves, even if these have already been discussed earlier in the chapter. If called upon to give a verdict on any stone purporting to be a diamond it is wise first of all to clean the stone —easily done with a clean handkerchief if the stone is loose, or with a soft toothbrush and warm water with a little liquid detergent in it should the stone be mounted. Diamond has a great affinity for grease (hence the grease tables!) and it is quite a task to clean it well and keep it that way in daily use, but well worth the trouble in the resulting splendour of the cleaned stone. A (clean) diamond then shows, when examined with a lens, brilliant 'hard'-looking facets meeting in sharp edges. Looking through the specimen there is no trace of 'doubling' of back-facet edges, but a pronounced 'shallow' look to the stone on account of its high refractive index. Fire is there certainly, but not overdone. The girdle is often very distinctive and may show small nicks which follow the lines of cleavage and often little patches called 'naturals' which represent parts of the original outer surface of the diamond crystal. These are often deliberately left by the cutter to enable him to check the direction of the 'grain'. When seen these are absolutely distinctive. The clarity and the adamantine lustre signal 'diamond' to the eye. There should be no traces of any scratches on the surface or bruises on the corners. If a polished piece of corundum is available a test of a corner of the diamond against its surface will serve to prove whether its hardness is truly 10. Only diamond (apart from carborundum) can scratch sapphire, so this is a stringent test and need hardly be destructive at all.

Before dealing with the main synthetic substitutes two old-time fakes must be mentioned. The first is paste, the common name in the trade for a showy form of lead glass which has a good lustre and considerable fire and was, and still is, a very effective and cheap material for costume jewellery, *diamanté* dresses, etc. In Victorian times some delightfully designed jewellery exploited this material, and it has its own beauty, its own special usefulness, and does not seriously attempt to rival diamond. A hard file is fatal to a surface of this glass and it should not be necessary to use it.

A much scarcer diamond substitute is a diamond doublet in which the crown of the stone consists of a thin piece of diamond and the base of synthetic white sapphire or some other suitable substance. These artifacts were a means of using up diamond crystals too thin for normal exploitation, and when mounted in a closed setting could be quite deceptive since the hardness and 'look' of diamond itself were there to see, and any hardness test abortive. There is a curiously phoney look about these doublets, however, and if the stone be tilted slightly a reflection of the edges of the table facet can be seen in the plane dividing the two materials.

Now for the synthetic substitutes. Though nowadays diamond itself is produced synthetically in large quantity the product consists of tiny impure crystals suitable only for industrial use. A few clear diamond crystals of gem quality and of carat size have been manufactured by the scientists of the General Electric Company in the U.S.A., but the cost of production of these made natural diamonds seem cheap. The synthetic substitutes we are referring to do not consist of diamond but of substances having only a superficial resemblance to the true gemstone.

The commercial success of these substitutes depends more upon publicity and clever advertising (and upon the gullibility of the public) than upon their intrinsic merits. The first to be exploited was synthetic white spinel, which in the mid-thirties was boosted as being 'virtually indistinguishable from diamond' and sold in expensive settings in West End stores by an enterprising gentleman called Jourado. Such a fuss was made about this stone (which was not even very new) that reassuring announcements had to be made over the radio by the Precious Stone Section of the London Chamber of Commerce to prevent damage to legitimate diamond trade. Synthetic white spinel is a compound of magnesium and aluminium with refractive index 1·728 against diamond's 2·417, hardness 8 of Mohs's scale to diamond's enormously higher hardness. In its favour was excellent transparency and freedom from colour and the fact that its crystallisation being cubic it is singly refracting. Cleverly mounted in the form of supporting baguettes or in eternity rings it can still be troublesome, but has faded out very much in the face of what was to follow.

The next furore was caused by the production of the enormously showy synthetic rutile or titania. Rutile is crystallised titanium dioxide and in nature best known as the hair-brown fibres seen so often in quartz. It has a very high refractive index, very high double refraction, and very high dispersion. Its hardness is $6\frac{1}{2}$. Rutile is very liable to lose oxygen when heated and become black, so that its synthetic production in 1949 in yellowish and several more attractive colours was something of a technical triumph. The huge double refraction and gaudy fire made rutile a sitting duck to recognise even without a lens, but again it was heavily advertised. Soon it was superseded by a much more dangerous newcomer, strontium titanate. This is not found in nature at all, has the *same* refractive index as diamond for yellow light, and though four times more dispersive is not nearly so absurdly gaudy as rutile. Moreover it is cubic and therefore singly refracting. Its density is high, 5·12, and the hardness is low, $5\frac{1}{2}$, and this constitutes its Achilles' heel. Undoubtedly this can be dangerously deceptive material until one gets to know it, when its excessive display of fire gives it away. A gentle prod with a needle below the girdle of a mounted stone will leave a mark and confirm suspicions.

Later still we have had to suffer publicity in connection with yet another contender for the 'indistinguishable from diamond even by a jeweller, without scientific tests' crown. In this case it is an yttrium aluminate not found in nature and labelled YAG standing for yttrium aluminium garnet, because it has the same crystal structure as garnet. This is singly refractive, reasonably hard (8 on Mohs's scale), very clear and colourless, and with a dispersion rather more than half that of diamond. The refractive index is 1·834 which makes it beyond the range of the normal refractometer. The density is 4·54, but this is useless as a test in a mounted stone. YAG had added publicity when chosen as the material for a replica of a large pear-shaped diamond weighing 69·42 carats which Richard Burton gave to Elizabeth Taylor. It has been sold under the name 'diamonair' and other fancy names. While YAG and strontium titanate resemble diamond quite closely in appearance, the reader must not be misled by clever advertising into thinking that the position of diamond itself is in any way threatened.

These synthetic materials will be described further in the last chapter of the book, together with some ingenious doublets in which YAG or synthetic-spinel crowns are cemented to a pavilion of strontium titanate, whereby the crown is hard enough to withstand wear or a simple hardness test, while the base provides fire.

CHAPTER TWELVE

RUBY AND SAPPHIRE

WHEN WE LEAVE the diamond scene and turn to consider other gemstones we enter a completely different world. Not only diamonds themselves, but their mining, grading, marketing, cutting and sales organisation are things entirely on their own. Dealings in all other stones are, by comparison, unorganised, sporadic, fluctuating in fortune and subject to the vagaries of fashion. And for most of us, even in a world diminished by jet travel and brought into our homes on television, there is still a feeling of romance attached to precious stones from the ancient mines and markets of the East, the wild interior of Brazil or the foothills of the Andes.

Ruby and sapphire, to be considered in this chapter, are two gem varieties of the same mineral, corundum. But while in the case of all other gemstones the species name is at least a possible one under which to sell a precious stone, everyone seems to jib at using 'red corundum' for ruby, or 'blue corundum' for sapphire except in a scientific treatise. The sound of the word is curiously abrasive—largely I think because it reminds one of the trade name for silicon carbide, 'carborundum', so familiar in the form of grindstones and hones. This is rather ironical, as the manufacturer's name 'carborundum' was itself derived from carbon (of which it partly consists) and corundum, which is hard enough to rank as 9 on Mohs's famous scale.

Actually, long before the days of manufactured abrasives, corundum, in the crude granular form known as emery, was one of the most popular and efficient grinding agents known, and emery paper is, of course, still very much in use, available in different degrees of fineness to suit each purpose. Emery owes its name to Cape Emeri on the Greek island of Naxos where it has been mined for many hundreds of years.

It is a dark grey material consisting of about 70 per cent corundum, with magnetite and other iron oxides.

It is fortunate indeed that a mineral so suited by its hardness to be used as a precious stone should be found (even if very rarely) in varieties having possibly the finest colours in mineral nature. The names of each of these varieties refer to their colours—ruby from the Latin *ruber* (red), in its later form *rubinus,* and sapphire from the Latin *sapphirus,* itself derived from an old Sanskrit word meaning blue. The name sapphire was in fact first used for lapis lazuli, and perhaps for other opaque blue minerals. In present-day practice, except for ruby, all the corundums used as gemstones are termed 'sapphire' with a suitable colour prefix, thus we have white sapphire, for the colourless variety, yellow, green, and even pink sapphires. In the case of pink sapphire there is a troublesome disputable margin between a rather pale ruby and a deep pink sapphire (see Plate C).

Because of their extreme rarity, rubies are a good deal more valuable than sapphires of comparable quality. A 5 carat Burma ruby may easily sell at £2000 per carat or more, whereas a sapphire of this size would have to be an exceptional stone to realise £500 per carat. Again, whereas top quality rubies over 10 carats are practically unobtainable, sapphires of well over 100 carats are by no means unknown. Of the other corundum gemstones the yellow sapphires are probably the most popular; the green varieties have rather a sombre tint, whereas the pinks, purples and violets, though bright and attractive, do not conform in the public mind with what a sapphire should look like, and are thus not in much demand. White sapphire is seldom completely free from colour or perfectly transparent. It has virtually no fire and, if a cheap substitute for diamond is required, synthetic white sapphire or synthetic spinel would be a more sensible substitute.

Star-rubies and star-sapphires which show a six-pointed star by reflected light when suitably cut in *cabochon* form fetch high prices when of good quality. Unfortunately the best star-effect is usually found in stones of pale colour. A number of other gems show asterism, as it is called, or the allied effect, chatoyancy which gives us cat's-eyes.

Corundum consists essentially of aluminium oxide which, if pure, would be a colourless substance. The magnificent red of ruby is due to small amounts (less than 1 per cent) of chromic oxide, which replaces some of the alumina in the crystal lattice. The colour of sapphire can be ascribed to titanium and iron, and some of the yellow stones, at least, owe their colour to ferric iron. Aluminium is the third in terms of abundance of the elements found in the earth's crust, but for the most part it is found combined with other elements in important rock-forming minerals such as the feldspars and garnets.

Though corundum is found as a constituent (sometimes a main constituent) of igneous rocks, the gem material has nearly all been formed in crystalline limestones which have been subjected to metamorphic action involving extreme heat and pressure, and recovered from alluvial gravels and sands derived from these rocks. Spinel, being a magnesium aluminate, is very commonly associated with corundum in both rocks and gravels as well as a number of other gem minerals.

Corundum crystals are not usually very attractive, being often misshapen and with rough and ribbed surfaces. The crystals commonly have a hexagonal outline, but their trigonal symmetry is frequently betrayed by raised triangular markings on their basal planes and by the rhombohedral form of some of their crystals—the rhombohedron being so typically a trigonal form that the system is often known as the rhombohedral system.

In Ceylon the usual shape of the sapphires is a bipyramid, tapering and striated horizontally. The colour is seldom even throughout, bands of intense blue often alternating with areas of yellowish-green. The bipyramids are sometimes truncated at either end by the basal pinacoid, giving them the 'barrel' shape which is particularly common in non-gem corundum. The fact that the crystals have retained their shapes at all after millions of years of wear and tear in being transported from the pre-Cambrian rocks in the north of the island to the gem gravels in the south, where they are recovered, indicates how hard and how tough the mineral is. The large variety of other gems found in the gravel, in which zircons, spinels, and tourmalines preponderate, have been so rolled and water-worn that one could not guess the shapes of their original crystals.

In the Mogok district north of Mandalay where the world's finest rubies are found the crystals are often tabular, sometimes in short hexagonal prisms striated horizontally, terminated by basal pinacoids. These basal planes are seldom flat, but more often terraced, giving a series of more or less parallel contour lines which are highly characteristic for the mineral in this locality. Another characteristic is multiple twinning, which gives rise to lines intersecting at 60° on the surface and results in a tendency to split parallel to the basal plane. This is known to mineralogists as a basal 'parting' which differs from cleavage in that the layers are not of molecular dimensions and do not depend upon the weakness of bonds within the crystal itself but on a secondary cause.

In the Mogok district not only fine rubies but also excellent sapphires are found, but it is as a ruby-mining centre that Mogok acquired its tremendous reputation. Both these varieties of corundum are recovered from alluvial deposits rather than from the rocks in which they originate which curiously are not the same, ruby coming from crystalline lime-stones and sapphire from an igneous rock. The Mogok deposits are described more fully in Chapter 3.

In the case of the deposits in Thailand the reverse is true: sapphires from this district have a very high reputation whereas the so-called 'Siam rubies' are regarded as being an inferior type and do not command the prices asked for their brethren from Burma. The stones from Thailand are on the whole darker and sometimes look much like gar-nets, but the best specimens can vie with rubies from Burma for beauty, and their value should depend upon the excellence of their colour and not upon where they were mined. In cases where doubt exists a dealer would ask a far higher price if he could obtain a laboratory certificate that the stone was a 'Burma ruby', but such certificates are in principle not issued, at least in London, as they would establish an undesirable precedent. The principle would be extended to Colombian emeralds, Siberian alexandrites, Kashmir sapphires, or whatever was considered the 'best' locality for the stones concerned. Provided the stone is a natural one its value should rest purely on its quality.

As it happens, a good gemmologist would never rely on colour to any extent in placing the origin of a stone, since its inclusions provide a far more certain means of doing this, and purely for his own purposes he finds a knowledge of such things extremely useful. There is always the lurking fear that new forms of synthetic gemstone might appear which were indistinguishable from nature's products, and the best safe-guard against deception is to know the typical internal features of each and every locality of each and every gem species.

Mining in Thailand follows the rather haphazard pattern common to alluvial gem fields the world over, being carried out by groups and families (mostly Burmese) who sink pits through the twenty feet or so of overburden to the gem-bearing sands below. The ruby deposits are mostly in the Province of Chantabun, bordering the Gulf of Siam, and the town of Chantabun is the marketing centre. The sapphires sold as Siamese have often come from the West and originated in Burma or from the district of Bo Pie Rin in Battambang in Cambodia. Sapphires of good quality also come from the Phailin mines of Cambodia which was once Siamese territory. Some fine yellow sapphires are found in

Thailand as well as a curious brown variety showing a bright star-effect when *cabochon* cut.

The gem gravels of Ceylon are rich in sapphires embracing every possible colour except, perhaps, a true ruby-red. As mentioned above, the colour particularly of the blue sapphires is seldom homogeneous, patches or layers of the deepest blue alternating with much paler portions of yellow or green. The native lapidaries are skilled in exploiting such stones to the best advantage. In some cases a spot of deep colour is placed at the base of the stone near the culet with the result that rays reflected from the back of the stone are universally coloured blue. More commonly a thin sharply defined layer of deep colour is disposed so as to cover the whole table-area of the stone, or an entire flank, and again the effect to the eye, especially in a mounted stone, is that of a completely blue specimen. A thin sharply delineated blue zone forming the table of the stone can easily be mistaken for a doublet when immersed in liquid and viewed in profile.

What has been said must not be taken to mean that no Ceylon sapphires are blue throughout. Some of the world's finest blue sapphires are, in fact, found in the island, and many so-called Kashmir sapphires really have their origin in Ceylon.

The yellow sapphires from these gravels are usually rather too pale to be valuable, but the occasional golden stone is one of the truly lovely gems of the world. It has a warmer, richer tint than its rivals from Thailand or Australia, and does not, as these do, owe its colour to iron but to some unfathomed cause. It is distinguished by an apricot-coloured fluorescence under ultra-violet light, whereas the others are inert.

Pink Ceylon sapphires are bright and attractive stones and occasionally are red enough to be sold as 'Ceylon rubies'.

There are several other important localities for sapphire of which those in Kashmir deserve pride of place for the superb colour of some of the best crystals. These deposits are higher above sea-level than any other gem-field in the world. The rocks themselves, which are granite-pegmatites, are found at an altitude of 14,800 feet, and are in fact very near the permanent snowline, and thus they can only be worked at certain times of the year. The sapphire crystals were first exposed by a rock-fall in the year 1881 and later were found on the floor of the valley which is still pretty high (13,200 feet) and were readily picked up and sold as blue quartz or amethyst for quite small sums of money. The stones occur as fairly large crystals, together with brown or green tourmaline. When it was realised that they were sapphires the price went up to £20 per ounce and considerable efforts were made to prevent Europeans from finding out where they came from. The main fault of Kashmir sapphires is their milkiness—very seldom are they quite transparent. But so fine (at best) is their colour that this defect almost becomes a merit. Cornflower-blue is the description given to the best of these delightful sapphires.

Corundums of a very distinctive steely blue are mined in Montana in deposits some 85 miles east of Helena. These were first discovered during gold-washing operations, and again were not at first recognised for what they were. The stones are usually pale in tint, and include yellows and greens. There are a number of other corundum deposits in the U.S.A. which sometimes produce stones of gem quality, but these are not commercially important.

We next move to Australia, where in the gemfields near Anakie in Queensland sapphires in a very wide range of colours including some fine yellow stones and star-stones are recovered. Australian (blue) sapphires have the reputation of being too dark in colour, and at night may appear practically black. They have in fact a relatively large percentage of iron in their composition which accounts for the sombre greenish colour, and is recognisable in the absorption spectrum, which shows a group of heavy absorption bands in the blue region. Most natural sapphires show the strongest of these bands (at 4500 Å) and this forms a most useful laboratory test, since no trace of this iron band can be found in a synthetic sapphire.

A fairly recent field where gem corundums of many shades of colour have been found is known as the Umba mine in the Korogwe/Tanga district on the upper reaches of the Umba river in Tanzania. There is ruby here of a sort in quite large sizes, but rather deficient in chromium and thus not a rich crimson but rather garnet-like in tint. This causes some confusion to the lapidary, as fine rhodolite garnets are found in the same mine, as well as green chrome tourmaline, zircons, etc. Some of the sapphires have the curious property of appearing green in daylight and reddish in tungsten light. As alexandrite chrysoberyl is famed for this type of colour-change the term alexandrite sapphire is sometimes used for these stones. This is not a wise name to use, however, as it is bound to cause confusion. Also in Tanzania are found hexagonal ruby crystals sometimes many inches across, which, though chrome-rich, are translucent or opaque and have a rather peculiar purplish-red hue like raw meat. These are embedded in a bright green granular mineral resembling jade, but which is actually a form of zoisite. Polished slabs of the corundum zoisite rock make a spectacular ornamental stone and this has been used for ash-trays and the like.

The rubies are extensively laminated by multiple 'twinning' and many attempts have been made to isolate small clear pieces from crystals shattered by heating them and suddenly quenching them in water. A few very small rubies of deep red colour have in fact been cut, but the exercise as a whole has very little commercial importance.

Perhaps the most ancient source of ruby was in the Badakshan district of Afghanistan, south of the upper course of the Oxus, where it occurred with its customary companion, red spinel, in crystalline limestones very similar to those in Burma. The old name for Badakshan was Balaskia, and it is thought that the term Balas or Balais ruby, which was extensively used for red spinel, was derived from this locality name. Some of the vast treasures amassed by the Great Mogul, Akbar, in the sixteenth century are said to have come from these mines, but specimens from this locality are hard to find today, even in museums.

There are certain hallmarks which enable experienced gemmologists to recognise corundums from the various well-known localities. In the case of ruby there are only two sources which have commercial significance—Burma and Thailand. Apart from differences in colour, the Burma rubies can usually be relied upon to show small patches of 'silk' consisting of fine needles of rutile intersecting at 60°. These have a 'silky' appearance by reflected light. Silk of this kind is not found in Siam rubies, the most typical features of which are round black inclusions surrounded by a lace-like circular 'feather'. Ceylon corundums of all colours are rich in 'feathers' consisting of droplets of the mother-liquid from which the crystal formed. Crystals of zircon surrounded by strain-cracks, are particular features of Ceylon stones and not of corundums only. 'Silk' is also found in sapphires from Ceylon, but the rutile needles are finer and longer than those in Burma rubies. When this form of 'silk' exists throughout the stone a star-sapphire can be produced by cutting a stone *en cabochon* with its base parallel to the plane of the needles. Sapphires from Thailand have circular feathers surrounding a dark inclusion very similar to those seen in Siam rubies. Kashmir sapphires at their best are a very pure blue and usually have a very faint milkiness. Australian sapphires tend to be dark and greenish; zones of green and blue can often be seen. To study such internal features properly one needs to immerse the stone in liquid and examine it under a low-power microscope. If the reader has such an instrument available he will find a new world of beauty within all these coloured corundums.

Gem-quality corundum has a fairly constant density and refractive indices as one might expect from a mineral with so simple a composition. The density of pure corundum is 3·99 and the refractive indices 1·760–1·768. Traces of chromium in ruby and iron in sapphire raise these figures slightly, but the density seldom exceeds 4·00 despite statements to the contrary in many textbooks. The dispersion is low, and white (colourless) sapphires, whether synthetic or natural, have practically no fire.

Colour in both ruby and sapphire is of course of prime importance, and the lapidary has to use all his skills to get the best from given material without losing too much weight. Stones usually arrive in this country already cut. Often the best possible use has been made of the colour possibilities, but the stone may be lumpy or even lop-sided in an endeavour to retain as much weight as possible. It may be decided to re-cut the stone in the hope that the enhanced value per carat will more than make up for the loss.

The importance of dichroism in the case of ruby has already been explained in Chapter 8, and its effect in the case of sapphire is almost equally significant. Both stones are strongly dichroic: in ruby the two colours are a fine blood-red on the one hand, and a far less pleasing yellowish-red on the other, while in sapphire the twin colours are rich dark blue and a paler yellowish-blue. Most fortunately the fine colour in each case belongs to the ordinary ray which means that if the lapidary cuts his stone so that the table facet is parallel to the basal plane of the original crystal the only colour seen when looking down on the finished stone is the best colour, since all rays travelling parallel to the optic axis are ordinary rays. In the case of ruby, at any rate, the lapidary is lucky in the habit of the crystals being mainly tabular, so that cutting the stones in the manner most desirable optically is also the least wasteful in material.

The most common and deceptive substitutes for natural rubies and sapphires are the synthetic corundums so cheaply manufactured by the Verneuil process described in Chapter 25. In cutting these stones the optical orientation is not usually considered, with the result that cut specimens are not shown to their best colour advantage and show strong dichroism through the table facet, where natural rubies and sapphires normally should not. It should be mentioned that in Siam rubies there is very little dichroism so that the criteria for cutting the stones are not so critical. It has already been remarked that the distribution of colour in corundum is seldom even, giving an added problem to the lapidary.

The best way to see how the colour lies is to immerse the stones, whether cut or uncut, in a dish of liquid. Water is better than nothing, but either bromoform or methylene iodide (liquids recommended in Chapter 10 in connection with density determination) are much more efficient, as their refractive indices approach more closely to those of corundum. Such immersed stones can also be distinguished more readily from synthetic ruby and sapphire which reveal curved growth-lines, though a low-power microscope may be needed to see these in the case of ruby.

In Chapter 8 the bright red fluorescence of ruby was described and the manner in which it can be stimulated by ordinary light filtered through copper sulphate solution and viewed through a red filter. Long-wave ultra-violet light has a similar effect; and under short-wave ultra-violet light synthetic rubies show more brightly than the natural stones, while Siam rubies are virtually inert. Short-wave lamps are useful in detecting synthetic blue sapphires, which show a bluish or greenish-white glow, while natural stones show no effect.

Which leads us to discuss other stones, apart from their synthetic counterparts, which might be confused with ruby or sapphire. To begin with, of course, there are glass imitations or 'pastes' which can be made in suitable colours to match any gemstone. Since synthetic stones were made in quantity the use of pastes dwindled, and they are easily recognised by their lack of dichroism, lower refractive indices, included bubbles, etc. Doublets are a little more difficult—either the old-fashioned types in which a thin slice of almandine garnet is fused to a glass base of appropriate colour, or, in recent more sinister attempts to deceive even the skilled gemmologist, the crown of the stone consists of inferior-quality Australian sapphire which is skilfully cemented to a base of synthetic ruby or synthetic sapphire. The table facet in these nasty deceptions gives a true corundum reading on the refractometer and reveals natural inclusions when inspected with a lens. Cleverly mounted to conceal the join these artefacts call for the skills of a laboratory gemmologist, who with the aid of a suspicious mind and a good microscope should be able to find the answer.

Of natural stones resembling ruby, red spinel, garnets of the pyrope-almandine series, or red tourmaline are the most likely to deceive the eye. The first two, being cubic, are singly refracting and thus non-dichroic. Spinel is always closely associated with ruby and the huge historical stones known as the Black Prince's ruby and the Timur ruby, both of which are amongst the Crown Jewels in London, are in fact spinels. To the trained eye, the red of spinel, though pleasing, is more of a brick-red than the crimson hue of ruby. Tourmaline only needs a refractometer test, or if loose a trial in methylene iodide in which it floats while ruby sinks rapidly. As my colleague, Mr. A. E. Farn, has pointed out to me, while the colour of ruby looks better in tungsten light, with tourmaline daylight gives the better effect.

There are very few transparent minerals which are found in varieties of sapphire blue. Iolite is one of them, but is easily distinguished by its low refractive indices (1·54–1·55) and astonishing dichroism, one ray being nearly colourless, as can be seen with the naked eye when the stone is turned. Kyanite can show a lovely blue tint, but is flaky in structure and does not cut well. The recently discovered blue zoisite for which Tiffany coined the varietal name 'Tanzanite' is probably the most like a rather purplish fine sapphire. The refractometer is the best answer here, where the indices 1·692–1·700 are not to be compared with the 1·765–1·773 of sapphire. Blue spinel should also be mentioned. This has a rather steely blue tint and its single refractive index is near 1·72. One feature which is unique to corundum gems (though more often seen in synthetic stones since in these the cutting process is more hastily carried out) is a series of ripple-like surface markings which lapidaries call 'fire-marks'. They are caused by local overheating when the gem is being polished on the wheel.

In choosing a sapphire ring or other jewel it is important to make sure that it will show a good colour not only in daylight but in artificial light. Mercury strip-lighting is flattering to sapphires, but tungsten lighting is not, being richer in red rays and poorer in blue and violet light. Stones from Kashmir and Ceylon hold their blue colour well in artificial (tungsten) light, but many sapphires from other localities which appear a full-bodied blue in daylight, become almost black in electric light. Ruby, on the other hand, responds well in tungsten light which gives it an extra fine glow. Mercury strip-lighting, however, is not the lighting for rubies, as it lacks a red component. An understanding of these factors will help anyone choosing a ruby or sapphire ornament, and perhaps also in deciding on which jewellery to wear for a given occasion.

———————— ◇ ————————

CHAPTER THIRTEEN

CHRYSOBERYL, TOPAZ AND SPINEL

Chrysoberyl

As well as being an order of scratch-hardness, Mohs's scale can be taken as a rough guide to the importance of the various gemstones. And having taken the first and largest step from diamond at 10 to corundum at 9, we may as well continue the downward progression and proceed to describe chrysoberyl, topaz and spinel. Topaz is Mohs's official number 8, and spinel is equally hard, while chrysoberyl is the only mineral with a hardness between 9 and 8, and is thus generally listed as $8\frac{1}{2}$.

As a precious stone, chrysoberyl is known in three very different forms. The first, and least-valued commercially, is a golden, brownish or greenish-yellow transparent stone which at one time was sold under the name chrysolite. The second is an opalescent honey-coloured or greenish-brown form known as cymophane or cat's-eye chrysoberyl because it displays a sharply delineated silvery ray of light when it is suitably cut in *cabochon* form. The third and most valuable form which is known as alexandrite has the curious faculty of appearing green in daylight and red or purple in artificial (tungsten) light.

The names are easily explained: chrysoberyl simply means golden beryl and chrysolite, golden stone. The name chrysolite was originally applied to topaz and later to olivine and on account of its ambiguity is better avoided. Cymophane, from two Greek words 'wave' and 'appear' is not much used in the trade, which finds 'cat's-eye' sufficiently descriptive, though, since stones of many other species show this effect of chatoyancy, it is better to add the species name to avoid possible confusion. The derivation of alexandrite is not nearly so obvious. It so happened that this curious variety of chrysoberyl was first discovered in the Ural mountains on the very day that the young Prince and future Tsar Alexander II came of age. Added to this, the colours that the stone showed—green by day and red by lamplight—happened to be the Russian national military colours, and these facts combined to make it seem appropriate to name the new gemstone after the young Prince. Until the mines in the Sverdlovsk (then Ekaterinburg) district became virtually exhausted, alexandrite was peculiarly a Russian gem, and hardly known or considered elsewhere.

The mineral chrysoberyl can be described either as a beryllium—aluminium oxide, or as beryllium aluminate, having the formula $Be Al_2 O_4$. This would seem to bring it closely in line with spinel ($Mg Al_2 O_4$), but in fact its structure is not cubic like spinel but orthorhombic, and closely akin to that of peridot. The mineral is colourless if pure, and in fact 'white' chrysoberyls as they are called, are found in several localities, but are hardly considered worth the cutting since though the mineral polishes well and has a bright appearance which makes yellow varieties extremely attractive stones, there is a lack of the fire which is needed to make a colourless gem interesting. It must be appreciated that though to the keen amateur lapidary almost any transparent mineral serves as an invitation to indulge in a faceting adventure, the skilled professional finds his time and energies far too valuable to be spent on any stones which are not commercially viable. A rather pleasing exception to this rule is found in the markets of Rangoon where charming little sets of local stones such as sapphires, spinels, zircons and peridot cut in uniform size and shape and arranged in shallow felt-lined native-made boxes, are offered for sale. These are the spare-time products of the native lapidaries, using waste material from the gemfields of Mogok, and are of course designed to attract the tourist. To the gemmologist they provide a rare opportunity of obtaining stones from a known locality at a reasonable price.

Traces of iron give chrysoberyl its customary pale yellow, golden and greenish colours, while alexandrite owes its colours of green and red to the element chromium, which is able to replace aluminium in the crystal lattice without disturbing the structure of the mineral.

Chromium, as we have seen, is the colouring agent in ruby and in emerald, the colour seen in each case being largely governed by the position and extent of a broad absorption band in the middle of the spectrum. In ruby this is very extensive and allows mainly red and a little blue light to be transmitted, while in emerald the band is narrower and obscures the yellow and leaves most of the green part of the spectrum unabsorbed. In alexandrite the same general pattern of absorption is found, but in this case the central band occupies a balanced position, such that in daylight the colour appears almost emerald-green whereas in artificial light, richer in red rays, the effect is raspberry-red. It may have been noticed that reference is often made to 'tungsten' light instead of merely 'artificial' light. This is because of the growing use in these days of strip-lighting based on mercury-vapour lamps in tubes lined with various fluorescent powders. These can give light of various tints, but they never have the preponderance of red rays which was a noted feature of candlelight, lamplight, and to a lesser extent of light from a bulb with a tungsten filament.

Chrysoberyl is orthorhombic and often forms crystals resembling peridot in form, with prisms, pinacoids and pyramids with the main pinacoid face vertically striated. There is a strong tendency for their crystals to join in a 'triple twin' giving the crystal a tabular hexagonal aspect, though the v-shaped striations on the main face and six small re-entrant angles in the perimeter of the stone give the show away. The mineral has its origin in granite and gneiss but is chiefly recovered from alluvial deposits derived from these rocks. The principal sources are in Brazil in the Minas Novas district of Minas Gerais, associated minerals being quartz, tourmaline, garnet and spinel.

In the Ceylon gem gravels all types of chrysoberyl are found, including the finest cat's-eyes and most of the alexandrites now on the market. Ceylon alexandrites, though larger and clearer than the old Siberian stones do not even at their best show so emphatic a colour-change.

The properties of gem-quality chrysoberyl are fairly constant. The density is 3·71–3·72 and refractive indices are always near to 1·744 for the lowest index and 1·754 for the highest, giving a birefringence of 0·010. These latter figures are only a little below those for corundum and careful readings are needed if mistakes are to be avoided. The dispersion at 0·015 is surprisingly low for a mineral with so high a refractive index and explains the absence of fire even in a brilliant-cut specimen.

The pleochroism is only noticeable in the alexandrite variety, but here it reveals a surprising range of colours (two at a time) through the dichroscope: purple-red and green are to be expected, but the third colour, an orange-yellow, would not be suspected without some polarising equipment to enable one to see it as an isolated colour. This makes the lapidary's work very tricky in getting the best colour from a given piece of rough. Alexandrite, too, has a typical chromium spectrum of very fine lines in the red and a broad absorption band in the green. The chromium lines in the red form a useful criterion for separating ordinary brownish-green Ceylon chrysoberyls from those which do not show enough colour-change in tungsten light to warrant the term 'alexandrite' being used.

Really fine alexandrites showing a good emerald-green in daylight and a rich purple by artificial light are among the world's rarest stones, particularly in sizes over 5 carats. They may be valued at hundreds or even a thousand pounds a carat. I must confess that in terms of beauty such high prices hardly seem to be justified. Fine chrysoberyl cat's-eyes, on the other hand, are for me the most beautiful of all gemstones. The 'silk' within the stone which causes the silvery ray consists of incredibly fine rutile needles packed in parallel formation, to the tune of some 100,000 to the square inch. It is their fineness which makes the ray so sharp, silvery and opalescent. The body-colour of the stone may be greenish-yellow or honey colour, and the stone should be translucent but not too nearly transparent, or the ray will be an enfeebled one. Probably the most favoured style of cutting for these is a rather steep oval *cabochon*. The lapidary has to be at pains to ensure not only that the base of the *cabochon* is parallel to the direction of the fibres, but also that the long axis of the *cabochon* is exactly coincident with the cat's-eye ray. In this particular, a round *cabochon* requires less critical care in the cutting. The base of the stone is left unpolished to conserve the weight and prevent light from the rear of the stone from interfering with the chatoyant effect. As with all cat's-eyes and star-stones a single source of light is necessary to achieve the sharpest and best effect. Direct sunlight, in fact, is the best lighting for all such stones and strip-lighting the worst. If a strip-light is the only source available and one wants to display a cat's-eye the best one can do is to orient the stone so that the cat's-eye ray is parallel to the length of the fluorescent tube.

When yellow gemstones are mentioned topaz is the name which naturally springs to mind, with citrine quartz as a cheaper and commoner substitute. But in fact there are a number of gem species which produce attractive yellow stones—sapphire, chrysoberyl, beryl, tourmaline, to mention a few. If one arranged fine specimens of each of these in a row they would be difficult to separate by eye: topaz might claim the subtlest and most satisfying golden tint, beryl the yellowest yellow and the greatest limpidity, but chrysoberyl I feel would score on the grounds of brightness of lustre. Few stones take a better polish, and the hardness is high enough to ensure that this will not soon be spoiled.

The term yellow chrysoberyl covers a wide range of tints from a rather wishy-washy straw or pale green colour, through golden to brown or green. The paler types were much used in Victorian jewellery, in gem-set crosses, cluster rings, etc., and were often shallow cut and improved in appearance and colour by being mounted on a gold backing. These 'chrysolites' had a curious charm. One would expect that the far finer specimens available from Brazil or Ceylon would be highly popular, but this is not so, more's the pity. Yellow chrysoberyl is usually mixed cut (brilliant top, step-cut base) and oval or cushion-shaped in outline.

The finest faceted chrysoberyl known is from the Hope Collection, and can be seen in the Mineral Gallery of the Natural History Museum in South Kensington. This is a yellowish-green, flawless stone weighing 45 carats. It is cut as an almost circular brilliant, is exceptionally transparent, and its colour approaches that of peridot.

Some of the stones most likely to be confused with yellow chrysoberyl have been mentioned above. So far as colour goes yellow chrysoberyls almost always have a distinct greenish shade, which differentiates them from yellow sapphire, topaz or citrine. If a refractometer is available a careful check in sodium light will definitely identify the stone, and the spectroscope will record the broad band at 4450 Å in the blue-violet found in all chrysoberyls.

The true alexandrite with its marked change from green to red in tungsten light is very distinctive, but a so-called 'synthetic alexandrite' is an extremely prevalent fake which deceives more people than it should, as its appearance, in daylight at least, does not remotely resemble the real thing. These pretenders are in reality synthetic sapphires coloured by the addition of vanadium which gives them a peculiar greyish-mauve colour which changes in lamplight to an emphatic purple. Once seen, these artefacts can easily be recognised and should hold no terrors. Commonsense should warn would-be bargain-hunters that large specimens of one of the world's rarest gemstones are unlikely to be offered at a fraction of their market value. Those of my readers who travel widely should be warned that the most dangerous places in the world to purchase gems are those such as Colombo in Ceylon, Hong Kong on the doorstep of China, or Rangoon, the capital of Burma, which are in close proximity to well-known sources of gem material. Huge quantities of coloured synthetic corundums and spinels are shipped to such places for sale to gullible tourists and there is no redress for the purchaser, as there would be for a falsely described gem bought from a reputable European jeweller.

So far as cat's-eyes are concerned, the most dangerous contender is the chatoyant variety of quartz. The colour here is usually fawn instead of the honey or greenish-yellow of the chrysoberyl, and the ray, being caused by relatively coarse asbestos-like fibres, is by comparison diffuse and ill-defined. If the stone is unset a trial in bromoform or methylene iodide will quickly settle the issue: quartz will float on the surface, while chrysoberyl will rapidly sink.

Topaz

Topaz is one of the best-known and most coveted gems in the jewellers' repertoire. The name has so fine and ancient a ring to it, and has been so long accepted in the public mind as the prototype of all yellow gemstones, that it is rather disturbing to learn that Pliny in his *Natural History* used 'topazius' as a name of a green mineral which was probably peridot. Topazius was a mysterious fog-bound island in the Red Sea on which pirates found the peridot when searching for water. Our present-day topaz was classed by Pliny as a chrysolite.

It was not until the late eighteenth century that the name topaz was finally settled by mineralogists on what we think of as the 'right' mineral, but it was more than a century before the trade could be induced to abandon entirely so popular a name for other yellow gemstones. True topaz was described as 'Brazilian topaz' or 'Saxony topaz' (after a famous locality at Schneckenstein): 'Oriental topaz' or sometimes 'King topaz' was used for yellow sapphire; while 'Occidental topaz' was reserved for the yellow quartz, citrine.

For a century or more the stone merchants of Idar-Oberstein, which is the chief cutting centre not only for Germany but for the whole of Europe, carried on an enormous trade in citrine, selling it under the name 'quartz-topaz' or 'topaz-quartz', which was tactfully transmuted into plain 'topaz' by the time it reached the jeweller's window. True topaz, on the other hand, formed an infinitesimal part of their trade, and their resistance to abandoning entirely the popular name topaz in connection with their main product was understandable.

Even after fifty years of trade education, the corrective influence of textbooks on gemmology, and such enforceable legislation as the Trade Descriptions Act, 1968, there is a reluctance by dealers to be content with just plain 'topaz' in describing this mineral. Most of them would prefer to add a corroborative adjective and put 'precious topaz' or 'Brazilian topaz' on their packets or invoices.

Topaz has a more complex chemical nature than the minerals so far described, being a fluosilicate of aluminium in which some of the fluorine has been replaced by water in the form of the hydroxyl (OH) group. Thus the formula can be written as $(Al(FOH))_2SiO_4$. The presence of fluorine gives the clue to the genesis of the mineral under the influence of fluorine and water vapours during the formation of granites and similar igneous rocks resulting in pockets and veins of minerals such as beryl, tinstone, etc., in addition to topaz itself.

Fluorine is known to have a depressing effect on the refractive index of a mineral—note, for instance, the very low index (1·434) of the calcium fluoride we know as fluorspar. In consequence not only do all topaz crystals have refractive indices which are relatively low in consideration of their high density, but those topaz crystals (and they include all colourless and blue topaz) in which fluorine greatly preponderates over hydroxyl are found to have lower indices than those of the yellow gem, topaz, of Brazil which contains hydroxyl in greater amount. The density works the other way: the more fluorine the higher the density.

The figures can be given as density 3·56 and refractive indices 1·61–1·62 for colourless and blue stones; 3·53 and 1·63–1·64 for the yellow stones from Ouro Preto in Brazil and the pink stones derived from these by heat treatment, which are the varieties most valued in commerce.

As already stated, topaz is the standard number 8 on Mohs's scale of hardness, and when cut takes an exceptionally high polish, making it slippery to the touch, an effect which can be distinctive to anyone who is sensitive to such things. The well-known Victorian gemmologist, Sir Arthur Church, had an amusing story to tell about this quality of slipperiness. A jeweller friend offered him the pick, at half-a-crown a time, of stones from a bag containing a mixture of topaz and citrines. Church inserted his hand, and by 'applying the inner aspect of a well-educated thumb' to each stone in turn he was able to extract the topaz stones, leaving the citrines in the bag.

Topaz has a very perfect cleavage parallel to the basal plane resulting in unusually smooth surfaces. The pearly lustre of a cleavage plane and a few lines marking the edges of very shallow 'steps' are clear indications that one is not dealing with a crystal face or a polished surface. Not uncommonly a film of air follows an incipient cleavage plane in a crystal or stone and gives rise to a play of interference colours. This rather easy cleavage makes it necessary to handle topaz jewellery with special care. A sudden shock such as that occasioned by dropping the jewel on to the plate-glass surface of a dressing-table can have the disconcerting effect of causing a stone to snap in two.

Topaz exhibits both frictional and pyroelectricity to a greater extent than any other gemstone except tourmaline. A brisk rub of the stone on the sleeve will make it capable of attracting small pieces of paper, and the same effect is noticeable when it is heated and allowed to cool slowly. Crystals are orthorhombic in symmetry and commonly show a combination of two rhombic prisms, vertically striated, forming eight-sided columns terminated at one end only by pyramids or domes, the base of the crystal where it was attached to the matrix being represented by a cleavage plane. In some localities, notably Burma and the Urals, there is a basal pinacoid which is characteristically rough and pitted.

Clear white topaz crystals from alluvial deposits may show vestiges of the original crystal form, or be completely water-worn into oval pebbles with a frosted surface. Since these are so hard and have a density very near that of diamond, inexperienced prospectors are often led to hope that they have made a discovery of diamonds of fabulous size and quality. In consequence many such pebbles are sent in hopefully for a scientific test in a gem-testing laboratory. Their shape and appearance are extremely typical and a density test giving a value of 3·56, in addition to a check for double refraction under a polariscope, are all that is needed to prove that one's suspicion is correct.

I remember a case where an elderly prospector simply would not believe these tests had any validity, and obstinately maintained that his stones must be diamond, since (he claimed) one could not break them even by hitting them with a hammer. It seemed that the only way to convince him that he was mistaken was to do just this, and we very successfully shattered one of his stones in front of his eyes. This, the crudest and least scientific test we had ever performed, was entirely effective psychologically and the old man departed sad in the knowledge that we were right.

One large white topaz of exceptional quality which was found in Brazil about 1740, and when cut was said to weigh as much as 1680 carats, was accepted as a diamond and found its way into the Portuguese regalia. This is hard to credit, since though white topaz can be clear and bright and takes an excellent polish, it has a very low dispersion and shows none of the fire so typical of diamond. The low value put upon this material by the trade can be gauged by the fact that a huge piece weighing ten pounds or more was given to the Hatton Garden Laboratory by a dealer when he was clearing his office of unwanted 'rubbish' before moving into new premises.

Before the advent of synthetic white sapphire or spinel, white topaz was considered an ideal material on which apprentice lapidaries could practise their craft. I have in my possession a brilliant-cut topaz which was the prize-winning entry in a lapidary competition held in 1851 in connection with the Great Exhibition of that year for which the Crystal Palace was designed and erected in Hyde Park, in the position now occupied by that other masterpiece of Victoriana, the Albert Memorial.

While one can understand why colourless topaz should have no market value, the lack of interest in blue topaz is rather puzzling, even in the rare cases where the colour is deep enough to resemble the best-quality aquamarine: this, despite the fact that fine blue topaz is rather harder and more lustrous than the beryl it resembles. One can of course appreciate that the higher density of topaz means that a 12 carat topaz has only the size of a 9 carat aquamarine.

Knowing what the weight 'ought' to be for a stone of given size is a useful piece of practical knowledge for anyone dealing in precious stones. Dealers in diamonds can usually estimate within a few points the weight of a brilliant if it is within the common commercial range of, say, $\frac{1}{2}$ carat to 5 carats. In this he is aided, of course, by the standard form of cutting. But I remember being told by the owner of a high-class jewellery shop in Rio de Janeiro which dealt almost entirely in fine aquamarines, that girls checking the weight of aquamarines before putting them into stock soon learned to spot the occasional 'rogue' blue topaz by the fact that its weight was considerably more than it would be if it had the lower density of a beryl.

The only colour apart from yellow that is popular in topaz is the pink variety, and it is doubtful whether this ever exists in nature, the pink topaz of commerce being produced from the sherry-yellow or yellow-brown crystals mined in Ouro Preto by heating them carefully to temperatures between 300 and 450°C. At higher temperatures the stones become colourless. Traces of chromium in these Brazilian stones are the cause of the pink colour, and the heat treatment seems to settle the chromium ions into the lattice in replacement of some of the aluminium. The presence of chromium is signalled by a narrow line in the red end of the spectrum (at 6820 Å) which can be seen either as an absorption or a fluorescence line depending upon conditions—and there is a fairly bright red fluorescence when the stone is examined under crossed filters (see Chapter 8).

The name Ouro Preto has already been mentioned several times as the source of the finest yellow and pink topaz. Ouro Preto is the capital of the State of Minas Gerais, and at the time when yellow topaz was first discovered in the district (1760) was known as Villa Rica. The topaz is found in a band of clay slates a few hundred yards wide which extends through a chain of hills to the south-west of the town for six miles or more. The slates are decomposed by weathering into a soft clayey mass, and here and there nests of detached topaz crystals are found embedded in brown clay or kaolin. The crystals vary in shade from pale yellow to dark wine-yellow, and are commonly a few inches long. They are released from the surrounding clay by playing a stream of water over them. The accompanying minerals include smoky quartz, black tourmaline, rutile and zircon. The most profitable mines were on estates at Bon Vista and Capao de Lana. The annual output at one time was said to be 18 hundredweight, with fifty miners operating, but later there was a decline and the valley shows remains of many abandoned mines.

We are not accustomed to thinking that Western Europe can provide much in the way of gem materials other than Baltic amber, but the Schneckenstein near Auerbach in Saxony was the chief source of yellow topaz in the eighteenth century. The Schneckenstein is a wall of rock like a ruined fortress composed of a quartz and topaz breccia within which are cavities lined with crystals of topaz, quartz and tourmaline, and partly filled with kaolin. The crystals recovered averaged about half an inch in length, but some were as much as four inches long. These varied from colourless to dark wine-yellow, with sometimes a greenish shade.

Apart from the mines in the Ouro Preto district, there are many other Brazilian localities for topaz. White and blue topaz is found in association with diamond in Minas Novas and in the Arrasuahy district in the north-east of the State of Minas Gerais, but always as rolled pebbles, associated with garnet, chrysoberyl, aquamarine, tourmaline, etc.

Fine crystals of topaz in various colours are found in many parts of the world, most notably perhaps in Russia, where it is invariably associated with beryl. The Mogok district in Burma, South West Africa, Nigeria, Japan and several localities in the U.S.A. have yielded gem-quality topaz, but not in the coveted yellow or pink shades. A curious pale brown colour seen in topaz crystals from Utah (U.S.A.), Mogok, Japan and eastern Siberia is unstable, and fades on exposure to strong sunlight.

Partly on account of the elongated habit of the original crystals, topaz is usually cut in long oval shapes or as pendeloques for ear-rings, etc. Usually the stones are mixed cut (that is with brilliant-cut crown and step-cut base), but elongated step-cut forms are sometimes used. When it comes to purchasing topaz specimens or topaz jewellery one has to be cautious unless the source of supply is a very reliable one. One must remember that Brazilian topaz is a decidedly rare gemstone and that a 'topaz' brooch or ring or necklace which is being offered in some second-hand shop at a moderate price (say £5–£20) is far more likely to be yellow quartz or even paste than the real thing, which would be worth some ten times this amount. A paste can usually be recognised on careful examination with a lens on account of the moulded appearance of the facet junctions as against the sharp edges of a properly cut gemstone. Any air bubbles seen glistening within the stone are another damning indication, also the lack of sharp extinction positions when the stone is rotated in a polariscope (i.e. between crossed polaroids). A very experienced eye is needed if one is to be sure of distinguishing citrine quartz from true topaz. Quite often in a 'topaz' necklace some of the stones are indeed topaz, and others quartz, and one has to admit that they match in pretty well. If the reader enjoys simple forms of scientific testing he may care to invest in some di-bromoethane (B.D.H. Chemicals, Poole, Dorset, can supply), and immerse his doubtful stones (mounted or not) in a half-tumblerful of this liquid, which has an ethereal smell but is not unduly poisonous. The fluid has a refractive index of 1·54 which so closely matches that of quartz that if a faceted citrine is immersed in it its facet edges and its outline practically disappear. A trial in this liquid with a specimen of rock-crystal forms an amusing experiment and a lesson in simple gemmology quite aside from any practical value it may have. All stones lose much of their relief when immersed in a fluid of fairly high R.I. but the greater the difference between the index of the fluid and that of the stone the stronger the relief becomes.

With corundum gems methylene iodide (recommended in Chapter 10), which has the high index of 1·745, is a very close match which helps to prove their nature when a white or yellow sapphire is involved, which reminds me that a very plausible substitute for yellow topaz can be yellow synthetic sapphire, which is manufactured specially in just the right warm shade of yellow, and is a bright and attractive stone. Pink topaz can also be plausibly represented by substitutes, synthetic pink sapphire being the most likely to encounter. This will show a brilliant red fluorescence under crossed filters or a long-wave ultra-violet lamp.

The above suggestions do not pretend to provide conclusive proof such as can be obtained in a properly equipped laboratory where a good refractometer reading can prove a stone to be topaz in a matter of minutes. To place any reliance on one's first fumbling tries at gem testing would be most unwise. All initial trials and experiments should be on known specimens in one's own collection or borrowed from some kind friend. Where big money is involved a reliable source or a laboratory test are the only true safeguards.

SPINEL

Spinel might with some justice be thought of as the Cinderella among gemstones. As a gem species it has much to commend it, but its name fails to give rise to any attractive image in the mind, and its merits are constantly being belittled by comparison with its more richly coloured companion mineral, corundum. Were there no ruby, red spinel would be the most sought after red gemstone: were there no sapphire, a fine blue spinel would be in high demand. But comparison with the corundum gems must always prove damaging and give the impression that a spinel is a 'second-best' stone.

It is ironic that even in the few cases where by reasons of size and circumstance red spinels have earned the right to be thought of historic importance the 'credit titles' have been given to the better-known species, and the public is told of the Black Prince's 'ruby' and the Timur 'ruby', and is apt not to read the small print where it is explained that these two famous stones are both, in fact, spinels.

It is useless to try and avoid these comparisons: the two minerals are created in the same sorts of rock and later become assembled in the same gem gravels—and the two most favoured colours of each are the same, blue and red. Spinel has slightly lower refractivity, is slightly less hard, and the one property where it 'scores' slightly over corundum, its dispersion; the greater fire this gives only assumes importance in giving *synthetic* white spinel a more lively colour-play than the comparable synthetic white sapphire.

The name spinel is said to be derived from the Latin *spinella* (meaning a little thorn) with reference to the spiky octahedral crystals in which it occurs. The name 'balas' or 'balais' ruby by which in the past red spinel was known to distinguish it from true ruby comes from the Latin Balascus, an Arabic rendering of the Badakshan, the district in Afghanistan from whence came the finest red spinels in earlier times. The variety-name 'rubicelle', which was at one time applied to an orange spinel, was clearly unsatisfactory, and has suffered a quiet death. Precious spinel is a magnesium aluminate, $MgAl_2O_4$, but the name spinel is also used to cover a group of minerals having the same crystal structure in which both the magnesium and the aluminium ions can be replaced by elements such as iron and zinc. Ceylonite and pleonaste are names given to opaque black forms of spinel rich in iron, and gahnospinel is a name I and my colleague C. J. Payne gave to blue spinels containing considerable amounts of zinc, which we were the first to discover in the Ceylon gem gravels. The pure zinc spinel, gahnite, was named after its discoverer, Gahn, a Swedish chemist.

Spinel crystallises in the cubic system, usually as simple octahedra developed evenly on all sides, as is possible in a mineral formed in a metamorphic rock. Sometimes the edges of the octahedron are replaced by faces of the rhombic dodecahedron: this is seen in dark red spinels from Burma which have an unusually large trace of chromium in their composition. Twinned octahedra in which one face of the octahedron is common to the two crystals are also common, as their name 'spinel twins' suggests. These are the 'macles' of the diamond world and have already been described in Chapter 11.

As stated at the beginning of this chapter, the hardness of spinel is reckoned as being equal to that of topaz; that is, 8 on Mohs's scale. The density is fairly constant at 3·60 and refractive index at 1·715, unless there is considerable replacement by iron or by zinc. Where iron is present in more than traces the stone becomes black and opaque and is known as 'ceylonite' or 'pleonaste'. Typical figures for such stones, which curiously enough are sometimes cut for mourning jewellery, are 3·8 for the density and 1·78 for the refractive index. The zinc-rich types we call gahnospinel are invariably blue and seem to be confined to the gem gravels of Ceylon. There is nothing in their appearance to suggest that they are anything else than pure magnesium spinels with just a little iron to account for their blue colour. But even a little zinc has a marked effect in increasing their density and refractive index. The highest figures we have so far recorded for these being 4·06 and 1·754, probably representing a zinc content of some 20 per cent.

Nearly pure gahnite, green in colour and transparent, has been recently found and cut as a gemstone. One such specimen in my collection weighing 4·67 carats, has a density of 4·64 and R.I. 1·798.

Spinel as a gemstone has a wide range of colour, but apart from the best red or blue specimens, these are more shades than colours: chiefly pinks, mauves and purples. The two main colouring agents are chromium and iron, chromium alone for the purest reds and iron for blue, while a mixture of the two produces the purple tints.

The red of spinel is not the red of ruby, and when examining hundreds of small rubies under the microscope in search of synthetics the occasional intrusion of a red spinel is at once noticeable for its brick-red shade compared with the rich crimson of ruby. Very pleasant, but different. Similarly the blue of spinel tends to be a grey or steely-blue when compared with sapphire at its best.

Colours are notoriously difficult to describe, and comparisons with well-known flowers, blood, the sea or the sky are often made to try and convey the desired mental image of the colour concerned. It is easy to ridicule such over-worked similes as 'pigeon's-blood' red for the finest Burma rubies, 'pistachio-green' for an epidote, 'clove-brown' for an axinite, and so on, since the blood of a pigeon, or a pistachio nut are not normally at hand for comparison. Even such a term as 'grass-green' to describe the colour of emerald, or 'sea-green' for an aquamarine, if taken literally must depend in one case on such factors as the time of year, whether the grass has been fertilised, or recently cut, and in the other case, whether the sea is the blue of the Mediterranean under a clear sky, or the indescribable tint of the English Channel on a sunless day.

And yet I personally would prefer these terms to a careful 'scientific' description of the colours in question in terms of saturation, brilliance and hue. The comparisons were originally coined on the basis of truth, or they would not have been generally accepted and hardened into clichés. The term 'brick-red', for instance, used above in connection with spinel, does not bear close analysis in terms of actual bricks, at least as commonly used; but all who know spinel would agree that the stone has 'this sort of red', and know that the term could never be applied to that of ruby.

While discussing colour, I might mention here a convention which the reader may have already noticed and found puzzling. That is the use of the term 'white' for transparent gemstones free from colour, when 'colourless' seems to be more truly descriptive. In normal parlance, snow is 'white', whereas ice is 'colourless', and one would expect therefore that while marble could be described as 'white', one would speak of 'colourless' zircon, sapphire or diamond. Probably the root of the matter lay in the relative commercial advantage of the two names. 'Colourless' sounds insipid, while 'white' sounds bright and pure. Be that as it may, the convention is too deeply rooted to alter, and must be accepted as 'one of those things' peculiar to the trade in precious stones.

While maintaining that the reds and blues found in spinel are not quite the same as those of ruby and sapphire, one cannot of course rely purely on colour-judgement to separate the two species. Even with the meagre equipment I have suggested that the reader of this book might find it worth while having on hand, the distinction is quite simple. Spinel is cubic and therefore shows no double refraction: it follows that when turned between crossed polaroids spinel gems will not show the four positions of sharp extinction shown by ruby and sapphire. In carrying out this test it would be wise to hold the stone on edge, as properly cut rubies and sapphires have their optic axis at right angles to the table facet, and rotating the stone in the plane of the table facet would maintain it in the one direction of single refraction. If a ruby or sapphire is free from its setting and immersed in methylene iodide its facet edges almost disappear. If the cell is placed between two crossed polaroids and the stone examined through a pocket lens placed just above it one should have the pleasure of seeing a black cross surrounded by a series of dark circles, which is technically known as an 'uniaxial interference figure'. Is this asking too much? If so, forget it: but if you do try and succeed you will have earned the pleasure of observing one more of the special tricks that can be performed with precious stones, and you will incidentally have proved with fair certainty that your ruby or your sapphire is a natural stone, as the cutting of their synthetic counterparts is optically at random, and such stones are most unlikely to have their optic axis at right angles to the table.

Another simple test depends upon dichroism. If a well-lit ruby or sapphire be placed on a sheet of white blotting-paper and examined through a polaroid disc held close to the eye, one should be able to notice a marked change of colour when the disc is turned while with spinel no such effect can be seen.

Both ruby and red spinel show a bright red fluorescence under ultraviolet light, and the effect is even stronger under the 'crossed filter' arrangement described in Chapter 8. The fluorescence may seem the same, but a small hand spectroscope will reveal a striking difference. With ruby the light can be seen to come almost entirely from a single bright line in the deep red, while in natural red spinels there is a group of five to seven bright lines, of which the strongest are in the centre. This 'organ-pipe' appearance is one of the most sensitive and useful tests for red spinel and can be applied to uncut as well as to cut stones, and of course to stones mounted in jewellery.

On the whole spinels are more free from inclusions than are the corundum gems; 'silk', for instance, is infrequent and though one occasionally sees a star-effect in *cabochon*-cut blue spinels (which indicates the presence of oriented 'silk') this is usually feeble. The most typical inclusions in red spinel are tiny octahedra often arranged in patterns.

A more serious difficulty than in the separation of spinel and ruby can be the distinction between red spinel and pyrope garnet. In most gem species the constants of density and refractive index are fairly well fixed, but with minerals which form part of an isomorphous series the composition, and therefore the constants, can vary rather widely. Both spinel and garnet are members of such a group and moreover both are cubic minerals, so that a test for birefringence is of no avail. Normally the R.I. and density are distinctly lower than the lowest figures for pyrope garnet and there is no problem, but an occasional chrome-rich spinel can reach the garnet level, and in such cases even the fluorescence test is unreliable: some spinels fail to glow and some garnets (against all the rules) do show some fluorescence. This matter fortunately has no commercial importance and can safely be left to the professional gemmologist.

Synthetic spinels are made in large quantities by the Verneuil process in a manner similar to that used for corundum gems. But these are not designed to imitate the natural spinels, but to form effective substitutes for aquamarine, sapphire, and even diamond. To grow these stones successfully a composition of $MgO.3Al_2O_3$ is found most effective, and this gives them a refractive index of 1·727 which is rather distinctive. Moreover the stones show a grid-like pattern of light and dark between crossed polaroids, and the blue examples appear red through the Chelsea filter. More details of these attractive synthetics will be given in Chapter 25.

A final word should perhaps be said about the origins of gem spinels. There are virtually only two commercial sources—the Mogok district of Burma supplies the reds and pinks, while blue, lavender and purple spinels are common in the gem gravels of Ceylon. The ancient mines of Badakshan are of historical importance only.

CHAPTER FOURTEEN

BERYL

BERYL HAS A deservedly high ranking amongst the minerals which provide gem material. Emerald, possibly the most costly of all gemstones, is a grass-green beryl; aquamarine, the clear sea-blue variety, is amongst the most popular of gemstones, and lovely clear stones of pink and yellow are also part of the beryl range. Beryl is, in fact, a typically allochromatic mineral in being intrinsically colourless but revealing the presence of oxides such as those of chromium and iron in terms of colour.

The name beryl is an ancient one and seems always to have been associated with the same mineral, which is rather unusual. In composition it is a silicate of the two light metals, beryllium and aluminium, and its chemical formula can be written $3BeOAl_2O_36SiO_2$; but there are nearly always small amounts of alkali metals present and also sometimes water, while chromic oxide (in emerald) and ferric oxide (in aquamarine) in small amounts can replace some of the alumina in the crystal lattice.

Beryl has full hexagonal symmetry and its crystal structure consists of rings formed by six silicon-oxygen tetrahedra stitched together, so to speak, by the atoms of beryllium and aluminium. The structure, in fact, resembles a honeycomb with open channels parallel to the symmetry axis, and it is within these channels that the alkali atoms potassium, rubidium and caesium can be held and water molecules also.

Beryl is one of those rewarding minerals which crystallise well and in forms which clearly show their hexagonal symmetry. In fact it is the simplest possible hexagonal forms which are those most frequently seen, in which rather elongated six-sided prisms are terminated by a flat basal plane. The chief modification of this simple habit consists in pyramid faces bevelling the corners or edges of the prisms: the basal plane however is always present. Usually only one end of the crystal is developed, the other end showing a broken surface where it was attached to the vein or cavity in which the crystal grew.

The crystal faces are usually fairly smooth: any striations present being parallel to the length of the prisms—that is, parallel to the hexagonal axis of the crystal. In some localities the faces are heavily etched, perhaps as the result of attack by hot fluorine vapours in the last stages of the crystal's growth. One may note here that pits or etch marks on the faces sometimes give a useful indication of the symmetry of the crystal. Small hexagonal pits, for instance, are often visible on the basal plane of a beryl crystal and serve to show that there is a six-fold axis of symmetry at right angles to this plane. In trigonal crystals such as corundum and tourmaline any such marking would be triangular in shape, indicating that the main axis has only three-fold symmetry.

The two most important gem varieties of beryl, emerald and aqua-marine, have already been mentioned. Three of the less well-known varieties have been given special names. Colourless beryl, which is scarcely worth the cutting, is sometimes known as goshenite, yellow beryl as heliodor, and pink beryl as morganite; but these variety names are seldom used. Green beryls of a tint which cannot be classed either as aquamarine or as emerald are also not uncommon.

The mineral's properties next. The hardness is usually listed as $7\frac{1}{2}$ as it stands between quartz and topaz on Mohs's scale. Both density and refractive index vary a good deal chiefly owing to the varying amount of alkalies present. The pink varieties have more than the normal share of these, and while the purest synthetic forms of beryl have a density almost exactly that of quartz (2·65) and refractive indices 1·560–1·563, some pink varieties have figures as high as 2·84 for specific gravity and 1·592–1·600 for refractive indices. The values for aquamarine and for yellow beryl are at the lower end of the scale, with densities 2·68–2·70 and refractive indices 1·57–1·58, with a birefringence of 0·006. When it comes to emerald the figures for density and refractive indices are found to be fairly characteristic for each locality, and assume practical importance in distinguishing between natural stones and the several forms of synthetic emerald which are now on the market. As this is not a technical treatise I will not enter fully into this extremely complex matter, but rest content with giving the figures for emeralds from three commercially important localities. For stones from the Muzo mine of Colombia typical values are 2·71 for density and 1·577–1·583 for refrac-tive indices; for those from Siberia the figures are 2·74 and 1·581–1·588; and for the dark green emeralds from Sandawana, Rhodesia, 2·75 and

1·585–1·592. Perhaps I should point out that the two figures mentioned for refractive indices represent the lower and upper index in each case.

The most commonly met with synthetic emeralds are made by crystallisation from a melt, and these have the low-density and refractive indices mentioned above (2·65:1·560–1·563), which distinguishes them from any natural emerald. Synthetics made by other processes cannot be separated by such simple measurements, but rather by a careful study of their inclusions under the microscope. This is one of the fields where the professional gemmologist must be consulted, especially as the cost of emerald is so high that any mistake is bound to be a costly matter.

Dispersion in beryl is only 0·014 and too low to give any effect of fire. For this reason colourless beryls, though clear and limpid, are seldom cut for use in jewellery. Both aquamarine and emerald show quite strong dichroism, and this makes the orientation of the table facet of the stone with regard to the original crystal a matter of some importance. In aquamarine the finest blue colour unfortunately belongs to the extraordinary ray, and it is tantalising that the fine colour as seen through a polaroid film-set with its vibration direction parallel to the axis of the crystal cannot be isolated without such an optical aid, and must always be diluted to the extent of at least 50 per cent by the ubiquitous ordinary ray, which has a feeble yellowish tint. The best that can be done is to cut the table facet parallel to the prism faces, thus ensuring a full 50 per cent of the desired blue colour. Luckily the habit of the crystal makes this the natural thing for the lapidary to do, and rectangular step-cut stones are the most frequently seen.

In emerald the deeper colour also belongs to the extraordinary ray, but this is a dark bluish-green, and many people, myself included, prefer the rather paler jade-green which is seen in the ordinary ray, and can be isolated by cutting a stone with its table at right angles to the axis of the crystal. These optical factors are of course not the only, or even the most important, considerations when cutting a gemstone. The shape of the crystal often dictates the direction and the style of cutting, while the depth of the colour and the nature and position of flaws or inclusions are also very important factors. Emerald is so commonly cut in the octagonal step-cut style which best displays its colour, that this type is often known as 'emerald-cut' in consequence.

Beryls of the other most fancied colours, golden yellow and deep rose-pink, are also most often step-cut. Beryl takes a beautiful polish, and flawless gems of the paler varieties have a peculiar liquid-like beauty which is not quite like that seen in any other gem.

Emeralds have their origin in rocks of a very different type from those which give rise to the other gem beryls. The mining of emerald in Colombia, where the finest stones in the world are found, has already been described in Chapter 5. These South American stones are exceptional in being recovered from calcite veins in a bituminous limestone, for in almost all other localities the mother-rock is a mica-schist.

The earliest known occurrence of emerald was in the so-called Cleopatra's emerald mines in Upper Egypt at Jebel Sikiat some 15 miles from the West Coast of the Red Sea in a depression in a long range of mountains. These were lost for more than a milliennium and rediscovered by Cailliaud early in the nineteenth century as partly surface and partly underground workings. Very ancient appliances and tools were found, some dating back to 1650 B.C., revealing that Cleopatra's use of the mines came comparatively late in the day. We do know, however, that this famous queen used stones from the locality, since emeralds from the mine engraved with her image were presented to those she wished to please.

The stones from this ancient mine were of good colour but rather pale: the occurrence is only mentioned here because for over 3000 years this was presumably the only source of emeralds except for a few stones derived from an almost inaccessible source in the Austrian Alps. This is at a height of 7500 feet above sea-level in a ravine leading out of the Habachtal, and though most of the stones from this commercially unimportant locality are pale and full of inclusions, a few fine stones are recovered even today.

The most important source for emerald apart from the Colombian mines lies in the Ural mountains on the right bank of the Takovaya river, and the emerald crystals are found in the same chrome-rich mica-schist rocks in which the alexandrite variety of chrysoberyl was later recovered. The mines were discovered accidentally in 1830 and were opened up under Government control in a difficult region of marsh and forest some 50 miles north-east of the town of Sverdlovsk, which was formerly known as Ekaterinburg. After twenty years' working the mines were closed; but the high price of emeralds made it worth while to open them again in the present century. Apart from emerald and alexandrite yet another beryllium mineral, phenakite, comes from these mica-schists. Actinolite and mica are amongst the minerals found with the emeralds, and crystals of these form typical inclusions by which these Russian emeralds can be recognised.

An occurrence of emerald (again in mica-schist) at Leydsdorp in eastern Transvaal, was discovered in 1927 and quite extensively mined. These South African stones have never been very popular in the trade as their colour is poor and the stones are usually full of mica inclusions. Thirty years later a more valuable source of fine emeralds was discovered in Rhodesia by two South African prospectors, Constat and Oosthuitzen, during a wide-ranging search for beryl, tantalite, and other ore minerals associated with pegmatites in the remoter parts of Southern Rhodesia. After finding poor-quality emeralds in 1955 they notified the Department of Mines. Then in May 1957 an amazing strike of deep green crystals was found associated with very ancient tremolite schists. The first emeralds were small and flawed, but a sample received so favourable a report from an American valuer that the Southern Rhodesian Government decided to pass an ordinance in 1958 extending control regulations for all precious stones discovered in Rhodesia, similar to those which the South African Government had found necessary for the ordered control of diamond discoveries.

The locality where the best quality emeralds were to be found proved to be quite small in area, in the midst of bush country rich in game but poor in water. A large crocodile which considered itself 'lord of the manor' resented their presence and had to be shot, but another which succeeded him was allowed, and even encouraged, to remain as a deterrent against inquisitive journalists. Too often the discoverers of a new gem deposit are robbed of their just reward by other more financially powerful interests muscling in and gaining control. In this case the two prospectors behaved with good sense and restraint and received their due reward. An adequate sample of small calibré-cut emeralds from the new deposit was submitted to Dr. Edward Gübelin of Lucerne for examination and report, and the experienced services of Mr. Dan E. Mayers were secured to act as managing director of the newly formed promoting company. Dr. Gübelin found the stones (which ranged from 0·15 to 0·38 carat) to have a quality which was both superb and unique. Moreover the high density and refractive index of the stones and their numerous hair-like inclusions of tremolite made them easily distinguishable from all other emeralds. He suggested that it would aid in the promotion of these new emeralds to give them a locality name, and put forward 'Sandawana' emeralds as euphonious and appropriate, as Sandawana was the name of the valley in which the prospectors camped on the night before the discovery was made.

When the new mine was in full production, and before U.D.I. spoiled relations with Britain, the complete monthly output of the

Sandawana mines was sent to London by air, graded in bags according to size and quality, and under Customs' seal to be checked and valued before being sent abroad for cutting. I was asked as an independent authority to check the weights of all these crystals, and thus became familiar with the appearance of the Sandawana rough, which was not very prepossessing at first sight, nor very perfectly crystallised. Only when dipped in oil and held to the light could one appreciate the superb colour of the stones. The depth and intensity of the green made Sandawana emeralds ideal for small calibré stones: for large stones the colour was too dark to be effective.

The space given to the above description of the Sandawana emerald discovery may seem disproportionately large, but it provides one of the few cases where the truth about an important gem locality can be recounted from its birth and one full account is more interesting to the reader than whole lists of locality names of the sort that students have to learn for examination purposes. The main localities for emerald have now been described, but stones of reasonable quality have been found in India near Udaipur (which is also a famous cutting centre for precious stones) and in western Pakistan. Rather pale but sizable emeralds from Bom Jesus in Bahia (Brazil) have been known since 1913, but other Brazilian localities have been proclaimed more recently: some of these though pleasing in colour are more properly classed as green beryl than as true emerald.

The distinction between emerald beryl, which owes its rich colour mainly to the presence of traces of chromium, and green beryl, which has a sadder colour due to iron, is normally easy and can be safely left to the dealer. The issue is blurred when the element vanadium is present to an appreciable extent, since this can also produce beryls of an almost emerald-green, and in fact is usually present to some extent in what are undoubtedly true emeralds.

In some of the difficult cases laboratory advice has been sought, and the issue is one of considerable commercial importance. When chromium is present in beryl, even in amounts of a tenth of 1 per cent, the fact is signalled not only by the resultant characteristic emerald-green tint induced in the mineral, but also by the presence of narrow lines in the red area of its absorption spectrum, by a red glow under crossed filters, and by a red tint when viewed under the Chelsea colour filter. When these signs are forthcoming a laboratory verdict can be given with a clear conscience; but there are admittedly borderline cases where a subjective judgement has to be made. However, the 'chromium criterion' as I have called it, does at least give a guide-line. Without it there would be a free-for-all, with nothing to prevent *any* green beryl being sold as an emerald. It must be emphasised that all the famous sources for emerald through the centuries produced stones in which the colour and the *quality* of the colour is undoubtedly due to chromium, and the Sandawana emeralds described above contain more than most, and have the finest colour. Also, with the exception of some experimental 'vanadium emeralds' made by Dr. A. M. Taylor, all manufacturers of synthetic emeralds have used chromium as their sole 'colouring agent'.

Beryl, apart from emerald, is found in large fine crystals of gem quality in many parts of the globe. The Sverdlovsk district in the Urals has provided a quantity of aquamarine, where it is associated with topaz, amethyst and tourmaline in druses partly filled with clay. Crystals two feet long and ten inches thick are occasionally found. Brazil has even richer sources of aquamarine and is undoubtedly the main supplier of these stones, most of which find their way to Idar-Oberstein in Germany for heat treatment to improve their colour, and subsequent cutting.

The largest gem-quality aquamarine crystal recorded was found in Marambaya, Minas Gerais, Brazil, and weighed 110·5 kg, which is equivalent to more than 1 cwt! Madagascar, the home of many beautiful gemstones, provides beryl in profusion in all colours except emerald-green, and is particularly noted as a source for the rose-coloured beryl, Morganite, which typically crystallises in hexagonal prisms bevelled by pyramid faces and more tabular in habit than the elongated shapes favoured by aquamarine. Morganite is also found in San Diego County, California, though usually paler in tint than the Malagasy stones. South West Africa is another famous source for gem beryls, beautiful green and golden-yellow stones being found in pegmatite veins at Klein Spitzkopje.

Probably the largest crystals of opaque beryl are to be found in Norway, where specimens may reach several tons in weight. The mineral has considerable commercial value as the main source of the element beryllium, which has an atomic weight of only 9, and the very low specific gravity of 1·9 compared, for instance, with aluminium's 2·7. It forms useful light alloys for aircraft manufacture, and 5 per cent of beryllium added to copper forms an alloy of great strength and malleability which is resistant to attack by the atmosphere.

There are many green gemstones but very few which approach emerald in colour: heat-treated tourmaline and fluorspar are perhaps the nearest. Demantoid garnet has a yellower green and is a far more lustrous and lively stone. Stained green chalcedony and fine green jadeite often are deceptively like emerald so far as colour goes. These are cloudy and translucent and would only be met with in the form of beads or *cabochon* stones, but even translucent emeralds of fine colour are also sometimes used in this way, so that care must be observed. The chalcedony material often owes its green colour to staining with chromium salts and has a pink appearance under the Chelsea filter, which adds to the confusion with emerald, and there are woolly lines in the red due to chromium when viewed through the spectroscope. The trained gemmologist, however, should not confuse these with the far sharper spectrum of emerald. The density and refractive index of chalcedony are lower than those of emerald. But not much lower, so that the distinction is not a job for a beginner. Jadeite has a distinctive texture and shows slight dimpling on a polished surface which one comes to recognise. The density of jade is 3·33 and it thus sinks rapidly in bromoform, while emerald floats.

If there are only a few natural gemstones which can be confused with emerald, the reverse is true when it comes to synthetics, doublets, and glass imitations, since emerald owing to its high value has long been a target for fraud of all kinds as well as for synthetic substitutes quite openly sold as such.

The earliest forms of imitation emerald were simply glass, but often none the less effective for that. Emerald itself has a vitreous lustre and the colour presented no great problem as the technology of coloured glass is an ancient one, and virtually any colour seen in mineral nature can be simulated very closely in this material. The illusion is cleverly enhanced by the inclusion of small air bubbles in strings and sheets which have the appearance of the feathers and flaws commonly associated with emerald. A careful scrutiny with a 10× lens should serve to reveal the bubbles for what they are: bubbles of this kind are *never* seen in any natural stone. A test between crossed polaroids should also show the lack of true birefringence in glass, though a crude extinction cross is often seen, due to strain in the glass following the moulding operation, which usually forms the 'facets'. The old-time jeweller would sometimes scar such deceptions with a hard file—a quite unnecessary piece of brutality.

More subtle imitations of emerald were composite stones consisting of a crown and base of pale beryl, or, more often, colourless quartz, cemented together with a green balsam which gave to the stone an emerald-green colour.

This type of imitation would resist a test with the file, and if beryl was used the refractometer would fail to give warning of the fraud. More recent makers of these 'soudé emeralds' as they were often called have made still further steps to deceive the gemmologist by using a faceted, poor-quality emerald, slicing it across the girdle and re-assembling the halves with green cement. This provides a stone with emerald-type inclusions which continue apparently without a break through the entire depth of the stone, and refractive indices to match.

Any of these doublets can be easily detected if they are not mounted by viewing them sideways—or when immersed in a suitable fluid (even water will do) against a white background. But when mounted so as to conceal the junction (which is usually at the girdle in such stones) these beryl or emerald doublets need the suspicious mind and professional skill of a trained gemmologist to identify them for what they are. Quartz soudés, of course, reveal their nature when a refractometer reading is taken, while to the trained eye the emerald absorption lines, if present at all, would be very faint in the doublet as compared with those seen in true emerald.

So much for imitation stones, which are nuisance enough. But emerald is one of the precious stones which have been successfully grown as crystals in the laboratory, and there are now several types of these synthetic emeralds available on the market. The processes of manufacture are slow and costly so that these synthetics, though costing perhaps only a tenth of the price asked for their natural equivalents, are by no means cheap to buy. This fact enhances their prestige and raises them in the public estimation to a level far above that of synthetic rubies, sapphires or spinels made by the inverted blowpipe process which is now seventy years old.

Details of the manufacture of these, and all other, man-made gem-stones will be found in Chapter 25 devoted to synthetics. Suffice it to say that so far the specialised laboratories have kept abreast of each new type of synthetic as it made its appearance, and have established means of distinguishing them from natural emeralds. Thus by dealing with reputable jewellers customers can be assured that the emeralds for which they have to pay so high a price are indeed natural stones.

One further word of warning however. Many of the poorer class of emeralds are marred by flaws which reach the surface of the stone. The appearance of such stones is considerably improved by soaking them in rape-seed oil, or some other light vegetable oil, which enters the cracks and renders them virtually invisible. It is not surprising (though in my view regrettable) that the cheaper grades of emerald are almost universally 'oiled' before selling them for mounting to the manufacturing jeweller, and so long as no colouring matter is added to the oil the practice is not considered illegal. Stones so treated may retain a good appearance for many years unless they are exposed to warm detergent solutions such as the housewife might use when washing up, which will tend to leach out the oil and reveal the hidden flaws. The effect is far more disastrous if the jewel containing the stone finds its way into an ultrasonic cleaner. I should therefore like to warn any owner of emerald jewellery not to immerse their stones in detergent or soapy liquid, or, in fact, in liquid of any kind. Even if the stone has not been oiled such treatment is liable to spoil the look of the stone. And, if thinking of paying a high price for an emerald-set jewel it would be a wise precaution to ask the jeweller to examine the stone or stones carefully with his lens to enable him to assure you that any flaws present do not reach the surface of the stone.

As for beryls of other colours (aquamarine, morganite and heliodor) one is entitled here to expect a stone which is completely flawless to the eye. Thin rod-like 'rain' inclusions are frequent in aquamarine and if not obtrusive can be considered a hallmark rather than a blemish. The similarity of blue topaz to aquamarine has already been commented upon. If unmounted, a trial in bromoform will settle that issue, aquamarine floating and topaz sinking very decisively in the liquid. A test with a polariscope (or crossed polaroids) will ensure the specimen is not some form of glass. A handsome and prevalent imitation of aquamarine is a pale blue synthetic spinel in which the colouring agent is cobalt. This ensures that the fake material shows a distinct reddish appearance when viewed through the Chelsea filter, whereas aquamarines are notable for giving a green effect under the filter due to the fact that this variety of beryl cuts off the red rays from light transmitted through them. For all beryls except emerald a refractometer measurement giving 1·57–1·58 for the refractive indices provides virtually complete proof that the stone concerned is a natural beryl. A yellow transparent form of labradorite feldspar has admittedly similar indices but is straw-coloured rather than golden yellow. It is also decidedly rare, so that a keen gemmologist if sold the feldspar by mistake would probably feel satisfied rather than dissatisfied with his bargain.

CHAPTER FIFTEEN

---◆---

THE GARNET GROUP

ALTHOUGH AMONGST the red stones used in jewellery ruby deservedly has pride of place in terms of beauty and costliness, with red spinel as runner-up, the red garnets have played an honourable part in providing stones of large size and of a colour, though dark, of a rich crimson or purple-red. These, when cut in *cabochon* form and lightened by backing with foil, have given an effect of barbaric splendour to many a cathedral chalice or royal crown and sceptre. Few stones indeed are so enhanced by setting in gold, or so add grandeur to the gold in which they are set.

The old name for these *cabochons* of almandine garnet was carbuncle from the Latin *carbunculus,* meaning 'little spark', and in one of the least credible of all legends Noah was said to have used a huge carbuncle to light the interior of his ark.

But there are in fact many types of garnet, and by no means all of them are red. They provide the perfect example of an isomorphous family of minerals. All share the same crystal structure and crystal form, and all have a basically similar chemical formula. This is almost infinitely variable, as the constituent metallic ions are of nearly the same dimensions and chemical affinities and can interchange with one another very freely. They are all double silicates of a divalent and trivalent metal and have a general formula which can be written as $A_3B_2(SiO_4)_3$. The rugger-scrum 'three-two-three' formation can be a useful mnemonic here. In this queer-looking formula, A can be represented by magnesium, divalent iron, or divalent manganese, while B may be aluminium, trivalent iron, or chromium.

The garnets all have the same strong tendency to crystallise in rhombic dodecahedra (twelve rhomb-shaped faces), icositetrahedra (twenty-four trapeze-shaped faces), or combinations of the two. These are usually found in perfect geometrical shapes with little distortion, and are more like textbook illustrations of crystals than any others in mineral nature. This is because they are formed under metamorphic pressure and are totally surrounded by the rocky matrix in which they are found.

Although the interchangeability of the atoms means that almost all the garnets found in nature are to some extent mixtures, six recognisably distinct garnet species emerge, and synthesis of the pure minerals enable us to know their properties—in particular their refractive indices and densities—and this in turn enables us to estimate the probable composition of any garnet found in nature by measuring its density and refractive index, since the influence on these properties of each garnet molecule is so well understood.

Here are the names and theoretical compositions of the six garnet species, together with their properties as found in pure synthetically made specimens. The properties of those found in nature will be given later when each species is fully described.

Name	Composition	Density	R. Index	Colour
Almandine	$Fe_3Al_2Si_3O_{12}$	4·32	1·830	Red
Pyrope	$Mg_3Al_2Si_3O_{12}$	3·58	1·714	Red
Spessartine	$Mn_3Al_2Si_3O_{12}$	4·19	1·800	Orange
Andradite	$Ca_3Fe_2Si_3O_{12}$	3·86	1·887	Green
Grossular	$Ca_3Al_2Si_3O_{12}$	3·59	1·734	Green
Uvarovite	$Ca_3Cr_2Si_3O_{12}$	3·90	1·86	Green

Before going further I had better explain the origin of some of these names. The word garnet itself is probably derived from the Latin *granatus,* a pomegranate, which has a garnet-red fruit pulp. Almandine is said to take its name from *Alabanda* in Asia Minor whence came the alabandic carbuncles (garnets cut *en cabochon*) mentioned by Pliny. Andradite was named after a Portuguese mineralogist; uvarovite after a Russian scientist; grossular from the botanical name for a gooseberry; pyrope from a Greek word meaning fire-like, and spessartine from a locality at Spessart in Bavaria.

ALMANDINE AND PYROPE

The two red garnets, almandine and pyrope, have been used as gem-stones through the centuries more than any others of the garnet family, with the result that the word garnet inevitably conjures up the image of a red stone to the mind. Both these species are treated together here because their molecules are usually so completely intermingled that it is only at each end of the range that we can properly speak of an almandine or a pyrope: most red gem garnets are, to be at all exact, 'almandine-pyropes'. Fortunately, in this particular range the term 'garnet' is usually sufficient for trade purposes. Some years ago I suggested the term 'pyrandine' (pronounced 'pirrandeen') as being a useful contraction for these mixed garnets, but this has not been universally accepted.

Another name for an intermediate red garnet is rhodolite. This was originally coined to describe some attractive rose-red or rhododendron-coloured garnets from Cowee Creek in North Carolina, and is to some extent objectionable as sounding so much like the manganese mineral, rhodonite. The rhodolites from Carolina were limited in quantity and made little impact on the trade. The name itself was moribund until recently the discovery of garnets of a similar colour in Tanzania brought it once more into use. Just now it has become a fashionable best-selling name and tends to be applied to almost any red garnet, regardless of colour.

Rhodolite from the type locality consisted of approximately two molecules of pyrope to one of almandine, and had a density of 3·84 and refractive index 1·76.

As a matter of interest, the lowest constants I have recorded for pyrope garnet have been 3·65 for the density and 1·730 for the refractive index, which suggests a garnet which is 90 per cent pure pyrope. It is useful to know this low limit, because there is the possibility of confusion between garnet and spinel in this area. Normally there is a distinct gap between their constants, but in the case of chrome-rich spinels, they *can* overlap, at least so far as refractive index goes. At the almandine end of the series the highest figures for garnets suitable for jewellery are about 4·20 for the density and 1·81 for the refractive index. Such stones contain rather more than 80 per cent of the almandine molecule, though this matter of judging composition from the constants is really not quite so simple, since other garnet molecules such as grossular are apt to intrude to some extent.

One might expect the colour of the red garnets to give an indication of their composition. In theory, pure pyrope should be colourless since neither magnesium nor aluminium have any colouring effect on the minerals in which they occur, while almandine, having iron as an essential ingredient, must inevitably be coloured. But in fact no pyrope has been found in a pure enough state to be lacking in colour: there is always enough iron present to give them quite a deep red tint, while in the most attractive types, such as the pyropes from Arizona and South Africa, chromium has stepped in to provide a much brighter and more pleasant shade of red. The most typical colour for almandine is a red tinged with purple or violet, perhaps best described as 'columbine red', and this is admittedly not very attractive. Stones of this hue may have a refractive index of anything between 1·76 and 1·79. Then at the upper end of the scale with refractive index 1·79 to 1·81, the colour becomes deeper and richer, and it is garnets of this kind which provide the finest carbuncles to which I gave words of praise at the beginning of this chapter. All the red garnets tend to absorb a great deal of light, and at the pure almandine end the colour is so dark as to become black. With the carbuncle garnets the best that can be done is to hollow the back of the *cabochon* and place gold foil behind it in the setting, which reflects light to show the glow of red.

The Bohemian pyropes which were in the past so extensively mined and so much used in Victorian jewellery are also rather too dark to be really beautiful. Though here there are no signs of the violet tinge of almandine, there is a hint of yellow or brown which makes them inferior to the pyropes from South Africa and Arizona where chromium enters in and enriches the colour sufficiently to make the terms 'Cape ruby' and 'Arizona ruby' popular as local names.

Average properties for all these pyropes, as well as for those found in Ceylon, are about the same: 1·745 for refractive index and 3·75 for density, though the mixed nature of these stones makes it inevitable that there is more variation than in a 'fixed' species. The hardness of pyrope is just a little above that of quartz, while that of almandine is a little higher still. The figures can be written as $7\frac{1}{4}$ and $7\frac{1}{2}$ on Mohs's scale so long as one remembers that these values are not quantitative and merely represent a hardness *order*.

One remarkable feature of almandine garnet is that light transmitted through it shows three strong broad absorption bands when examined through a hand spectroscope. Actually there are nine bands to be seen, but by far the most prominent are the three centred at 5760 Å in the yellow, and 5270 and 5050 Å in the green. In dark specimens the two green bands tend to coalesce into one very broad absorption region. The 5050 band is the most persistent, and can be seen even in pyropes where a broad chromium absorption band covers and masks the 5760 and 5270 bands. It can also be detected in 'doublets' in which a thin slice of almandine is fused on to a base of any required colour to represent ruby, sapphire or emerald, etc. Before the days of synthetic stones, such doublets were the most effective simulants of genuine gems, since when in a setting they defied a hardness test with a file and showed natural inclusions. Even today garnet-topped doublets are frequently met with in jewellery and can be a nuisance, especially if mixed in with natural rubies or natural sapphires, etc. More will be said about these fakes in Chapter 25.

While pyrope can be very free from inclusions and flaws, almandine usually contains needle-like inclusions running parallel to the edges of the dodecahedron and thus intersecting at angles of 110° and 70°. When these needles are fine and frequent, a stone polished *en cabochon* and correctly oriented may show a four-rayed or a six-rayed star by reflected light. Even under the most favourable conditions, e.g. direct sunlight or a single bright lamp, such stars are quite hard to see and have more value as a curiosity than as an enhancement of the stone's beauty. These needles were formerly thought to consist of hornblende, but have been proved by Professor Mellis of Stockholm to be rutile—the titanium oxide mineral already familiar as the 'silk' in Burma ruby and the red-gold fibres in rutilated quartz.

Garnet is typically a mineral of metamorphic rocks and is found in its characteristically ball-like crystals in mica-schist, hornblende-gneiss, etc. Curiously, however, pyrope garnet is not found in well-shaped crystals, but rather as irregular grains or lumps, never very large in size. This seems true whether the source be in the old kingdom of Bohemia (now Czechoslovakia), Arizona, or South Africa.

During the nineteenth century the mining, cutting and marketing of pyrope garnets was almost exclusively a Bohemian industry. The stones were found over an area of many square miles in the neighbourhood of Trebnitz. The origin of the stones was in olivine or serpentine rocks, but the grains of garnet had become detached from their original matrix and were found loose in gravel deposits which were usually covered by a layer of soil a few feet in thickness. Pits were sunk in the most favourable districts, the garnets washed free from their surrounding clay, sieved and sorted into various sizes. These were never very large, and stones too small for cutting were used as abrasives, or even as gravel for garden paths—which gives some idea of the enormous quantities available.

Pyropes of rather larger size and occasionally of a very fine blood-red colour were found when searching for diamond in the 'river diggings' along the Vaal river in South Africa. These were less commonly found amongst the heavy mineral concentrates from the 'dry diggings'—that is, from the diamond pipes themselves. The close association of pyrope garnet with diamond has been used as a pointer to diamond deposits in many parts of the world—both being derived from olivine or serpentine rocks.

The occurrence of pyrope of fine quality in the United States has already been mentioned, the most important sources being in Arizona and New Mexico, where the stones are loose in the desert sands and are frequently brought to the surface by ants and are recovered from the giant ant-hills by the Navaho Indians.

Almandine is a commoner form of garnet than pyrope, but material of gem quality is rather scarce. The red garnets found in the Ceylon gem gravels have the violet tinge of almandine but are of intermediate 'pyrandine' grade, with refractive index around $1 \cdot 76$. True almandines have been mined in various parts of India, in particular in the neighbourhood of Jaipur where the almandine is found embedded in micaschists. The city of Jaipur is a great cutting centre not only for garnets but for emeralds and precious stones of all kinds.

There are not many stones with which these red garnets are likely to be confused. Only in exceptional cases are the constants of spinel high enough, or those of pyrope low enough, to cause mistakes in identification. The 'pyrandine' garnets may have the same refractive index as ruby and in colour can resemble Siam rubies very closely—but they have only a single refractive index, and their distinctive absorption spectrum is of great assistance in resolving any doubts. In warning, however, it should be mentioned that between crossed polarisers almandine frequently shows 'anomalous' double refraction due to strain, which might well cause some puzzlement to a beginner.

GROSSULAR

Though the name grossular is hardly known to the general public, it has earned itself a quite important place in jewellery in its orange or brownish-yellow form of hessonite or cinnamon stone, as found extensively in the Ceylon gem gravels, and quite recently as transparent green stones from Tanzania and Pakistan. It also occurs in massive green forms which can closely resemble jade, though these belong properly to the 'hydrogrossular' series, and are also frequently intermingled with idocrase.

Grossular is a calcium-aluminium silicate, and as such has no intrinsic colour. Unlike pyrope, which is in similar case, it does occasionally occur in colourless form, and quite frequently in very pale shades of green, yellow or brown. It is also unlike pyrope in having, when transparent, almost invariable constants, with refractive index 1·743 and density 3·65. The dispersion is 0·027 which is a good deal higher than spinel (0·020) but falls far behind demantoid garnet with its phenomenal 0·057, which considerably exceeds that of diamond.

Bracelets or necklets set with mixed Ceylon gemstones are not infrequently seen, and these are both attractive to the eye and interesting to the gemmologist. Nearly always, amongst the sapphires and zircons which are the mainstay of such ornaments, specimens of brownish-yellow hessonite grossular will be found. These are very distinctive, and rank amongst those gemstones which can be identified with certainty merely by inspection with a lens. They have, for one thing, a curious treacly appearance, and also very numerous rod-like transparent inclusions of diopside, while the colour itself is fairly characteristic. In the past there was a confusion between these stones and zircons of similar colour, which are also inhabitants of the Ceylon gem gravels. These were known as jacinth or hyacinth, and the name was also less properly applied to the garnets, to which the name cinnamon stone was also given. Nowadays more care is taken in naming stones correctly, and names of dubious meaning are avoided altogether. Thus the zircons are simply known as zircons with an appropriate colour-tag, while the orange garnets are known as hessonite garnets. All the other forms of this calcium garnet are known by their species name of grossular, and the public will probably become gradually accustomed to this as a name to be reckoned with.

Two of the most exciting districts for producing new gem localities during the past two decades or so have been Pakistan and south-east Africa (Rhodesia, Tanzania, Mozambique, Kenya), though it is often not possible to obtain any exact information as to the place and nature of the occurrence. Those who have made a lucky find, even when they have staked a claim officially, are anxious not to have others muscling in. Too often really big money talks and finds a way to override legal niceties, and gets what it wants. I remember in 1952, when the first of the large opaque ruby crystals in their green zoisite matrix were discovered in Tanzania, the only hint that the man involved in exploiting this astonishing material would give was to say that it was found 'in rhino country'. And it so happens that both Pakistan and Tanzania have recently provided new sources for emerald and for gem-quality grossular.

From Pakistan, grossular, interesting to the gemmologist, comes in two forms. The first consists of translucent green (or white mottled with bright green) pieces which closely resemble jadeite, the second form being green and transparent. I examined a number of the translucent pieces in 1965 and found that they were in fact a mixture of grossular with idocrase, a mineral of very similar composition and crystal structure. An older source for jade-like grossular is in South Africa near Pretoria, and it was formerly offered for sale under the misleading name of 'Transvaal jade'. This material is found in shades of pink as well as green, and can be most attractive when cut as beads, since it takes a high polish and has a fair degree of translucency. Black particles of magnetite or chromite are typical, and help to differentiate it at sight from jade.

The refractive index of these massive grossulars is near 1·72 which is lower than for hessonite, while the density varies, according to Robert Webster, between 3·36 and 3·57 for the Transvaal stones, while my determinations on the Pakistan pieces give a range of 3·28 and 3·52. The lower values belong to stones having a considerable idocrase content, which is conveniently signalled for the gemmologist by the presence of a strong absorption band in the blue part of the spectrum at 4610 Å.

The mineralogist now prefers to use the term 'hydro-grossular' for these massive types of the garnet as the (OH) group is present to some extent, but such niceties need not worry the gemmologist.

Reverting to the transparent green type of grossular, this, if it can be found in sufficient quantity, will prove a very welcome addition to the stones available for jewellery. As we shall see later in this chapter the green andradite garnet, demantoid, is the most sought-after and costly of all garnets, but good specimens are very scarce, and a supply of fine green grossulars would be most useful. Admittedly the dispersion of grossular is only half that of demantoid, but is still high enough to make a very lively stone. Tanzania and Pakistan have provided some excellent specimens, and in each case the constants are those of nearly pure grossular with density 3·62 and refractive index 1·742.

Very attractive transparent crystals of hessonite grossular have been found at Asbestos, in Quebec Province, Canada, but I have not yet seen cut stones derived from these crystals.

One other type of grossular should be mentioned, which consists of large translucent pink crystals set in a calcite matrix forming a decorative marble. This is found in Xalostoc, Mexico, and has been named 'xalostocite' after this locality. The material is distinctive enough to be recognised at sight when one has once seen it.

Those who work in gem-testing laboratories are always glad to know of any special characters by which a given species can be identified. In the case of the massive types of grossular such a welcome distinctive test is provided by exposing the stone to X-rays, as the stone then shows a strong orange-yellow fluorescence. So far we have no clue as to the cause of this behaviour—we only know that it never fails, and are duly grateful.

SPESSARTINE

The manganese-aluminium garnet, spessartine, is too scarce in its occurrence to make it an important gemstone commercially, but its attractive appearance makes it much sought after and valued by collectors and keen gemmologists.

At its most typical it has a delightful colour to which the description 'aurora-red' is often given—aurora being the colour of the sky at dawn. Here is another instance to add to those previously given where a descriptive adjective given to the colour of a gemstone somehow fits the case so well that it is universally adopted and becomes a cliché—like the 'pigeon's-blood' red of Burma ruby, or analogous, one might say, to Homer's invariably 'wine-dark' sea.

Being a manganese mineral one might expect the colour of this garnet to show something of the rose-red tints so much admired in the manganese-silicate mineral rhodonite or the carbonate rhodochrosite. But though it often has a blush of pink in it the colour is mostly a warm yellow or brown resembling closely the tints shown by the hessonite variety of grossular. The purest spessartines amongst those which come from the famous locality of Amelia, Virginia, are indeed a very pale yellow.

Although it is one of those garnets which can be found in specimens which conform pretty closely to their theoretical composition, spessartine can mix very freely with the almandine molecule, which naturally influences its colour towards reddish hues, but does not greatly affect its properties, while admixture with grossular does affect its properties, but does not influence its colour.

The properties of gem-quality spessartines can be said to range from 4·10–4·20 for their density and 1·79 to 1·81 for refractive index, while the hardness is 7 or fractionally higher on Mohs's scale.

For the laboratory gemmologist the most useful means of recognising spessartite is provided by the spectroscope which reveals a series of absorption bands, two of which are in the blue at 4950 and 4850 Å, with a stronger band at 4620 Å, and a very powerful one at 4320 Å in the violet. There are further strong bands at 4240 and 4120 Å, but these can only be seen in pale specimens and by using a powerful light-source. Where almandine is also present the almandine absorption bands can of course be seen in addition, and there must occasionally be a difficult decision made as to whether to certify the stone as a spessartine pure and simple, thereby enhancing its saleability, or whether there is too much almandine present to disregard in giving the stone a name.

In the early days of the Hatton Garden Gem Testing Laboratory we were able to 'rescue' a fine 12 carat spessartine from a parcel of hessonites by means of its absorption spectrum and physical constants. This stone had a certain amount of almandine in it but was, without doubt, essentially a spessartine. It is now to be seen in the fine collection of gemstones displayed in the Museum of the Institute of Geological Sciences in South Kensington, London (see Plate F).

Spessartine is unusual amongst the garnets in its geological occurrence, being recovered chiefly from granitic pegmatites, as opposed to the metamorphic rocks, such as mica-schists, in which the red garnets are found. A curious feature of spessartite crystals is an etched pattern on the faces of the dodecahedron showing lines and ridges parallel to the edges of the face, the whole looking like the plan of a maze, or the ruins of some ancient city. Even fragments of spessartine showing no complete crystal form can be recognised by this characteristic pattern.

Andradite

Andradite is the name given by mineralogists to the calcium-iron garnet which was also known as melanite or common black garnet. Not a promising mineral to use as a gemstone, one would say, except perhaps for mourning jewellery as an alternative to black spinel, black tourmaline, black onyx or jet.

The situation was changed in startling fashion late in the nineteenth century. Around 1860, greenish-white, nearly colourless pebbles were found in the gold-washings of Nischne Tagilsk in the Ural mountains which were precursors to the beautiful yellow-green to emerald-green transparent crystals found in the stream Bobrowka (also in the Urals) south of the town of Sverdlovsk. It was not established for some time that these 'Bobrowka garnets' were a pure form of andradite, enriched, in the emerald-green varieties, by the presence of chromium. The stones have since that time been known by many misleading names, the most persistent in the British trade being olivine, which properly belongs to the family of minerals of which peridot is a member. The origin of the name demantoid is rather obscure, but fortunately has a fine ring to it and is not likely to be confused with that of any other gemstone.

An alternative name is, simply enough, 'green garnet', and this being certainly true could hardly be objected to. But the arrival of transparent green grossular on the market means that this is likely to lead to some problems, since this too can lay fair claim to be 'green garnet'.

The demantoid found in and around the Bobrowka was recovered either as loose grains or as nodules up to about two inches across embedded in asbestos veins in a serpentine rock. The nodules themselves are built up of irregular grains packed closely together but separated by a coating of clay or serpentine. Distinct crystals are seldom found, but the shape of the grains suggests that they are based on combinations of the rhombic dodecahedron and icositetrahedron which seem to be the invariable habit of the garnet family.

The characters of demantoid are pretty constant, as they are essentially pure andradites with little intrusion of other garnet molecules. The density is always near $3 \cdot 85$, and the refractive index $1 \cdot 888$, which is well outside the range of the normal refractometer. Its crowning glory lies in its exceptionally high dispersion, $0 \cdot 057$, which is a good deal higher than the $0 \cdot 044$ of diamond. The colour of the stone masks its fire somewhat, but the high refractive index gives the stone an almost adamantine lustre, and in cases where the colour is also a rich chromium green the stone is amongst the most handsome of all gems.

Two weaknesses prevent demantoid from being one of the most important of precious stones, one incurable, the other possibly to be mitigated by future discoveries. The first refers to its low hardness of $6\frac{1}{2}$, it being decidedly softer than any other form of garnet. So long as the stone is not exposed to heavy wear such as in a ring which is constantly worn, but confined to such jewels as brooches, ear-rings, or pendants, this lack of hardness is not vitally important. The second disadvantage referred to is its scarcity. Up to a point, rarity is recognised as a factor which increases the value of a precious stone, but to be truly viable commercially a constant source of supply should be available.

Though demantoids of good quality have been found in the Congo there seems no continuing supply from that quarter, and the Urals are virtually our only source. Demantoids of large size are almost unknown: a specimen in the Smithsonian Institution weighing $10\frac{1}{2}$ carats must be considered pretty phenomenal. Some thirty-five years ago I had the enviable task of checking the dispersion of a pair of fine demantoids weighing some 6 or 7 carats apiece—but I have not seen their like again. An unfortunate feature of the gem seems to be that only stones of about a carat and under have a really fine colour; the larger ones appear often to be short on chromium and have a sadder tinge to them.

Demantoids are one of the easiest stones to recognise merely by inspection with a good lens. This is due to the fact that they almost invariably contain bunches of the fine asbestos fibres which are their matrix, usually spreading out from a single nucleus, the whole effect very much resembling a horse's tail flowing in the wind. These inclusions are, in fact, affectionately known to students as 'horsetail' inclusions.

As an example of the frequency of their occurrence I may mention a test carried out on a parcel of 106 demantoids in which I found 'horsetails', or a few wisps from such, in 100 out of the 106 stones. No other stone which at all resembles demantoid shows inclusions of precisely this nature so their presence, combined with the appearance of the stone, makes an experienced gemmologist as sure of his ground as though he had in his hands a full chemical and X-ray analysis.

Yellow transparent forms of andradite are occasionally found, notably in the Ala valley in Piedmont (Italy). But these are hardly of cuttable quality, and even if they were it would be better to describe them as yellow demantoids than encourage the fancy name 'topazolite' which falsely suggests an affinity with topaz.

Uvarovite

The one remaining garnet, uvarovite, is a calcium-chromium silicate, and as such has a built-in (idiochromatic) rich green colour. This is a rare mineral, but has been found in crusts of small dodecahedral crystals which make attractive specimens. Its density is 3·77, refractive index 1·87, and the hardness $7\frac{1}{2}$ on Mohs's scale. So far, no crystals large enough to cut as gems have been discovered.

Before bidding farewell to this famous family of gemstones, it should perhaps be mentioned that some of the varieties—those which contain iron or manganese in any quantity—are distinctly magnetic. Not magnetic enough to be actually picked up by even a powerful permanent magnet, but quite enough to lessen the apparent weight of a specimen in poise on a balance when a small but powerful magnet is placed immediately above it. Very occasionally a property such as this is worth remembering as it may assist in differentiating between green metamict zircon and demantoid; orange metamict zircon and spessartite, red spinel and pyrope. In each case the first stone mentioned is non-magnetic as compared with the garnets.

CHAPTER SIXTEEN

— ◊ —

TOURMALINE AND ZIRCON

TOURMALINE

APART FROM HAVING a similar hardness (just over 7 on Mohs's scale) tourmaline and zircon have nothing particular in common with one another and are bracketed together in the same chapter only as a matter of convenience. It is certainly true of both these minerals that they not only have considerable attractiveness and importance as gemstones, but are also of unusual interest to the scientist. Let's deal with tourmaline first.

Tourmaline can perhaps boast of having the greatest range of colour of any gemstone, though corundum and beryl run it very close. It can certainly be said to have the most complex chemical composition. Its pleasantly euphonious name is derived from the Sinhalese word *turmali* and dates, so far as Europe is concerned, from the early eighteenth century, when the first stones of this kind reached Amsterdam from Ceylon. One has to admit that in Ceylon (at least amongst the less educated dealers) the name has been used pretty indiscriminately for other pebbles of gem quality found in the gravels, such as zircon. An earlier name, schorl, which now belongs exclusively to black tourmaline, was originally, in its German form of *schörl*, used by miners for a number of different minerals, each distinguished by a suitable colour prefix. As remarked earlier, the exact naming of minerals came fairly late in the history of science: for those who are, in Meredith's phrase, 'hot for certainties in this our life', it is best to consult a modern textbook. Even as late as the twentieth century, jewellers have been careless in their use of names, but now they can't afford to be, thanks to the Trade Descriptions Act.

Although tourmaline can vary widely in colour and composition, the habit of its crystals is so distinctive that it is one of the easiest minerals to recognise in its natural state. It belongs to the trigonal system, and whereas many trigonal crystals such as those of quartz and corundum give the appearance of hexagonal symmetry, with tourmaline the threefold symmetry of the principal axis is made clearly visible since almost all the crystals show a triangular cross-section, slightly rounded. Crystals are typically prismatic and heavily striated parallel to their length. When green they remind one of angelica, when pink, of rhubarb. And there is yet another characteristic—a particoloration in which the crystal changes its colour abruptly either half-way down its length or in more or less concentric zones round the main axis. The two colours involved in this very curious peculiarity are usually green and pink. In one typical instance the core of the crystal is red surrounded by a colourless zone and finally a green zone on the outside. The term 'watermelon' tourmaline is aptly applied to such crystals in the U.S.A., where they are particularly common.

There is no lateral plane of symmetry in tourmaline crystals, which means that the two ends of the crystal are noticeably dissimilar in character. One end may show a basal plane and the other a pyramid. The 'polarity' of the crystals thus made visible in their shape can be demonstrated in other ways. When warmed, for instance, a tourmaline crystal becomes electrically charged; negatively at one end, positively at the other. As a lecture experiment, this can be shown by sifting a mixture of red lead and sulphur through muslin on to a cooling tourmaline crystal: the yellow sulphur is attracted to the positive pole and the red lead to the negative. This curious feature of tourmaline crystals was well known to Dutch traders in the eighteenth century, who called them *aschtrekker* from their gift of attracting tobacco ashes when thrust into the hot bowl of a pipe. Even in faceted tourmalines mounted in jewellery this pyroelectric effect can be noticed if such stones are on display in a jeweller's window. The heat of the sun or of strip-lighting in the window is quite enough to induce electrical charges on the stones with the result that the tourmalines are noticeably coated with dust in contrast with specimens of any other gemstones shown in the same window.

Another marked feature of tourmaline, at least in the brown and dark green varieties, is its strong dichroism. The ordinary ray is almost completely absorbed in such stones, and crystals which are quite transparent when viewed laterally are virtually opaque when looking down the length of the crystal. Before the advent of 'polaroid' this effect was exploited in the construction of 'tourmaline tongs' in which two polished slices of brown tourmaline, cut parallel to the main axis, were mounted in wooden discs on wires forming flexible 'tongs' which enabled stones to be examined between 'crossed tourmalines' in the same way as 'crossed polaroids' are used at the present time.

I have already commented on the great variety of colours seen in tourmaline: let us examine these in detail. The range runs in fact all the way from white to black; white or colourless tourmaline being known as achroite and the black as schorl. Green is probably the colour most seen in gem-quality tourmaline. In nature this tends to be a rather dark bottle-green, but this is nowadays usually 'improved' by heat treatment, which tends to produce brighter clearer greens that are not so dichroic and from some localities may even approach the coveted green of emerald. After green, pink and red are the tints most typical of tourmaline—and very often, as we have seen, parts of the crystal are pink and parts green. In cases where the colour approaches a ruby-red the variety name, rubellite, is sometimes used—a name which is probably sufficiently different from ruby to cause no confusion. Rubellite can, in fact, quite easily be mistaken for ruby or deep pink sapphire when a really fine specimen is involved, though of course its properties differ greatly from those of the vastly more valuable stone. An interesting point to note is that whereas the colour of ruby looks at its richest in electric light, rubellite looks at its best in daylight.

The other colours seen in tourmaline are yellow, indigo blue and brown. Yellow tourmaline can be very bright and attractive, though the rich tints of topaz or yellow sapphire are not quite attained. Blue tourmaline, which has been given the variety name of indicolite, has usually too much of an inky or greenish-blue colour to commend it: it resembles Australian sapphire or blue spinel in this. Brown is a very common colour in Ceylon tourmalines, but stones of this tint are lacking in beauty or sparkle and are seldom used in European jewellery.

Now a look at the composition of tourmaline, which I have already referred to as 'complex'. Students of gemmology sitting for an examination are usually advised by their teachers to describe it as 'an extremely complex borosilicate of aluminium and other metals' if the question arises. A determined attempt to produce an ordered chemical statement has resulted in the general formula $NaR_3Al_6B_3Si_6O_{27}(OH)_4$. In this 'R' is a symbol which can represent chiefly magnesium or lithium or iron, and the names 'dravite', 'elbaite' and 'schorl' have been used for the resultant three types which, of course, intermingle in most cases to some extent. Dravites are brown and schorl is black, thus it is the alkali-bearing elbaite tourmalines that give rise to the gem varieties. Rather mysteriously, lithium has a way of producing pink minerals and certainly influences tourmaline in that direction. Crystals of pink tourmaline are in fact often found in matrix of a pink lithium mica known as lepidolite, and together the two minerals make very handsome specimens for the collector. In the greens and the blues the colour is influenced by iron.

Since colour is a sensitive indicator of composition it is not surprising to find the properties of tourmaline varying a little according to their colour-variety. Red and pink tourmalines, for instance, have the lowest density, 3·01 to 3·05; green varieties usually fall within the range 3·05 to 3·10; yellow and blue stones are a little higher, while black tourmalines, being rich in iron, may have a considerably greater density.

The refractive indices are usually near 1·64 for the upper (ordinary) ray, and 1·62 for the lower, the double refraction most commonly being 0·018, though it may vary between 0·014 and 0·021 in the gem tourmalines. With black stones, again, the indices and double refraction can be much higher. For the record, however, it should be mentioned that small dark red tourmaline crystals recently discovered in Kenya by Dr. John Saul have shown the startlingly high birefringence of 0·032. The density (3·07) of these tourmalines is normal, and chemical and X-ray analysis have failed so far to explain their optical peculiarity.

The double refraction of 0·018 is strong enough to be clearly seen when a faceted tourmaline is examined with a 10× lens. The edges of the rear facets are plainly 'doubled' at least when viewed from certain angles through the stone. This simple observation is of very great value in gem identification without the use of instruments.

Tourmaline is seldom quite free from inclusions and these are fairly typical, being thin liquid films which look black and opaque at certain angles and clear and colourless at others, the black effect being due to total reflection and not to any true opacity of the film.

Tourmaline is a common mineral in granites and their attendant pegmatites, and thus its occurrence is very widespread, and the favoured localities are for the most part the same as they are for other pegmatite minerals such as beryl and topaz. Particularly fine crystals in the three main colours of pink and green and blue are found in the Sverdlovsk district of the Urals and near Nerchinsk in Siberia. Red and green and particoloured crystals are found in the north-east parts of Minas Gerais, Brazil, and magnificent crystals occur in many parts of the United States, the most notable localities perhaps being the pegmatite dykes near Pala and Mesa Grande in California, where large transparent crystals of tourmaline in greens and blues, as well as in red and yellow, are accompanied by kunzite and lepidolite, as might be expected since these are lithium minerals. Madagascar and South West Africa are also famous for their tourmalines, while Elba, from which the name elbaite was taken, provides many coloured tourmalines, some crystals having a black cap to them, earning the local name of 'niggerheads'.

An interesting variety coloured a fine green by vanadium has been found in Tanzania and some coloured by chromium are also found there. The dark red variety found in Kenya with the curiously high birefringence of 0·032 has been mentioned earlier. So far the crystals of this strange type are rather small and the colour very deep. Although the original gem tourmalines came from the Ceylon gem gravels these are mostly yellowish or brown, and cannot compare in beauty with the clear greens and pinks of the other localities described.

For those who enjoy collecting minerals in Britain, quite good crystals of the black tourmaline, schorl, can be found on the fringes of Dartmoor, Bovey Tracey being the best-known locality.

There are not many gemstones which are likely to be confused with tourmaline. The 'doubling' of the back facet-edges is a very useful clue and the fact that it sinks in bromoform and floats readily in methylene iodide separates it from quartz, beryl, topaz or the corundum gems. Where zones of pink and green are to be seen, tourmaline is the only possible answer.

ZIRCON

Zircon is a widely distributed mineral, being found in many igneous rocks and in gravels and sands derived from these. In its transparent varieties it has many attributes such as a high lustre, a good display of fire, and satisfying colours, which would place it very high in the ranks of the gem minerals were it not for some defects which have a damaging effect on its reputation. These include a peculiar brittleness which renders the girdle and facet-edges of zircon likely to be easily chipped and abraded; another is a tendency to milkiness or slight cloudiness in place of the complete transparency which is needed if a stone is to rank as a gem of the highest class, and lastly zircons of sky-blue tint (which is its most popular colour) are notoriously liable to fade to a most unsightly brownish colour. As a mineral of scientific interest, zircon may be said to have even more to offer than tourmaline, as I hope to show.

The name zircon probably derives from the Persian word *zargun*, meaning gold-coloured, another and once popular version of the name being jargoon. Hyacinth or jacinth were also names formerly used for zircon of reddish-brown tint as found in the Ceylon gem gravels alongside hessonite garnets of very similar appearance. The clearly fallacious term 'Matura diamond' was also in use for colourless heat-treated zircons from Ceylon, but is now preserved only in books. This matter of old names which are best forgotten is a difficult one for authors. If they are mentioned in the text as a matter of historic record they tend to be perpetuated, whilst if they are omitted the reader may feel that the book is not so informative as it should be. An appendix containing a sort of scrap-heap of best-forgotten names is one solution to this problem.

An extraordinary change in the status of zircon as a gemstone took place in the years following 1912 when for the first time beautiful sky-blue zircons were shipped to London from Bangkok in Thailand. Until then, zircon had been almost exclusively a gemstone of Ceylon, where enormous quantities of the mineral are to be found in the celebrated gem gravels or 'illam'. Here the mineral is found chiefly in shades of green or yellow, or occasionally in the more attractive reddish-brown 'jacinth' colour already mentioned. The only sign of other possibilities lay in the colourless stones produced by heat treatment referred to above, which were used as a substitute for diamond. The actual origin of these magnificent blue zircons, the appearance of which was enhanced by excellent cutting, was not known until after the First World War, when a young German mineralogist called W. F. Eppler visited the localities concerned and was able to give an authentic account of the matter. Eppler (now Professor Eppler) actually wrote the thesis for his doctorate on the subject of zircon and has since that time become one of the most respected of the world's gemmologists, author of several fine books and of countless articles on precious stones. Eppler found that while the first of these spectacular zircons had their origin in Chantabun in south-east Thailand, that source had been exhausted, and since 1921 the raw material had been obtained from gravels situated between two tributaries of the great Mekong river a little south of the junction of Cambodia, Laos and Annam, the territory being known locally as 'Moung-Kha'. The Mekong (which is properly pronounced 'Maykong') is one of the world's great rivers, and from being a name hardly known in Europe has in recent years become tragically familiar as a major feature in the bitter warfare in South Vietnam, in which the forces of the U.S.A. have been so deeply involved. The river rises in Tibet and flows through Yunnan, Burma, Thailand and Cambodia before emptying by a giant delta into the China Sea, a total flow of some 2,600 miles.

This source of zircon was found by immigrant Burmese who undertook the mining, and transported the rough stones to Bangkok for treatment and cutting. Stones of a similar nature were also found near Bassac some 100 miles north-west of the first deposit at Moung-Kha.

The recovery of the stones from the gravels was carried out in the usual primitive manner by sinking pits, sieving and washing the material to concentrate the heavier minerals, amongst which zircon with its density near 4·7 certainly belongs, and finally hand-picking. As found these zircons are of an uninteresting brown colour and result in not very attractive gems even when cut and polished. The natives, however, discovered by trial-and-error methods of heat treatment which resulted in stones of far more pleasing appearance. The procedures and apparatus used were crude and simple enough—but as in all matters involving 'cooking' a great deal of know-how was needed to obtain the desired outcome, and even so there were unpredictable failures due partly to slight variations in the composition of the rough crystals.

The charcoal stoves used for the heating process were crude clay affairs employed by the Thai natives for cooking purposes. These had a grate on which the charcoal was burnt and an aperture below this for the draught. There was an iron chimney, and for the highest temperatures the height of this was increased and an enforced draught provided by means of a ventilator fan.

Various chemical mixtures were employed in which the stones were embedded while being roasted, and analysis showed that these 'secret' concoctions contained a whole range of reagents which probably had little influence on the resultant colour of the zircons. The important factors were (a) the nature of the raw material; (b) the temperature reached while firing and (c) whether the heating was carried out in an oxidising or a reducing atmosphere.

Eppler's findings were that heating the rough at 900°–1000°C for two hours in a reducing atmosphere (that is, in crucibles packed with wood charcoal) resulted mainly in the production of blue colours, some colourless stones, and a good deal of poor-coloured material. Zircons heated in an open oven and crucible at 850°–900°C yielded reddish, yellow and colourless stones, and some of the 'failures' from the reducing heating produced yellow or colourless stones worthy of cutting when reheated under these conditions.

The blue zircons from these processes were obviously the most in demand—their great drawback being a tendency to 'revert' especially when exposed to sunlight. Responsible Bangkok dealers realising this fact took the precaution of exposing all their good blue stones to full sunlight for many hours, reheating those which reverted to a brownish tint and finally only selling those in which the colour seemed stable. Precautions of this kind ensured that there was no trouble due to loss of colour in the early stones to reach the markets of Europe and the U.S.A. But after the war the demand for blue zircons became so great that it was tempting to curtail or abandon these precautionary tests, with the result that many of the imported stones 'reverted' and in consequence soon acquired a bad reputation. White (colourless) zircons suffered somewhat from the same trouble. I remember well an occasion when I was studying the emission spectrum of a large parcel of white zircons which glowed with a yellow light under an ultra-violet lamp in our laboratory. When eventually the ultra-violet rays were switched off and I saw the stones in daylight I was horrified to see that they had all turned a nasty brownish colour. At that time the Laboratory was not equipped with a furnace, so I took the stones home and heated them in the hot oven of our Aga cooker for several hours. Mercifully this treatment restored them to their original condition. A few of the stones tested on the hot plate in the dark showed a distinct phosphorescent glow.

As already mentioned briefly the final cachet on these zircons exported from Bangkok was provided by the high quality of the cutting— very far removed from the lumpish stones with badly finished facets seen in most zircons from Ceylon. This was due to a team of German lapidaries in Bangkok who employed the flat skives and fine polishing techniques used when faceting diamonds. Hence the proportions of the stones were good and the facets truly flat. The supply was so plentiful that eventually these 'Bangkok' zircons became quite cheap (I can remember a time when one could buy cut white zircons for 12s 6d a carat) and they were very popular for use in inexpensive jewellery, but the tendency to 'revert' and the brittleness already mentioned prevented their being used in high-class pieces. To avoid damage due to stones jostling against each other in a packet, it was found worth while to wrap each stone individually in a screw of tissue paper.

In recent years, owing to the continuous fighting over and around the zircon-bearing localities, stones of this type have become very scarce and have consequently risen in price.

Zircon is one of the few gemstones that crystallise in the tetragonal system, and unless they are badly water-worn its crystals clearly advertise the fact, consisting of square tetragonal prisms capped (often at both ends) with a four-faced pyramid. The basal plane is very seldom seen and in this it differs from idocrase which is the only other tetragonal gemstone one is likely to encounter. In idocrase the tetragonal form is also often well displayed, but the prisms are vertically striated and the pyramids are almost always truncated at the summit by a square basal plane. In idocrase indeed sometimes the basal plane is predominant and a second order prism may bevel the junctions of the main four tetragonal prism faces.

But apart from crystal form, the lustre of zircon crystals is sufficiently high to be an outstanding and recognisable feature. This is due to the high refractive index of the mineral, which except for diamond is the highest of any gemstone in common use.

Before embarking on the long and complicated story of the physical properties of zircon, let us deal with its chemical composition. Essentially it is a silicate of zirconium, and its formula can be written very simply as $ZrSiO_4$; a pleasant contrast to the complex formula of tourmaline. But the element hafnium, which was not discovered until 1923, was found to be present in all zircons in amounts up to as much as 4 per cent. The names of the elements zirconium and hafnium may well be new to my readers, though in fact in the composition of the rocks they are a good deal commoner than silver or gold. They belong to a group of metallic elements of which titanium is the best-known member. In addition to zirconium, hafnium and silica there are always traces of other elements in zircon, including the radioactive uranium and thorium, and various rare-earths, and these, as we shall see later, have important effects on the properties of the mineral.

If we were dealing only with normal fully crystallised zircons of the type found in Thailand and Cambodia the tale of their properties could soon be told. The density varies little from the high figure of 4·68, while the refractive indices are 1·925 for the ordinary ray and 1·984 for the extraordinary, giving the high birefringence of 0·059, making the 'doubling' of the back facet-edges in a cut zircon a very easy matter to observe with even a low power lens.

But it must be remembered that until well after the beginning of this century all the zircons used in jewellery came from Ceylon, and the properties of these stones were found to vary in the most extraordinary manner. The density in some cases was found to be as low as 3·95, and the refractive index as low as 1·78, with little or no sign of birefringence. In a few cases the figures were almost as high as those quoted above, while for the majority of these Ceylon stones the properties ranged between the two extremes. No changes could be found in the composition to account for these wide variations in properties, and for more than seventy years the matter remained a major mystery and a subject for more or less inconclusive research, though some significant facts were established. The answer to the mystery came in 1936 when Chudoba and Stackelberg found by the use of X-ray crystal analysis that in zircons of the lowest density the orderly crystal structure of the stone had completely disappeared and given place to an amorphous mixture of silicon and zirconium oxide. These workers also found that by prolonged heating at 1450°C these 'low' zircons could be restored to stones having the normal high density. The reason for this breakdown in structure is now understood.

The zircons in the Ceylon gem gravels originated in ancient pre-Cambrian rocks, which are thought to be 600 million years old. They also contain the radioactive element uranium in amounts of 6400 parts per million. This means that for all those millions of years the crystal lattice of these stones has been bombarded by alpha-particles hurled out by the slow decay of the uranium atoms in their midst. Alpha-particles are in effect helium nuclei, four times as heavy as a hydrogen atom and are pretty damaging as missiles, so that it is not surprising that the tetragonal lattice should be largely destroyed, leaving an amorphous wreckage of silicon and zirconium oxides which, since they occupy a larger volume than when neatly packed as a crystal, have a much lower density. The vibrations and mobility of the atoms are increased on heating, hence prolonged heating may enable the silica and zirconia to re-arrange themselves into their original positions in the crystal, with a corresponding increase in density and refractive index. The name 'metamict' has been applied to such broken-down crystals of which zircon is only one example. It is curious that such internally disordered stones seem to be mostly green in colour, and it may be recalled that bombarded diamonds assume a green tint. Incidentally the density of heavily bombarded diamonds is also appreciably lowered.

Many Ceylon gemstones contain small crystals of zircon as a natural inclusion and these are typically surrounded by one or more halo-like cracks. The reason for this is that ages after its enclosure the zircon became a metamict and had in consequence to expand—hence the strain-cracks surrounding it. This type of inclusion when seen has therefore come to be regarded as a hallmark of a Ceylon gemstone.

The defect of slight milkiness previously mentioned is particularly noticeable in Ceylon zircons and spoils their appearance, and only stones of the clearest yellow and orange have sufficient appeal to warrant their being properly cut and mounted. Mixed in with other stones in a multi-gem brooch or bracelet they can, however, be very attractive. *Cabochon* zircons of typical Ceylon green and yellow colours can be used to very good effect in jewellery, their high lustre making a glittering show when imaginatively mounted. Very seldom however are such things seen: convention has an exceedingly strong hold. Some enterprising designer would do well to accumulate a supply of *cabochon* zircons, and set a new fashion in mounting them in clusters.

The dispersion of zircon is 0·038 for the B-G range and this is not far below the 0·044 of diamond. Well-cut white zircons thus have, in addition to a bright (though slightly greasy) lustre, a considerable degree of fire when brilliant-cut, which has made them of all natural stones the most likely to be mistaken for diamond. One case in which zircons were used fraudulently to represent diamond has already been described in the chapter on diamond.

Actually, confusion between diamond and white zircon should only be possible where the stones are not critically examined. There is no stone more easily recognisable with a lens than white zircon. The large double refraction makes the doubling of the back facet-edges quite obvious even in small stones.

Another interesting property of zircon which enables the gemmologist to identify it with ease and complete certainty is its absorption spectrum. When light which has passed through the stone is examined through a small spectroscope the ribbon of rainbow colours is crossed by a series of rather narrow dark bands—a very striking effect. This was first observed by Sir Arthur Church in 1866 and was described by him, together with the bands seen in almandine garnet, in a rather obscure journal called the *Intellectual Observer*. Three years later a well-known mineralogist of that time, H. C. Sorby, unaware of Church's discovery, also saw the dark bands in the spectrum of zircon and ascribed them to a new element, which he called 'jargonium'. This gave rise to a rather unseemly argument between the two scientists. To Sorby, however, goes the credit of discovering, after further research, that the absorption bands seen through the spectroscope were caused by traces of uranium in the mineral. It should be noted that both uranium and thorium compounds are isomorphous with those of zirconium, and their almost invariable presence in zircon crystals is thus explained.

It will be recalled that the only zircons available as gemstones in the last century were those from Ceylon, and it is in these stones (and in the rarely seen zircons from Burma) that these striking dark bands are most clearly visible (Fig. 8(3)). It is interesting to see how one can gauge the degree of deterioration in the crystal structure in zircon by the degree of sharpness of these bands. In fully crystalline zircon they are remarkably sharp, but they become vaguer and vaguer in the lower-density stones until finally, in metamict green zircons, one can see only a vague band in the orange-red with perhaps a single narrower band in the green part of the spectrum.

If zircons in the intermediate range are heated to redness not only does their density increase but the absorption bands become noticeably sharper. To me it was a surprising discovery to find that heat treatment of completely metamict stones caused a slight *lowering* of the density and the development of an entirely new series of sharp absorption bands which are not those of zircon at all, but of cubic or tetragonal zirconium oxide.

The fact that the absorption spectrum of zircon is an extremely sensitive indicator of structure is also shown in the blue, white or golden zircons from Cambodia which are marketed in Bangkok. These contain very little uranium compared with those from Ceylon and in the rough state show no sign of absorption bands. But the heat-treated blue and white zircons derived from this rough invariably *do* show narrow absorption lines in the red and orange part of the spectrum by reflected light, and for the gemmologist this forms a most useful test.

Amongst the other peculiarities of zircon are the facts that only in blue zircon is there appreciable dichroism, and that in green zircons of low density a curious 'zoning' is often visible of straight lines meeting at an angle of about 97°. This is not colour-zoning, as seen for instance in sapphire, but a structure effect which is entirely characteristic for this type of zircon.

Since the refractive index of zircon is outside the range of the normal refractometer it is fortunate for the gemmologist that thanks to its absorption spectrum and the strong double refraction of the zircons most used in jewellery, it is amongst the easiest of stones to identify.

For those who wish to see the full range of colours displayed by zircon one can recommend a visit to Sir Arthur Church's collection in the Natural History Museum, South Kensington, while in the Geological Museum (now styled the Institute of Geological Sciences) which is nearby, some remarkably fine zircons are on display.

The only attempt to imitate zircon that I have seen is in the use of synthetic blue spinel to represent blue zircon. The colour was nearly right, but the lustre, fire and strong double refraction were missing.

CHAPTER SEVENTEEN

———————— ◦◊◦ ————————

QUARTZ, AGATE AND CHALCEDONY

Quartz

IT MIGHT FAIRLY be claimed that, apart from diamond, quartz in its many varieties is the most important of all the gem minerals since it is the only species in which the necessary qualities of hardness and beauty are allied to so plentiful a supply of raw material that the cost is low enough for ordinary people like you and me to afford.

In the opening chapter of this book I described granite as a typical rock, and quartz and feldspar as two of its main constituents, pointing out that in some of their varieties both these important minerals are valued as gemstones. Feldspar, at least as a rock constituent, is actually the commonest of all minerals and quartz the next. It has been calculated from a study of 700 igneous rocks that quartz accounts for some 12 per cent of the earth's rocky crust (i.e. the lithosphere) to feldspar's 60 per cent. Its hardness and lack of cleavage and, even more, its chemical stability under the influences of weathering, makes it the last residue of a great variety of rocks—hence the sands of the seashore and the major deserts of the world consist almost entirely of quartz grains.

Obviously, quartz in the form of grains in rocks and sands, however plentiful, would be of no importance to the jeweller. But, in addition to its role as a rock-forming mineral, quartz is to be found in almost any mineral vein or cavity in the rocks—often on its own, but also providing a bright spangled coating for other minerals, or growing alongside them in friendly competition. A search among the flint pebbles on a beach (which are derived from the veins of flint in the chalk cliffs above) will soon reveal some with little cavities lined with quartz crystals, and the white veins of quartz in many a quarry will show clear crystals where the vein is not completely filled. Under favourable conditions in pegmatite rocks crystals of colourless, smoky, or amethyst quartz may grow to giant proportions and weigh several hundredweights, but not, I fear, in this country!

As a gemstone quartz is better known under other names both in its clear crystalline forms such as rock-crystal, amethyst and citrine, and in the enormous variety of cryptocrystalline aggregates which have provided the Bible and other literature with such resounding names as chrysoprase, sardonyx, jasper, heliotrope and prase. In the Book of Revelations (Chapter 21) where the walls of the New Jerusalem are, in St. John's imagination, 'adorned with all manner of precious stones' no fewer than six of the twelve stones mentioned are the names of quartz varieties.

Thus it would be a great mistake to scorn quartz because it is plentiful, as it has an honourable place amongst the most handsome products of the mineral world. In all its varieties it would in fact make a good beginning to a mineral collection. Indeed, not only a beginning: the quartz family alone could well repay a lifetime of study.

It has been already remarked in Chapter 9 that the hardness of quartz—the standard 7 on Mohs's scale—has a critical significance, since the gritty particles in dust consist mainly of quartz fragments, and gemstones of lower hardness are liable to become scratched by these during daily wear. Quartz has a very simple chemical composition, being pure silica (silicon dioxide) with the formula SiO_2.

The name is an old German mining term and may have originally been applied to milky veins of the mineral crossing the rock as 'Querklufterz', which became abbreviated to 'Querertz' and finally to Quartz. Only when the veins or cavities in rocks are completely filled with the silica mineral are crystals lacking. Whenever there is space and free silica present, quartz is ready to oblige with beautiful crystals. Crystals of quartz vary very little in habit, and any budding mineralogist should make himself familiar with them. At first glance they appear to be hexagonal as their most prominent features are the six prism faces, intersecting at 120°, which are heavily striated horizontally. But the symmetry is really trigonal, and the hexagonal 'pyramid' with which the crystals are always terminated is really a combination of two sets of three rhombohedral faces. More often than not these 'pyramid' faces are of very different sizes, the smaller faces then appearing as triangles which have angles of 70° at their base and 40° at the apex, with the sides nearly one and a half times the length of the base. The prism faces are characteristically striated at right angles to their length, and this is a very valuable aid to identification and to the correct orientation of a distorted crystal.

A feature of quartz which is unique amongst the gem minerals is the spiral arrangement of the atoms along the main (trigonal) axis, which has the effect of rotating the plane of a ray of polarised light passing along the direction of this axis. Externally this 'screw' arrangement is made visible by the presence of small 'extra' faces either at the top right-hand corner or the top left-hand corner of alternate prism faces. These faces can be seen in the drawings in Fig. 17(1), one of which shows a 'right-handed' crystal, and the other a 'left-handed' crystal. Even when the two sets of rhombohedra forming the 'pyramid' are equally developed and the crystal appears to have hexagonal symmetry, etching with alkalis or with hydrofluoric acid will reveal differences between them in the surface patterns produced.

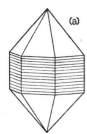  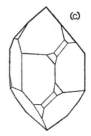

17 (1). Diagrams of quartz crystals:
    (a) simple form showing horizontal striations on prism faces
    (b) unequal development of rhombohedral faces
    (c) small extra faces revealing spiral development

Very often what appear to be simple crystals of quartz are inter-penetrant twins, and such crystals are of no value for technical purposes such as maintaining the wavelength of broadcast emissions or in the construction of very accurate timepieces, which depend upon the piezo-electric properties of quartz. During the war the need for suitable natural quartz for these important purposes led to the destruction of many beautiful crystals. The supply of suitable untwinned crystals is now assured by the large-scale production of synthetic quartz crystals. The growth of these is a slow process, but by the choice of suitable crystal plates as 'seeds' the producer can at least ensure that the resulting crystals are not twinned.

Though the normal 'habit' of quartz crystals is to show rather slender prisms capped by a 'pyramid' at one end, and the other end either attached or broken away from the matrix on which it formed, there are local variations on this theme. In some localities doubly terminated crystals are found, notably in Herkimer County, New York, where crystals of unusual brilliance and limpidity occur loose in cavities or embedded in powdered anthracite which can be seen as a frequent inclusion in the crystals, or at Compostella in Spain, where small doubly terminated crystals are coloured rust-red by inclusions of ferruginous clay.

Where, in any locality, small lustrous quartz crystals are found in quantity they gain for themselves names such as 'Bristol diamonds', 'Cornish diamonds', etc.: reprehensible, of course, but hardly likely to be seriously misleading. In the amethyst variety of quartz the prism faces are hardly developed to any extent and the colour is concentrated in the 'caps' of the crystals. This is one piece of evidence in favour of the theory that the colour of amethyst is due to traces of iron plus exposure to natural radiation from surrounding minerals. In the milky-pink variety known as rose-quartz signs of crystal faces are usually lacking.

However clear and limpid quartz crystals may seem one can usually find crystals of other minerals included, either with the naked eye or under lens examination. Cavities containing liquid are especially common, and often the cavities have the shape of a 'negative' quartz crystal. A bubble of carbon dioxide is frequently seen in the liquid-filled cavity, and sometimes a cube of rock-salt, making a 'three-phase' inclusion. Milky quartz owes its cloudiness to the presence of millions of such tiny inclusions. When strongly heated in a flame quartz containing such minute cavities is liable to 'decrepitate' in a series of tiny explosions as the contents of the cavities burst their bounds—each explosion being accompanied by a flash of yellow sodium light in the flame.

The best-known and most spectacular solid inclusions in quartz consist of golden-brown needles of rutile (titanium dioxide) sometimes in parallel formation, but more often curved and randomly arranged. Very occasionally a bunch of rutile needles will be found emerging from the crystal like a shaving-brush. Other needle-like inclusions consist of dark brown tourmaline or green actinolite. Greenish flakes of chlorite are common both on the surface and within quartz, especially in Swiss specimens, and little platelets of foethite, appearing red by transmitted light, are also often seen, particularly in amethyst.

Owing to the purity of its crystals and its simple (silicon dioxide) composition, quartz has the most constant properties of any mineral. Wherever it is found, one can be sure that a water-clear sample of quartz will have a density of 2·651 and refractive indices of 1·544 and 1·553 for the two rays. Using the hydrostatic method seven specimens of pure flawless quartz pieces carefully measured for density in our Hatton Garden Laboratory gave values of 2·6507, 2·6506, 2·6511, 2·6514, 2·6508, 2·6509 and 2·6506, giving an average of 2·6509. Some superb early work by French scientists between 1905 and 1910 involved cutting and polishing two cubes of quartz of 4 and 5 cm edge precisely and then weighing these. These measurements gave 2·6507 for the S.G. of the pure mineral. The most accurate refractive index measurements have given values of 1·5443 for the ordinary and 1·5534 for the extraordinary ray (reduced to four places of decimals) using a Hilger spectrometer reading to one second on specially prepared prisms.

To strive for such accuracy is, of course, an academic exercise and unrelated to everyday gem testing, but I quote the figures here to show how superbly precise crystal architecture can be in a pure material such as quartz, and also to show how reliable is a piece of clear rock-crystal as a standard for checking the accuracy of one's density techniques and the scales of refractometers. If a pure quartz specimen is measured and gives results in figures other than the above, you can be quite sure that the error is with you and not with the quartz!

Although colourless rock crystal is sometimes used effectively in the form of spherical or faceted bead necklaces, as rondels between beads of other stones, for crystal balls of the fortune-teller type, for small boxes or carvings of animals, and so on, it has nothing like the important position as a stone for jewellery as the yellow and violet blue varieties known as citrine and amethyst. Natural citrine is quite rare in nature, and the vast quantities of yellow, brown and reddish-brown quartzes which emanate from the great German cutting centre of Idar-Oberstein are for the most part heat-treated stones originally either smoky quartz or amethyst. The term 'burnt amethyst' is often used in the trade for such material. The temperature employed is usually between 470° and 560°C, which represents a dull red heat. The natural citrine is usually more insipid in colour than the 'burnt' stones, and thus commercially less popular. It may be distinguished from the heated stones by its distinct dichroism, since the heat-treated stones have none. However, as the colours produced by the heat-treatment are permanent and richer in tint, and since the heating process is so universally carried out, no one bothers very much about distinguishing between the two.

Citrine, as its name suggests, properly applies to rather pale yellow stones. The browner types grade into 'smoky quartz' which is fairly common in nature. The name, cairngorm, which properly belongs to a local variety of brown or smoky quartz found in the Cairngorm mountains north-west of Braemar in Scotland, has a good sound to it and makes a useful variety name where citrine seems unsuitable. Purists, however, object to the name being used for brown quartz which has not come from this locality, and it seems probable that such stones have long ago been exhausted and replaced, for the tourist trade, by imported material.

The colour of natural citrine is thought to be due to traces of trivalent iron which have been found by careful analysis.

Amethyst is the most highly valued of the quartz varieties, and varies in colour from a pale mauve or violet to a very deep violet or purple. Under tungsten light the deeper colours appear reddish-purple against the violet-blue colour shown in daylight or fluorescent lighting.

Stones of the richest colour are often claimed as 'Siberian' in the trade, and Uruguay amethyst comes next in their estimation. No other stone quite matches the colour of fine amethyst, though the tint is not admired by everybody. Purple sapphire, for which the misleading name 'oriental amethyst' was used in the past, comes near to it, and naturally is a far brighter-looking stone, while the recently discovered blue variety of zoisite (to which the name 'tanzanite' has been given) can also resemble amethyst, though it is decidedly bluer in shade. The name amethyst is derived from the Greek and means 'not drunken'. Wearers of the stone were said to be immune from the effect of strong liquors, and amethyst rings were in consequence much used by bishops.

One difficulty facing the lapidary in cutting an amethyst is the banding of colour which is a common feature of the stone. When such banding is visible through the table facet the appearance of the stone is largely spoiled. Amethyst frequently shows a curious 'thumbprint' or 'tiger-stripe' inclusion, which is quite distinctive. This consists of nearly straight alternating dark and light stripes with zigzag edges. Under high magnification these are resolved (according to W. F. Eppler) into pale liquid inclusions and darker negative crystals.

Not long ago it was discovered by accident that certain types of amethyst can be turned green by careful heat-treating, and such stones have been marketed under the name 'prasiolite'. Gemmologists who dislike the unnecessary intrusion of new names prefer to call this material 'greened amethyst'. The colour produced is a rather dull leek-green, and is unlikely to find much public favour.

The cause of colour in amethyst has long been a matter for research and argument. The fact that it changes colour on heating, becoming yellow, and, at higher temperatures, colourless, suggests that it is not a straightforward matter of a 'colouring oxide' of some transition element being present. It is true that the colour-depth has been found to go hand-in-hand with the iron-content in amethysts from a number of Japanese localities, and that the same is the case for smoky quartz. But the colour seems to develop only when the stone has been subjected to irradiation, which in nature can be derived from radioactive minerals, or in the laboratory supplied by artificial neutron bombardment.

Colours which alter under the action of heat and radiation are always difficult to 'explain' except in terms of highbrow physics. Quite tiny traces of impurities in the crystal lattice can act as 'colour centres', and these can usually be altered and finally destroyed by the action of sufficient heat. We see this type of reaction in the case of diamond and zircon as well as in quartz which we are now discussing. Colour in such stones as ruby, emerald and the garnets is a much more straightforward affair. The main concern for the jeweller and his customer (apart from the obvious one that the colour must be satisfying to the eye) is that the colour should be permanent under the ordinary conditions of living. The fact that a coloured stone one is wearing in a ring will lose its colour when subjected to a dull red heat need not bother one unduly, but if it is liable to fade when exposed to bright sunlight, this gives an uneasy sense of impermanence which is the last thing expected or desired in a precious stone. Fortunately, despite the changes due to heat described above the coloured quartzes can be expected to retain their colours indefinitely if worn and treated in a normal manner.

This is not so sure in the case of another coloured quartz—rose-quartz—now to be described. As this is never fully transparent it is hardly suitable for faceting, but is a lovely material for small carvings, snuff-bottles and the like, and as beads for necklaces. Both in rock-crystal and in rose-quartz the quality of the material is better shown if the beads used for the necklace are polished as spheres and not carved or faceted. In the case of rose-quartz this not only has the advantage of showing the colour and translucency to better effect, but enables one to see in many cases the effect of asterism which is quite common in this material though more pronounced in stones from certain localities than from others. If the beads are turned around under a strong single source of light (such as the sun or a 100 watt lamp) several of them are liable to show reflected rays which cross (at two points on the sphere) to form a six-rayed star. Even where the rays are not clearly visible there is usually a 'knot' of light (German, *lichtknolle*) to be seen at two points on the bead. Actually this faculty in rose-quartz is far more striking by transmitted than by reflected light and if a disc of suitable rose-quartz is cut at right angles to the main axis of the crystal and a distant light viewed through the disc held close to the eye the effect is both beautiful and startling, as six sharp bright rays are seen emanating from the light-source itself, which is seen as the centre point. If there be several lights and the disc is turned in front of the eye the effect is reminiscent of searchlights sweeping the sky in the midst of an air raid.

The star effect in rose-quartz was cleverly exploited during the Second World War by a London lapidary, when it proved to be quite a dollar-earner. Suitably oriented *cabochons* were cut from slabs of star-rose-quartz, and the bases of these were coated with a reflecting layer of dark blue enamel and finished off with a neatly ground disc of quartz. The effect under a single light was like that of a star sapphire, only far more spectacular. The 'give away' apart from this unnatural brilliance, was that a reflection of the light-source was clearly seen at the centre of the star; an effect not found in true star sapphires. Also if one were suspicious enough, one had only to view the stones sideways to see the pink colour of the rose-quartz.

The sharpness and perfection of these star effects in rose-quartz is due to the tiny size of the oriented needles of rutile which cause the phenomenon. Indeed the existence of such needles was not proven until an ingenious scientist dissolved some star-quartz material in hydro-fluoric acid and examined the residue under the enormous magnification of an electron microscope, when the submicroscopic needles of rutile were observed.

Rose-quartz is a 'massive' variety of the mineral, in which a number of similarly oriented quartz crystals are packed together and show no crystal faces. In 1960, however, some actual crystals of rose-quartz were found in Minas Gerais, Brazil, and since then a few other occurrences of the kind have been reported. The pink colour in this material was at one time ascribed to manganese, but is now thought to be due to minute quantities of titanium.

Quartz showing the cat's-eye phenomenon known as chatoyancy is also well known, though the ray is far less sharp and less opalescent than in the highly prized chrysoberyl cat's-eyes. These quartz cat's-eyes consist of translucent massive quartz, brownish in colour, which has crystallised round fibres of asbestos-like hornblende to which the cat's-eye ray is due. Such stones are usually cut in oval *cabochon* form with the base left matt. A check on the refractometer (using the 'spot' method) or in a heavy liquid such as bromoform if the stone be loose, will resolve any doubts in cases where a fine quartz cat's-eye might hopefully be a chrysoberyl.

A far sharper ray is seen in another variety of quartz known as 'tiger's-eye' or 'crocidolite', a handsome golden-brown material which was found during the latter part of the last century near Griqualand West, in South Africa. The material is found in thin slabs in which the fibres of the original asbestos-like mineral, crocidolite, are arranged perpendicularly to the surface of the plate. The crocidolite was originally blue in colour, but has not only been completely replaced by quartz, but the iron content has been oxidised, giving a golden tint. Polished pieces show an attractive banded appearance in which dark brown and paler golden stripes alternate. The name crocidolite (borrowed from the original mineral) is perhaps more commonly used than tiger's-eye quartz. Polished in the form of eggs or beads, or as *cabochon*-cut gems, tiger's-eye has a striking appearance which at first may seem quite magnificent, but which palls a little as one grows familiar with it. When it first appeared in Europe high prices were demanded, which tumbled rapidly when it became known what a vast quantity was available. In places the crocidolite has retained its original bluish tint and stones cut from this have been christened 'hawk's-eye'.

Replacement of one mineral by another while retaining its original crystal form is quite a commonplace in nature. The resulting material is known as a 'pseudomorph', and in mineralogical language tiger's-eye is a 'pseudomorph of quartz after crocidolite'. By heating the golden-brown tiger's-eye material a change from brown to red can be achieved as the iron content becomes oxidised to hematite.

Before passing on to the agate family which are known as 'crypto-crystalline' quartzes (because their crystal grains or fibres are too small to be visible to the naked eye), I had better describe aventurine, which is a granular form of quartz containing little leaflets of green mica, which has an attractive jade-like appearance. Granular quartz rock of this kind is known as a 'quartzite', and differs from sandstone which is a sedimentary deposit, in being a metamorphic rock. The little quartz grains are interlocking and the rock very tough and coherent. Aventurine quartz varies a good deal in appearance according to the amount of green mica present. Usually it can be recognised by examination under a lens when the mica leaflets can be observed. On a polished surface the mica leaves little hollows, being so much softer than the surrounding quartz. Aventurine is much used for ornaments and carvings, and also as beads for necklaces. The green is due to chromium in the mica and this ensures that the shade is a very pleasing one.

Something should be said about the chief localities for the crystallised quartzes used as gems, though the mineral is so ubiquitous that a complete list of sources would read like a gazeteer. Some of the most beautiful groups of crystallised quartz have been found in the Swiss Alps, from Bourg d'Oisans in France, and the famous marble quarries at Carrara in northern Italy. In former times, pebbles of clear quartz transported by rivers flowing from the Alps and recovered from the Rhine were polished in Idar-Oberstein and sold as 'Rhinestones'. Since that time the name has been debased and loosely used for glass imitation stones.

Although much fine quartz has come from Madagascar, from the United States and from Japan, there can be no doubt that Brazil has been the largest commercial producer, particularly of amethyst. The main area for amethyst is in Rio Grande do Sul and this extends into Uruguay, which is also noted for stones of fine colour.

Rose-quartz is not so widely spread as the other varieties, and is found only in pegmatites. The best material has been discovered in the north-east part of Minas Gerais, Brazil. There are numerous sources of rose-quartz amongst the pegmatites of Madagascar, also in North America in the States of Colorado, South Dakota and California. In deposits at Bedford and North Castle in the State of New York the rose-quartz is famous for its marked asterism.

Finally, the pegmatites of South West Africa, and near that great gem-mining centre of Sverdlovsk in the Urals, have produced large quantities of the mineral.

CHALCEDONY (AGATE) GROUP

When hot solutions rich in silica filter through the veins in rocks already formed and find their way into crevices and cavities they sometimes crystallise out as rock-crystal, but quite often form compact masses in which the crystals are so tiny that a microscope is needed to discern them. A general name for these cryptocrystalline quartzes is 'chalcedony', but where they have a concentric banded structure the more familiar name of 'agate' can be used. The term chalcedony is used for translucent grey, yellow, or brown masses having a rounded hummocky exterior surface for which mineralogists use the terms reniform or botryoidal, meaning, respectively, shaped like a kidney or a bunch of grapes.

Neither simile is very exact here, but it serves to give the general idea.

In the chalk cliffs of our south coast one can see dark layers of another common type of chalcedony which we call flint. Chalk itself is formed from the remains of millions of tiny shell-fish and is almost pure calcium carbonate, but the spicules of the fossil sponges which formed part of its mass were rich in silica and dissolved in the waters which percolated down through the joints in the rock, until saturation point in silica was reached and a layer of flint was deposited as a black band a few inches in thickness.

When chalk is weathered away the flints remain and form the pebbles and shingle which are so much part of our image of the seaside at our south coast resorts, and are sorted into coarse and fine pebbles by the action of the tides. The faculty for producing sparks when struck by steel gave rise to flint, steel and tinder being a much used means of producing fire, while flint-lock muskets using the same principle were in use for 200 years prior to 1840.

Flint is not used as an ornamental stone (though I have often thought how attractive the rich grey-black material might look if polished as beads), but was of enormous importance to early man as a material for tools, axes and arrow-heads, and also formed a durable building stone. It is mentioned here at some length because a diligent search amongst the broken surfaces of flints will often reveal cavities lined with tiny crystals of quartz and also pockets showing the typical botryoidal chalcedony growth described above. Also it seems to me a good thing if the reader should be able to link up at least some of the gemstones described in this book with stones he can readily see and handle in these islands.

Chalcedony is, however, formed more in volcanic rocks than in sedimentary, being formed there in cavities and pockets as an alteration product of the decomposing rock. When decomposition of the rock is complete the chalcedony nodules are set free and lie loose in the soil, or are carried away in streams to form pebbles in alluvial deposits. Where the chalcedony is of a uniform red colour, it is known as 'cornelian'; where brown, 'sard'. 'Plasma' is a dark green chalcedony which, when spotted with red, becomes heliotrope or bloodstone.

Much more important than these are the agates, in which the chalcedony is built up of layers of different colour and translucency. These layers, when examined in detail, are usually extremely thin, as many as 17,000 to the inch having been counted in one instance, but they group themselves into broader bands of similar colour or opacity. As used for ornament, agates are almost invariably stained chemically to make their colours brighter and more contrasted than the soft browns and greys met with in nature. The manner in which the fine layers in agate were produced is still a matter for debate. Their occurrence is most often in almond-shaped cavities in volcanic rocks, which are known as amygdales, and the shape of the agate nodules naturally conforms with that of the original cavity.

One theory of agate formation assumes the existence of hot intermittent springs such as are now found in the geysers of Iceland and in the Yellowstone Park in the U.S.A. Water from such springs would fill cavities in the rocks and then subside, leaving a thin film of silica which would harden under the influence of heat and be succeeded by another layer as the springs rose again. Most agates show the presence of one or more ducts through which hot solutions could enter, but some do not—and here an alternative suggestion, based on work by the German scientist Liesegang, may have some validity. He showed how banded precipitates could be formed by the diffusion of reagents into gels—a gel being the name for a coagulated jelly. In a simple experiment which illustrates the idea, a pool of 5 per cent gelatin gel containing a little potassium bichromate is allowed to 'set' on a glass plate. If a drop of silver nitrate solution is placed in the centre of the gel, a series of beautiful scarlet 'Liesegang' rings of silver bichromate will form, alternating with vacant zones.

A detailed explanation of this phenomenon of periodic precipitation would take too much of our space, but many examples can be produced experimentally. Thus it can be assumed that if a rock cavity has been completely filled with silica solution which stiffens to a jelly, and this is then exposed to a later solution which contains traces of chemicals which would react on impurities in the original silica gel, the conditions might be such as to form banded precipitates.

There is certainly no easy explanation, especially when one finds cases where the concentric arrangement of the layers is interrupted and a series of straight parallel bands appears at one end of the nodule, or where not the centre (where one expects it) but the periphery is occupied by crystalline quartz.

Agate nodules vary widely in dimensions from the size of a pea to giants weighing 40 hundredweights, but an average and commercially useful size seems to be from 4 to 6 inches in length.

It used to be assumed that the slight porosity of agate to chemical solutions which make its staining a simple matter was due to traces of opaline silica in the minute pores between the quartz fibres, but recent workers maintain that these submicroscopic pores contain nothing but dilute saline solutions.

The most important staining process carried out on agate, the production of black onyx, has been operated in Oberstein since 1819, and was said to have been imparted to an agate merchant by a customer from Rome where it had been known for a very long time. In this, suitable agate material is immersed in a solution of honey or sugar which is allowed to simmer for several weeks. The stones are then removed and washed before being transferred to another pot containing sulphuric acid. Sulphuric acid has a tremendous appetite for water and its effect on sugar, or sugar solutions, is a drastic 'charring' leaving a residue of carbon. The effect on the sugar-soaked agates, therefore, is to deposit grains of carbon in the pores of the stone, resulting in a satisfactory and permanent black colour. After this treatment the onyx is dried in an oven and finally cut and polished and soaked in oil, the surplus oil being later removed with bran. The white bands in agate are largely impervious so that the black and white banded onyx at one time so favoured for the cutting of cameos (enabling a white carving in relief to be made against a black background) is not difficult to prepare by the above process.

The name onyx, which is derived curiously from the Greek word for a finger-nail, has been used in the past for other banded minerals, especially the stalagmitic marbles which are so popular today for pen-trays, chessmen, etc., and described as 'Mexican onyx', 'Brazilian onyx', etc. A preferable term for this much softer material is 'onyx-marble', where the term onyx is used as an adjective to indicate a banded structure.

Two other staining processes which are frequently carried out, though more with unbanded chalcedony than with striped agate material, are treatment with ferrous sulphate solution followed by heat, which produces a reddish-brown 'cornelian' colour (not so pleasing as the quieter tints of the undyed stone), and impregnation with chromic acid followed by heating, which results in an apple-green or almost emerald-green stone resembling chrysoprase. Stained chalcedony of lavender-blue is also frequently seen, though what it is meant to represent is something of a mystery.

Chalcedony and agate have a slightly lower density than fully crystallised quartz, the values ranging from 2·58 to 2·64, 2·60 being a good average. The refractive indices are also lower (1·533 and 1·539), and the small amount of birefringence shown is due to the structure. The hardness and toughness of agate make it a valuable material for laboratory purposes such as supporting the knife-edges of delicate balances, or for pestles and mortars. In Idar-Oberstein where there is really a glut of coloured agates, cut and polished in hundreds of workshops, ingenuity is strained to the utmost to find saleable objects which can reasonably be fashioned from agate: penholders and paper-knives, ash-trays and umbrella handles, book-ends and paper-weights. It does not seem to occur to the promoters of these souvenir-type objects that there exists a large public for which a fine agate, untouched except by the polishing of one major surface, provides a desirable ornament in its own right which any kind of artificial attachments only debase and spoil.

Some of the special agate varieties should be mentioned by name. Onyx, as we have seen, can either be a black and white agate in alternating straight bands, or it can be entirely black. Sard is a red or reddish-brown chalcedony, and sardonyx an agate with straight bands of red and white. Moss agate, sometimes called mocha stone, is a milky off-white chalcedony in which dendritic or moss-like inclusions of a dark mineral are seen giving a very pretty pattern. This is the result of iron, or more often manganese compounds diffusing through the silica gel before it solidified as chalcedony. The consequent 'tree' or 'moss' usually consists of a manganese mineral with the almost unpronounceable name of psilomelane, which as hand specimens is black and glistening rather like hematite. It is really somewhat strange that the term 'agate' should have been applied to these decorative stones, as they are not notably banded.

Two members of the quartz family, chrysoprase and jasper, which stand rather apart from the chalcedony group, have not yet been described. Chrysoprase is an attractive apple-green stone consisting of micro-granular rather than fibrous quartz, and owes its colour to the presence of nickel. It is quite rare, and good specimens are more costly than other varieties of the compact forms of quartz. It is used a good deal in *cabochon* form for ring-stones, and is extensively imitated by chalcedony which has been stained green with chromium salts. There is also a natural green chrome-chalcedony (discovered in Rhodesia in 1955) to complicate the issue. Both this and the stained material appear red or pink under the Chelsea filter, whereas chrysoprase remains green, and this serves as a useful rough and ready test. The reader must be warned that there are numerous translucent green minerals somewhat or 'more than somewhat' resembling jade, and even an expert sometimes has all his work cut out to identify them. The best thing an enthusiastic beginner can do is to make a collection of authentic pieces of each of these stones and study their appearance and behaviour as thoroughly as possible. It will be found that while some, once seen, are easily recognisable, others need skilled testing before a sure identification can be made.

Jasper, though hardly a gem material, should receive brief mention. It is a very impure form of massive quartz and derives its colours (mostly browns and greens) from the minerals it encloses, which may be present to the extent of 20 per cent of the stone. The only intrusion of jasper into jewellery is when, under a false colour, it pretends to be lapis lazuli. For this particular fake (which is surprisingly effective at first sight) a pale brownish jasper is chosen, which is found at Nunkirchen near Idar-Oberstein in Germany. This is heavily stained with Prussian blue, which is an iron ferrocyanide. The 'Swiss lapis' (which is its nick-name in this country) contains little lakes of crystalline quartz here and there, which can be seen with a lens and at once reveal its nature. True lapis lazuli has a more violet blue and contains little brassy specks of iron pyrites.

The main occurrences of the chalcedony minerals must briefly be given. So far as Europe goes, as already indicated, the agate industry belongs essentially to the twin townships of Idar and Oberstein, on the river Nahe, a tributary of the Rhine. Here in the local rocks was an abundant supply of the raw material and, since the time of invaders from Rome, cutting and polishing agate was carried out by a high proportion of the inhabitants. In the old days the grinding and polishing was done on huge sandstone wheels driven by water power. The workers lay almost prone on their stomachs on a low bench, with their toes braced against pegs or struts fixed in the floor, to enable them to press the stones against the wet surface of the wheel. A more health-destroying activity could hardly be imagined, and for many years only a few of these crude workshops have survived, and at times are in operation for the amusement of tourists. Slitting, grinding and polishing are now carried out in comfort with electrically driven cutting discs and wheels.

During the nineteenth century the unthinkable happened: the local supply of agate material virtually dried up, and some of the more venturesome Idar lapidaries and dealers emigrated to Brazil in search of gems. It was in 1827 that the discovery of agates and other quartz minerals lying on or near the surface was first made by a native of Oberstein. The finding of amygdales in vast supply in melaphyre rocks in Rio Grande do Sul came in time to save their home industry in Idar-Oberstein, and the numerous varieties of fine gemstones imported from Brazil enabled workers there to extend their skills to more profitable fields of lapidary work.

Other fields rich in agates are found in Madagascar, in the Deccan trap area of India, and in various parts of North America, such as Oregon, Texas and Colorado. There are even small agates to be found on the beaches in Ayrshire and Kincardineshire, which have come from the local lavas. Various localities in Silesia were for a long time the chief commercial sources of chrysoprase. It occurs there in thin veins or flat plates, embedded in serpentine from which it derived its nickel content. It grades into inferior material of essentially the same kind, known as hornstone.

Deposits of chrysoprase, again as veins in serpentine, have been discovered in the State of Goias, Brazil, and at Marlborough Creek, Queensland, Australia. This last deposit was first found in 1963, the chrysoprase veins covering a wide area on a plateau 1350 feet above sea level. The chrysoprase here contains some 2·4 per cent of nickel and is of an exceptionally deep and jade-like green. Large quantities have been exported to the Orient where anything resembling jade is readily accepted as material for carvings, and as readily bought by visitors to Hong Kong in the fond hope that they are in fact jade.

The different forms of quartz crop up so frequently wherever gemstones are bought or sold or collected that it is useful to have some simple tests available. With the transparent varieties the most likely substitute is glass, and a test between crossed polaroids, or in a polariscope, will soon settle that issue. With the popular yellow or citrine varieties confusion with the much rarer and more costly topaz is likely. It is worth while having on hand a 'quartz' liquid, as recommended in Chapter 10; that is, a bromoform solution diluted with benzene to match the density of quartz, preferably kept in a corked bottle in a dark cupboard with a small beaker or tumbler nearby into which it can be poured for the actual experiment. A small quartz 'indicator' should be used to ensure that the fluid has the exact density of quartz. For loose stones this constitutes a sure test for the quartz gemstones, which will remain suspended in such a liquid alongside the indicator. It is also useful as a check on the chalcedony gems. Actually undiluted bromoform, or methylene iodide, can serve to resolve the 'topaz' issue, as true topaz will sink in both these liquids, where quartz will bob briskly to the surface.

Of course for those who have a refractometer this provides a more rapid and positive test than those suggested above, since quartz has indices 1·544 and 1·553, and yellow topaz the higher values 1·63 and

1·64, but I do not expect the majority of readers to have indulged in so expensive an instrument.

Where spherical quartz beads are concerned a simple and completely conclusive test can be suggested which is worth while carrying out because it involves so pretty an effect. It was explained early in this chapter that the silica molecules in a crystal of quartz are arranged in a spiral pattern, and this causes a rotation of the plane of rays of polarised light passing along the main (three-fold) axis of the crystal. Whereas in all other uniaxial gemstones placed between crossed polars with their optic axis vertical and viewed from above in convergent light an 'interference figure' is seen consisting of a black cross centred in a series of concentric rings, with quartz the cross has a hollow centre. With quartz beads or spheres between crossed polaroids or, more conveniently, in a polariscope (see Chapter 9) the shape of the beads themselves provides the 'convergent' light, and one only has to turn them into the correct position to see the distinctive interference pattern with a coloured hollow centre.

Even the very brief summary just given may daunt the non-scientific reader, but I hope that, despite this, some will at least take the trouble to put some quartz beads between crossed polaroids, shine a light through them, and enjoy the effect. It is not only a useful practical test, but an excellent example of the sort of extra enjoyment gemstones can give over and above the mere attractiveness of their appearance.

CHAPTER EIGHTEEN

OPAL

THERE ARE THOSE who claim that opal, with its wonderful vivid play of iridescent colours, is the most beautiful of all gemstones, and it is difficult to argue against this opinion. 'Provided always', as the lawyers like to add, that the opal concerned is of fine quality, since few gems can vary so widely in their appearance in ranging from the worthless to the priceless. But comparison with other gemstones is really in this case hardly possible since such criteria as transparency, lustre, dispersion and body-colour, which most other gems possess in varying degree and upon which their charm depends, no longer have significance. In this respect opal is akin to pearl, another highly prized gem material which stands apart from others and calls for separate and special standards of appreciation.

It is not only in appearance that opal is quite distinct from other gems. For one thing, except for amber which is a fossil resin, opal is the only gemstone which is amorphous, i.e., lacking in crystal structure. It is, in fact, a colloidal substance formed by the gradual solidification and hardening of a silica jelly deposited by hot silica-rich waters in cavities in volcanic rocks or fissures in sandstone. In its composition and manner of formation it would thus seem closely akin to agate, but in the latter case conditions allowed the silica to crystallise, if only in micro form, and the only water content in the final solid is held in tiny cavities between the quartz crystallites.

Opal, then, consists of silica with a variable amount of water, 10 per cent being an average value. Being amorphous, it has no regular external crystal form, but is found in rounded nodules, as encrustations and as veins of varying thickness. It has a lower density than quartz; the lowest indeed of any valuable gem, varying between 2·0 and 2·12. The refractive index is also very low, being near 1·45, and the hardness is about 6 on Mohs's scale. This low hardness does not greatly impair its value as a gemstone as it is usually *cabochon*-cut and non-transparent, so that a few scratches do not constitute an obtrusive blemish. Nevertheless, opal is not the most robust of gems and is more suited for use in pendants, earrings and brooches than for the harder wear to be expected in a ringstone.

In its ordinary form the mineral has no particular charm, being a translucent milky-white substance, or yellowish, brownish or green if coloured by impurities. A general term for opal which is not of gem quality is 'common' opal, whereas gem opal is termed 'precious' opal: in older times the term 'noble' opal was sometimes used, possibly by analogy with the German word *edel* which means both 'noble' and 'precious'.

Precious opal, naturally, is what concerns us here, and this can be conveniently divided into four different categories: white opal, black opal, fire opal and water opal.

White opal is the most usual form of precious opal and is the type which has made the stone famous in past ages, being the only form available until comparatively recent times. In this the play of iridescent colours is seen emerging from the milky-white or pale yellowish background. In black opal, which is unique to certain districts in Australia, the flashes of rainbow colours are seen against the dark grey bodycolour of the stone, which makes for a more spectacular effect. This is by far the rarest and most coveted form of opal and good pieces, with evenly sized patches of pure and varied colour, can fetch hundreds of pounds per carat. Fire opal stands apart in being valued for its magnificent flame-red hue rather than for an iridescent play of colour, though some stones have this also. Fire opals can be nearly transparent and are then faceted, usually with a slightly domed table. Water opals are less well known and appreciated and they, like fire opals, come chiefly from Mexico. They are virtually transparent and by transmitted light merely show an uninteresting yellowish tint. By reflected light, especially against a dark background, spangles of vivid colours spring into life changing constantly with the angle from which they are viewed and with no cloudiness to dim their brilliance. Jelly opal is another name for these fascinating gems.

In judging the value of black or white opals connoisseurs pay great attention to the size of the coloured patches forming the mosaic, the brilliance and variety of the colours and the evenness of distribution.

Stones showing very numerous small-scale patches (the so-called harlequin opal) are less prized than those where the little sheets of colour are about 2 or 3 mm across in stones up to an inch in length, and rather larger in bigger stones. As for the colours themselves, red or orange flashes are essential to add contrast to the more common blues and greens if the stone is to appear really exciting. Most opals when looked at closely under a good light, especially if a lens is employed, will show enough to delight the beholder. But to be effective in jewellery an opal must be capable of displaying its attractions under indifferent lighting and at a not too intimate distance.

The usual style of cutting for opal is a rather shallow oval *cabochon*. The iridescent patchwork is usually confined to a fairly thin layer which precludes too steep a *cabochon,* and the underpart of the stone is seldom of 'precious' quality, and is sometimes referred to as 'potch'. Because of the extreme thinness of the 'precious' layers it is a common practice to cement a thin slice showing fine colours to a base of 'potch' or even of onyx, forming a 'doublet' of handsome appearance and quite suitable to be used in jewellery. A further improvement in appearance can be achieved by cementing a dome of rock-crystal on top of the 'precious' layer which has the double virtue of magnifying the patches of colour and of protecting the surface of the opal from scratches. Such composite stones are commercially legitimate so long as they are bought and sold for what they are. Naturally they are available at much lower prices than solid one-piece opals, which is all to the good: it would be a pity if the loveliness which opal displays should be available only to the very wealthy.

Opal doublets and triplets all aim at giving the effects to be seen in fine black opals: white opals are seldom imitated or enhanced and the iridescent patches are more often embedded to some depth within the stone so that a doublet backing is not necessary. Another artificial means of representing the true black opal has come to the fore very much in the last decade, although a recipe for 'treating' opals in such a manner is to be found in the 1823 edition of John Mawe's famous little book *A Treatise on Diamonds and Precious Stones.* Mawe wrote: 'Many impositions have been practised in forming imitations, or enhancing the effect, of the opal. The first I shall describe . . . is effected by warming the stone, and immersing it in oil or grease, which is afterwards burnt off. The rents which had absorbed the grease by this means become dark and agreeably contrast with the beautiful iridescence of the stone, which now assumes the name of black or green opal.'

Mawe was thus acknowledging the superior appearance of opal having a dark background nearly a century before the first natural black opals were found at Lightning Ridge in New South Wales. The modern treated opals have probably been 'doctored' in the same sort of way which is used to form black onyx, that is by soaking in sugar solutions and later 'carbonising' the sugar-soaked pieces by immersion in sulphuric acid. Indifferent white opal from Andamooka seems to be the chief raw material, having pin-point patches of iridescent colour. The treated stones show a very distinctive *cloisonné* appearance when examined with a lens, the coloured spangles being fragmented and quite unlike the little striated sheets typical of true black opals. Little black spots are visible all over the surface. Again there is no harm in the use of such stones, provided they are sold as 'treated' at a pound or two for the stone instead of, maybe, a hundred times that amount.

Anyone interested in collecting opals would do well to obtain samples of treated stones and also of the usual forms of doublet, as careful inspection of these will do a good deal to ensure one against being swindled. Free from their setting doublets should be easy game, though one should be cautioned that natural black opals may show quite a sharp division between their 'fancy' top surface and the dull blue-grey base. In such cases, however, going round the junction with a lens will reveal certain points at which the fiery particles dip down into the potch, thus crossing the imagined junction line. Much greater difficulty is experienced where the stone is in a closed setting with the possible junction line concealed. Even laboratory workers may find proof hard to come by in some cases. If the base can be seen to be onyx the stone is, of course, certainly a doublet. If the surface is flat or nearly so a doublet may be suspected, and under the microscope small flattened bubbles marking the junction layer may be noticeable by focusing through the spangled layer under a good light. Another trick is to punch a powerful beam of light through the entire stone when, in a doublet, little points of light, denoting bubbles, may be seen against the opaque background of the remainder of the stone.

The threat of a completely synthetic opal has recently been implemented in commercial practice by the enterprising firm of Gilson operating in the Pas de Calais. These synthetic opals have similar R.I. to natural stones but are a little softer. They have a texture like tapioca pudding and a far shorter afterglow than have natural white opals after exposure to ultra-violet light. Because of these possibilities the reader will once more understand the need to buy only from sources one can trust, and also the need the trade has for a specialised laboratory to safeguard them against acquiring 'wrong' stones for their stocks.

The exact cause for the brilliant colours reflected from precious opal has only been revealed (thanks to the enormous magnifications possible in the electron microscope) during the past decade. It was always realised that these rainbow tints owed nothing to absorption but were the products of some form of 'interference' of light whereby some wavelengths (colours) are enhanced and others destroyed by waves which have 'got out of step' with one another. Common examples of colours produced by interference are films of oil on water and thin soap bubbles in which rays of light reflected at the surface of such thin films become out of phase (out of step) with those which have passed into the film and been reflected from its further side. And there are cases more akin to those found in opal (since they involve regularly spaced structures rather than films) such as the iridescent hues of tropical butterflies' wings or beetles' wing-cases. Even the bright blue on a jay's wing-feathers is not due to pigment but to peculiarities of structure. If light reflected from a patch of colour in an opal is examined though a spectroscope it will be seen to consist of quite a narrow band of wavelengths, that is to be spectrally very 'pure'. And if light which has passed through a precious opal be so examined a series of shadows unlike normal absorption bands will be seen crossing the spectrum, and these will move as the stone is moved and represent gaps in the transmitted light caused by these preferential reflections.

Formerly the most popular and plausible theory was that the interference effects in opal were caused by groups of thin parallel cracks or parallel layers of opal material of slightly differing refractive index, but German and Australian scientists working independently, using electron-microscope photographs, have found that the structure of precious opal consists of millions of tiny spheres of cristobalite (one form of crystallised silica) which are uniform in size and closely packed in the manner of atoms in a crystal, though on a much larger scale. This provides a three-dimensioned grating which gives preferential reflection to certain wavelengths of light at certain angles, the actual colours produced depending upon the size of the spheres. To produce colours these must have diameters similar to the wavelengths of visible light. The longest wavelength of the flashes of colour produced was found to be about double the diameter of the spheres.

In common opal or in potch the little spheres were found to be uneven in size and thus packed together unevenly, giving rise to no selective reflections.

As for the localities for opal, these are remarkably few so far as material of gem quality is concerned. Until a century ago the only source of any consequence was near the village of Červenika, formerly in northern Hungary, but now included in Slovakia. The material has always been known as 'Hungarian opal' and it is convenient to continue to use this description. The opal from this district is found in a brownish-grey volcanic rock at the foot of the mountains Simonka and Litanka in a wild, forested region. The rock is extensively weathered and the opal is found in nests or pockets accompanied by much common opal and the minerals marcasite, pyrite, stibnite and barytes. It is almost certain that all the opals known to the Romans came from this source, though the circuitous routes by which the stones reached their markets led to stories of their being mined in Egypt, Arabia, and other romantic-sounding places. As a fact this opal was remarkable in being the only major gem material apart from Baltic amber which was mined on the continent of Europe.

The precious opal from the 'Hungarian' mines was white opal found in rather small pieces and spangled with small-scale patches of colour: in fact what today might be described as harlequin opal. Its reputation as the finest opal obtainable continued for some time after the discovery of opal at White Cliffs had revealed the first Australian opals to the world, and this European opal certainly delighted Pliny who wrote in his *Natural History* the Latin equivalent of the following description: 'Of all the most precious stones, opal is the most difficult to describe, since it displays at one time the piercing fire of carbuncle, the purple brilliance of amethyst and the green of emerald, blended together and refulgent with an incredible brightness.'

Curiously and unfortunately it seems difficult to find examples of Hungarian opals in the London museums, so that their reputation is by hearsay. Today Australian opal rules the market, though Mexico, Honduras, and recently Brazil, have contributed some fine material.

There are two main forms in which opal occurs in Australia, one known as 'boulder' opal, and the other as 'sandstone' or 'seam' opal. In boulder opal, veins of the coveted mineral are found encased in small boulders of siliceous ironstone which are tough and very hard to break, while sandstone or seam opal is found near the base of desert sandstone beds at its junction with the underlying clay, often as flat cakes which could be found free from surrounding matrix.

The first recorded occurrence of opal in Australia was in 1872, when deposits of boulder opal were discovered at Listowel Downs in central Queensland, but Australian opal was really put on the map when the seam opal of White Cliffs, some sixty miles north of Wilcannia in New South Wales, was found. This was in 1889 and was quite by accident. A party of kangaroo-shooters were following the trail of a wounded kangaroo when they came across a lump of opal on the surface of the ground giving a hint of the treasures below. Subsequently other samples were found strewn on the surface where they had been weathered out of the hillsides, and included fossil shells and bones, and also strange groups of opalised crystals looking like pineapples. The place was at first known as Kangaroo-Shooters Camp, and only later became famous under the name White Cliffs. The surface rock was mercifully soft, allowing small pits to be sunk to the opal-bearing layers which were at varying depths from five to fifty feet below the surface, or often non-existent. The entire field was eventually found to cover an area some fifteen miles long and two broad. Soon the fields were in full swing with seven hundred miners working, and well over a million pounds' worth of opal was raised before the supply began to fail.

Marketing the new opals, however, was not easy. To dealers in Hatton Garden accustomed to the paler 'Hungarian' opals, these new stones were not acceptable. And an even greater prejudice had to be overcome in the case of the black opals which were to follow, when stones which are now amongst the most costly in the world were sold (in the rough) at a few pounds per ounce!

This discovery of black opal took place in 1903 and was at Lightning Ridge near Walgett in northern New South Wales, and the rock formation is similar to that of White Cliffs, except that the opal is found more in isolated nodules instead of thin seams. Whereas in white opal the colours are for the most part seen in a regular chequer-board of pattern, which is restful and undisturbing, the pattern of colours in black opals is irregular and highly individual: each piece tends to be a thing on its own. But it took ten years or more to swing the opinion of the jewellery trade in its favour.

As with White Cliffs, supplies from Lightning Ridge began to dwindle when in 1915 important deposits of opal were found at Coober Pedy in the Stuart Range mountains of South Australia. Coober Pedy means 'man in a hole' in the Aboriginal tongue, and is aptly named, for the miners in the strange little community which exists there all live underground; this is for the very good reason that the surface temperature can be 120° or 130°F, whereas within their skilfully constructed underground dwellings this is reduced to 80°, which is more or less bearable. Planes shuttle to and from this remote spot bearing essential supplies and dealers, who rapidly assess the value of the bags of opal shown them, and pay cash on the spot. Stones from Coober Pedy are white opal, while those found at Andamooka, 270 miles to the south-east, can be classed as black. The discovery here took place in 1930, and the opals in this small field lie fairly close to the surface. A magnificent opal from Andamooka was presented to the Queen in 1949. In the rough this weighed 6 ounces, but it was finally cut into a *cabochon* stone nearly three inches long and weighing 203 carats.

There are several other opal localities in Australia, all probably below the shallow sea which once divided the continent into two islands, but in recent years the world's supply has been predominantly from Coober Pedy and Andamooka.

The opals of Mexico were known to the Aztecs 500 years ago and more. Especially famous are the flame-coloured fire opals found in a matrix of trachytic porphyry at Zimapan in the State of Hidalgo. There are many other sources for opal in Mexico and at some of these the completely colourless hyalite variety is found, which only becomes exciting as a gem when the internal iridescence entitles it to be called water opal, about which I have written enthusiastically earlier in this chapter.

Opals from Honduras and Guatemala have been used during last century but now have no importance. The most recent source to attract notice has been in Brazil where white opals of attractive appearance have been produced in some quantity.

Attempts to imitate precious opal using milky glass containing scraps of tinsel are so unconvincing as to be hardly worth mention. On the other hand fire opal can be very plausibly represented by a slightly cloudy orange-coloured glass. The low refractive index of opal serves to distinguish it from the artificial glasses. The much more serious problems posed by treated opals and by composite stones have been sufficiently discussed earlier.

Perhaps brief mention should be made of the superstition which persuades some people that opals are unlucky. There is, of course, no solid ground for such a belief. But it must be recognised that opals are by their nature less robust than most gemstones, and should be treated with rather special care. Drastic methods of cleaning, for instance (especially ultrasonic cleaning) should be avoided. It is well worth taking some trouble to preserve the beauty of this lovely gemstone.

———————— ◊ ————————

CHAPTER NINETEEN

PERIDOT, SINHALITE, ZOISITE AND SPODUMENE

Peridot

In those chapters describing the various gem minerals we have been climbing down the useful ladder of Mohs's scale and have now passed below the important rung which represents the hardness of quartz, which means that apart from certain 'collectors' stones' which are too rare or too soft to be used in commercial jewellery, pearl, amber and translucent or opaque stones such as jade and turquoise, this chapter represents the end of our story.

It is quite likely that of the four stones to be described in this chapter only peridot will be a name which is known to the reader. Kunzite and tanzanite which are names given to the most popular varieties of spodumene and zoisite may be slightly familiar, while sinhalite was until quite recently accepted as a form of peridot and so deserves inclusion here.

The lovely olive-green gemstone, peridot, has for centuries held an honourable position amongst precious stones. Peridot is the jeweller's name for the mineral, olivine, which plays a very important role in the formation of basic rocks—that is in those rocks poor in silica, such as basalt. It is indeed a main constituent of the rock known as peridotite, and another rock called dunite consists of olivine and nothing else.

Despite its wide distribution in the rocks, there are only three localities in the world where peridot of gem quality has been found in commercial quantities, as will be described later.

Peridot is a silicate of iron and magnesium, the chemical formula of which can be fairly simply written as $(MgFe)_2SiO_4$. The exact proportions of iron to magnesium are not fixed since olivine is a midway member of an isomorphous series of minerals stretching from the pure magnesium silicate forsterite to the iron silicate fayalite. I said a 'midway member', but the types of olivine which are used as the gemstone, peridot, are in fact nearer the magnesium end of the family and contain only some 10 per cent of ferrous oxide—enough to account for the fine green colour.

The hardness of peridot is about $6\frac{1}{2}$ on Mohs's scale, a reasonable hardness for all except ring-stones; the density is near 3·34 and lowest and highest refractive indices are commonly 1·654 to 1·690, which denotes the rather large double refraction of 0·036—quite sufficient to show a pronounced 'doubling' of the back facet-edges when these are examined (using a lens) through the front of the stone. This simple fact and the colour of the stone are enough to identify it with some certainty. Ideally the colour is a rich olive-green, but in some cases can be rather pale and insipid, and in others too brown to be really attractive (see Plate N). Golden-brown stones which were formerly thought to be an iron-rich form of peridot were found to belong to another and hitherto undescribed species now known as sinhalite, as I shall relate further on in this chapter.

Crystals of peridot are not often seen or easily obtainable. They are orthorhombic and have a rather flattened prismatic form very much like that seen in chrysoberyl.

Peridot is most usually step-cut, the form most calculated to display the colour of a gemstone to best effect at the sacrifice of some brilliance and fire, which in this case are not of importance. As with aquamarine, a peridot must be of fair size, say 5 to 20 carats, to make much impression, but within this range it can be mounted with very pleasing effect as the centre stone of a brooch or pendant. Common defects of the stone are a slight greasiness of the lustre due to difficulties in polishing, which requires a special technique, and a tendency to 'sleepiness' in Burma stones, which on the other hand have the richest colour. This lack of complete transparency is due to myriads of tiny needle-like inclusions: if not too pronounced, a slight cloudiness in the stone is acceptable when the colour is really good.

Traditionally the only important source for peridot was the Island of St. John's, or Zeberged, in the Red Sea some 40 miles offshore from the Egyptian port of Berenice, where crystals occur in veins of nickel ore in a decomposed peridotite rock. Magnificent stones of up to 80 carats were formerly cut from the crystals found in this source, but for a long time there was no known source for rough peridot, all the stones used in jewellery being derived from old stones recut and polished.

The main sources of peridot today include Arizona and New Mexico, where ants bring to the surface pretty bright green pebbles derived from decomposed peridotite below the desert sands, and the Bernardino valley, some 20 miles north of Mogok, where occasionally quite large stones of a fine rich green are quarried from the mountainside.

Amongst minor sources of the gem the beautiful little green pebbles recovered from the beaches of Hawaii are worth mentioning. These rather surprisingly contain traces of chromium which enhance their colour and enclose myriads of what appear to be bubbles, but are thought to be negative crystals. These sometimes form a pattern which outlines the geometrical shape of an olivine crystal. Arizona stones often show a delicate form of inclusion somewhat resembling a water-lily leaf—a rounded lace-like 'feather' surrounding a small opaque crystal which (according to W. F. Eppler) consists of a garnet.

Peridot is not enough in public demand for imitations of the stone to be frequently seen, though synthetic corundum and glass of approximately the right colour have been met with from time to time. A quick glance with a lens through the table facet would expose such impostors since they would fail to show the 'doubling' of the back facets which is so pronounced a feature of peridot. The only other green gemstone which might be expected to show such strong double refraction would be green zircon, but these are almost all metamicts, as explained in Chapter 16, and show no doubling to speak of.

Lastly it may be mentioned that for gemmologists practised in testing gemstones with the spectroscope, three evenly spaced absorption bands starting between the green and blue form a very distinctive feature in peridot.

SINHALITE

Despite the possible range in composition and hence of properties to be found in olivines of the peridot type there is in fact very little variation in the properties of peridots used in jewellery. Certain golden-brown or pale yellow stones, however, were met with occasionally in the course of our laboratory work which had decidedly higher density and refractive indices than normal green peridots. Though not happy in the colour and in certain optical details we, in common with other gemmologists, accepted such stones as iron-rich olivines until 1952, when Dr. G. Switzer of the U.S. National Museum in Washington found that the X-ray powder photograph of one of these specimens in the museum collection was definitely not that of olivine but of some new unknown mineral. Sir Frank Claringbull and Dr. M. H. Hey of the Mineral Department of the Natural History Museum in London followed this up and analysed the mineral, finding it to be a magnesium aluminium borate ($MgAlBO_4$) containing some 2 per cent of iron, to which the colour is due. The name sinhalite (from the Sanskrit name *Sinhala* for Ceylon) was chosen for the new mineral as all the specimens whose origin was known had come from that island. This was the second time within a few years that a mineral new to science had been established from a cut gemstone *before any samples of the rough had been found*. If the reader has any imagination I think he will realise that the chances of such a happening are pretty remote. Gemmologists were naturally agog to find more samples, and these were located mixed in with parcels of yellow chrysoberyls and golden zircons, which they resembled closely in appearance but in nothing else. Samples of the rough were before long discovered in the Ceylon gem gravels, including quite a big lump of some 60 carats, which I purchased and had cut into several very pleasing golden-yellow stones.

A year or two later a well-formed (orthorhombic) sinhalite crystal was discovered in the Mogok district and measured and described by my colleague, C. J. Payne. One could not help feeling that this was a bit of one-upmanship by the only possible rival to Ceylon in its claim to be the world's greatest storehouse of unusual gems! The very close similarity in refractive indices, density, hardness and even absorption spectra between minerals so chemically dissimilar showed once again the importance of structure in determining the properties of a mineral.

I realise that all that I have so far written about sinhalite can only really interest those with at least some scientific knowledge. But the practical effect for gem-lovers was that it brought to light a new gem mineral which has very considerable beauty, and was found to be plentiful enough to satisfy the needs of most collectors. Indeed, in an article written in the *Gemmologist* in 1952, only a few months after the first paper in the *Mineralogical Magazine* describing its discovery, C. J. Payne was able to quote full details of twenty-four cut specimens ranging in weight from 1·29 to 74·83 carats, and in colour from pale yellow to dark brown. These extreme colours are quite unattractive but fortunately the majority of specimens are a very pleasant golden-yellow, golden-brown, or greenish-yellow, clear, flawless, perfectly transparent. For any gem-lover who would like to present his wife with an attractive brooch or pendant featuring a stone that his next-door neighbour will not even have heard of, I suggest that a sinhalite is well worth considering!

ZOISITE

Zoisite is yet another mineral which has only quite recently moved into the ranks of important gemstones. It is closely related to the well-known mineral, epidote, but was claimed as a separate species by Werner in 1805 and named by him after Baron von Zois for the sufficiently good reason that the Baron gave him his first specimens. It is a silicate of calcium and aluminium containing some water, and crystallises in the orthorhombic system. Although it was occasionally found in transparent crystals the colour was usually greyish and uninteresting. In 1825 a rose-red massive variety owing its colour to manganese was discovered in Norway, and was christened thulite after the old name for that country. Later thulite was found in the U.S.A. and gained some favour as an ornamental mineral. Its next claim to fame in the world of gemstones was due to the discovery in 1954 of a handsome green zoisite rock in Tanganyika (now Tanzania) to the west of Mount Longido in which spectacular large crystals of opaque ruby corundum were imbedded. The resultant rock was certainly eye-catching and gave rise to a spate of ash-trays and similar objects. To me the combination of bright green and raw-meat-red is most unpleasant, but few seem to agree with me. The name 'anyolite' was coined for this green zoisite, derived from the Massai word for green.

But the first and utterly astonishing breakthrough of the mineral zoisite into the ranks of important gemstones came late in 1967. A few large transparent blue crystals thought to be dumortierite, reached London and were submitted to our laboratory for testing. Our friends in the Geological and Natural History Museums submitted samples to X-ray crystal analysis, which proved them to be an entirely new form of zoisite. Our measurements showed the crystals to have refractive indices of 1·692 and 1·701 for the lowest and highest readings, with 1·694 for the intermediate (beta) index, and a double refraction of 0·009. The density was found to be extremely constant at 3·355, and the hardness between $6\frac{1}{2}$ and 7 on Mohs's scale. A remarkable feature was the pleochroism shown by the deeper coloured crystals which exhibited as its three main colours a magnificent sapphire-blue, a rich purple and a rather indifferent sage-green. Vanadium was found amongst the trace elements, and seems a probable cause for the colour.

The news of this striking newcomer to the ranks of fine gemstones and, more important than this, an adequate supply of specimens suitable for cutting, spread to the main centres of the jewel trade with amazing speed, and Tiffany's of New York, always to the front in exploiting new gem materials, made a feature of the stone and coined a special name for it, 'tanzanite', which was at first frowned upon as unnecessary by scientists, but seems to have been welcomed by the trade as a better selling name than 'blue zoisite'. For details of this occurrence I am indebted to Mr. Rudolf E. Thurm, a skilled gemmologist working for Tanzania Gemstone Industries Ltd. in Moshi, and to articles by Professor Dr. Hermann Bank of Idar-Oberstein. The mines (at least three are in operation) are situated in the Merelani or Mirarani hills some 40 miles south-east of Arusha, and to the south-west of the famous 19,500 feet high mountain, Kilimanjaro, just south of the border with Kenya.

The zoisite occurs in pegmatite veins with graphite, sulphur, feldspar, calcite and quartz, which have a greenish colour due to the presence of a green grossular garnet, which is seldom of gem quality. The rocks emit a strong smell of hydrogen sulphide indicating volcanic action in the neighbourhood.

The tanzanite crystals are found sporadically in small pockets, and sometimes weeks may elapse without reward. Most of the crystals found are reddish-brown in colour, but these change to blue when suitably heated. Occasionally completely colourless zoisites are found. The blue crystals that do occur are said by the miners to be 'naturally burnt'. According to Thurm, it is the deep reddish-brown crystals that give the best blue stones after heating (see Plate N).

Rather surprisingly the treatment is carried out on stones which have been already cut and polished, and they have to be quite free of flaws or inclusions as these will become noticeably more evident after heat-treatment. The specimens are tightly packed in a screw-stoppered container with powdered gypsum and are heated in a charcoal fire for about twenty minutes before being slowly cooled. The heat apparently transforms the trivalent vanadium present into the tetravalent form, to which the blue colour is due. The pleochroism is markedly reduced which is advantageous in its use as a gemstone. The shape of the rough may not always make it possible for the ideal cutting direction (with the blue ray emerging from the table facet) to be followed.

In the few short years since its discovery this new form of zoisite has already established itself as an important and desirable gemstone. It is doubtful whether any other 'new' gemstone in the past has achieved such a rapid rise to fame. At its best it rivals the most superb Ceylon sapphires available, but lower grades might be mistaken for rather poor amethyst. The sincerest compliment (that of imitation) has already been paid to the new gemstone, synthetic sapphire having been manufactured with just the necessary hint of mauve to resemble the zoisite's typical hue.

Where available the refractometer provides the safest test for blue zoisite. In its absence the reddish appearance through the Chelsea filter may help. Mauve sapphire also appears red through the filter, but the colour is not the same. As always, direct experience with the stone itself is the surest guide. As a final note on this exciting gemstone I feel I should warn any owner of a blue zoisite jewel that subjecting it to ultrasonic cleaning is particularly harmful.

Spodumene

The mineral, spodumene, in its unexpected incursion into the world of gemstones has certain parallels with the zoisite just described. As a mineral it has been known since 1800, but the very name spodumene (meaning ash-coloured) suggests that its normal appearance is decidedly drab. There was a brief indication of its potential as a gemstone when in 1879 green transparent crystals of the mineral were discovered in North Carolina, but the supply of this 'hiddenite' variety was soon exhausted and the specimens became almost at once museum specimens or collectors' treasures rather than commercial gemstones. The real breakthrough into popular recognition came in 1902 when clear, lilac-pink crystals, up to 1000 g in weight, were found near Pala in San Diego County, California. This was named kunzite after the well-known gemmologist, G. F. Kunz, who first described it, while hiddenite was named after W. E. Hidden, its discoverer.

Other varieties of gem-quality spodumene, mercifully unnamed, are known. A clear yellow type, for instance, is not uncommon, while colourless and pale blue types have also been described.

The mineral spodumene is a lithium aluminium silicate closely analogous to the sodium aluminium silicate which is jadeite, the more precious form of jade. Both of these minerals are members of the famous family of minerals known as the pyroxenes. Spodumene in its common form is the only important ore of lithium, and occasionally occurs in giant crystals in pegmatite veins. One such crystal was estimated to weigh as much as 65 tons and was 42 feet in length! The crystals are monoclinic and very typical in appearance, being heavily ribbed and etched by hot acid vapours during or soon after their formation.

I have said that hiddenite had a short life, as only a single pocket of crystals was found in the occurrence in North Carolina, but paler and much larger specimens of gem-quality green spodumene have recently been recovered in Brazil, and as, like the earlier hiddenites, they owe their colour to chromium, it should be allowable to describe them by the same name.

The kunzite variety of spodumene has been found in several places in North America, and fine crystals have also been mined in Minas Gerais, Brazil, and in Madagascar. The accompanying minerals include beryl and tourmaline, which like spodumene, are typical products of pegmatite rocks.

The bluish-pink of kunzite is a lovely and distinctive colour, but is only seen at its best when the crystals are viewed in the direction of their prism-edge. Great skill is needed in their cutting, not only because of this directional need, but also on account of its very easy pinacoidal cleavage. It is fortunate that large crystals of kunzite are available, since stones of such a pale colour need to be of fair size and thickness to register.

The density of gem-quality spodumene is always near 3·18 and the refractive indices 1·660–1·675, giving a birefringence of 0·015. The hardness is 7 on Mohs's scale, or just a little lower. Kunzite is noted for its orange fluorescence under ultra-violet rays. Under X-rays an even stronger glow is seen with a strong and persistent afterglow. After such treatment the stone is seen to have changed its colour to green, but this is not permanent, being discharged by exposure to sunlight for a few hours or when heated at well below red heat. The irradiated stone if thus heated in the dark can be seen to emit an orange glow (thermo-phosphorescence). When this fades away it signifies that the kunzite has returned to its original colour.

While kunzite shows no absorption bands when examined through a hand spectroscope, hiddenite should show narrow lines in the deep red signifying the presence of chromium. Ordinary yellow spodumene owes its colour to iron and reveals its close kinship with its fellow pyroxene, jadeite, by showing a narrow band in the violet at 4370 Å, with a weaker band at 4350, a little further into the violet. This can be quite useful for identification.

There are quite a number of pale pink gemstones and it is by no means easy even for an expert to distinguish them from one another by sight. Thus in hoping to recognise a kunzite we have to consider pink beryl, pink topaz, pink tourmaline and pale amethyst amongst the natural stones, as well as synthetic pink spinel and paste. Here is a good opportunity to exercise a keen colour-sense, but of course one should first be familiar with the appearance of all these stones. For the gemmologist a test on the refractometer provides a quick and certain answer. For the interested amateur the extent of doubling of the back facets as seen with a lens may be distinctly helpful. Of the above only tourmaline will show so distinct a doubling, and tourmaline most commonly contains characteristic inclusions of its own.

As with all the gems described in this chapter the spodumene varieties are not suited for hard wear, and their easy cleavage renders them very vulnerable to damage by some accidental knock or jar. But they provide large, clear gemstones with a difference at not too great a cost, and for this we should be grateful.

CHAPTER TWENTY

——— ⟨⟩ ———

THE JADE MINERALS

JADE, IN ITS finest and most colourful qualities, is, despite its lack of transparency, one of the most valuable of precious stones at the present time. But our taste for what might be termed its 'prettiness' must seem trivial and superficial to students of the Chinese, Aztec and Maori cultures, as to these peoples jade meant so infinitely much more than it can to us today. Wherever in the world jade stones have occurred they have been gathered and worked with inexhaustible patience into useful and ornamental and symbolic forms. The Eskimos of the Arctic, the Maoris of New Zealand, the Aztecs of Mexico, the tribes of the Indus valley, and above all the Chinese; all have prized jade beyond any other stone.

Jade calls for deeper and more contemplative appreciation than do the gems that shine and glitter. Texture, translucency, patterning of colour, and the 'feel' of the polished pebble, all play their part. And for once, curiously enough, the Latins and the Greeks seem to have had no knowledge of this delectable material. The name jade was derived from the description *piedra de hijada,* that is 'stone of the flank or loins' given to it by a Spanish physician named Monardes in the sixteenth century. This was based on a superstition that the stone had a curative value for kidney troubles.

Any detailed account of jade is complicated by the fact that the name has been used, and will continue to be used, for two distinct minerals. How this came about is a long story, impossible to condense into a few words, and as most readers will be more interested in an account of the jade minerals themselves than in the tangled history of confusion in their naming, I will confine myself to the facts as we now know them.

Let it briefly be said that under the general term of 'jade' come two quite different minerals, nephrite and jadeite. Nephrite belongs to the amphibole group while jadeite is a member of what might be termed a rival rock-forming group called the pyroxenes, a family which includes the mineral spodumene, described in the last chapter. Both types of jade form rock-like masses of tiny interlocking crystals which make them extremely tough and ideally suited for making tools and weapons. Its only competitors in this field for Neolithic man were flint and the volcanic glass, obsidian. These would more easily produce sharp-edged axes, knives and arrow-heads, but such edges were brittle, whereas the polished axe-head of jade would endure for generations. And whereas flint and obsidian were prized only for their usefulness which ceased with the coming of iron, the appearance, the feel, the sound when struck, the colour and texture of jade lifted it at least for the Chinese far beyond utilitarian levels to become the most desired and honoured of all materials.

Of the jade-loving peoples, the Polynesians and the Eskimos worked in nephrite, the Aztecs mainly in jadeite, the Chinese in both. Each mineral served the needs of these peoples equally well: only to our pernickety scientific minds does it seem important to separate them into their different species.

Jadeite

I will deal with jadeite first as this is really the only form of jade which ranks as a stone suitable for use in jewellery. Jadeite was not recognised as a separate mineral species until 1863, when the French chemist Damour analysed various specimens of jade recently imported from China and found them to consist of two quite distinct minerals. Since nephrite was by then already firmly entrenched as 'jade', Damour coined the name jadeite for his newly established mineral. While the colours of nephrite tend to be quiet and sombre, those of jadeite are often clear and bright. In the shades of green for which both are famous, those of nephrite are due to iron and could in the main be described as spinach- or leaf-green; those of jadeite are due to chromium and range from what is popularly meant by jade-green to the brightest emerald-green.

The colours of jadeite jade are in fact many and varied, and samples in the form of oval *cabochons* showing a range of these colours, which can be obtained in Burma, are amongst the most attractive things a collector can desire. The cost of these is not prohibitive—say £20 for half a dozen stones weighing several carats apiece. Stones of the finest green are obviously not represented, as the inclusion of just one of these would send the price soaring into three figures.

Colours can be said to range from pure white to black. Typical shades are lavender, bright orange, brownish-red, pale greens which are fairly uniform over the area of the stone, and bright greens which are seen as patches or veins on a white background. Though never transparent, jadeite is often highly translucent. Polished surfaces have a delightful lustre and an attractive dimpled finish, owing to the uneven hardness of the grains. Sometimes the outlines of individual crystals can be clearly seen; in other cases the texture is finer and the stone appears to be homogeneous. A coarse-textured jadeite of a very saturated green colour is sometimes used in jewellery. This has less than the usual charm of Burma jade, though almost certainly comes from there. It has been called 'Yunnan' jade, which, if misleading as to locality, is a convenient label.

The composition of jadeite is fairly simple: it is a silicate of sodium and aluminium—closely analogous to spodumene, the silicate of lithium and aluminium described in the last chapter. The density is fairly constant between 3·30 and 3·35, the usual value of 3·33 almost exactly matching the density of that useful liquid, methylene iodide. The refractive indices of the individual grains are about 1·654 and 1·667, but in the massive microcrystalline form in which we meet it one can only hope to see a vague edge on the refractometer at about 1·66. The hardness is nearly 7 on Mohs's scale, and it has a low melting point.

An accurate determination of the density is the most generally useful non-destructive method for separating jadeite from nephrite and for discriminating between these and the many jade-like minerals which I shall have to mention below. An S.G. test can be quite awkward to carry out when large and elaborate carvings are concerned: in the Hatton Garden Laboratory we used spring balances of different strengths and a bucket, or sometimes a small dustbin, filled with water in which to immerse the specimen. With jadeite mounted in jewellery this test of course could not be applied, and we made great use of the spectroscope. With green jadeite narrow absorption bands due to chromium could be seen in the red, and with paler specimens a strong narrow band in the violet at 4370 Å was found to be completely diagnostic. We discovered this band early in 1935 and have found it enormously valuable as a test. It is a pity that nephrite jade has nothing so distinctive in its spectrum.

There is only one source for jadeite of gem quality, and this is in upper Burma. Though jadeite is often known as 'Chinese jade' (as distinct from 'New Zealand jade' meaning nephrite) no source for jadeite lies within the Chinese territories. This form of jade, indeed, was unknown in China before the eighteenth century, and all the early carvings made use of nephrite from eastern Turkistan. The important date is 1769 when a written agreement put an end to the prolonged wars between China and the fierce Kachin tribe who controlled the jadeite terrain.

This is in the neighbourhood of Mogaung in the Kachin hills, and is either quarried from jadeite-albite dikes or collected as water-worn boulders from the banks or bed of the Uru river, which is a tributary of the Irrawaddy. The most important quarry is at Tawmaw, a village perched 1600 feet above the river and six miles west of Sanka. The Tawmaw dike, which is some 20 feet thick, extends for several miles.

The rock is extremely tough, and was formerly quarried by lighting fires against the rock face. The rapid cooling in the cold night air caused the rock to crack in all directions making it possible to break it up further into pieces of manageable size. This treatment tended to lower the quality of the material and has been superseded by modern drilling and blasting techniques.

The jade recovered from the river beds or banks is of better quality but the yield of this material is relatively small. The boulders were originally part of a conglomerate and some of them may weigh as much as 10 tons.

The jade blocks are taken down to Mogaung and sent from there to Mandalay and Rangoon and thence to Hong Kong, Canton and other Chinese centres. An earlier route was by land through Yunnan province into China: hence the term 'Yunnan jade', though none actually is found in that province. The rough jade is sold by auction; each block having a small polished area 'mawed' on its side to give the purchaser some idea of its colour and quality—though what other parts of the block may reveal makes the transaction almost as much a matter of luck as of judgement. In the traditional Chinese auction bidding is secret. The auctioneer wears a long robe with wide sleeves and bids are made by grasping his hand in a special way. When a sufficiently high bid is made the auctioneer, whose memory never fails, announces the name of the buyer. When a much-fancied block of jade is for sale there may be a good deal of excited milling around by merchants each trying to get in first with their bid.

Penetration to the jade-bearing districts of upper Burma has always been difficult for the European. The country is mountainous and heavily forested, inhabited by tigers and infested by insects. But ten years ago a political decision by the Burmese Government whereby all Chinese owners of jade mines were outlawed led to disturbed conditions, abandoned mines, and outbreaks of banditry, which made any visit to the Mogaung area doubly hazardous.

In addition to the Chinese, with whom the use and appreciation of jade will always be most closely associated, the Aztecs, who were rulers of Mexico from the fourteenth to the sixteenth century, were another race who prized jade very highly, though their temperament and attitude was far less sensitive and contemplative than the Chinese, and their admiration stemmed more from its possible warlike and ritual uses than from a sensual and mystical appreciation of its quality and beauty. The Aztec name for the stone was *chalchihuitl*, and this was predominantly jadeite jade, often exhibiting bright emerald-green colours. Whence came their supplies of this material is still a mystery. The American mineralogist, W. F. Foshag, who concerned himself with this question, did succeed in finding jadeite, accompanied as usual by albite feldspar, in serpentine rocks near Manzanal in Guatemala, but there seems no proof that this was the origin of the stone so prized by the Aztecs.

A similar mystery exists in a number of jade axe-heads found in the British Isles, which Dr. W. Campbell-Smith investigated and found to be nearly all jadeite (though not of the quality found in Burma) in spite of the fact that no European source for the material is precisely known. This research involved much borrowing of specimens from museum and other collections in order to ensure that their nature had been correctly assessed. Traditionally, the mineralogist would resort to the examination of small fragments or thin sections under the microscope, or some form of chemical or X-ray analysis—all of which methods are to some extent destructive and thus naturally frowned upon by many curators. It was pleasing to find when examining some of these axe-heads in our laboratory that the diagnostic absorption line of jadeite at 4370 Å was clearly visible (when the artefact was examined through the spectroscope) by reflected light, and that by this rapid and non-destructive technique the mineral could be identified with certainty in a matter of seconds.

NEPHRITE

Nephrite, the amphibole variety of jade, was given its present name by Werner in 1780 by translation from its Latin equivalent, *lapis nephriticus,* which had prevailed since early in the previous century. This and the name jade itself are derived from the curious superstition that considered the stone when worn as an amulet to have a curative effect on kidney troubles. Nephrite is a silicate of calcium and magnesium containing some iron, to which the colour is due: it belongs to that tremolite-actinolite series. The texture is more 'felted' then jadeite, as the tiny crystals are longer. This makes the material very tough with a splintery fracture. Minerals of the amphibole group do, in fact, tend to crystallise in long blades or needles. An extreme case is that of asbestos, in which each long thread consists of a single crystal. The individual crystals in nephrite are monoclinic and have pronounced cleavages intersecting at 120° which can be seen and measured when a thin section is examined under the microscope. The crystals in jadeite are also monoclinic, but their cleavage planes intersect nearly at right angles (93° to be precise). These facts are mentioned because they provide positive methods of identification should other more convenient methods fail, and are the classic methods used by mineralogists.

The density of nephrite varies more than that of jadeite, the extreme range being 2·90 to 3·03. The higher values belong to dark green types, the S.G. of paler varieties being commonly near 2·95. The refractive indices are also lower than for jadeite, refractometer readings being near 1·61. The hardness is disconcertingly variable. Reputedly it ranks as $6\frac{1}{2}$ on Mohs's scale, but sometimes pieces yield to the point of a needle, placing them below 6 on the scale. Unfortunately nephrite has no distinctive spectrum, the most one can hope to see is a vague line between the green and the blue, and some indistinct chromium lines in the red in the brighter green pieces. Though a dull leaf-green is perhaps its most characteristic colour, nephrite that is free from iron (that is, almost pure tremolite) can be almost white and translucent. This, with its greasy lustre is aptly named 'mutton-fat' jade: it is probably the most highly valued of all the nephrite varieties.

Nephrite is far more widely spread than jadeite. The early Chinese sources lay beyond their western borders in Sinkiang, East Turkistan, and the Kuen-Lun mountains, and the recovery of the prized mineral from river bed and rockface, together with the vast and difficult journey of 1800 miles to Peking, was a heroic enterprise. The discovery of boulders of nephrite in rivers near the south-west end of Lake Baikal in Siberia, which was made in 1850, provided a more accessible source, but by that time jadeite from Burma, with its brighter colours, had won favour with the Chinese carvers.

Another well-known home of nephrite is New Zealand, where the Maoris have used it extensively in fashioning weapons, axes and adzes, as well as the curiously contorted and flattened carvings of the human figure known as *hei-tiki*. Amongst the Polynesian peoples the search for jade was a stimulus for exploration, much as the search for gold or diamonds has been for more 'civilized' men. To the Maori the name for nephrite was *pounamu* (which means greenstone) and this was collected from the west side of South Island in the form of pebbles and boulders in the rivers of Westland, and has been found *in situ* in parts of the southern Alps and in D'Urville Island, where it occurs in serpentine. In earlier days the Maoris spent an enormous amount of time and labour in fashioning and polishing their greenstone implements, most particularly the short war-club called the *mere,* which was handed down from generation to generation. The New Zealand nephrite is now never carved by the native peoples, but copies of the traditional *hei-tiki* neck ornaments are fashioned in Idar-Oberstein in thousands, for sale to visitors to New Zealand.

The largest deposits of nephrite available at the present time are probably those in North America, at Jade Mountain in Alaska and in the basins of the rivers Noatak and Kobuk, from British Columbia, Wyoming, California and Monterey. There are also deposits in Rhodesia and Taiwan. The only important European source for the mineral is at Jordansmühl in Silesia (now part of Poland) on the southern slope of the Steinberg, and there is proof that the deposits have been used in prehistoric times in the discovery of artifacts of undoubted Jordansmühl jade among the old lake dwellings of Lake Constance and as far west as Holland.

The main country rock at Jordansmühl is a grey-green serpentine, and it is on the borders of this that seams and great boulders of nephrite have been found. One mass weighing 5000 pounds was bought by G. F. Kunz in 1899 and shipped to the U.S.A. A feature of jade from this locality is the variation in colour from ivory-white to deep green: the white pieces with green translucent veins are most attractive. Along with the nephrite is found gem-quality apple-green chrysoprase.

A word as to the working of jade. In general it is true to say that in the higher manual arts tools of simple but effective design tend to persist in the face of modern mechanical inventions. Thus the very primitive-looking tools used by the Chinese craftsman of today probably differ very little from those used by his ancestors. There is a quality of patience in the Oriental which is quite foreign to our Western nature, and that certainly is needed, for instance, where blocks of jade are sawn by a wire charged with emery mounted across a large bow drawn by two operators with a small boy in the middle to replenish the cut with emery and water. In fashioning snuff bottles and small vases a drilling stick charged with abrasive is rotated by means of a bow-drill, and it is noteworthy that work on the inside surface is completed before work on the outside shape is begun. In work involving perforated patterns diamond drills are used to make the initial incisions, marking the corners of pieces to be removed. Into these holes the wire of a bow-saw is inserted, and the jade is sawn across from one hole to the next.

Wheels for polishing are made of strips of ox-hide rolled tightly into flat cylinders, and fine ruby dust is sometimes used as the polishing powder.

An astonishing feature in the craftsman's skill is his visual imagination, which enables him to foresee his final design after prolonged study of the block of jade to be worked, noting any spots of colour he wishes to exploit. No sketches are made and, apparently, no mistakes, and perfect symmetry and balance are maintained.

When it comes to jade identification we are faced with a wide range of possible substitutes, most of them consisting of natural microcrystalline minerals. Many of these resemble the true jades sufficiently closely to have been named 'jade' with some sort of qualification. It needed some vigilance and resolution on the part of gemmologists not to allow these to creep under the jade 'umbrella'.

One such stone is a massive form of hydrogrossular garnet; first found at Buffelsfontein in the Transvaal as a pale to medium green stone with black spots, it takes an excellent polish and is enough like jadeite to make the misnomer 'Transvaal jade' inevitable. This material has also been found in pink and grey forms. Its hardness is $6\frac{1}{2}$, density $3 \cdot 5$ with a certain amount of variation, and refractive index $1 \cdot 73$. Fortunately for the gemmologist this form of garnet shows a distinctive orange glow under X-rays. We don't yet know the cause, but are grateful for the fact.

Another jade-like material is massive idocrase to which the name 'californite' has been applied. Its constants are very similar to those of the hydrogrossular just mentioned, but it does show a helpful feature in the form of a powerful absorption band in the blue at 4610 Å and a weaker one at 5300 in the green. Both in composition and in structure idocrase and grossular are extremely similar, and nature, when in one of her cussed moods, sometimes mixes the two together in varying proportions. Material of this kind has been found in Pakistan, and looks extremely jade-like, especially a variety with bright green patches on a white background. The apple-green variety of serpentine known as bowenite, which at $5\frac{1}{2}$ is harder than most serpentines, has recently been used perhaps more than any other stone for misnamed 'new jade' or 'Korea jade' carvings from Hong Kong, and is a very attractive mineral in its own right, though a good deal softer than either of the two jades, and with a density of 2·6. The naming of bowenite is rather ironic since G. T. Bowen, the mineralogist thus immortalised, though he was indeed the first to describe it, mistakenly identified it as nephrite!

There are at least a dozen more types of greenstone which have been, or might be, mistaken for jade, but the list would only serve to confuse the reader. An adequate list and the properties of each stone will be found in my book *Gem Testing* or in Webster's *Gems*.

To determine the nature of each of these when they appear as ornamental eggs, snuff bottles, vases, goddesses or Buddhas can pose quite a problem even for the experienced gemmologist. A density determination and a discreet hardness test may provide the answer, but very often one must resort to X-ray crystal analysis on a tiny scraping of powder from the specimen. Jadeite itself, the only jade likely to be found in jewellery, is usually recognisable at sight by its dimpled surface and characteristic colouring, while the absorption band in the violet when seen provides proof positive. But there remains the further snag that in recent times many apparently finely coloured jadeite pieces owe their colour to staining. In the case of green jade the faked stones may be suspected when they show a pink colour through the Chelsea filter, whereas true green jade remains green through the filter. The spectroscope is more specific in the hands of an expert, who can see that the customary chromium lines have been masked and a 'foreign' absorption band in the orange introduced by the dyestuff used. Under magnification the introduced colour can be seen to follow interstices in the body of the stone. Lavender-coloured jade has also been 'improved' by staining, and this is difficult to detect. Stained jadeite fades in sunlight and the deliberate preparation and sale of such material is indefensible.

It should perhaps be mentioned that a dark, iron-rich form of jadeite known as chloromelanite has been claimed as a separate form of true jade by some authorities and allowed to shelter under the prestige-conferring jade 'umbrella'. In more than forty-five years of experience in our Hatton Garden Laboratory no example of this material was submitted for test. It can thus be safely ignored except by specialists.

Another stone connected with jadeite should really be classed as an ornamental rock. This is a bright green material mottled with very dark spots and streaks and is known in Burma, after its locality, as 'maw-sit-sit'. This has been thoroughly investigated by Dr. E. Gübelin and found to be albite feldspar impregnated with a very chrome-rich form of jadeite. 'Jade-albite' has been suggested as a name for this decorative rock. The average density was found to be 2·77 and refractive index readings varied between 1·52 and 1·54—essentially a feldspar reading.

In Chapter 17 I suggested that the quartz minerals were sufficiently varied to repay a lifetime's study, and being obtainable at reasonable prices would form a good field for a collector. I might make a similar suggestion with regard to jade and the numerous jade-like minerals. For the amateur lapidary, in particular, this would offer wonderful scope, since he could cut and polish his own pieces and thus take an added pride in his collection.

—————— ◈ ——————

CHAPTER TWENTY-ONE

TURQUOISE, LAPIS LAZULI AND THE FELDSPARS

TURQUOISE

BECAUSE THEIR attraction lies primarily in their colour it is not surprising that both turquoise and lapis lazuli were amongst the earliest materials to be prized as gems.

It may seem superfluous to describe the colour of turquoise since 'turquoise-blue' is a recognised descriptive name for a pale and slightly greenish-blue. At its best it is sky-blue: the colour of a hedge-sparrow's egg; the greenish tint which in some cases can be very pronounced, is far less desirable. It is almost opaque, its lustre tends to be waxy so that colour and a fair degree of hardness are all that can commend it. Undoubtedly it looks well with gold, and for those who like it, it provides a colour hardly met with in any other gem. But to the gemmologist who is frequently asked to give his verdict on turquoise in jewellery this is emphatically *not* a favourite stone, for reasons which will transpire later.

The name turquoise is supposedly derived from Turkey from whence it was exported, though the ancient sources were in Persia and Egypt. This is borne out by the name 'Turkey stone' applied to the mineral in the seventeenth century.

In composition turquoise is a hydrous phosphate of aluminium and copper, usually with some ferric iron to which the green shades are due.

In past centuries the main source for turquoise was Persia, in mines near Nishapur in the province of Khorassan, where the mineral is found in veins and pockets in porphyritic volcanic rocks which penetrate sedimentary strata such as sandstones, limestones and clay-slates. These are interbedded with thick deposits of gypsum and rock salt. The turquoise is mined from the southern slopes of Ali-Mirsai, a peak in a chain of mountains. There the village of Maaden is perched at 5100 feet above sea level in a valley which penetrates the mountainside. All the turquoise mines, present and past, are concentrated in this area, and all the inhabitants of the village earn their living in mining, polishing and selling the mineral.

The brecciated trachyte (which is a fine-grained basic rock) is found in blocks cemented together with veins of the iron oxide mineral, limonite, and turquoise in turn is often deposited on this limonite in the veins or mingled with it. The turquoise layers are commonly not more than a quarter of an inch thick, and never more than half an inch, so that this, the best source for fine turquoise, can only produce small stones, and these often marked by thin dark lines of limonite. Where there is much limonite, the stone is sold as 'turquoise matrix'.

Another ancient locality for turquoise which was exploited 5000 years ago by the Egyptians, lost, and then rediscovered in the nineteenth century, is in the Sinai peninsula not far from its west coast in the neighbourhood of Serbâl. Some turquoise is found in veins in the sandstone of the Meghara valley and some in porphyry outside the valley. The exact locality of the best-quality stones having the deepest and most permanent colour is kept secret by the Bedouins who market the precious mineral.

Other ancient mines existed in the New World, and some of those in Mexico were in use long before the Spanish conquests, the Aztecs valuing turquoise as highly as they valued gold. The same addiction to the mineral seems to be shared by the Pueblo and other Indian tribes surviving in turquoise country. The mines in the states of New Mexico, Arizona and Nevada are too numerous to describe in detail. Turquoise in North America is available in much larger pieces than it is in the Persian and Egyptian localities, but it is also softer, more porous and of poorer colour. The formation of the turquoise often seems to stem from the kaolin or china-clay remains of decomposed feldspars, in reaction with the calcium phosphate mineral, apatite.

The only spot where turquoise crystals have been found is at Lynch in Virginia: these were triclinic in symmetry. Normally turquoise is so compactly cryptocrystalline that there are no signs that it is anything but amorphous. The density of the small compact stones from the old mines in Persia and Egypt is remarkably constant for an aggregate, lying between 2·78 and 2·81: the hardness a little under 6. Under the microscope a rather characteristic structure is seen of white speckles and shreds against a uniform blue background. Occasionally neat little discs of darker blue are noticeable at the surface of the stones.

The American turquoise which comes in larger pieces and often free from matrix has a lower density ranging usually from 2·65 to 2·75. It is also porous to varying extents, and is almost always waxed on the surface of the polished *cabochons* to improve the finish and darken the colour somewhat. The practice is so universal that it is generally accepted as legitimate. But here is where the trouble begins for the trade and for the gemmologist. For with the paler and more porous types of turquoise which are virtually unsaleable as mined, it was found possible to impregnate them thoroughly with wax, or more effectively with plastic, and thus, starting with rubbish, make a saleable product available at a low price, while still being able to claim the stone as turquoise. In none of these processes was there any need to *dye* the material—the 'wetting' action of the impregnating wax or plastic automatically deepens the colour, just as does the action of rain on dry dust, or the sea on dry sand. The difficulty of detecting such malpractices (at least they are malpractices if undeclared) and of legislating against them, can be imagined. One has to admit that the plastic-impregnated turquoise is deeper in colour than the untreated American specimens, and that the colour will probably be permanent. But 'doctored' material clearly should not be sold on the same basis as the natural mineral. These extreme practices are fairly new, but we have for years seen all sorts of so-called 'synthetic' turquoise on the market under various names, most of it purely artificial, and to have these further problems with a stone that does not in any case lend itself to easy testing constitutes a real nuisance, and certainly the prestige of turquoise as a gemstone is lowered by having so many substitutes and fakes to contend with.

The latest blow comes from the house of Gilson, who have produced a 'synthetic turquoise' claimed, with some justification, to be indistinguishable from the natural mineral.

How can we attempt to cope with all these fakes and semi-fakes? Where the stone is, or can be obtained, free from its setting a density determination gives some valuable help: a value below 2·6 on the stone is hardly acceptable for true turquoise. When the turquoise has been plastic-bonded a careful trial with a penknife will show a tendency to peel rather than powder, and heating a fragment in a small glass tube will yield a typical odour, and an oily distillate will condense on the cooler part of the tube. Heavy waxing is also revealed by scraping, and a heated needle applied to the surface will melt the wax. An absorption band characteristic of turquoise, which was discovered in our laboratory in 1940, has also proved very helpful. The band is at 4320 Å in the violet and can be seen by practised eyes through a prism spectroscope in reflected light, especially if this has been filtered through a flask containing copper sulphate solution. A broader, weaker band is also visible in the blue at 4600 Å. If these bands are seen they at least provide a proof that turquoise is present: but if they are *clearly* seen, this is a sign of impregnation, as this process makes the bands appear at greater strength. The refractometer gives a vague reading near 1·62 with true turquoise: anything very different from this is a sign of some imitation such as glass, porcelain or made-up powder. R. Webster has found that all made-up imitation turquoise responds to a test with a drop of hydrochloric acid placed on the back of the specimen. In imitations this turns yellow and gives a yellow stain on white filter paper applied to the spot. No such effect is seen with true turquoise.

With the Gilson 'synthetic' turquoise the density is around 2·74, which is a plausible value, but the absorption band at 4320 Å could not be seen, and Webster observed under the microscope a surface structure of small angular blue grains against a whitish background, which was not like anything seen in natural turquoise.

The above is only a rough outline of the problems involved, but enough has, I think, been said to convince the reader that testing turquoise for authenticity is yet another matter for the expert, and one that the expert himself does not greatly relish.

Nothing has yet been said about the natural minerals which might be confused with turquoise. There are not in fact many of these. There is a so-called 'bone-turquoise' or odontolite, which is a fossil ivory, tooth or bone, which has become blue owing to the presence of the iron phosphate mineral, vivianite. This has a higher density than turquoise (3·00–3·25). Under a lens a striped appearance is visible, which gives a clue as to its organic origin. Also there is always about 10 per cent calcium carbonate present, so that a drop of dilute hydrochloric acid placed on the surface will effervesce briskly. As this will leave a dull spot on the polished surface a less harmful method of applying the test is to scrape a little powder from the edge on to a microscope slide and apply the acid to this.

That the fossil teeth of the mastodon and other extinct mammals, conveniently stained blue by nature, should be of common enough occurrence to be mined for profit, seems an unlikely story, but is in fact true. Deposits of these teeth and bones are, or were, especially abundant in the Miocene beds near Auch, and other places in the south of France. When the odontolite is first taken out of the ground it has a dull blue-grey colour, but after heating this becomes a fine turquoise-blue. The hardness is a little less than that of turquoise, but it takes a good polish.

The mineral most closely resembling turquoise is, perhaps, variscite, a hydrous phosphate of aluminium, but its colour is always green and thus it does not compete with turquoise of good quality. The greenish-blue translucent form of feldspar known as 'amazon stone' also bears a certain resemblance to turquoise, but its density and refractive index are lower, and it has a characteristic sheen of its own. More will be said of this mineral later in the chapter.

Lapis Lazuli

For some 5000 years lapis lazuli has been used and treasured for its intense deep blue colour. The colour of the stone is so strong that in pieces of any size it is apt to be almost overpowering unless streaked with the white of calcite which it normally contains, or sprinkled with the golden spangles of iron pyrites. The stone has little else than its colour to commend it, being opaque and not very hard. It lies in fact on the borderline between the stones used mainly in jewellery and those used solely for ornamental purposes, such as mosaics and inlays, vases and carvings. The name lapis lazuli simply means 'blue stone', the word lazuli being derived from an old Arabic word for blue, from which the French *azur* also stems. From the description given by Pliny and other writers in classic times it is certain that the Latin *sapphirus* referred, not to corundum, but to lapis lazuli. He refers to this blue stone being 'refulgent with spots like gold', meaning clearly the little brassy speckles of pyrites which, in practice, still serve as a useful sign of its authenticity. Sapphire continued to denote lapis right up to medieval times, which is hardly surprising since until then all knowledge was derived from the authority of ancient writings.

Lapis differs from other gemstones in being not a single mineral but a mixture of a number of minerals, that is, a rock. The nearest it comes to being homogeneous is when it consists of a blend of the so-called felspathoid minerals, sodalite, hauynite, lazurite, etc., which are formed when sodium, aluminium and calcium get together with not enough silica to form a feldspar. These minerals are all cubic and form an isomorphous series, which explains why on occasion dodecahedral crystals of lapis lazuli are found for all the world as though it were a single substance. Such purity and restraint are most unusual. In the material mined and handled as a gem several minerals other than the blue constituents are normally present—calcite, diopside and iron pyrites being the chief.

This you would expect from the manner in which the material is formed in nature—by the baking action of a white-hot granite intrusion in beds of impure limestone containing sodium and, most importantly, sulphur. We know the blue colour depends upon sulphur because of extensive experiments carried out by Gmelin and others aimed at making artificially the pigment ultramarine. This intense blue colouring matter was greatly esteemed by artists as providing them with a blue which was otherwise unobtainable and which had proved itself permanent. Hitherto fine samples of lapis lazuli had been the only source, and this was extremely expensive. The mineral was crushed and powdered and sifted and purified, often by the artist himself.

Gmelin's work largely put an end to this. Analysis had shown the stone to consist mainly of silica, alumina, lime (calcium), soda and sulphur, and after many experiments a process was perfected of producing ultramarine on a commercial scale quite cheaply by heating a mixture of clay, sodium salts, charcoal and sulphur in a furnace. The artificial ultramarine was hardly inferior in colour to powdered lapis, and in 1829, a year after the process was published, sold for £12 a pound. Early in this century the price had fallen to thirty shillings a hundredweight and the production was about 10,160 tons per annum. Obviously this total was not derived from the use of the pigment by studio artists. Its uses were (and are) widespread as a 'whitener' of paper, linen, sugar, and so on, by compensating for the natural yellowish tinge of such commodities. Though ultramarine is permanent to air and light, an acid quickly bleaches the colour with the discharge of sulphuretted hydrogen, giving the rotten-egg odour which earned for chemistry the name of 'stinks'. The particular constitution which enables sulphur to produce the intense colour is not properly understood, but by analogy with sulphur in blue glasses, it may be due to the S_2 molecule itself.

The finest lapis lazuli has always come from extremely ancient mines in Badakshan in north-east Afghanistan. The mines are in the upper reaches of the Koksha river which is a tributary of the fabled Oxus. It was in this general region, incidentally, that the earliest rubies and red spinels were recovered. Marco Polo visited these mines in 1271 in the course of his famous travels of which, fortunately for us, he left so good

1. **The 'Big Hole' at Kimberley.** Kimberley Mine as it is to-day: a typical
diamond pipe. Discovered in 1871 and finally abandoned in 1914, having
reached a depth of 3,600 feet. Total production amounted to 14 million carats
of diamond, valued at 47 million pounds. The surface area of the mine is 38
acres. *See page* 39.

2a. Underground working at Premier Diamond Mine. By drilling and controlled blasting, tunnels are driven across the mine. The ore scraped from the tunnels is loaded into trucks, which run to a crushing plant and thence to the main shaft to be raised to the surface. *See page* 40.

2b. Grease tables at the Premier Mine. Heavy concentrates from the crushed rock are finally washed over inclined tables coated with thick grease, to which only the diamonds adhere. *See page* 41.

3. Removing the overburden covering diamondiferous gravels on coast of South West Africa. Rotary bucket excavators remove 660 tons of sand per hour, which is conveyed to disposal areas. After clearing the sand, mining of the diamondiferous gravels can begin. *See page* 42.

4. Rough diamonds with blue ground. A jumble of rough diamonds of good industrial quality on which a few large gem quality crystals and pieces of blue ground have been placed. The bright, slightly greasy lustre of the rough diamonds is well shown. *See page* 124.

5a. **Cleaving a diamond crystal.** After careful inspection a small nick is made in the stone by another diamond at the appropriate point. The crystal is then cemented in a holder known as a 'dop', and a sharp blow given to the heavy steel cleaving knife the blade of which has been placed in the nick. *See page* 60.

5b. **Sawing a diamond crystal.** The phosphor-bronze sawing disc is charged at its slightly thickened edge with a paste of diamond-dust in olive oil. It rotates vertically at about 5500 revolutions per minute. An octahedron is usually sawn into two equal parts. It may take a working day to saw through a 1 carat crystal. *See page* 65.

6a. **Grinding a diamond into shape.** The stone to be shaped is mounted on a lathe, and another diamond, mounted on a long holder, held under the operator's arm, is pressed against it as it rotates. The final result is a peg-top shape having a frosted finish. *See page* 62.

6b. **Polishing facets to form a brilliant.** Three diamonds, held in mechanical dops, are here being polished facet by facet on a horizontal cast-iron scaife charged with diamond dust and rotating at 2000 to 2500 revolutions per minute. *See page* 62.

7a. **Inspecting brilliant during polishing operation.** Frequent inspection of each diamond is necessary during the polishing operation to ensure that the facets are true and evenly disposed. *See page* 63.

7b. **Models showing stages in cutting a brilliant.** This shows how a diamond octahedron is first sawn into two parts, each of which is ground into a peg-top shape, and the table and other main facets ground and polished in series until the completed brilliant has been fashioned. *See pages* 61–63.

8. Sorting diamond crystals in London Offices of De Beers. In the offices of the Central Selling Organisation in London, diamond crystals undergo their final sorting for size, shape, quality and colour in preparation for the monthly 'sights'. *See page* 130.

9. **Cleavage rhomb of calcite, showing strong double refraction.** This large clear cleavage rhombohedron of the 'Iceland Spar' variety of calcite from the British Museum (Natural History) collection shows clearly the effect of its strong double refraction. The two grey images of the printed name are each due to one of the polarised rays. Where the images overlap the full blackness of the print is revealed. A double image of the back edge of the block can also be seen on the left-hand side of the picture. Each face of the rhombohedron is a cleavage plane. So perfect are the three directions of cleavage in calcite that when fragments of a specimen which has been smashed with a hammer are examined, each will be found to consist of a cleavage rhombohedron. *See pages* 80 *and* 102.

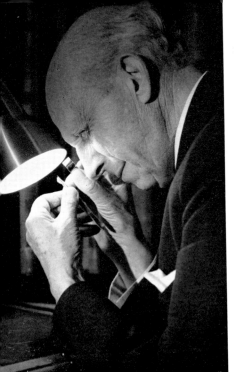

10a. **Author examining a gemstone with a 10 × lens.** It is worth noting the position of the light and the lens in relation to the stone, also the contact of the hands which serves to keep the stone steadily in focus. *See page* 100.

10b. **Diamond balance arranged for hydrostatic weighing.** Here two boxes (taller than the normal match box) loaded with tin-tacks for steadiness support a bridge made of a rectangle of plate-glass, on which stands a beaker of distilled water. A wire coil containing the stone is suspended from a hook at the top of the balance pan. *See page* 115.

11a. X-ray photograph of zircon and diamond rings. This was one of the actual photographs prepared by the author to serve as explanatory evidence in the Rex v. Rice case (see page 142). Five of the rings are set with white zircons which are opaque to the rays. In two cases a 'hole' where there is a stone missing can be seen. In the claw-set ring there was a diamond, so transparent to the X-rays as to be invisible.

11b. Octahedral face of diamond crystal showing 'trigons'. Every octahedral face in a diamond crystal will show the characteristic shallow triangular pits known as 'trigons', though seldom in such numbers and prominence as shown here. Note that the triangles are in reverse position to the triangle formed by the edges of the crystal face itself. *See page* 122.

12. **Group of beryl crystals.** This beryl group from Salinas, Minas Gerais, Brazil, is in the Natural History Museum. The crystals came from the wall of a pegmatite vein and are in random orientation. The hexagonal symmetry is clearly shown. Since prism faces are dominant such crystals are said to have a 'prismatic' habit. Each is terminated by a basal pinacoid with a slightly roughened (etched) surface. Small pyramid faces can also be seen at the intersections of the prisms. Cracks parallel to the base mark the presence of an imperfect basal cleavage. *See page* 172.

3a. **Group of quartz crystals.** A series of quartz crystals growing in roughly parallel orientation from the side of a mineral vein. These also are from the collection of the British Museum (Natural History). These milky crystals were chosen rather than water-clear specimens as they show more readily in a photograph the characteristic features of this ubiquitous mineral, which should enable it to be recognised by any keen collector: moreover the crystals are 'home-grown', coming from Cornwall. The hexagonal prisms are typically striated horizontally—i.e. at right angles to their length. The irregularly developed 'pyramid' faces are in fact a combination of rhombohedral forms. *See pages* 208 *and* 209.

3b. **Polished section of agate.** This specimen from Rio Grande do Sul, Brazil, shows the outline of the almond-shaped cavity or 'amygdale' which it filled. The thin layers of chalcedony have been deposited in an irregularly concentric manner, slight impurities in the silica giving rise on occasion to bands of darker colour. The centre cavity is lined with crystalline quartz. *See page* 218.

14. **Fluorspar crystal.** This cube of fluorspar, from Wheal Mary Ann, Liskeard, Cornwall, is seen from an unusual angle, perpendicular to one of its eight corners, i.e. at right angles to a potential octahedral surface. The picture has been chosen because it shows so well the cracks due to the easy octahedral cleavage and the characteristic tessellated surface of the cube, suggesting that the main cube is composed of numerous smaller units having slightly different orientations. The specimen is from the magnificent collection of British minerals bequeathed to the Natural History Museum by Sir Arthur Russell. The accessory minerals seen are calcite and galena. *See page* 275.

15a. Mining for blue zoisite in Tanzania. The photograph (kindly sent to me by Mr. Rudolf Thurm) shows the primitive methods used in the small open-cast mining of gemstones. *See page* 237.

15b. Zoisite crystals from Merelani Mine. A typical crop of zoisite crystals recovered from the mine shown in (15a). Some are nearly colourless, some reddish-brown, some a magnificent purplish-blue. The photograph (by Mr. Thurm) shows the crystals at about half their natural size. *See page* 237.

16. **Large-scale production of synthetic corundum.** The photograph shows the impressive ranks of Verneuil furnaces in the manufacturing hall of the great Djevahirdjian factory in Monthey, Switzerland.

The photograph was taken in 1954. Since then the furnaces have been enclosed to some extent, but are essentially the same. The annual output from this one factory is now 300 million carats of corundum, which is chiefly used for industrial purposes. *See page 316.*

a description. The lapis lazuli is found in pockets in a black and white limestone, beds of which lie at 1500 feet above the river, where the sides of the narrow valley rise as walls of bare rock. As well as the most prized deep blue material varieties of paler blue and of a green colour are found in these mines.

As with jade mining, the old method of breaking up the solid rock by lighting fires and quenching them with water was used; the rocks thus cracked by the sudden change in temperature were later assailed with heavy hammers, and the unwanted limestone removed. When a pocket of the lapis lazuli was encountered the rock was carefully grooved around the whole nest of material to enable it to be levered out intact with crowbars. Blocks of a hundredweight or more were often recovered in this way lying parallel to the bedding planes of the limestone. The iron pyrites, brassy spangles of which are so familiar to the gemmologist in lapis lazuli from this region, is also found in quite thick bands in the limestone from which it is mined.

The only other source for lapis of good quality is to the west of Lake Baikal in Siberia, where, true to form, the rock is found in a white granular limestone or marble along the line of contact with a granite intrusion. The deposits are found in valleys south of the village of Kultuk, and there is a good deal of variation in the colour and quality of the stone. Besides the desired dark blue variety, violet, green, and even red material is found, and there is less disseminated iron pyrites than in the lapis from Badakshan.

Lapis is also found in the Chilean Andes, again in limestone, but here the colour of the rock is far less intense and there are large white patches of calcite. The name 'Chile lapis' is, in consequence, used in the trade in a derogatory sense, as it is not of high enough quality to be used in jewellery. It so happens that it was my maternal grandfather, Frederick Field, who first analysed and identified this Chile material. He was at the time acting as analyst to a copper-mining company in Coquimbo when a load of this pale blue lapis rock was offered to the company as copper ore. Field's analysis soon showed that copper was entirely lacking in the sample, and its true nature was established.

Since the composition of lapis varies a good deal, its density is also rather variable. It is curious and rather alarming that for nearly 100 years practically every textbook gave 2·38–2·45 as the density of the stone—figures based on determinations made by the mineralogist Breithaupt on small isolated fragments of the blue constituent, which were taken up by the standard work, Dana's *System of Mineralogy*, and thereafter slavishly copied. In practice we found the density of the rock as used in jewellery to fall in almost all cases within the range 2·7–2·9 depending to a large extent on the proportion of pyrites present.

The hardness of lapis is about 6 on Mohs's scale—enough to take and retain quite a high polish on the *cabochon* forms in which the stone is cut. Lapis is too opaque to give good refractive index readings, but a vague edge at about 1·50 is usually visible.

There are hardly any minerals which can be confused with lapis lazuli (except perhaps sodalite which has a lower density and less intense colour), but it is extensively imitated in jasper stained with prussian blue. The jasper used is obtained from Nunkirchen near Idar-Oberstein in Germany, and the name used for the imitation stone is 'Swiss lapis', unless you happen to be Swiss, when with more justification the term employed is 'German lapis'. Though in its general aspect the stained jasper resembles lapis it does not stand up to scrutiny with a lens. In place of the spangles of pyrites little 'pools' of crystalline quartz are visible, moreover the dyed stone is harder and of lower density than true lapis. A more ambitious (and more expensive) representation of lapis lazuli appeared in 1954 when the firm of Degussa of Hamburg marketed a sintered synthetic spinel coloured with cobalt. This was very handsome material and could even be provided with speckles of gold to enhance the resemblance to lapis. Furthermore it made admirable seal-stones, and for that function had a vogue for a while. Distinction from lapis was easy on many counts. It was harder (8), denser (3·52), and had a higher refractive index (1·725). Moreover it appeared brilliantly red through the Chelsea filter (lapis appears brownish), and showed a very strong cobalt absorption spectrum.

One more fake to guard against is the 'improvement' of the colour of poor specimens of the natural rock by the surface application of wax and dyestuffs. This false colouring matter usually betrays its presence when a pad of cotton wool dipped in amyl acetate (nail-polish remover) is rubbed across the surface; if there is any dyestuff on the stone it will show as a blue stain on the wool.

THE FELDSPARS

In the opening chapter I stated that quartz and feldspar, the two most important minerals in that familiar rock, granite, were both potential gemstones. Quartz in all its varieties has been fully described in Chapter 17. Now it is feldspar's turn.

Feldspar is the general name for a large family of minerals, the names of which will probably be new to the reader until translated into the names of such gem varieties as moonstone, sunstone or amazon stone.

First there is orthoclase, a silicate of potassium and aluminium which can be written $K(AlSi_3O_8)$, which is the most prominent mineral in most granites with its large white or pinkish crystals. This is mono-clinic as suggested by its name, which signifies that it has two cleavages at right angles to one another. Then microcline, which has the same composition as orthoclase, but has cleavages at an angle slightly dif-ferent (microcline) from a right angle, a sign that it has slipped over into the lower symmetry of the triclinic system; and finally a closely knit group of triclinic feldspars collectively known as the plagioclases ('oblique cleavages') which range from the sodium feldspar, albite, $Na(AlSi_3O_8)$ at one end to the calcium feldspar, anorthite, $Ca(Al_2Si_2O_8)$ at the other. I won't bother the reader with further names in the plagioclase range at the moment, as I feel this would be too much.

Pure orthoclase is found as transparent crystals in the St. Gotthard region of Switzerland and is named adularia after the Adula Alps. This form of orthoclase is too insipid to be attractive as a gem material, but a variety in Madagascar containing iron is not only transparent but of fine yellow colour, and this has been cut fairly extensively, though it is admittedly more a stone for the collector than for the jeweller. This yellow orthoclase is found in quite large crystals and cut stones of 20 carats upwards, flawless and free from inclusions, are not uncommon.

However, it is not as a clear gemstone but in forms that show beauti-ful optical effects that feldspar is important. The best known of such stones is moonstone which, though colourless or faintly yellow by transmitted light shows a lovely silvery-blue sheen when viewed by reflected light. Moonstone consists of an intimate inter-growth of orthoclase and albite feldspars in thin alternating layers, and it is this structure which gives rise to the shimmering effect. When the layers are relatively thick the sheen is plain white (such as one can see in light reflected from a pile of microscope slides), but with very thin layers the reflected light has a beautiful blue glimmer. Moonstones are naturally cut in *cabochon* form or as beads to show off their particular beauty, and a moonstone necklace is almost as dainty and universally wearable as one of pearls. Ceylon is the best-known supplier of moonstones, and here they are found not only in the gem gravels in the south of the island, but are also found as crystals in pegmatites and dikes in the central province. Less known, but even more beautiful, are some of the moonstones which come from the Mogok region of upper Burma. These have a subtle play of colour almost like opal, and are treasured by collectors but too scarce to be known in commercial jewellery.

Thirty or forty years ago moonstones were in plentiful supply, but in recent years, at least in the form of necklaces, they seem to have disappeared from the market, which is a great pity.

The triclinic potash feldspar known to mineralogists as microcline has a distinctive blue-green colour, and though commonly nearly opaque can be used in jewellery in much the same way as turquoise or jade. To gemmologists it is commonly known as amazonite or amazon stone. Just why, it is difficult to say, as it is not known to come from the vicinity of the Amazon river. Amazonite is found in finely developed crystals in pegmatite rocks. There are several famous localities in the U.S.A., in particular Amelia in Virginia and in the Pike's Peak area of Colorado. It is also found in the Urals and in some districts of Brazil.

The cause of the very characteristic colour is not certain: it has much the same tint as verdigris and it has been suggested that a trace of copper may be the cause, but I have seen no mention of copper in any analysis of the mineral. Amazonite has a curious 'shredded' surface appearance, and shows a typical feldspar sheen at certain angles, due to multiple twin planes.

The physical properties of orthoclase and microcline are very similar, as one might expect. The hardness is the standard 6 on Mohs's scale, the density 2·56 and the mean refractive index 1·525, with a small double refraction of from 0·005 to 0·008.

Two other varieties of feldspar worth mentioning in the context of this book are sunstone and labradorite. Sunstone is a plagioclase feldspar (oligoclase) which contains thin crystals of the iron oxides haematite or goethite, giving a red or orange spangled effect by reflected light. Sometimes the name aventurine feldspar is used by analogy with aventurine glass and aventurine quartz. Being a plagioclase, the density is a little higher (2·64) and so are the refractive indices (1·54–1·55) than those of orthoclase.

Labradorite is another feldspar of the plagioclase series. It is best known for a type which shows areas of brilliant iridescent colours at certain angles by reflected light, while at other angles it looks grey and uninteresting. The material which shows these effects is only feebly translucent. The colours are due to interference, which is thought to be due to the fine lamellae caused by repeated twinning. Sometimes labradorite contains platelets of magnetite, which add to the effect. Labradorite is also found in a clear pale yellow form which can be cut as a rather nondescript gemstone.

Labradorite owes its name to the fact that masses of the mineral were found on the coast of Labrador near Nairn two centuries ago, and the specimens from this locality were the first to become famous. A very beautiful form of the mineral is found in Finland, and an attempt has been made to market it as something new by naming it 'spectrolite'. The density of labradorite is 2·70, and the refractive indices 1·56–1·57, thus some care is needed if one is not to confuse the transparent yellow variety with beryl of similar appearance.

Moonstone is the only one of these feldspars that has been imitated to any extent. Strongly heated amethyst has a rather similar appearance, and so has white chalcedony, but the most effective imitation seen is colourless synthetic spinel which has been strongly heated causing partial recrystallisation and a schiller effect. Examination of moonstone with a lens will often reveal attractive inclusions looking rather like an insect skeleton (if such a thing were possible). These are caused by stress cracks following cleavage directions.

Another type of white or yellowish moonstone seen in recent years has been called 'albite moonstone' and has shown a distinct cat's-eye effect, or in some cases a four-rayed star.

CHAPTER TWENTY-TWO

————— ◁◦▷ —————

SOME OTHER GEMSTONES

ALL THE MAJOR gemstones (apart from pearl and others of organic origin) have now been described, and I face the problem common to every author writing on this subject—what else to include and what to omit? Having worked for many years in Hatton Garden I know fairly well the range of stones available. This range has extended in recent years because more and more dealers try to cater for the growing demand from collectors for stones which are not in normal commercial use, and also because more unusual stones have become available. In this connection I confess to being amused to find a description of the potential gem mineral, painite, discovered in Burma in 1957, in at least three recent books on gemstones, although no cut stone of this species is known to exist. On this account, although my colleague, C. J. Payne, and I were concerned in establishing its nature, I have omitted painite from this chapter. But, with apparent inconsistency, I have included the almost equally rare gem, taaffeite, because the story of its discovery is so full of interest and of valuable lessons for the budding gemmologist.

The stones in this chapter will be treated in alphabetical order, since this is by far the most convenient for reference.

ANDALUSITE

There seems no adequate reason why andalusite should not have a small but honoured place in commercial jewellery since it has a hardness of $7\frac{1}{2}$, a pleasing if rather curious appearance, and is not any rarer, shall we say, than alexandrite chrysoberyl, which in some respects it resembles. What makes andalusite distinctive and appreciated by connoisseurs is the very strong pleochroism which causes flashes of red to appear at the ends of a properly cut specimen in striking contrast to the brownish-green of the body-colour of the stone. Both the particular shade of green and these red flashes are so distinctive that they almost in themselves serve to distinguish this species. To display the red rays to best effect the table facet of the stone must be cut at right angles to the edges of the prism. Andalusite is an aluminium silicate (Al_2SiO_5) crystallising in the orthorhombic system. Two other minerals having the same formula are fibrolite (also orthorhombic), and kyanite, which is triclinic and bright blue. All three polymorphs are occasionally cut as gemstones.

In appearance and properties andalusite is close enough to some forms of tourmaline to cause possible confusion. A collector's search for an andalusite is apt to cause a sudden emergence of tourmalines from the stock of dealers anxious to oblige. The double refraction of tourmaline, however, is twice that of andalusite, and the density distinctly lower. Normal figures for andalusite are 3·15 for the density, and 1·635–1·645 for refractive indices. There is an absorption band in the blue at 4550 Å. A bright green type of andalusite found in Brazil has a striking absorption spectrum featuring a group of lines with a sharp edge at 5535 in the green and another line at 5175 Å. This spectrum is typical of a manganese-rich type of the mineral called viridine, and must thus be ascribed to manganese, though unusual for this element.

Chiastolite or 'cross stone' is the name given to an opaque form of andalusite which shows a dark cross on a whitish background when the crystal is cut at right angles to the prism.

Andalusite has been found as one of the minerals in the Ceylon gem gravels, but most of the stones cut as gems come from the states of Minas Gerais and Esperito Santo of Brazil. The name andalusite stems from its occurrence at Almeria in Andalusia.

APATITE

Apatite takes its name from the Greek word *apate,* meaning deceit, indicating the ease with which it can be confused with crystals of beryl, calcite or quartz. As we have seen, most of the gem minerals are silicates, but apatite contains no silica, being a phosphate of calcium containing variable amounts of fluorine, chlorine and hydroxyl. These last three ions can interchange with one another in the crystal lattice causing slight variations in the properties of the mineral.

Crystals of apatite belong to the hexagonal system and are usually a well-developed combination of hexagonal prisms, pyramids and basal plane. When pure it is white, but traces of impurities give it a variety of colour, the most frequently seen being yellow, violet, blue and green. When transparent these form quite attractive gems, though too soft for general use in jewellery. The hardness of apatite is in fact the standard 5 of Mohs's scale. The density varies between 3·18 and 3·22, and the average refractive indices are 1·635–1·638, with the notably low double refraction of 0·003.

Greenish-yellow apatite, sometimes called 'asparagus stone', is found in Spain, and also comes from Durango in Mexico. Burma is a well-known source for apatites of very pleasing blue; these are strongly dichroic with, unfortunately, the extraordinary ray having the fine colour, the ordinary being yellowish. These blue Burma apatites often have fibrous inclusions giving rise to quite good cat's-eyes when cut *en cabochon*. They also have other most interesting inclusions which look for all the world like gas-bubbles as seen in glass, but are really negative crystals. Recently greenish-brown apatite cat's-eyes have been coming from Brazil, which at first sight are remarkably like the prized chryso-beryl cat's-eyes, but lack their brilliant lustre.

Apatite is one of many gemstones in which calcium is a main consti-tuent and which in consequence contain traces of rare-earth elements, which are so chemically similar to calcium that they follow it around in all its reactions in the laboratory of the rocks, and finally take their place with it in the crystal. By far the most frequent of these rare-earth elements to infiltrate in this way are neodymium and praseodymium, which are so difficult to separate that it is convenient for most purposes to treat them as a single unit and call them 'didymium', which was the name originally given them by Mosander in 1841.

Why these otherwise unimportant traces of didymium are mentioned here is that they have a characteristic and sharp line-absorption spectrum which signals to the keen gemmologist that the gem in which he has seen them is a calcium mineral, and if he has seen them in any strength that the stone concerned is apatite, since in the other gems in which they occur (danburite, sphene, scheelite) the lines are exceedingly faint.

If the reader happens to use Crookes's lenses in his spectacles to cut out glare, all he has to do is look through a small spectroscope without removing his spectacles to see these didymium lines very plainly. Sir William Crookes, the great Victorian scientist, was a pioneer in the use of the spectroscope, and it was he who, having noted that didymium in glass showed a group of absorption bands in the yellow part of the spectrum, which is the main cause of 'glare', suggested the usefulness of this glass as a filter. There is a group of lines in the yellow of which bands at 5950, 5850, 5750 Å are the strongest, and in the green at 5280, 5230 Å etc.

Blue apatite from Burma has quite a different sort of spectrum—chiefly in the pale-coloured ordinary ray, i.e. down the length of the crystal. There are two weak bands in the orange at 6288 and 6189 Å, a strong sharp band at the end of the green at 5110 Å and another at 4884 in the blue. It has been suggested that these are praseodymium bands, but they do not tally with the known spectra of that element.

Apatite is admittedly of minor significance as a gemstone, but is vitally important to life on this planet as it is the only major source of phosphate, without which no vegetation would be possible, and our bones and teeth lack the essential mineral ingredient which gives them hardness and strength.

BENITOITE

Benitoite, which at its best is a gemstone with the bright blue of sapphire and the fire of diamond, would undoubtedly be counted amongst the most attractive of gemstones were it not for the fact that relatively few and small crystals were found in its only known locality. This is in San Benito County, California, from whence comes its name.

It was at first mistaken for sapphire and, astonishingly, many stones were cut and sold as such, which points to a good deal of impercipience all round. It was a gemmologist in a jeweller's shop who first queried their identity on account of their tremendous dichroism, and Dr. G. D. Louderback of the University of California who identified it as a new mineral. This was in 1907, and benitoite is the first of the several new minerals discovered during the present century which are also gemstones.

The mineral is found as bright blue tabular trigonal crystals embedded in natrolite in veins of serpentine and copper minerals. The mine is some 4800 feet above sea level in the Diablo Range.

Benitoite is a barium titano-silicate, and thus has a chemical similarity to another rare gemstone, sphene, which is a calcium titano-silicate. The density is 3·65, the refractive indices 1·757 and 1·804, with the unusually high birefringence of 0·047, and even more surprisingly high dispersion for the two rays of 0·039 and 0·046, which puts it on a par with diamond in this respect. The stones are for the most part quite small, and a cut specimen of $1\frac{1}{2}$ carats is exceptional, while the largest of all weighed a little over 7 carats. The twin colours seen in a dichroscope are deep blue and colourless.

Benitoite is another of those unfortunate minerals in which the best colour belongs to the extraordinary ray, and inevitably must always be diluted to the extent of 50 per cent by the ordinary ray which cannot be eliminated however the stone be cut. The colour in any case is a bit tricky, for though it presumably owes its blue to the titanium which is an essential element in the stone, there are often parts of a crystal which appear colourless in any direction. And though the blue is bright enough it seems to lack the richness to be found in the blue of sapphire.

The best style of cutting for benitoite is the brilliant form, as this enables the fire to show itself even if masked somewhat by the blue colour. Some years ago there was a report of another source for benitoite from which a pink specimen was recovered. If, one day, a locality for the stone is found where crystals of important size exist, benitoite might well spring into prominence in the way that tanzanite did a few years ago. The world of jewellery has a need of further transparent blue stones as alternatives to the ubiquitous sapphire.

BLENDE

Whether the term blende or its alternative sphalerite is used, here is yet another of those minerals owing their name to Greek words for deceit—in this case apparently because lead-miners were apt to mistake the mineral for the lead-ore, galena, and were disappointed when it yielded no lead. Without being too uncharitable, that such a mistake could be made by miners accustomed to handling the bright steely-grey crystals of galena speaks very poorly for their powers of observation.

Whilst galena is a sulphide of lead, blende is a sulphide of zinc, and equally a most important ore. Its hardness of only $3\frac{1}{2}$ to 4 on Mohs's scale, and its ready cleavability parallel to the six directions of the dodecahedron, at once put paid to its use in jewellery. But on the other hand its high refractive index (2·37) and tremendous dispersion of 0·156 bestow on transparent varieties, when cut by a skilled lapidary, a truly magnificent appearance, and this makes blende a favourite with some collectors of unusual stones.

Blende, in common with many of the sulphide minerals, is cubic in symmetry and commonly crystallises in lustrous groups of highly complex crystals showing dodecahedral and cube faces, and is black or dark brown in colour. When pure it is colourless, but more often the transparent forms are golden brown or greenish gold. The chief localities for such cuttable material are Picos de Europa in Spain and Sonora in Mexico. At one time I purchased a number of handsome cleavage pieces from these sources with a view to using them to form the hemisphere of an experimental refractometer in the hope that the high index of the blende would enable readings to be taken of stones beyond the range of the normal instrument. Thanks to the skill of the designers and workers in the optical firm of Rayner & Keeler, an experimental model was eventually made employing not a hemisphere, but a prism of blende, and on this instrument my colleague, C. J. Payne, and I were able for the first time to take direct refractive index readings on a series of cut zircons with indices ranging between 1·79 and 1·99. The contact liquid used was a self-inflammable phosphorus mixture, emphatically not recommended for general use. This little blende model, which I still retain, did later lead to standard Rayner refractometers using glass prisms, which have had world-wide recognition ever since their first appearance in the late thirties, and also to special models incorporating synthetic white spinel and even diamond. Diamond is indeed the ideal material for a refractometer, not only on account of its high refractive index, but because of its mechanical and chemical invulnerability, but the cost of production is too high for the average person's pocket.

Zinc blende has, curiously enough, a similar crystal structure to diamond, with zinc and sulphur substituting for the carbon atoms in the lattice. It is curious that this should be responsible for such a lowering of hardness and a dodecahedral rather than an octahedral cleavage.

Authors are apt to stress the very high dispersion of blende, but actually it is only comparison with the very low dispersion displayed by diamond (in relation to its refractive index) which makes blende seem so exceptional: comparison with other materials of high index, such as strontium titanate and rutile, makes the dispersion of blende appear quite ordinary.

BRAZILIANITE

In brazilianite we have the second discovery of the century of a new mineral which could also be claimed as a gem material. Greenish-yellow transparent crystals of the stone were recovered from a pegmatite in Minas Gerais, Brazil, during the Second World War, and were recognised as a new mineral by Dr. F. H. Pough when visiting the district, and later (1945) described by him and E. P. Henderson, who analysed the mineral. The name brazilianite was given to the mineral in honour of the country where it was first found. Fine crystals of the new species were also collected by Frondel and Lindberg in 1947 in the Palermo mine in Grafton County, New Hampshire, U.S.A.

Brazilianite is a hydrous sodium-aluminium phosphate crystallising in well-developed monoclinic crystals of a yellowish-green ('Chartreuse') colour resembling that found in apatite or chrysoberyl. The hardness is $5\frac{1}{2}$, density 2·99 and refractive indices 1·602–1·623, giving a double refraction of 0·021. There is a perfect pinacoidal cleavage. Brazilianite has no distinctive absorption spectrum and no fluorescence, but can be identified with certainty by its colour combined with a careful refractometer reading.

Apart from the novelty of its recent appearance on the scene it has no particular claims on the collector's attention, and certainly will never be a commercial gemstone.

CALCITE AND ARAGONITE

The crystallised carbonate of calcium known as calcite is one of the commonest and best-known minerals, but could certainly not be classed as a gemstone in the ordinary way. However, in some of its massive forms such as the 'onyx' marbles, it has recently become a fashionable decorative stone for the designing of lampstands, ornamental boxes, chessmen, inlaid tables, and the like, which make it worth mention here. Moreover the clear colourless Iceland spar variety has had great importance in mineralogy since its huge double refraction (0·172) and optical clarity made it possible for the well-known Nicol prism to be constructed, whereby pure plane-polarised light was made available for the first time, providing a powerful tool for analysing the optical properties of crystals and gemstones.

Calcite, $CaCO_3$, crystallises in the trigonal system and has a density of 2·710, refractive indices 1·486 and 1·658 respectively for the extraordinary and ordinary rays, and a hardness which is the standard 3 on Mohs's scale. Its rhombohedral cleavage is so perfect that if any piece of calcite be smashed with a hammer or crushed in a mortar each little fragment will be seen under magnification to be a parallelepiped bounded by rhombohedral cleavage planes.

In its clear colourless form calcite has very constant properties and can be used to check the accuracy of a refractometer, or as a density indicator at a very useful point on the scale where slight differences between synthetic and natural emeralds from different localities are in question.

To digress for a moment: if any reader has access to a refractometer he might find it an interesting exercise to take readings on the smooth surface of a calcite cleavage flake. One shadow-edge at 1·658 will remain fixed whatever the position of the specimen. The second edge, belonging to the extraordinary ray, may be seen at 1·486 or 1·566, or at any position between these critical readings according to the orientation of the specimen. When this is slowly rotated, the observer should note that in the critical positions just mentioned this second shadow-edge is seen as a strictly horizontal line across the scale, whereas in intermediate positions the line of the shadow-edge is tilted. This curious phenomenon is true for the extraordinary readings on any uniaxial mineral, and for both rays on any biaxial mineral (where the shadow is only truly horizontal in three critical positions), but in most stones the amount of birefringence is too small for the effect to be noticeable. With calcite, it will be found impossible to obtain a higher reading than 1·566 for the lower ray when using a cleavage surface. If the polished face were parallel to the trigonal axis the shadow-edge of the extraordinary ray would be seen to travel the whole range from 1·486 to coincidence with the ordinary ray reading at 1·658 while the specimen was being turned through a right angle. If, on the other hand, the polished surface were parallel to the basal plane of the crystal, the two edges would each remain stationary at their fullest separation.

I must apologise to the non-scientific reader for this digression, but these detailed phenomena are not mentioned in textbooks, and this seemed an appropriate opportunity to draw attention to them. Such observations are quite easily made on calcite and carry with them some very useful insights into the optics of crystals.

Although calcite under ordinary conditions is the stable crystalline form of calcium carbonate, another version, so to speak, exists in the shape of the mineral aragonite, which crystallises in the orthorhombic system. Aragonite is denser (2·94), and a little harder (3½ to 4) than calcite, and its lowest and highest refractive indices are 1·530 and 1·686, giving a double refraction of 0·155—nearly as great as that of calcite. A large double refraction is in fact a feature of carbonates, being bound up with the planar structure of the CO_3 group.

Although its crystals are orthorhombic, aragonite has a strong tendency to crystallise in pseudo-hexagonal twinned forms, in this resembling another orthorhombic mineral—chrysoberyl. To the gemmologist, aragonite is important as being the form that calcium carbonate assumes in pearl and mother-of-pearl.

Calcite is the main constituent of the stalagmites and stalactites which give such spectacular beauty to some of the caverns found in limestone districts in Britain and in many other parts of the world. Water containing some carbon dioxide in solution filters through the joints in the limestone and drips on to the floor of the cavern where it evaporates and crystallises in the shape of stalagmitic columns. Evaporation and crystallisation also takes place on the roof whence come the slowly forming drips, and the kind of mineral 'icicle' is formed which we call a stalactite. Traces of impurity cause variations in colour and a beautiful translucency. Marble, of which there are countless varieties, is a crystalline limestone consisting of calcite in massive form, which has been used for many centuries as a material for sculpture and the decorative interior of buildings.

The banded or 'onyx' marbles, popularly but misleadingly called 'Mexican onyx', 'Brazilian onyx', and so on according to their place of origin, are of stalagmitic origin. The material has also been called 'oriental alabaster' and 'alabaster onyx'. The name alabaster properly belongs to a massive gypsum which is a hydrous calcium sulphate and a much softer substance, while 'onyx', of course, should be reserved for the straight-banded form of agate. In the now usual general name 'onyx marble' for the decorative stalagmitic marbles, the term onyx is employed in an adjectival sense, meaning 'banded'.

DANBURITE

Danburite was first discovered in 1839 embedded with feldspar in a dolomite rock at Danbury, Connecticut, and its name derives from that locality.

In composition it is a calcium borosilicate and it crystallises in the orthorhombic system. In this and in many other ways it resembles topaz, but lacks the charm and fine colour of the better-known mineral. Its hardness is 7, but, though it has no distinct cleavage, it is extremely brittle. The density is easy to remember, being almost exactly 3·00, while the refractive indices are 1·630 and 1·636. Danburite when pure is colourless and is often found in this condition. The best specimens come from Mogok where occasionally quite large clean stones of an attractive yellow are discovered. A step-cut stone of this description in the Natural History Museum in South Kensington weighs 138·61 carats.

There seems little prospect that the stone will be used in commercial jewellery. One interesting property of the stone is that it shows a sky-blue fluorescence under long-wave ultra-violet light, the cause of which is not understood.

DIOPSIDE

Diopside is a well-known member of the pyroxene family of rock-forming minerals which includes several other gemstones including jadeite and spodumene. It is a silicate of calcium and magnesium crystal-lising in the monoclinic system: some iron inevitably replaces the magnesium. The name comes from two Greek words meaning 'double appearance' in reference to the rather strong birefringence of the stone. The density is near 3·30 and the refractive indices near 1·68 and 1·71 for gem quality stones. The hardness is between 5 and 6, and the colour usually a rather dull green.

Diopside provides some attractive mineral specimens but has hardly been used in jewellery until recent years, when about 1960 nearly black stones cut *en cabochon* and showing a bright four-rayed star made their appearance on the market. These came from southern India and have attained considerable popularity. The arms of the star intersect at angles of 73° and 107°, and the oriented inclusions causing the effect can be seen with a lens. It was found that these consisted of magnetite and as a result the stones are quite noticeably attracted by one of the small power-ful magnets which are now available from ironmongers. Very few gem-stones are so strongly magnetic, so that this forms a simple and useful test.

The best green diopsides contain some 1–2 per cent chromium and are then known as chrome diopside. Stones of this variety have been found in Outokemper, Finland, and have been cut for collectors, while attractive chrome-diopside cat's-eyes have come from the Mogok district.

Apart from the above, the appearance of diopside is usually rather dull and uninteresting, resembling bottle-glass or the natural glass called moldavite. Its properties are near those of peridot, but its refrac-tive indices are distinctly higher and its density a little lower, as a trial in pure methylene iodide will conveniently show.

ENSTATITE

Amongst the minerals found in the famous blue ground in which diamonds were recovered in Kimberley were some attractive blood-red pebbles and rather angular fragments of a green mineral. Despite their small size these for a time achieved popularity as Cape ruby and green garnet. Their true names were pyrope garnet and enstatite, and continued popularity became impossible when the heavy mineral concentrates from the diamond pipes ceased to provide these nicely coloured specimens.

Enstatite is yet another of the pyroxene group, and is essentially a magnesium silicate, though it commonly contains some iron and thereby grades into hypersthene. It is an orthorhombic mineral, shows the typical two cleavage directions intersecting at nearly 90° to all pyroxenes, has a density of 3·26 and a hardness of 5½ on Mohs's scale. The refractive indices are 1·665 and 1·674 for the green varieties, and the small birefringence of 0·009 effectively prevents confusion with diopside or peridot. Enstatite also has a very distinctive clear-cut line in its absorption spectrum between the green and the blue at 5060 Å. This line becomes even stronger in the brown types which contain iron, and weaker bands in the green and blue appear. The South African stones contain a touch of chromium which adds quality to the colour, and faint lines in the red end of its spectrum.

Epidote

Epidote is a fairly common mineral which is often found in extremely attractive lustrous groups of crystals of a dark brownish-green colour (sometimes referred to as 'pistachio-green') which is very typical of the species.

It is a typical iron colour and like that of brown tourmaline soaks up too much light to be anything but a sombre gem when faceted. The related mineral clinozoisite has a more pleasing colour and is a more rewarding stone to cut.

Epidote is a member of an isomorphous group and can thus vary quite a lot in composition, but it is fundamentally a silicate of calcium and aluminium containing variable amounts of iron and magnesium. It is monoclinic, and the crystals are very complex: they are usually striated parallel to their length. Their density is about 3·4, refractive indices 1·733 and 1·768, and hardness 6½, but these figures can vary. There is a very strong absorption band at 4550 Å in the blue in epidote, and in its associated minerals (including zoisite) which sometimes aids identification. The name epidote is from a Greek word for 'increase' in reference to the supposed fact that the base of the prism has one side longer than the other.

EUCLASE

The name euclase is very apt since it means 'good cleavage' and, as the lapidary knows to his cost, this otherwise promising gem material has a very easy pinacoidal cleavage which makes it difficult to cut. Euclase has an unusual composition being an aluminium borosilicate containing water. It is monoclinic, quite adequately hard ($7\frac{1}{2}$), with a density of 3·10 and refractive indices 1·653 and 1·673 for the lowest and highest rays. The readings on the refractometer might well cause euclase to be mistaken for another rare gem mineral of similar colour—fibrolite, the description of which follows next. The indices of fibrolite are slightly higher, but the birefringence is very nearly the same.

The chief source of euclase of gem quality is in the area of Ouro Preto in Minas Gerais, Brazil. This district is chiefly famous as being the only source for fine yellow topaz. The occurrence of euclase is in fact very similar to that of topaz since it is found in a matrix of quartz in the veins of crystalline schists. Blende and cinnabar are accompanying minerals.

Euclase often contains traces of chromium, giving rise to a doublet in the deep red and a red glow under crossed filters. Although I once had the good fortune to encounter a fine euclase mounted as a brooch, surrounded by small stones of the same ilk, the stone is more prized by collectors than by jewellers, who in most cases are not aware of its existence.

FIBROLITE (SILLIMANITE)

Fibrolite is an aluminium silicate crystallising in the orthorhombic system and is trimorphous with andalusite and with kyanite. It is equally well known to mineralogists as sillimanite, this being one of the awkward cases where one name cannot be said to be more 'correct' than the other. Sillimanite derives from an American mineralogist, B. Silliman, while fibrolite refers to the tendency of the mineral to appear in fibrous forms. Grey and greenish massive varieties have served similar purposes to jade in the making of axe-heads and the like, and translucent fibrous pieces have been polished and used as cat's-eye gemstones. But the fibrolite gems most coveted by the collector are the clear blue stones occasionally recovered from the ruby mines of Burma, a superb example of which weighing nearly 20 carats is the pride of the Geological Museum collection in South Kensington.

Fibrolite in this form has a hardness of $7\frac{1}{2}$ and a constant density of 3·25, with 1·659 and 1·678 for the least and greatest refractive indices. Measurements taken on pieces from the Ceylon gravels, where the gem is also sometimes found, gave the slightly higher values of 1·663 and 1·684—the birefringence of 0·021 being the same in each case. The stone is strongly dichroic, the best blue colour being seen down the length of the crystals.

Weak absorption bands at 4620 and 4410 Å in the blue, and a powerful band at 4100 Å in the obscurity of the violet, may be of assistance in distinguishing fibrolite from euclase, which is optically so similar. Owing to traces of chromium in the mineral, it may show a weak red fluorescence under crossed filters. In this respect it resembles euclase, and a density test is undoubtedly the best means of distinction.

Fibrolite is yet another gemstone in which the (pinacoidal) cleavage is far too perfect and easily developed for comfort. One promising crystal which I asked a lapidary to cut for me was returned in the form of a stack of cleavage sheets looking more like a transparent sliced loaf, or a pack of playing cards, than a promising gemstone!

FLUORSPAR

Fluorspar (or fluorite, or simply fluor) is one of the most attractive of all the common minerals, its large transparent cubic crystals in a wide variety of colours gracing many a mineral gallery. And, pleasing to relate, some of the world's finest fluorspar crystals have come from these islands, the counties of Cornwall, Durham and Cumberland being particularly favoured, while a famous banded massive variety, known as 'blue-john', comes only from Derbyshire, though now the supply is practically exhausted.

Fluorspar is a fluoride of calcium, CaF_2, has a density of 3·18, and a very low refractive index (1·434). It represents the standard 4 on Mohs's scale of hardness. It is interesting to note that the element fluorine has a depressing effect on the refractivity of minerals, but not on their density, thus both fluorspar and topaz have refractive indices decidedly low in relation to their density compared with the majority of minerals, while (stepping outside the realm of gemstones) the mineral cryolite, which is a fluoride of sodium and aluminium, has an index of only 1·334, which practically matches that of water! Fluorspar is colourless when pure, but is found in a range of beautiful colours including blue-violet, green, yellow and rose-pink.

Stones cut from clear crystals make attractive enough gems, but the low refractive index means that its reflectivity is poor, and the low hardness prevents a brilliant polish being applied or retained. Curiously enough one comes across faceted fluorspar gems in some old pieces of jewellery.

Crystals of fluorspar are almost invariably unmodified cubes, but the perfect cleavage is octahedral—so easily produced that specimens of coloured fluorspars artificially cleaved into octahedra are sometimes offered for sale. As I stated in an earlier chapter the cleavage surfaces of fluor are characteristically rough because the cubes from which they are derived so often consist of a series of cubes not quite in parallel formation. Cracks following the cleavage planes are almost always visible in crystals of fluorspar and can spoil the appearance of a specimen when they become obtrusive. Exposure to the heat of the sun if the crystals are on a window-ledge or in other ways subjected to fluctuating temperatures can cause a worsening of these cleavage cracks, in the same way as it can with barytes and other readily cleavable minerals. Another peculiarity of fluorspar crystals is their tendency to show vicinal faces which take the form of very low pyramids on the cube faces. At the apex of these low pyramids the edge or corner of an interpenetrating cube will be seen emerging. So far as I know nobody has offered a satisfactory explanation of these idiosyncrasies.

The name fluorspar derives from the Latin *fluere,* to flow, and refers to fluorspar's efficiency as a flux to lower the melting-point of ores, etc. And fluorspar itself gave rise to the name 'fluorescence' being coined by Stokes in 1852 for the emission of light from a substance when exposed to rays of shorter wavelength, such as ultra-violet rays, since many (but not all) specimens of this mineral are noted for the vivid violet glow they display when suitably stimulated. A knowledge of the derivation of the term should prevent students making one of their most frequent spelling mistakes, i.e. 'flourescence', for the phenomenon.

The fluorescence of fluorspar is due to various rare-earth elements which can sometimes be identified by characteristic emission lines in the spectrum of the fluorescent light. An interesting fact is that after the mineral has ceased to give a luminous glow the crystals may continue to phosphoresce with invisible (ultra-violet) rays, as can be proved by placing the specimen on a photographic film or paper in the darkroom for some hours, and then developing it. Apparatus isn't always needed for observing fluorescence: there are many green crystals of fluorite which appear violet by reflected light due to its strong fluorescence in ordinary light. The best-known decorative variety of fluorspar, blue-john, with its jagged bands of fibrous crystals ranging from dark violet to nearly white, is quite inert under ultra-violet rays.

IDOCRASE (VESUVIANITE)

The name idocrase is another of those which betray a certain worry about identification, as it is taken from two Greek words meaning 'form' and 'mixing', suggesting that its shape resembles that of other minerals. Personally I find its well-formed tetragonal habit very easy to recognise. Tetragonal minerals are in fact rather uncommon in nature: of those likely to be encountered, rutile and cassiterite have a metallic lustre, leaving zircon as the only one which has crystals resembling idocrase. Of these two, crystals of idocrase are commonly terminated by a basal pinacoid face, seldom seen in zircon; and in idocrase the prism faces are often vertically striated—in zircon, not. The sub-adamantine lustre and heft of zircon are also very distinctive. Two other names for idocrase, vesuvianite and californite, have a more obvious derivation, and yet a fourth name for a yellowish variety, xanthite, is only useful when one is wanting to complete an alphabet of gemstones.

It has already been remarked when describing the calcium aluminium garnet, grossular, how similar in composition this was to idocrase. No more need be said on that score. The hardness of idocrase is $6\frac{1}{2}$ on Mohs's scale, the density varies between 3·38 and 3·42 for the transparent varieties, which are golden-brown to green in colour, and near 3·30 for the massive jade-like californite varieties. The refractive indices are a little above 1·70 and show a notably small degree of double refraction (0·005). A useful feature in identification is a strong absorption band in the blue at 4610 Å which is due to iron.

Like the garnets, idocrase is usually formed by contact metamorphism, being found chiefly in altered limestones. Attractive green crystals are found in Piedmont and at Mount Vesuvius in Italy, and a golden-brown variety which has produced some good cut specimens, occurs in the Laurentian mountains of Canada. It is chiefly in its jade-like californite varieties that idocrase is liable to be used in jewellery, and that aspect of the mineral has already been sufficiently discussed in the section on grossular in Chapter 15.

IOLITE (CORDIERITE)

In a world where transparent, hard and well-coloured gemstones are in short supply I have always been surprised at the comparative neglect of iolite, which, when properly cut, provides stones of a beautiful violet-blue, is adequately hard and not in really short supply. This is another of the minerals which have alternative names. Iolite, from the Greek word for violet, is preferred by English-speaking gemmologists: cordierite (after a nineteenth-century mineralogist) is preferred by most mineralogists, while a third name, dichroite, which has an obvious derivation, has also been extensively used. In addition there are what might be called nicknames such as 'water sapphire' and 'lynx sapphire', which are misleading and thus should certainly not be used in these scientifically enlightened days.

Iolite is a silicate of magnesium, iron and aluminium, crystallising in the orthorhombic system. Its physical properties are very close to those of quartz, with hardness 7 or just over, density 2·58–2·62, and refractive indices 1·54–1·55, with double refraction 0·008. Confusion with amethyst is obviously likely to happen in mounted pieces, but the intense pleochroism should leave no doubt where iolite is concerned.

The colours belonging to each of the three principal rays are yellowish, light blue, and an intense violet-blue. Without knowing anything about optics it is obvious to the lapidary that the table facet of the stone must be oriented at right angles to the direction of best colour, which lies parallel to the prism edge. The colour of iolite cannot really compare with sapphire in richness or intensity, but it is a very *pretty* stone, and the startling change of colour when viewed from different directions should, one imagines, add a special interest and distinction to the gem. Apart from its well-known occurrence in the Ceylon gem gravels, fine quality iolite has been found in Rhodesia, Kenya, Burma and Madagascar. A curious variety found in Ceylon contained masses of reddish platelets of biotite mica, and a similar appearance in stones from Madras contained pseudo-hexagonal platelets which (according to Eppler) consisted of chrome-chlorite.

Iolite has a fairly rich absorption spectrum which naturally in so pleochroic a mineral varies a great deal with direction. In testing a small sackful of iolite rough in search of a few blue zoisite crystals with which they were said to be mixed, I found the most easily recognised features in iolite were two bands in the yellow at 5920 Å and 5860 Å which, together with a band in the green at 5350 Å formed an unmistakable pattern. These bands were best seen when the iolite was turned into its 'yellow' position. As always, when using the spectroscope for identification, it is the pattern of absorption bands that matters, rather than a painstaking measurement of wavelengths.

KORNERUPINE

The rare mineral kornerupine was first discovered at Fiskernaes on the west coast of Greenland by the Danish mineralogist, J. Lorenzen. He announced his discovery in 1884, and named the new mineral after his close friend, A. N. Kornerup, who had recently died at the early age of twenty-six. It is sad to record that Lorenzen himself died at sea in the same year that his paper was published: he was only twenty-nine.

The first kornerupines of gem quality were found by A. Lacroix in two localities in Madagascar, in 1912 and 1922. The stones were pale sage-green, transparent and capable of being cut into small gemstones. That a cut kornerupine of this type should be recovered from an antique dealer's junk-box would seem as near the impossible as the finding of a golden half-sovereign on the shores of Loch Katrine, and yet I know as a fact that both these things did happen.

In the late thirties my colleague, C. J. Payne, and I were able to establish that kornerupine of gem quality, though of quite different type and colour, was also to be found in the gem gravels of Ceylon.

To give full details of the story would take too much space in dealing with a gemstone of very minor importance, and would only interest fellow gemmologists. Let it just be said that several brownish-green cut gemstones in our possession, and one weighing 9·18 carats (labelled 'enstatite') in the Natural History Museum, which we had good reasons to suppose emanated from Ceylon, were proved to be a new type of kornerupine and analysed by Dr. M. H. Hey. Proof positive came when we sorted through samples of the 'illam' from the Matale district of Ceylon, kindly sent to us by Mr. Hans Van Starrex, and found two pebbles which were indubitably kornerupine.

The hunt was now on, and our friend, E. H. Rutland, was able to recover quite a number of such stones from unregarded pebbles from Ceylon which were in the hands of London lapidaries. We were later able to add a further locality for the mineral when a beautiful green kornerupine, known to be from Burma, was tested in our laboratory and found to match a small stone previously of unknown origin which we had held for many years.

Kornerupine is a silicate of magnesium and aluminium containing variable amounts of iron, upon which its colour and other optical properties depend. It also contains boron and about 1 per cent of water. The presence of boron had not been suspected by earlier analysts and Dr. Hey (who is probably the best analyst in the world today) did a major job in establishing the complex chemistry of the mineral.

The hardness of kornerupine is rated at $6\frac{1}{2}$, the density lies between 3·30 and 3·35, and refractive indices near 1·67 and 1·68, with a double refraction of 0·012. The Ceylon stones are brown or greenish-brown and are very dichroic; they resemble tourmaline or zircon from the same locality, but a trial with the spectroscope eliminated the possibility of zircon, while its behaviour in methylene iodide, the density of which it closely matched, eliminated the possibility of tourmaline.

The green stones from Burma have a lovely colour between that of peridot and demantoid garnet: if there were more of them kornerupine might become a popular gem, and some bright salesman would think up a good selling name for the variety. To most people kornerupine may seem an ungainly name, but the interest of a keen gemmologist of my acquaintance in its unfolding story was such that he named his new house 'Kornerupine' in its honour!

KYANITE

Kyanite can be numbered amongst the very few gemstones which can emulate the pure intense blue of sapphire, and its name is derived from the Greek word, *kyanos,* for blue. But its other physical characters are such that it seems almost impossible to produce cut stones from the mineral which do not have a flawed and flaky appearance.

This is due partly to two prismatic cleavages and to an extraordinary grained structure almost like wood, leading to a hardness of nearly 7 across the prisms, but little more than 4 down their length. Kyanite forms beautiful sky-blue prismatic crystals—and this curious grained structure can easily be demonstrated with the point of an ordinary pin, which makes no impression across the specimen, but can be felt to 'bite' quite easily down the length of the prism. Please note that hardness tests of this kind should neither be employed on cut specimens nor on fine crystal surfaces; but with controlled technique and the careful choice of a suitable place on a rough specimen, it can be used without any perceptible harm. The 'directional' hardness of kyanite is actually the basis for an alternative name, 'disthene', from Greek words meaning 'double' and 'strength'.

As mentioned in describing andalusite and fibrolite above, kyanite is the third and triclinic member of the three crystallised forms of aluminium oxide found in nature. Its density is 3·67 with slight variations, and refractive indices 1·712 and 1·728. The pleochroism is strong; the colours for the three principal rays being colourless, violet-blue, and cobalt-blue. The cause of the colour is rather obscure as pure aluminium silicate should be colourless, and indeed parts at least of kyanite crystals are devoid of colour. Green specimens are also met with, and the typical blue crystals vary in depth of tint from sky-blue to a dark violet-blue. Analysis of a fine blue kyanite from St. Gotthard showed the presence of 1·2 per cent of ferric iron, but some Rhodesian kyanite I examined showed a strong chromium spectrum, with the customary doublet in the deep red at 7060 Å. Most kyanites show absorption bands in the blue at 4460 and 4330 Å, and a photograph of the spectrum also revealed bands in the near ultra-violet. Stones containing traces of chromium show a distinct red fluorescence under crossed filters.

The bladed crystals of kyanite occur in crystalline schists, often accompanied by brown crystals of staurolite in several Swiss localities, and form very pretty mineral specimens. Gem quality kyanite has been found in Kashmir, Burma, Rhodesia, Kenya and Montana.

Confusion of kyanite with sapphire is unlikely on account of the parallel cracks almost always visible in cut stones; and if the stone is faceted a refractometer reading will identify it with certainty.

MALACHITE

The basic copper carbonate known as malachite is a mineral with a rounded nodular structure, which when cut across and polished produces the well-known agate-like pattern of circles and bands in shades of dark and pale green which makes it such a favourite amongst ornamental stones. The green of malachite is often interspersed with dark blue bands of azurite, which is another carbonate of copper containing only 5 per cent of water compared with the 8 per cent of malachite. Azurite is also found on its own in beautiful crystals of very dark blue.

Both minerals have a density near 3·8, and being carbonates they fizz when touched with a drop of hydrochloric acid. With a hardness of only $3\frac{1}{2}$ they are unsuitable for use in jewellery though occasionally made into bead necklaces, ear-rings, etc.

Malachite is fairly abundant and is used as an ore of copper. The finest material for carving into vases and for other large-scale decorative purposes has come from localities in the Urals, which are very rich in copper. Amongst other large suppliers are the Burra Burra district of South Australia and Katanga in the Congo.

Both malachite and azurite owe their names to their colour, malachite from the Greek word for mallow, which has leaves of similar green, and azurite from the word for blue.

MOLDAVITE AND OBSIDIAN

Because of their similar nature and also by their alphabetical proximity, moldavite and obsidian can be treated together. Both are forms of natural glass and have very similar physical properties, but their origins are very different. We know very well how obsidian is formed, but the origin of moldavite and other similar bodies (known as tektites) which have reached us from outside the atmosphere remain uncertain. Obsidian is simply a form of volcanic glass, derived from a rapid cooling from the molten magma, and thus being 'frozen' into a rigid form before crystals of any size had time to develop. It is usually of so dark a brown colour as to appear black, but types with more decorative colours, or with masses of tiny inclusions causing iridescence, or with attractive white patches, have been cut and polished for decorative purposes. Ancient man valued the sharp, if rather brittle, cutting edge that made skilfully broken obsidian an ideal material for arrow heads, spears and knives.

Moldavite, which is a bottle green or brownish-green glass, was first discovered at the end of the eighteenth century near the Moldau river in what was then known as Bohemia, and derives its name from the river. This was an area far removed from volcanic activity, and an alternative notion that the scattered pieces were the remains of an ancient glass factory was ingenious but hardly tenable. Thousands of little glass nodules were later found in many parts of South Australia, in Tasmania, and on Billiton Island where the name billitonite was given to them. These have a very characteristic rough exterior surface and are customarily about the size of a large walnut and slightly oval in shape.

Two other naturally occurring glasses of mysterious origin may be mentioned here. One is a nearly pure silica glass, pale yellow-green in colour, which was first discovered in 1932 lying in irregular lumps on the surface of the Libyan desert. The other is the so-called 'pit glass', which is found amongst the mineral pebbles in the Ceylon gem gravels. These are of varying colours of brown and green, which might pass as artificial bottle-glass except for their situation which seems to make this impossible.

Moldavite and obsidian have very similar physical properties with a hardness of $5\frac{1}{2}$, density 2·38 and refractive index 1·49. The silica glass from the Libyan desert has lower figures, with specific gravity 2·21 and refractive index 1·46. The hardness is 6 on Mohs's scale.

Moldavite contains large bubbles, round and elliptical, together with treacly swirls suggesting rapid fusion on its entry into our atmosphere and rapid cooling. In the yellow glass from Libya there are cavities of such irregular shape that the term 'bubble' seems hardly to apply.

PHENAKITE

In phenakite we have a mineral of beautiful clarity and sufficient hardness ($7\frac{1}{2}$) to be a recognised gemstone: its only real lack is that of colour. Colourless gemstones suffer from the great drawback that they are compared in the mind's eye with diamond—inevitably to their disadvantage.

The mineral owes its name to yet another confession of weakness in identification that seemed to afflict early mineralogists, since it stems from the Greek word *phenao* for deceit. Being clear and colourless, apparently, was enough reason for it to be confused with quartz or white topaz. It is a beryllium silicate and crystallises in rather squat prismatic crystals belonging to the trigonal system. The density is fractionally under 3; the refractive indices are 1·654 and 1·670, giving a (positive) double refraction of 0·016 and the dispersion 0·015. I mention the latter as with colourless stones it is important. Actually, despite its rather low refractive indices and dispersion phenakite has a noticeably bright and pleasing appearance.

Amongst gemmologists, when phenakite crystals are seen inside an emerald this may serve as a warning sign that the stone is synthetic, as being a beryllium silicate it is a logical product where any imbalance of this constituent in the ingredients is concerned.

Phenakite of gem quality comes chiefly from Brazil, and also from the Urals, Rhodesia, Tanzania, and localities in the U.S.A.

Not long ago a huge colourless phenakite weighing 1470 carats in the rough was brought for testing to the Gem Trade Laboratory, New York. From this a proportionately immense cut stone of 569 carats was produced. Phenakites of pale yellow, pale red, and greenish-blue have been reported, but I have never been fortunate enough to see such stones.

PYRITE

Pyrite or 'iron pyrites' with its bright and brassy lustre is one of the best-known of the world's minerals. In jewellery it was once extensively cut, chiefly in rose-cut form, and mounted in brooches, lapel clips and the like, under the name marcasite, which the trade like to pronounce as 'marcazeet'. Marcasite is actually another mineral having the same composition but different crystal structure, and being more liable to decompose by oxidation than its commoner cousin. Pyrites is iron sulphide, FeS_2, and crystallises in the cubic system. The crystals themselves are more often than not well-developed cubes, but striations on the cube faces betray the fact that it hasn't the full cubic symmetry. The striations denote the incipient growth of a curious twelve-sided form in which each face has a pentagonal outline. Hence this form is known as a pentagonal dodecahedron or, with reference to the mineral in which it so typically occurs, a pyritohedron. Though hardly true gold in colour, pyrites used to be nicknamed 'fool's gold', for the hopes its glint could raise in the inexperienced prospector's breast. When filling his coal-scuttle the householder may have noticed thin brassy sheets of pyrites on the surfaces where the lumps of coal have broken. This is not a welcome sight as any appreciable amount of pyrites in one's coal may provoke minor explosions in the grate. The mineral is of less value as an ore of iron than as a source of the sulphur needed in the large-scale production of sulphuric acid, which sounds more deadly under its old title of 'oil of vitriol'.

The reflectivity of a polished surface of pyrite is very constant at 54·5 per cent, and for this reason it is used as a standard in ore microscopy. The hardness of iron pyrites is $6\frac{1}{2}$ on Mohs's scale, and its density 5·0.

The derivation of the name from the Greek word for fire has a sounder basis than many of the other derivations I have felt bound to give the reader, since its ability to emit sparks when struck by iron is more reliable than that of flint under like provocation. The 'flints' used in the older forms of cigarette-lighter consisted, in fact, of small rods of compacted iron pyrites. Pyrite is to be found in all parts of the world. In England those who dwell in chalk country may be familiar with the heavy nodules of iron pyrites to be found in the soft white rock. These have a rusty-looking exterior, but when broken across reveal radiating brassy fibres of this iron sulphide mineral.

RHODOCHROSITE AND RHODONITE

These two manganese minerals can be treated together because in appearance they are almost exactly alike and serve much the same decorative purposes. They each have a particularly pleasing rose-red colour, which to the experienced eye speaks of manganese. Rhodonite is a manganese silicate and has the advantage in hardness over rhodochrosite which is manganese carbonate, but to many (myself included) the softer material has a slight edge in terms of beauty. Rhodonite is a pyroxene (that family of which jadeite, spodumene and enstatite are also members) and crystallises in the triclinic system. A beautiful transparent cut stone in my collection has the appearance of a very fine spessartine garnet. This has a density of 3·70, refractive indices 1·738–1·752, and shows a broad absorption band in the green at 5480 Å, a narrow and strong band between the green and blue at 5030, and one at 4550 Å in the blue. It is typical of manganese absorption bands that the strongest bands of all are in the deep violet and near ultra-violet. In some specimens both of rhodonite and rhodochrosite there is an intense band near 4120 Å, but this is very difficult to see. The spectra of the two minerals are so alike that they cannot be separated by this means, and the same is true of the density which in each case ranges from 3·40 to 3·70. The refractive index of clear pieces would form a firm basis for identification since rhodochrosite has the usual large double refraction of a carbonate, with indices 1·600–1·820: but in their common massive state each gives a vague refractometer reading near 1·73. In theory a trial with a drop of dilute hydrochloric acid would do the trick as rhodochrosite should fizz as it is attacked by the acid, but rhodonite, too, may contain some carbonate and behave in a similar manner. One is left with the difference in hardness and the sheer *appearance* of the specimen. Rhodochrosite yields to the point of a needle gently applied: rhodonite does not. Rhodochrosite is typically stalagmitic in structure—that is, concentrically banded with a radiating crystal growth: it is also more translucent and richer in colour than the pyroxene mineral. And where rhodonite very frequently encloses black veins and patches of the manganese oxide pyrolusite or of psilomelane, rhodochrosite is remarkably free from these blemishes.

The best samples of rhodochrosite probably come from Catamara and San Luis in the Argentine, while rhodonite has been mined in large quantity in the Urals near Sverdlovsk, and is also found in fine quality in New South Wales and in California.

Scapolite

Scapolite is the general name for a family of minerals closely analogous to the feldspars ranging from a sodium aluminium silicate (containing some chlorine) to which the name marialite has been given, to a calcium aluminium silicate (containing some sulphate and carbonate) known as meionite. This has to be said to explain the considerable differences to be found in the properties of the various gem-quality scapolites decribed below.

The name scapolite comes from the Greek for a rod or column in allusion to the customary shape of the crystals. The family all belong to the tetragonal system and crystals are prismatic in their development and show two directions of easy cleavage at right angles to each other.

Though the mineral group has been known for more than a century the first inkling that it might furnish gem material did not come until 1913, when the first of a range of very beautiful cat's-eyes were forthcoming from the Mogok stone tract in Burma. The first to appear were a delicate pink in colour and were offered as 'pink moonstones' with some plausibility. Later, colourless, mauve and deep blue scapolite cat's-eyes made their appearance. The cat's-eye effect was caused by included slender parallel crystals of an unidentified, doubly refracting mineral, and was more clear-cut than in most chatoyant stones apart from chrysoberyl.

Then in 1920 transparent yellow scapolites were found in Madagascar, and years later similar stones of deeper colour from Esperito Santo in Brazil. These yellow scapolites are notable for being remarkably clear and free from inclusions. They resemble beryl both in appearance and properties, though the large double refraction makes distinction easy.

All types of scapolite have a hardness near 6. The density for the pink cat's-eyes is 2·67, and refractive indices 1·549 to 1·570, the violet cat's-eyes giving values rather lower than these. The yellow transparent stones have a density of 2·7, and refractive indices 1·553–1·574, with a negative double refraction of 0·021.

An interesting characteristic of many scapolites, in particular a massive yellow variety from Ontario in Canada, is the yellow fluorescent glow they exhibit under ultra-violet light. When this yellow light is examined through a spectroscope a number of evenly spaced discrete bands are visible which we had assumed were caused by traces of uranium in the mineral, banding of a similar nature being a familiar feature in the light emitted from 'Canary' uranium glass. Quite recently Dr. W. A. Runciman of the Australian National University, following some research carried out in Russia, has been able to prove that our assumption was wrong; the activating impurity being a sulphur ion.

SMITHSONITE

Smithsonite is a zinc carbonate mineral which is occasionally found in translucent banded pieces having very attractive green, yellow and light blue colours. To some extent it can resemble jade and turquoise, and the colours are almost certainly due to staining by some copper compound.

The hardness is about 5 and the density is noticeably high when the stone is held in the hand, being about 4·35. The refractive indices show the usual huge double refraction of a carbonate, being 1·621 and 1·849, but these do not help to identify a stone which is always cut *en cabochon*. A drop of acid on a trace of powder scraped from an inconspicuous part of the stone will fizz and confirm that the specimen is a carbonate. Green smithsonite was first marketed by a firm called Goodfriend Brothers of New York, who used a gallicised version of their own name 'bonamite' for the material. In London this fancy name is still used in preference to the more scientifically correct smithsonite.

SPHENE

Sphene, or titanite as it has also been called, is one of the most sought-after of collector's gemstones, and its fame has even spread into the ranks of commercial dealers (who have never seen one in their lives), as something to be coveted. This is partly due to the rarity of really fine specimens and partly on account of the extreme beauty of lustre, colour and fire that this stone can display. Sphene is a calcium-titanium silicate crystallising in the monoclinic system in flat tapered crystals, crystals from which in fact its name is derived, i.e. from the Greek word for a wedge. Normally it is found as dark brown opaque crystals, and when transparent yellow, green, or brown sphenes are found in plutonic or metamorphic rocks they are seldom of a size to yield cut stones of more than a carat or so.

The hardness is $5\frac{1}{2}$ on Mohs's scale, the density practically the same as diamond (3·52) and the refractive indices beyond the limit of the normal refractometer, being 1·90 and 2·03. However, the large double refraction of 0·13, which is more than twice that of zircon, should enable an experienced gemmologist to identify sphene merely by inspection with a lens. In trying to gauge the degree of double refraction in a cut stone (which is a very valuable skill to acquire) one must examine the stone from a number of angles to ensure that the position of maximum doubling has been found and then, of course, also take into consideration the size of the specimen, since the doubling effect is very much increased if the stone is a large one.

Apart from its pleasing yellow and green colours, the two factors which make sphene so attractive to the eye are the high refractive index, giving a bright surface lustre, and a dispersion of 0·051 (compared with the 0·044 of diamond), which gives it plenty of fire. Apart from diamond, the only yellow or green stone of similar liveliness is demantoid garnet. All in all one can well understand its attraction to the collector.

Switzerland and the Austrian Tyrol have produced many good sphenes; but more as mineral specimens than as raw material for cut gemstones. Recently there have been some profitable discoveries of transparent sphene in San Diego County, California, and in Baja California, Mexico, where specimens containing up to 1 per cent of chromium have resulted in stones of a bright green colour.

Taaffeite

In introducing this chapter with its gallimaufry of lesser-known gem varieties I defended the inclusion of the exceedingly rare mineral taaffeite on account of the quite extraordinary story of its discovery which depended entirely upon a piece of acute observation by an enthusiastic amateur gemmologist.

This was Count Taaffe (pronounced Täf), who was born in Bohemia in 1898 and died in Dublin in 1967. He was the only son of the 12th Viscount Taaffe of Corran, Baron of Ballymote, County Sligo—a resounding enough title, which belonged to the Taaffe family from 1628 until 1919, when it was removed from the roll of peers of Ireland, as the Taaffes had by then become Austrians and thereby 'enemy aliens'. The 11th Count Taaffe was, in fact, the Austrian Prime Minister from 1879 to 1893, and his grandson, the Taaffe of our story, was the first of his family permitted to return to their ancient home of Ireland.

Taaffe was a prickly and eccentric man, but honourable and generous to his friends, amongst whom I was fortunate to be numbered on account of my sympathy and encouragement when, late in life, he decided to enter for the examinations of the Gemmological Association.

To supplement his meagre income and enlarge his experience of gemstones, Taaffe did a certain amount of buying and selling and had found that a rewarding and inexpensive source of interesting pieces could be the box of oddments that most jewellers had accumulated through the years.

In October 1945 Taaffe picked out some hundreds of stones from such a box belonging to a jeweller named Robert Dobbie, to whom he paid £14. These stones had for the most part been broken out of old jewellery over a period of some twenty years. Having taken the stones home Taaffe followed his usual procedure by first thoroughly cleaning them, and secondly sorting them out into little groups according to colour. The third stage was to hold each stone in tweezers and examine it carefully under a Bausch & Lomb binocular microscope at a magnification of twenty diameters.

The microscope had no stage, and Taaffe's habit was to examine the stones from all angles over a sheet of white paper, under a 100 watt bulb in a flexible desk-lamp. Evidence of double refraction was one of the things that he particularly looked for, and on this occasion one of the stones, weighing 1·42 carats, from the group containing violet and mauve specimens caught his attention because 'every speck of dust on the back and every scratch appeared double, like on a badly wobbled snapshot.'

Taaffe had no refractometer, but in appearance and in all the other tests he could apply, including an astonishingly accurate density determination using (of all things) a hand-held balance, his mystery stone behaved like a spinel. He confirmed the double refraction by observing a clear extinction at 90° between crossed nicols, was naturally extremely puzzled, and on 1 November 1945, posted this unique stone to me at the laboratory with a covering letter: 'This time a new riddle: what is this mauve stone? It seems to me to answer all the characteristics of spinel, yet it shows double refraction.'

It was now our turn to be puzzled. The refractometer readings were 1·718–1·723, and showed a double refraction of 0·0047, but the density (3·61), hardness (8), and what we could see of the absorption spectrum agreed with those of spinel. No known mineral had such properties, and a preliminary X-ray test by Sir Frank Claringbull at the Natural History Museum confirmed that the stone was not spinel.

Taaffe courageously allowed a small slice to be removed from the culet of the stone for more detailed X-ray work, and a preliminary chemical analysis. This showed that the mineral was hexagonal of a rare symmetry class to which only a special form of quartz had previously been known to belong. It also showed the presence of magnesium, aluminium and beryllium, and up till then no mineral containing beryllium and magnesium as essential constituents had been encountered.

Then came a long delay during which we in the laboratory and the Museum staff were searching keenly for further specimens of the new mineral, concentrating particularly on parcels of mauve spinels and, the news having spread, many of our gemmological friends were joining the search. At last, four years later, a second taaffeite (as we had already christened the new mineral) was discovered by C. J. Payne in the course of a routine test on a mixed collection of unusual stones which were clearly mostly from Ceylon. There were green sapphires, an attractive green kornerupine, and a mauve stone weighing 0·86 carat, showing refractive indices 1·717 and 1·721 and a uniaxial interference figure. This was taaffeite number two!

There followed some tricky bargaining with the owner of the stones (in which the kornerupine was included to distract attention a little from the true prize) before landing both stones for a sum of £20.

Before the new mineral could be officially christened and established in a full scientific paper a further sacrifice was necessary of part of Taaffe's stone in order to complete a full chemical analysis. The first reduction had been from 1·42 to 0·95 carats; the second sacrifice reduced the stone (after refaceting) to 0·56 carat. Dr. Max Hey, the museum's brilliant analyst, had only 12 mg with which to carry out a preliminary and final analysis, in which he found Al_2O_3 70·0%, Fe_2 5·9%, MgO 13·4%, BeO 11·0—showing taaffeite to be essentially a magnesium beryllium aluminate, intermediate in composition, that is, between the cubic mineral spinel, and the orthorhombic chrysoberyl. The colour of the stone can be ascribed to the iron, and in the second specimen, which was paler in colour and had slightly lower refractive indices and density, there must be less iron present.

After this there was a further long interval before a third specimen of taaffeite was discovered. This was a stone of 0·84 carat, and was found by Robert Crowningshield of the Gem Trade Laboratory, New York, while testing a parcel of varicoloured spinels on Christmas Eve, 1957. A fourth taaffeite, and by far the largest yet, came to light in America in 1967. This was a purple cushion-cut stone, presumed from Ceylon, weighing 5·34 carats.

Taaffe's original stone was purchased after his death (with other stones from his collection) by Mr. R. K. Mitchell, to whom stone-dealing is a profession, and gemmology an addiction. The second taaffeite is appropriately in the Mineral Department of the Natural History Museum in South Kensington, where so much of the skilled work was done to establish the new mineral, while taaffeite number four is said to be in the Smithsonian Institution in Washington, which possesses probably the world's finest collection of gemstones.

Since then, small prismatic crystals of taaffeite have been found in the Chinese province of Hunnan, and tiny green transparent crystals from the Musgrave Range of central Australia have proved to be closely related to taaffeite. These discoveries are of great interest to crystallographers, but I am convinced that one day it will be the gem gravels of Ceylon that will yield the first rough taaffeite pebble of gem quality.

There rests for now the taaffeite story. The ripples from that first keen observation by a lone gemmologist in Dublin have already spread very far, and will doubtless spread further before they die away altogether.

CHAPTER TWENTY-THREE

---◈---

PEARLS AND CULTURED PEARLS

So FAR, all the gems I have been describing have been minerals, but there are certain organic products such as pearl, coral and amber, which by virtue of their beauty have earned a place alongside the gemstones. Of these pearl is, of course, supreme and at one time was even comparable in value with diamond, ruby, sapphire and emerald.

Pearls are abnormal secretions made by molluscs known as pearl-oysters and pearl-mussels. These all have the power to secrete calcareous substances from the waters in which they live, which enables them to build protective shells in which to house their soft and vulnerable bodies. These shells are lined with the smooth lustrous and iridescent material we know as nacre or mother-of-pearl. Any shellfish which produces nacre can also, in certain circumstances, give rise to the shining spheres we know as pearls.

The soft body of the mollusc is enveloped in two flaps of tissue known as the mantle, and it is the outer epithelial cells of this which have the power to secrete all the substances needed for the building of the shell. The outer zone of cells produces a dark horny substance known as conchiolin which acts as a waterproof covering to the calcareous prisms which are built by the second zone of cells. This is the 'prismatic' layer, and consists of tiny columns of calcite set in a framework of conchiolin: it gives bulk and strength to the shell. Lastly comes the fine nacreous lining to the shell which is deposited by the innermost zone of epithelial cells. All these operations are carried on simultaneously during the growth of the molluscs. The 'spat', as the tiny embryo oysters are called, are at first free-swimming in the ocean, but if they are to develop to maturity they must find some rocky base on the sea's bed to which they can anchor themselves. Inspection of the pearl banks or 'paars' has shown that one reason for failures in pearl production may be the absence of this rocky 'culch' at depths suitable for the maturing oysters. This can easily happen under the influence of rapid currents.

When the larval stage of a tiny parasitic worm or similar irritant intrudes into the body of the mollusc there is a strong tendency for the animal to isolate the intruder in a 'pearl sac' lined with epithelial cells of the type found on the mantle, and once this has happened the secretion of conchiolin and nacre follows automatically in a series of extremely fine laminae resulting in a more or less spherical pearl. From a study of the shape of natural pearls it is obvious that during growth there has been a continual rotary motion of the growing pearl. Many pearls indeed have an external shape which resembles a lump of clay after it has been turned and shaped on the potter's wheel. If it is not spherical, the pearl whether it be elliptical, drop or button-shaped, will be symmetrical about an axis of rotation. On the other hand many pearls (which have not grown in a sac) have an entirely irregular shape—these are known as 'baroque' pearls.

If the pearly lining of a shell is studied under the microscope it will be seen to consist of myriads of exceedingly thin overlapping platelets, the edges of which are finely serrated—rather as though trains of tiny waves had suddenly become frozen as they advanced. It is these piles of very thin translucent plates of aragonite which give to mother-of-pearl its beautiful silvery lustre, while the effect of the more or less parallel serrated edges of the laminae act as a grating and break up the incident light into iridescent colours. The surface of a fine pearl has the same structure (modified of course by its spherical shape), and it is this which gives rise to the 'orient' of pearl which is the basis of its beauty. In each of the nacre layers there are microscopic prisms of aragonite perpendicular to the layers, set in a fine network of conchiolin. A sectioned pearl shows a number of major layers of growth like an onion, representing seasons. The structure of a pearl is thus both concentric and radial.

It is found that the normal healthy oyster as a rule contains no pearls. Those which are distorted and have obviously been victims of parasitic attacks are those in which pearls are most frequently found. Many pearls are malformed, over-rich in conchiolin, or too tiny to be usable, so that the discovery of a fine pearl is quite a rare event, and millions of oysters die a wasted death during each major pearl fishery, though in some areas the shells themselves are the main source of revenue.

The names given by scientists to the pearl oysters and mussels have changed more than once during the past fifty years, but there now seems to be some guarantee of permanence under the present International Rules of Zoological Nomenclature, which state that the pearl-bearing oysters all come under the species name *pinctada,* while the freshwater pearl mussels are all to be classed as varieties of *margaritifera. Margaritifera* simply means 'pearl-bearing': the origin of *pinctada* I haven't been able to ascertain.

The finest pearls have been fished for two millennia in the Persian Gulf near the island of Bahrein, while other famous fisheries were in the Gulf of Manaar between Ceylon and southern India. In each case the pearl oyster is the *pinctada vulgaris,* a small mollusc only some three or four inches in diameter and with a thin shell which makes it of little value as a source of mother-of-pearl.

During the nineteenth century there were thirty-six fisheries held off the coast of Ceylon. Then came three in successive years culminating in a record-breaking one in 1905 in which eighty-one million oysters were taken. Maybe the banks were overfished on that occasion, or currents altered the formation of the sea floor and left no banks of culch at a suitable depth for the oysters to thrive. Whatever the reasons there have since that time been only three fisheries in these once-favoured waters, the last being in 1956, when the headquarters were at Tuticorin on the Indian side of the Gulf, and thus under the control of the Government of Madras. Fishing in the Persian Gulf continued seasonally at least until the thirties. The world trade depression, the war, and the competition for labour provided by the great oil industry which thrived in the Gulf, all served to diminish the supply from these waters also.

Until quite recently the fishing methods employed in harvesting the pearls have persisted unchanged through the centuries. Sentimentalists (myself included) may regret the passing of the ancient ways which seemed to work so well, but it must be admitted that in older days the Arab divers were little better than slaves in the hands of the wealthy boat-owners and merchants. For the sake of their families they 'sold their souls to the company's store', and the health even of their lean and hardy bodies was before long undermined by their over-frequent dives to depths of thirty feet or more.

In the early years of the century Government control had to some extent prevented such extreme exploitation, but when aqualung and other diving equipment is available (and is used extensively with success by Japanese divers in Australian waters) the old skin-diving methods do seem unnecessarily primitive.

In the Ceylon fisheries of which we have record, the decision whether or not to hold a fishery in any year was made very responsibly by the Government inspectors on the basis of extensive sampling from which not only the number of oysters available but the probable value of the pearls therefrom was estimated. If the results were favourable the extent of the fishing grounds was marked by buoys bearing a red flag, while buoys with white flags marked promising spots for the boats to cluster and carry out their diving.

The coming fishery was then advertised in local papers reaching as far as the Persian Gulf and the southern coasts of India, which resulted in an enormous assembly of divers, speculators, merchants and general hangers-on gathering at the shanty-town of Marichchikkaddi, which for a few months became the pearl headquarters of the world. For that short time the waste land between the jungle and the ocean became a sizable city with government offices, hospitals, post offices, court-houses, and prisons, while Orientals of all kinds squatted on mats in open-fronted stalls selling gems of all sorts, and showed themselves extremely shrewd judges of the weight, quality and value of pearls.

Each evening saw the picturesque homeward race of ruddy-sailed craft from the fishing grounds, each eager to get in first with its booty. The load of each vessel was counted and divided into three piles—two for the Government, and one to be shared amongst the divers, who were besieged on their way home by natives keen to buy even a few oysters with which to try their luck. The unopened oysters were also readily accepted as currency by shopkeepers—a sort of gambling fever spread throughout this temporary town.

It is known that a good deal of revenue was lost to the Government during the transit of the oysters from the boats to the shore, as many of the finest pearls lurked just inside the lip of the shells, and some of these would inevitably fall out, or be helped out, and be secreted by the boat crews.

In the 1956 fishery, based on Tuticorin, motor vessels and divers using aqualungs largely replaced the small teak boats with their naked divers, and large dredging sacks of heavy netting were used to collect the oysters in place of the small string bag slung round the neck of each diver which traditionally used to hold the catch. The dredging nets were emptied on deck and the oysters sorted in order that the smaller molluscs could be returned to the sea in the hope that later they would become the bearers of pearls.

It is better not to dwell on the methods used for recovering the pearls from the shells. It must have been an exceedingly smelly business, which began by allowing the shells to rot and allowing blow-flies to get to work on the decaying flesh, which they did with nauseating efficiency, soon aided by their voracious grubs. Eventually, however, all was washed and clean and tidy.

In the first three decades of this century at least, the finest pearls were prepared for the European market in the city of Bombay. Here the pearls were cleaned, bleached, drilled, graded for size and matched for colour, and finally presented in the form of 'bunches', in which short strings of graded pearls were bound and braided with silver wire terminating in silver tassels, the whole being folded in blue silk and provided with a neat parchment label bearing the number and weights of each group of pearls in the bunch. The numbers of pearls in each bunch might vary from a hundred to several thousands, according to the size of the pearls involved. These bunches formed the raw materials from which fine pearl necklaces were assembled by experts, carefully graded for size and matched for colour.

In pearls even more than in stones the weight is very important. The unit of weight is the 'pearl grain' which is fixed at a quarter of a carat, and the value of pearls increases according to the *square of the weight in grains,* or, in the case of a group of nearly equal size, according to the *average weight multiplied by the total weight* of pearls in a group. The resulting figure was known as 'once the weight', and to obtain from this the actual cost of the pearls, one had to multiply this by the 'base' value of the pearls, which depended on their quality in terms of colour, shape, lustre, and so on.

The classical 'base' method for calculating the value of pearls in graduated groups or sizes will be easier to follow if I show an actual example of a fairly steeply graduated necklace valued in this way. In this case there were 129 pearls weighing 182·30 grains. The pearls were separated into five sizes and the calculation carried out as follows:

Pearls	Grains	Average	Once the Weight
1	8·20	8·20	67·24
4	20·80	5·20	108·16
16	41·64	2·60	108·26
42	59·64	1·42	84·68
66	52·00	0·78	40·56
—	—		—
129	182·30		408·90
—	—		—

In pre-war days the base price was always reckoned in shillings and that total figure of 408·90 was also the price at a base of 1s = £20 8s 10d; at a base price of 20s = £408 18s 0d, and at a top-quality base of 100s the necklace would be valued at £2044 10s 0d.

In these days of decimal coinage the same calculation would be used, but the 'once the weight' figure of 408·90 would have to be multiplied in the context of the decimal pound. So to obtain the value at the old 1s base, one would multiply 408·90 by 0·05, and the top base value obtainable now would be about £1.00, so that the necklace formerly priced at about £2000 would now be worth about £400.

To give some idea of the very high prices paid for fine pearls even as late as June 1938, I can quote a short news item published in that month by the *News Chronicle*: 'A £10,000 pearl, found by a native diver off the coast of Broome, Western Australia, has arrived in London by air and will shortly be offered for sale. It is a remarkably pure specimen and weighs 103 grains. An official of the Australian Pearl Company told a *News Chronicle* reporter last night, "It is the finest pearl we have handled for fifteen years, and, despite its great value, we anticipate no great difficulty in disposing of it".'

In the jewellery trade of the twenties the Oriental pearl was queen, famed for its special beauty, its age-long prestige, and full of profit-making possibilities. Periodic visits to Hatton Garden were paid by Ali Reza, the great Arab pearl-dealer, who walked down that street of gems in lordly style wearing a burnous and protected by an obsequious attendant carrying a large parasol against the sun, or an even larger umbrella against the rain. These visits were followed in due course by an influx of pearls (beautifully mounted in 'Bombay bunches') to the big importing houses, whose names were then household words in the 'Garden', but now alas, are mostly forgotten: Max Mayer, Mendes da Costa, A. Tanburn, Jerwood & Ward. . . . Every dealer and big jeweller had his own pearl-stringer, and two 'pearl-doctors', the Brockmans, father and son, were kept busy skinning, polishing and drilling pearls.

But a cloud was on the horizon. In 1921 the first whole 'cultured' pearls had appeared on the market. These were the outcome of long years of ingenious experiments by Japanese workers, of which Kokichi Mikimoto (at one time a noodle seller) was the most successful.

This was a logical development from the centuries-old practice of the Chinese of inserting flattened metal images of Buddha between the soft body and the shell of freshwater mussels, enabling them to recover, two years or so later, a shell decorated with pearl-coated images. The first commercial success for the Japanese was to induce the formation of large 'blister' pearls on this same principle, formed on mother-of-pearl threequarter spheres cemented to the inside of the shells of their local marine oysters, kept captive in wire cages suspended from rafts in some of the sheltered bays of their eastern coast. After returning the oysters to their cages for two years or so the artificially induced blisters were removed from the shells and backed with mother-of-pearl, and ground into shape to form a complete sphere. A sophisticated version of the same idea is still very much in use in the form of 'Mabe' pearls, which will be described later.

Mikimoto's achievement was to induce the pearl-bearing oysters to form complete 'cultured' pearls on mother-of-pearl beads inserted into the soft parts of the oyster's body, the bead being wrapped in mantle tissue taken from another oyster. The molluscs used were the small pearl-oysters known to scientists as *pinctada martensii,* which were fished when young and farmed in cages.

The earliest whole cultured pearls to appear (in 1921) were at first presented as natural pearls from a new source, and when some of these were sectioned and found to consist of a mother-of-pearl bead coated with a thin layer of pearl substance there was naturally considerable consternation amongst pearl-dealers and fishers, and a great deal of argument went on as to the name under which these new products could be legitimately sold. Eventually the term 'culture' or 'cultured' pearls was agreed upon, the simple name 'pearl' being reserved strictly for the natural product of the oyster.

Experiment showed that these early cultured pearls gave a distinctive greenish or mustardy fluorescent glow under ultra-violet rays, in contrast to the sky-blue effect shown by most natural pearls, and soon large black wooden boxes containing a mercury-vapour lamp and a dark purple Wood's glass filter for carrying out this test were to be seen lurking in many a pearl merchant's premises. This simple test soon proved unsatisfactory, however, and the hunt was on (a hunt which I was asked to join) for any non-destructive method by which natural could be distinguished from these new cultured pearls.

By 1925 things had reached such a point that the Committee of the Diamond, Pearl and Precious Stone Trade Section of the London Chamber of Commerce decided to instal a special pearl-testing laboratory, which I was asked to organise and operate. A degree in chemistry and mineralogy was not at first much help in tackling a problem of which I knew nothing. But with the help of advice and ingenious apparatus from Paris, and a rapidly acquired knowledge of pearl structures and habits, I was able within six months to issue certificates with 100 per cent certainty on drilled pearls, stating whether these were natural or cultured, while a few years later, installed in new premises, with special X-ray equipment and C. J. Payne, a fellow graduate from King's College, London, to assist me, we were able to test all types of pearl, drilled, half-drilled, or undrilled. We were the first independent laboratory of its kind to be established and so 'got in on the ground floor' in pearl-testing, and a little later in gem-testing also.

After the war, the increasing menace of synthetic gemstones made it necessary for us to double our staff by enlisting the already well-known gemmologist, Robert Webster, and A. E. Farn, who is now in charge of the laboratory. This phalanx of four, as I liked to call it, remained for twenty-five years, when each in their turn the three seniors retired. Now, nearly fifty years on, the laboratory still flourishes in Hatton Garden with a team of four, having tested some four million pearls and a million gemstones, on which more than 85,000 certificates have been issued, thus safeguarding the trade and the public against fraud.

It seemed appropriate to introduce this brief sketch of the Chamber of Commerce Laboratory which has been referred to in passing many times in the earlier parts of this book. To have referred to it under its full title as the 'Gem Testing Laboratory of the Diamond, Pearl and Precious Stone Trade Section of the London Chamber of Commerce and Industry' on each occasion would have seemed unduly pompous and consumed valuable space.

A number of ingenious ideas were put forward and apparatus contrived for the purpose of distinguishing natural from cultured pearls without harming them in any way: but in London we soon became convinced that only two of these were satisfactory and sufficient. The first, for drilled pearls only, was invented in Paris by Chilowsky and Perrin, and was known as the 'Endoscope'; the second, for use primarily for partly drilled or undrilled pearls, entailed the use of X-rays to determine either the crystal arrangement within the pearl by diffraction methods, or the presence of a foreign bead by direct radiography of the same general type as that used in dentistry and medicine.

X-rays were, of course, an obvious choice when the problem first arose, but a great deal of experiment was necessary before they could be used with sure success, and the apparatus was expensive, potentially dangerous, and only suitable for use in specialised laboratories. Many contributed to their eventual success, but the name of the French scientist, Dauvillier, in connection with diffraction methods, and of A. E. Alexander in the U.S.A., for advancing our skills in radiography, deserve mention.

Details of the techniques of pearl-testing would be out of place in this book: for those interested they can be found in my book *Gem Testing*, or in Robert Webster's *Gems*.

In the case of run-of-the-mill cultured pearls that one sees in shops, an expert eye can recognise them for what they are without benefit of apparatus. The general 'look' in itself is revealing, and if rotated under a a strong electric light, some of the beads will have a thin enough skin to show a sudden 'gleam' as the mother-of-pearl in the underlying bead reaches an orientation in which its peculiar sheen is visible. Even where no actual sheen is to be seen, cultured pearls vary in lustre as they are turned under a light, while in natural pearls there is no reason why this should be so. If a cultured pearl is unstrung, or the pearl loose enough on its thread for a lens examination to be possible down its drill-hole, a sharp line of demarcation should be visible about $\frac{1}{2}$–1 mm down the canal followed by a structureless centre, having a colour and texture reminiscent of candle-wax. If natural pearls are examined in this way a series of structure lines should be apparent within the canal, and the interior will show a warm yellow or brownish tint often with a dark patch of conchiolin right at the centre.

Cultured pearls of low quality have the merest film of pearl substance over the bead, show varicose-like wrinkles on the surface, and a tendency to exhibit a little 'snout' at one end of the pearl. Good imitation pearls are much to be preferred to such monstrosities.

Despite their vast commercial success, owing to their rise coinciding with the decline in natural pearl production, the producers of cultured pearls have had to face many problems. The first was the degradation of the cultured pearl reputation which followed the flooding of the market with poor quality cultured pearls selling in London stores just before the war, at something like 30s a string. To prevent this happening meant organisation and discipline amongst the pearl-farmers and marketing authorities, with powers to destroy all cultured pearls of inferior quality. There are now special Cultured Pearl Inspection Offices in Kobe and Tokyo which serve that function.

The next problem is linked with the small size and short life-span of the Japanese pearl-oyster, *pinctada martensii*. This mollusc has a diameter of only three or four inches (though a larger strain is now being developed) and an effective life-span of only seven years. The oysters are not ready for the nucleus operation until they are three years old. During the maximum three and a half available for the growth of the nacre the deposit normally amounts to about o·5 mm in thickness, adding 1 mm to the diameter of the original bead. In the warmest waters available to Japanese fisheries (Kyushu) the growth is more rapid, and an 8 mm bead may have increased to 10 mm diameter in the completed cultured pearl.

There are also periodic troubles with adequate food supply for the captive oysters, with disease, and with the supply of suitable mother-of-pearl for forming the bead nuclei, which comes from Mississippi mussels and is imported from the U.S.A.

After the war a new type of cultured pearl appeared which at first caused a good deal of consternation, because in these there was no bead nucleus. These are produced in shallow freshwater basins round Lake Biwa in Japan, and the pearls are induced to grow in large freshwater mussels having the official title *hyriopsis schlegeli,* by inserting strips from the pearl-secreting mantle of one mussel into the edge of the mantle of a second mussel, which is then returned to the water in a cage suspended from a raft in the manner so long practised with the seawater-cultured pearls. This 'tissue-culture' method of pearl production was not invented under the urge of a fiendish desire to deceive, but because these lumpish mussels are so full of viscera that they are not suited for seeding with bead nuclei.

The Biwa cultured pearls have a very distinctive lustre and shape which reveal their nature to an expert. They tend to be oval or baroque in shape. They show a very bright fluorescence under X-rays and small distinctive markings and hollows or conchiolin patches on an X-ray photograph.

The finest cultured pearls have come from waters off the north Australian coast and some of the Pacific islands. The oyster used here is the large *pinctada maxima.* The resultant cultured pearls are also large and have very thick skins. Considerable skill is needed to detect the presence of the bead nucleus or the signs of tissue culture. But even as acknowledged cultured pearls these fine pearls are extremely expensive, and they are too large for use in necklaces.

Reference was made earlier to the cultured blister pearls, sold as 'Japanese' pearls, which were popular before the advent of the whole cultured pearl. These were big and blatant, and suited more for the knobs of hatpins, or for costume jewellery than as a serious replacement for true pearls. Nevertheless, the modern equivalents known as 'Mabe' pearls (from a slang term for the oyster originally used in their production) have a considerable popularity, about half a million pieces being exported annually from Australia to Japan for finishing. The chief markets are in Spain, Mexico and Hong Kong.

Specimens of *pinctada maxima* in the Australian cultured pearl fisheries which have ejected the full bead with which they were at first inoculated, are selected for the more humble task of making blister pearls. Hemispheres of soapstone (steatite), carefully measured for height, are inserted and the blister pearls formed are cut from the shell by a circular saw. To prepare the blister for the market the steatite 'former' is removed, the thin pearly blister bleached and cleaned, filled with resin, and cemented to a mother-of-pearl base. The size of the finished blister varies from 12 to 22 mm diameter. As exported from Japan the wholesale price for these 'Mabe' pearls is about £1 apiece.

IMITATION PEARLS

Imitation is the sincerest form of flattery, and for a very long time the natural pearl has been so flattered. There is, after all, nothing so becoming to a woman as a pearl necklace, and as natural pearls, even today, are very expensive, the widespread sale and use of cultured and imitation pearls is quite understandable. The older, cheaper type of imitation pearl consisted of hollow beads of translucent glass, lined with a pearly 'essence' made from fish-scales or some substitute concoction, and filled with wax. The better types of imitation pearl are formed of solid glass beads provided with a number of coatings of the special 'essence' and carefully burnished. Imitation pearls of the more expensive kinds are very attractive and suitable for their purpose. They do not, or should not, deceive anyone when closely inspected. Under a lens, instead of the delicately serrated edges of nacre, the surface texture is like shining blotting-paper, and under a lens the canal-holes will usually show signs of some peeling of the applied skins, and the glassy lustre of the bead itself where its rim lies exposed.

Before closing this chapter on pearls it should be mentioned that in addition to Oriental pearls from the Persian Gulf and the Gulf of Manaar, there have been successful fisheries off the north and north-west coasts of Australia where *pinctada margaritifera* and *pinctada maxima* provided large silvery pearls as well as valuable shell for the mother-of-pearl industry; there are black pearls fished from Mexican waters in the Gulf of California, and very translucent white pearls off the coasts of Venezuela.

The term black pearls gives an inadequate idea of their beauty, which lies in a bronze or gun-metal basic colour with a subdued peacock sheen which is very lovely indeed. A famous black pearl necklace belonging some time before the war to Lady Cowdray, was valued at something like £100,000. Inferior pearls are sometimes stained to represent true black pearls, using silver nitrate solution which causes a black deposit of metallic silver when the solution enters the drill-hole and seeps along the layers near the surface of the pearl. This type of fraud can luckily be detected by means of X-rays.

Pearls are also produced by freshwater mussels in many of the rivers in Europe and the U.S.A. Small-scale but persistent fishing for pearls is still carried on in some Scottish rivers, and a really fine and valuable pearl is occasionally recovered. The method of fishing is simple but requires great patience. The worker, clad in waders, searches the bed of the stream by means of a glass-bottomed bucket which enables him to see below the surface of the water. The mussel here is *unio margaritifera*. To collect together enough freshwater pearls to form a necklet of good quality takes a long time, but to the educated eye the soft lustre and beautiful pastel shades of these pearls have a very special loveliness.

A final note may be added about a quite different type of pearl which is found in the giant conch *strombus gigas* found off the coasts of Florida. The well-known decorative shells of this great shellfish are not lined with nacre but with a beautiful pink porcellanous substance, and the 'conch pearls' or 'pink pearls' which are recovered from these shells are a delicate shade of pink and have a characteristic flame-like pattern on their surface which is not nacreous but has a fascination of its own. These pink pearls are considerably denser than the Oriental pearl—2·85 as against 2·70. This high density enables a distinction to be made between pink pearls and imitations made from coral, which has a density near 2·69. The value of conch pearls is naturally not to be compared with that of Oriental pearls, but good specimens will always find a ready sale. Their shape is usually oval or elliptical, and they are thus well suited for pendants or for drop ear-rings.

CHAPTER TWENTY-FOUR

AMBER, CORAL AND JET

Amber

BESIDES PEARL, there are several other substances used in jewellery which cannot be classed as minerals since they owe their being to organic nature.

Amber is one of the few gem materials which is found principally in Europe. It comes mainly from the shores of the Baltic Sea, and until 1939 its mining and working was very much a German monopoly. But centuries before Germany existed there was an important trade in amber, and regular routes were organised between the dwellers on the Baltic shores and the rest of Europe, the traffic extending indeed to the Mediterranean countries and to Egypt.

It was natural that fishermen should treasure these transparent yellow lumps which were flung up by the sea, the low density of amber (1·08) enabling it almost to float on the salt water of the ocean. Amber beads are found in thousands of ancient tombs and burial grounds dating back to the Bronze Age.

Amber is the fossilised resin exuded by pine trees which flourished in the Eocene period, some seventy million years ago. Baltic amber is alone amongst other fossil resins found in different parts of the world (including Sicily, Rumania and Burma) to contain succinic acid—about 5 per cent. Indeed it is described in Dana's *System of Mineralogy* under the name 'succinite'. Here amber is said to be 'tasteless', thus suggesting a test that never in my life have I applied to any gemstone!

As already stated, the density of amber is 1·08, unless filled with numerous cavities, when naturally the value is lower: the hardness is $2\frac{1}{2}$ on Mohs's scale. Its refractive index is 1·54 and, though singly refracting, it shows bright interference colours between crossed polars. Being a poor conductor, it feels notably warm to the touch, and when rubbed it has the curious faculty of picking up little bits of paper or other light objects, a fact which, incidentally, was well known to the Greeks, who called the substance *electrum*, from which our word electricity is derived. This power of developing frictional electricity is in reality not very useful as a test since so many insulators show the same effect if not quite to such a strong degree.

Though not so easily fusible as modern resins such as copal, amber melts between 250° and 300°C, and then boils quietly, giving off the choking fumes typical of succinic acid. The colour is characteristically yellow, though sometimes it is almost white and sometimes brown. It is transparent to nearly opaque.

It is a widely known fact that amber often includes ants, spiders, flies, and fragments of pine needles, etc., which were trapped when it was first exuded as a sticky mass all those millions of years ago. This has provided a wonderful opportunity for entomologists to study insect life of that period, which has been preserved in every detail, whereas normally of course such flimsy creatures would die without leaving any fossil traces. Unfortunately, however, the insects in question have shown no significant differences from their modern counterparts, nor have any species unique to the Eocene period been discovered. The remains of no fewer than 163 species of plants found in amber have been identified by Göppert.

In addition to the chance supplies of amber thrown up on the Baltic coast, and even on the shores of Norfolk, Suffolk and Essex, amber has been, and is, extensively mined in what was formerly east Prussia, from beds of glauconite (blue earth) at Palmnicken near Königsberg. The waste amber scraps are heated and compressed to form 'pressed amber', which provides a cheap substitute for true 'block amber'.

The gemmologist has to distinguish pressed amber, or 'ambroid' from block amber, on account of the price difference: he also has to separate amber from more recent fossil resins such as copal or kauri gum, and (an easy task) from bakelite and other synthetic resins, which are by far the most usual imitations met with.

Pressed amber when closely examined shows evidence of flow under pressure, the bubbles being compressed in one direction instead of being spherical. Copal and Kauri gum are perceptibly softer and more friable than amber when touched gently with a knife blade. The surface of copal is typically 'crazed' with fine cracks, it feels sticky to the touch after rubbing, and it softens more easily than amber under a drop of ether. Bakelite (often seen as 'amber' necklaces), has a distinctive golden-brown or reddish-brown colour, is very resistant when touched with a knife blade and, in common with other plastics, *peels* rather than crumbles as amber does. It is perceptibly heavier (1·26) in the hand, and a specific gravity test of the whole necklace, taken by dangling it in a bucket of water in a spring balance, provides a completely conclusive proof.

CORAL

Coral might be described as the collective skeletons of a vast number of the curious little organisms known as coral polyps. These begin life as tiny free-swimming very primitive organisms living in the warm waters of the sea at depths of 10 to 500 feet or so, which eventually attach themselves to a previous coralline growth where it forms part of a vast colony in which the individuals share a common gelatinous base known as the cœnosarc. It is from a membrane at the lower part of the cœnosarc that the growth of the coral 'skeleton' takes place. It is, in fact, an external and communal skeleton.

The coral substance is essentially calcium carbonate in the form of calcite with some 3 per cent magnesium carbonate, organic matter, and traces of iron. The density is 2·68, a little lower than that of pearl, and its hardness is usually given as $3\frac{3}{4}$ on Mohs's scale, fractionally softer, that is, than fluorite.

Coral is found in very many varieties, but that most used in jewellery is *corallium rubrum* or *corallium nobile* and the most favoured colours are pink and red, though white coral also is frequently made into necklaces.

The material has played an important part in jewellery for two thousand years, and was particularly popular with the Romans. For them it was in a sense a local industry, since the chief source of precious coral from the earliest times to the present day has been the Mediterranean Sea, where it is extensively dredged off the coasts of Algeria, Tunis, Corsica, Sardinia, Sicily and Spain. The Japanese home waters have also provided suitable coral, especially of an ox-blood colour. But it is the Italians who have always had almost a monopoly in the fashioning and trading in coral jewellery.

When polished, coral has a characteristic grained structure and a typical colour range. Both these can, unfortunately, be imitated very closely by plastics. However, the density of plastics is very much lower, as can be judged by simply balancing them in the hand, and a trace of coral powder scraped on to a glass slide will effervesce briskly when a drop of acid is placed on it, in the very helpful manner of all carbonates. Other plausible imitations may be made from porcelain, and coral itself may be used to ape the more highly prized pink conch pearl.

JET

One might be rather startled to see someone wearing a necklace consisting of polished lumps of coal: yet one cannot avoid the fact that jet, which was once so popular in Victorian jewellery, is merely a variety of lignite coal. Not, admittedly, the type of coal which is to be found in the coal-measures of carboniferous times from whence is derived our fuel, but a geologically much younger fossil, a mere 180 million years old or so. Jet is in fact thought to have been formed from driftwood which eventually reached the sea-bed and was there covered with layers of silt, which in due course became hardened and compressed into shales in which the jet is found in compact masses.

In England we chiefly connect jet with the town of Whitby in Yorkshire where, on the nearby coast there were, and are, considerable deposits of jet rock in the upper Lias beds. These have been worked since Roman times by tunnelling into the cliffs or neighbouring hills. Whitby became so famed a centre for the trade that material was even imported from the Continent to be fashioned there. Records show that in 1870 there were 1400 jet workers in that small town, and even today a few occupied in the old craft still linger on.

Jet is, or should be, lustrous when polished, and pure black in colour. It is easily worked but also easily scratched and broken. The hardness is from 3 to 4 on Mohs's scale, and the density about 1·35. The exact refractive index is difficult to judge on so opaque a substance, but the refractometer gives a vague reading near 1·65.

Being a form of coal, a splinter of jet will ignite quite readily and burn with a smoky flame and coal-like smell. This, of course, is a pretty crude test to use on carved and polished pieces, but a more refined version can sometimes be employed with virtually no damage, by applying a red-hot needle to some inconspicuous part of the object and noticing the odour produced by the operation. Vulcanite, the sulphur-hardened black form of rubber, can be eliminated by this method, as it emits a strong smell of rubber under the hot needle. Other plastic imitations will each give a characteristic reaction, none of which resembles that supplied by jet. Imitations in black glass or onyx are not nearly so likely to deceive, as they are so much heavier and harder, and colder to the touch.

The Whitby deposits are by no means the only source of jet in the world. There are deposits in Württemberg in Germany, in the Department of Aude in France, in Spain, and in the mountains of Utah in the U.S.A.

The name seems to have come from the Latin term *gagates,* which in turn was derived from the Greek name for a place or river of Asia Minor where the jet was found. The German version, *gagat,* is clearly from the Latin. The modern French word is *jais,* but an earlier style, *iaiet,* was probably the route by which our word became accepted into the English language.

◦◊◦

CHAPTER TWENTY-FIVE

IMITATION, COMPOSITE AND SYNTHETIC GEMSTONES

IMITATION STONES

IMITATION GEMS can be defined as those which are made to resemble natural stones in appearance, but which are quite different from them in their composition and properties. Synthetic gemstones, on the other hand, are man-made stones which have essentially the same composition, crystal structure and properties as those found in nature. While composite stones, as their name suggests, are stones assembled from two or more pieces, which are intended to represent a complete gem.

The ingenuity and cupidity of man ensure that any valuable object or product is, before long, copied or imitated in some way, either to provide the masses with a substitute at a price they can afford (Van Gogh's *Sunflowers* in half a million homes), or for the more sinister purpose of deceiving the jeweller or dealer, and milking him of his money.

For imitating gemstones, glass, in its many forms and colours, is pre-eminently suitable, and even in classical times was extensively used to represent not only the transparent varieties of gems, but translucent and opaque stones also. Thus we learn from that invaluable informant, Pliny, that glass was in his day made to resemble obsidian, jasper, agate (complete with stripes), onyx (in three contrasted layers), and lapis lazuli, as well as sapphire and other transparent gems. Owing to the fragile nature of glass, few of these elaborate fakes have survived, but enough of the artefacts remain to provoke astonishment at the ancient glass-blower's skill. Occasionally and rather amusingly, he would feel the urge to outdo nature and, after a spell of patiently copying the sedate curved banding of an agate, would go berserk and show the world what an agate *could* be like if it were constructed in more bizarre patterns and in brighter colours.

Glass is, in effect, a supercooled liquid, its extreme viscosity allowing it to resemble a solid, and preventing its constituents from crystallising as they would if they had the necessary mobility. All man-made glass is much the same in the manner of its making: the oxides of calcium and the alkali metals, with sometimes the addition of lead, are fused with silica in the form of pure sand, and later cooled under controlled conditions—slowly enough to avoid strains within the glass, but rapidly enough to avoid the risk of crystallisation, which would impair its transparency.

Although there are a number of types of glass, by far the commonest are *crown glass* (otherwise known as window-glass or plate-glass) which consists of silica, potash, soda and lime; and *flint glass,* in which lead takes the place, in varying degree, of the calcium in the crown-glass formula. Crown glass is relatively hard (about $5\frac{1}{2}$ on the scale) and has a refractive index about 1·51 to 1·53, and density 2·4–2·5. It has a very low dispersion and lacks fire. The flint glasses have a refractive index, density and dispersion which rise progressively with the proportion of lead in their composition, but the hardness becomes lower and lower, and they have an increasing tendency to tarnish in the atmosphere. In practice a refractive index of 1·70 is virtually the upper limit for glasses used to imitate gemstones, and 1·50 the lower limit. Since it so happens that *no singly refracting gemstones of any importance have refractive indices between these limits* any jewel showing a single refractive index within this range is automatically suspect.

The hardest type of glass is a *borosilicate crown glass* which has a hardness near 7 and density 2·35, with refractive index 1·50 (all figures given for glass are bound to be approximate). A pale blue version of this has been used a good deal to imitate aquamarine. Glasses can also be made from fused beryl, and these too are rather hard, with refractive index about 1·51 and density 2·45, but there is no particular advantage in a stone having the same *composition* as beryl when its properties are so different. It is worth while in passing to note that any glass made by the fusion of a crystalline mineral will always have a density and refractive index a good deal lower than those of the corresponding crystal. The disorderly arrangement of the atoms in glass naturally takes up more room than the neatly packed atoms of a crystallised solid. The possibility of preparing a glass to match almost any colour is, of course, a great advantage when it comes to imitating gemstones. Colour in glass is least successful perhaps in the reds and blues. Red is most commonly provided by adding selenium, but this is rather a weak colour and is recognisable by an absorption band in the green at about 5550 Å. Red glass coloured by copper is too saturated, and that formed by colloidal gold too costly. Didymium used in some strength can provide quite a fair imitation of ruby, but recognition is easy since the spectrum is very formidably banded. As for blue, an attractive pale blue is furnished by copper, but the most usual sapphire-blue glass is that containing cobalt, which gives a very distinctive colour not seen in nature, showing reddish reflections, and a strong three-band spectrum which is very characteristic.

As against these partial failures the green of emerald can be very well simulated in glass by means of copper compounds or chromium salts, and an added emerald-like appearance is given by contrived inclusions consisting of bubble formations which to the unaided eye resemble the mossy flaws to be seen in most emeralds. Yellow, pink and violet are also well represented in glass, and opaque white and black glasses can be used to stand in for agate and onyx. The common trade name for glass imitation gemstones is 'paste', which is curiously derived from the Italian *pasta* meaning 'dough'. Another term, though one seldom used today, is 'strass', which properly applied only to a special lead glass manufactured by an Austrian, Josef Strass, for the express purpose of imitating diamond. This contained about 50 per cent lead oxide and various other ingredients such as boron and arsenic, designed to add brilliancy and fire. This product had a density about 3·74 and refractive index 1·635.

To give a brilliant effect on imitation diamonds made from a cheaper, harder glass, metal foil is applied to the pavilion facets. Such stones are known as 'chatons', and were not intended to deceive, but to give a strikingly flashy effect in costume and stage jewellery.

To save in cost of production, pastes are commonly moulded into the required shape instead of being faceted by a lapidary. This causes the stone to have an insipid appearance and is one of the points to notice when inspecting a doubtful piece with a lens. The facet edges in a moulded stone are invariably rounded instead of sharp. Improvement in appearance is gained by cutting the crown facets only of a moulded paste on a lap, using tin oxide as the polishing agent. The resulting pieces are described as 'half tin cut', or, if the whole stone is so treated, 'full tin cut'.

In the 'bad old days' the jeweller was accused (with some justification) of brutality in applying the edge of a hard file to any stone which he suspected might be a paste. This practice had the disadvantage of irretrievably damaging what might be an attractive piece of paste jewellery, and also was quite likely to harm some of the softer natural gems such as demantoid or sphene, or even fracture the edges of certain hard but brittle gems such as emerald. In these days we try always to use non-destructive methods, and if there is any need to resort to hardness testing, to take pride in accomplishing this without any apparent harm to the stone.

Let me now suggest some of the ways in which glass imitation gems can be detected. First (under lens examination) if the moulded effect mentioned above is seen, this almost certainly proves the stone to be a paste. Secondly, the inclusion of bubbles, singly or in chains, is a damning feature. Synthetic stones also contain gas bubbles, but on a much smaller scale. Bubbles in glass may be either completely spherical if the glass has cooled in a static condition, or elliptical if there was some flow during cooling. In stretched or spun glasses the bubbles may be elongated into tubes. Thirdly, a search for small fractures on the girdle or facet edges may be rewarding. Bright conchoidal (shell-shaped) fractures are particularly typical of glass, though they are also seen on some natural gemstones. Fourthly, the presence of striae or flow structures are a conclusive sign.

Naturally, during the course of a lens inspection contra-indications may have been noticed, such as doubling of the facet edges or crystal inclusions, or zoned bands of colour, any of which will put paid to any thought of a paste. One has to learn from experience how to distinguish gas bubbles from included crystals which, though usually angular in outline, may sometimes be deceptively rounded in shape. Crossed polaroids provide a useful further test. Pastes are singly refracting, but often show interference colours in polarised light due to strain, and when looking down at the table facet a paste between crossed polars may show a very typical 'interference cross' shaped like a curved x.

On the refractometer, glass will show a single reading, and this will probably be in a region where no natural singly refractive stone has its index, that is between 1·50 and 1·70, as explained above. On a standard refractometer lead glasses show a sharper reading than a stone in white light, whereas on a spinel refractometer they will show a colour-fringe effect due to their higher dispersion. Finally, to an experienced gemmologist a paste usually 'looks wrong', by which is meant that it hasn't *quite* got the colour or the lustre of the stone it represents.

COMPOSITE STONES

Composite or assembled stones most usually consist of two pieces only and are then known as doublets. Though strictly incorrect, this simple and well-understood term is nowadays commonly extended to cover stones constructed from three pieces also. There are several basic ideas behind the construction of doublets. One is to join two separate pieces of a gemstone together to make a more important and valuable-looking stone than could be made from the two used separately. This may have been done occasionally with diamond, but I have never seen it. Another is to construct a doublet in which the crown consists of the stone represented, and thus gives the proper reactions for hardness, refractive index, lustre and so on, while the pavilion is made of some inferior natural stone, or of synthetic material, or even of glass. This is found in most diamond doublets, the crown being of diamond, and the pavilion of synthetic white sapphire, or rock-crystal, etc. A rather special case is that of opal doublets in which a thin slice of precious opal is cemented to a solid base of 'potch' opal or to black onyx. These are legitimately sold as such, and only later when mounted can they be used in an attempt to deceive. But in the commonest doublets of all no part of the assembled stone consists of the gem represented: the aim is merely to provide a paste of the appropriate colour with a protective crown of some hard stone which will enable it to withstand wear and resist a hardness test with the file. The stone chosen to act as the crown was almost invariably an almandine garnet, to slices of which it was found quite easy to fuse glasses of various colours, the composite mass being then suitably faceted. In such doublets it is astonishing how little the thin garnet slice affects the colour of the stone.

In the trade these garnet-topped doublets are very familiar, but none the less a nuisance, as they can easily escape detection, particularly when mixed with genuine rubies or sapphires in, say, a five-stone ring, or in a brooch. Garnet-topped doublets have a long history behind them, as shown in an account written by Camillo in 1502 of the various forgeries practised by Italian jewellers of his time. Besides making exact counterfeits in paste of the true gems they used 'such illusive processes as that of cutting a garnet very thin and backing it with crystal to pass as a ruby'.

Another composite stone of some antiquity is the so-called '*soudé* emerald' (meaning 'soldered' emerald), which in its usual form was composed of quartz at the top and bottom, carefully chosen for its 'natural-looking' flaws, with a slice of emerald green glass between the two. The junction layer would usually be hidden by the setting, but in any case was not so obvious as one would expect. A more convincing '*soudé*' had a beryl crown, which defeated a refractive index test, which in a quartz '*soudé*' is of course a revealing feature.

Forty or fifty years ago doublets were considered rather 'old hat', and had hardly varied in their nature for a generation or more. Since then the tempo has quickened and the nuisance value of the many doublets now made is considerable.

A development tried some twenty years ago was to use synthetic colourless spinel as the crown and base for composite stones of many colours, the required tint being introduced by a thin layer of colouring matter in the plane of the girdle where the crown and pavilion were cemented together. This made it possible to produce a bigger range of colours in these spurious stones than was feasible in synthetic spinel itself. Some of the nastiest recently devised doublets from the gemmologist's point of view have been those representing natural sapphires, in which the crown consists of poor quality greenish-blue Australian sapphire cemented (almost invisibly) to a pavilion of blue synthetic sapphire, giving the impression of a natural sapphire of good quality. The natural inclusions to be seen near the surface of the stone, and even the 'natural' absorption spectrum, seemed sufficient proof to the unwary that the whole stone was genuine. 'Rubies' have been made in the same way—the base of the stone in this case being made from synthetic ruby, the colour of which overpowers the greenish-blue tint of the natural sapphire crown. Some dealers were bamboozled into paying £60 a carat for unmounted parcels of these fakes, which are definitely aimed at deceit.

As another example, pale emeralds have been cut into a faceted stone, sliced at the girdle, and then carefully cemented together again, with the colour enhanced by a layer of green. These, when mounted, present to the observer the appearance of good quality emeralds, with the correct refractive index and birefringence, and typical emerald inclusions which seem to be continuous throughout the stone.

Doublets involving two kinds of synthetic stone have also been evolved to exploit the special qualities and protect the weaknesses of each. For example, a crown of synthetic white spinel has been backed by a pavilion of strontium titanate, the junction being below the girdle. As a result, the softness of the strontium titanate has been protected, but its dispersion has added fire to the spinel. And so it will go on so long as there is profit to be made by dishonesty on one hand and gullibility or carelessness on the other.

Apparently some 'doubleteers' have become so in love with doublet-making, or so convinced that doublets are 'the thing' that stones have been assembled which consist of a synthetic ruby crown cemented to a synthetic ruby base, without any gain in appearance or plausibility.

Suggestions have been made in earlier chapters for detecting diamond and opal doublets, while garnet-topped doublets can almost always be identified even in a setting by noticing under a lens the change in lustre where the edge of the garnet slice abuts on the coloured glass below— the garnet top usually being so thin that it does not reach to the level of the girdle. Placing the stones in a cell of methylene iodide (or even water will serve) and viewing them edgeways, will show up the dark red garnet crown with startling clarity.

But it will be obvious to the reader that where stones have been so elaborately faked as to deceive a jeweller, and even worry an expert, the ordinary member of the public cannot possibly play the detective with any hope of success. His best guarantee is to deal with a reliable jeweller who can, if desired, have any doubtful stone submitted for a laboratory test and written report.

SYNTHETIC GEMSTONES

The term 'synthetic' as descriptive of all man-made gemstones worries some purists and infuriates some of those who spend their days and skills in manufacturing gems. But a dictionary definition fits the case precisely when it states that a synthetic product is one which is 'artificially produced but of like nature with, not a mere substitute for, the natural product'.

It would serve little purpose in a book of this kind to go into details of the many attempts which were made by chemists of the nineteenth century to produce precious gems by laboratory methods. These attempts were a sort of continuation of the alchemist's dream of turning base metal into gold, but with a far greater possibility of success. Success there was on a small scale in producing rubies and emeralds, but the first production in commercial quantity of factory-made gemstones did not get under way until the present century.

The man who accomplished this breakthrough was the French scientist, Auguste Verneuil (1856–1913), whose ingenious method for producing ruby and other gemstones is still very much in use at the present time.

The Verneuil apparatus consisted essentially of an inverted oxy-hydrogen blowpipe, through the immensely hot flame of which finely powdered aluminium oxide containing traces of chromic oxide is systematically fed in small sprinklings. The powder melts as it passes through the flame and forms as droplets on a pipe-clay stem placed in an enclosed chamber below the blowpipe. On this pedestal under careful control of the flame and powder an inverted pear-shaped stalagmite (known when completed as a 'boule') begins to grow, and in the course of less than two hours has become a tapered cylinder of pure synthetic ruby weighing, perhaps, 150 carats.

Stated thus briefly it sounds an easy enough process, but years of research and organisation were needed before a trouble-free operation could be assured. To begin with, the alumina used for the process must be exceptionally pure, and so must the gases used in the furnaces. The gases are manufactured on the premises and the alumina is produced from calcining ammonium alum which has been recrystallised several times. When this is heated at about 1100°C ammonia and sulphur dioxide are driven off and make their escape through tall chimneys. The pure alum is used if colourless corundum is required; for ruby, some 8 per cent of red chromic oxide is placed in the centre of each circular dishful of the white powder, giving the appearance of a series of poached eggs. After calcining, the powder is tumbled to an impalpable powder and portions placed in a hopper at the head of each furnace. At the bottom of the container is a fine sieve through which the powder sifts in small amounts under the influence of taps from a small hammer which is electromagnetically controlled (see Fig. 25 (1)).

There are separate inlets for the hydrogen and oxygen gases. In operation the hydrogen is first turned on and ignited, and then the oxygen admitted in one furnace after the other, welcomed on each occasion by a curious yelping noise. Then the hammers are started, first at about 80 taps per minute, causing a spray of molten droplets of alumina, looking like golden rain, which accumulates as a cone of crystallised corundum on the pedestal below the flame. The melting point of alumina is high (2050°C), and the flame, of course, must be considerably hotter than this. The critical point comes when the operator, who wears dark glasses and can see what is happening in the furnace chambers, adjusts the position and temperature of the flame until at the centre of the cone of deposited alumina a single stem begins to grow and, under control of the powder supply, slowly swells to a diameter of about three quarters of an inch and is then allowed to grow in the form of a cylinder until the requisite size of boule is achieved. It is a strange sight to see this operation in process. There are ranks of robot-like furnaces in the large dimly lit hall, empty except for a few slippered acolytes who silently control the furnaces. Where things are seen to be

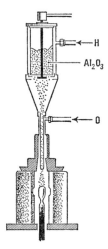

25 (1). Diagram showing principle of Verneuil furnace

going wrong in any furnace the gas supply is switched off, the furnace door opened, and the offending boule yanked from its position with long pincers. Ruby was the first target and the first success; production starting about 1904. After some six years it was found possible to produce blue sapphires by adding iron and titanium to the alumina, and corundums of other colours, yellow, green and purple among them were added to the list.

Before attempting to cut the corundum boules, whether for industry (their major purpose), or as gemstones, it has been found necessary to nip the stem of the boule and give it a slight tap with a hammer, which causes it to split longitudinally into halves. This releases the tensions developed during the very rapid growth and cooling. Enormous quantities of synthetic rubies are needed in industry for the bearings of meters, the 'jewels' of watches, and so on. Every aircraft, for instance, must have thousands of ruby bearings for its instruments. It is found that the crystal orientation must be correct if these bearings are to wear well. To give some idea of the huge growth in the output of these Verneuil synthetics, I can quote Professor W. F. Eppler, who was for many years in technical control of a large production plant. He states that in 1924 world production ran at 160 million carats, or 32 tons. In 1952 this had increased to 550 million carats, and by 1970 even this figure had approximately doubled.

That it should be possible to grow large single crystals at such a rapid rate, and by a process so unlike any in mineral nature, was very astonishing, and for many years it was considered that only corundum would allow itself to be 'brutalised' into crystals in this way. The substance concerned needs to pass very quickly from the molten to the crystalline state. Garnet or beryl or quartz, for instance, would form a glass when fused and quickly cooled. There had, however, been early indications that spinel might be made by this 'flame-fusion' Verneuil technique, and in the mid-twenties production of spinel boules began on a considerable scale. It was found necessary, though, for the boules to grow easily, to alter the ratio of alumina to magnesia to about 3:1, instead of the 1:1 proportions found in the natural mineral. The boules were in fact mixed crystals of spinel and the cubic form of aluminium oxide known as 'gamma' alumina. This meant, amongst other things, that red spinel, the most prized variety, could not be produced, as in the 3:1 mixture chromium produced a green stone, and not a very bright green at that.

The curious situation thus arose that these synthetic spinels (as it is convenient to call them) were, and still are, deliberately manufactured in colours to represent stones of another species, in particular, aquamarine, green tourmaline, diamond, and, more occasionally, sapphire. Traces of cobalt, and sometimes of manganese, resulted in pale, slightly mauvish-blue stones which closely resemble aquamarine in appearance, and these are in very wide circulation. They are readily distinguishable by a reading on the refractometer which is constant at near 1·728, that is, rather higher than the figure for pure natural spinel, and of course far away from the aquamarine value. They also show a characteristic orange-red through the Chelsea filter, where aquamarine appears distinctly green, and display through the spectroscope the three broad bands typical of cobalt. All synthetic spinels, owing to internal strains, show a patchy grid-like pattern between crossed polars, which has been rather happily described as 'tabby extinction'.

The claim to resemble diamond might, on the face of it, seem very far-fetched but, owing to clever promotion, caused quite an unreasonable scare in 1935 when they were being offered for sale as 'Jourado diamonds'. These white spinels have superb transparency, are completely free from colour, and have a dispersion of 0·020 which, though far below the 0·044 of diamond, is just enough to give a hint of fire. They also take an excellent polish. But as brilliants they are entirely unlike diamond, though when cleverly step-cut or fashioned as baguettes or batons they can be quite effective.

It should be mentioned that in 1950 red synthetic spinels were produced commercially, though only as quite small stones. Obviously the $MgO:Al_2O_3$ ratio of 1:1 did not allow large boules to be formed. These stones were easily distinguishable on account of the curved swathes of colour they displayed, and seem to be no longer on the market.

The fact that a man-made stone should be used to represent a gem species other than its own is not, in fact, confined to synthetic spinel, but in doing so they are functioning as *imitations* of the stone represented. By far the most common representation on the market, for instance, of that rare form of chrysoberyl called alexandrite, is not a 'synthetic alexandrite' as it is so often described in the trade, but a synthetic corundum coloured by vanadium, which in daylight is a curious plum colour and by artificial light a purplish-red. Synthetic yellow sapphires, too, are deliberately coloured to resemble topaz, while in others the aim is to resemble garnet, amethyst and even peridot.

The Verneuil synthetic corundums have certain features which betray their origin. In the first place, because of the discontinuous, periodic nature of their growth, they have a delicate layered internal structure revealing itself as a series of parallel slightly curved striae when viewed at the correct angle under a low-power microscope. In synthetic rubies the striae are very closely spaced, and when properly seen with the stone immersed in methylene iodide, or other suitable liquid, resemble the lines on a gramophone record. In blue sapphires these lines also exist, but broader curved swathes of blue alternating with nearly colourless portions are what are more clearly seen, and these are more effectively spotted with the naked eye, or with a pocket lens, over a sheet of white paper, than under the microscope.

The purple 'alexandrite' type tends to show the 'gramophone' lines very clearly, but yellow synthetic sapphires are grown more slowly, and in these the curved striae are seldom visible. Another feature in Verneuil corundums which assists the gemmologist is the frequent presence of small gas bubbles either as 'single spies' or in small groups. Some of these are spherical, others show a highly typical tadpole shape, with a small plump body and tapering and often twisted tail.

Bubbles in a stone (*true* bubbles, not rounded negative crystals) if not enclosed in a liquid-filled cavity, are a sure sign that it is either a glass, a doublet, or some form of synthetic. To the experienced eye the nature and grouping of bubbles is very revealing, and well worth study. Those in glass tend to be rather large and luscious, and frequently show pointed elliptical forms which are never seen, for instance, in Verneuil synthetics. Bubbles in synthetic spinel are sparse and rather thread-like, though sometimes enclosed with liquid in little triangular cavities, or even quite large and displaying the beginnings of negative crystal outlines. These last are sometimes known as 'profiled' bubbles. In a doublet bubbles tend to be flattened and therefore their outer rim is less heavily defined than is the case with a spherical bubble where (on account of the low refractive index of the included gas) the only light transmitted is a small spot in the centre.

The successes of the Verneuil furnace did not stop with corundum and spinel. In 1947 the firm of Linde Air Products in New York found it possible to grow effective star-rubies and star-sapphires by adding a small percentage of titanium (2·5 per cent) to the mixture forming the boule, and then annealing at about 1200°C, when tiny rods of titanium oxide crystallised out in the form of rutile intersecting at angles of 60° in accordance with the symmetry of the host crystal of corundum. The result, when suitably oriented *cabochons* of the stone were cut, was a very spectacular star-effect, much more defined than in a natural stone. Apart from the sharpness of the star, a clue to these synthetics is given by the neatly finished base of the stone, whereas natural stars are left with a lumpy base to retain as much weight as possible.

At about the same time, a modified version of the furnace was used to prepare synthetic rutile. It was found that an outer oxygen envelope to the customary oxy-hydrogen torch was needed to prevent excessive reduction of the TiO_2, while a vibrator in place of the customary 'tapper' gave a constant flow of feed which prevented strain in the crystal and avoided the layered structure typical of corundums made by the Verneuil process. Though the rutile boules are black and opaque when grown in this way there is no appreciable difference in density and crystal structure between these and transparent rutile, and by heating the black boules in a stream of oxygen they gradually change to pale yellow, passing through dark blue, green, and orange-coloured stages. Intense absorption in the violet prevents synthetic rutile from becoming truly colourless, though as a pigment, titanium oxide makes a satisfactory white paint. The blue and orange intermediate stages make very lovely gems when cut, but these colours have never been commercially exploited. The optical properties of this 'Titania' synthetic were outstanding. Refractive indices were 2·61 and 2·90 for the ordinary and extraordinary rays, giving a double refraction of 0·287—a good deal higher, that is, than for calcite. The dispersion even for the lower ray was 0·300, or about seven times that of diamond. And the two together made a brilliant-cut rutile look like something out of this world. But not, except to the purblind, in the least like diamond. To complete the record, the hardness of this rutile was 6, and its density 4·25.

Synthetic rutile was hardly more than a nine days' wonder; it looked so obviously phoney that it could not be thought of in terms of true gemstones. Far otherwise was the next gem product from the Verneuil furnaces, which really did resemble diamond pretty closely. This was strontium titanate, a substance not known in nature, which was first produced in 1953 by the National Lead Company in America. As with rutile, the boules are black when they leave the furnace, but they become virtually colourless when annealed in oxygen.

Strontium titanate has the advantage (so far as representing diamond is concerned) of being cubic in its crystal structure and therefore singly refracting. Its refractive index is almost the same as that of diamond—2·41 for sodium light, and the dispersion about five times higher, at 0·220. This is quite enough to give a degree of fire which to the trained eye puts diamond out of the question, but the plain fact remains that many a diamond dealer has been deceived by these stones, when nothing was said or done to put him on his guard. The great weakness of strontium titanate is its low hardness (about 5½) which means that a needle point can mark it, and any little scratch that appears on this material has a curious and very typical centipede-like structure. As a rule the facets of a cut strontium titanate have rather rounded edges quite unlike the sharp incisive edges of a cut diamond. With loose stones the high specific gravity of strontium titanate (5·13) differentiates it at once from diamond, and that without carrying out a specific gravity test. First, there is the noticeably heavy 'feel' in the hand, and next the evidence of a diamond gauge, with which the estimates of weight are completely haywire when applied to the titanate material.

One of the many troubles a new synthetic brings with it is the spate of fancy names invented by its promoters when 'selling' it to the public.

Thus with strontium titanate we have had 'starilian', 'fabulite' and 'diagem' pushed at us in turn. Fortunately each of these is clearly *not* a name which would be given to a true gemstone.

OTHER METHODS OF CRYSTAL GROWTH

Where the 'flame-fusion' method using the Verneuil blowpipe fails, other and gentler methods of persuading crystals to grow from their molten state have proved surprisingly effective. In the Czochralski or 'pulling' method, a seed crystal of the substance concerned is dipped into a crucible of the molten material and very slowly withdrawn at a controlled rate. Large single crystals of fluorite, scheelite, and crystals of garnet structure unknown in nature have been made by this technique.

The other successful method is known as the Bridgman-Stockbarger technique (what a pity that these scientists don't have shorter names!). In this a crucible containing the molten material is very gradually lowered into a cooler part of the vertical furnace and 'freezes' into a crystal as it goes. These techniques were developed primarily to produce crystals which might act as lasers or be of use for other technological purposes: their use as artificial gemstones has been more or less a by-product.

From the gemmological point of view the most important crystals grown by the 'pulling' method have been rare-earth aluminates or so-called rare-earth 'garnets' in which the only connection with true garnets is that they have the same crystal structure. None of these rare-earth aluminates, in fact, has any counterpart in nature. They are very striking substances, hard, transparent, and with a high, single refractive index, and it is hardly surprising that one of them in particular has been boosted as a diamond substitute.

This is an yttrium aluminate ($Y_3Al_5O_{12}$) which is absolutely colourless when pure. Its hardness is 8 on Mohs's scale, density 4·54, refractive index 1·834, and dispersion 0·028. Its use as an effective diamond substitute has been mentioned (together with other contenders) in Chapter 11. This first became prominent in 1969 and has since been extensively exploited under such names as 'diamonair', 'cirolite', etc.

In reading the cleverly worded advertisements for recent diamond substitutes one has to study the claims made for the product very carefully to realise which particular material is in question. There are several more compounds waiting in the wings which will probably be pushed at the public in due course. Yttrium oxide, for instance, which has hardness $7\frac{1}{2}$, refractive index 1·92, and a dispersion a little higher than diamond at 0·050. Its high density of 4·84, however, will serve to identify an unmounted sample.

GROWTH FROM SOLUTION

So far the methods for making crystals which I have described have been crystallisation direct from the molten solid. But minerals such as quartz and beryl (emerald) can only successfully be grown from solution.

In the case of quartz large clear untwinned crystals have great industrial importance, and for many years synthetic quartz has supplied the needs of the nations. But recently some of the coloured quartzes have been manufactured for gem purposes on a big scale, so that a brief description of the hydrothermal manufacturing process should properly be given in this chapter.

Water is nature's universal solvent. Although at atmospheric temperatures and pressures its solvent action on most minerals is very slight so that the wearing away of rocks by rain is imperceptibly slow, superheated water under pressure is a very vigorous solvent even of robust rocks like granite, and of minerals like quartz.

For growing quartz a strong pressure-chamber known as an 'autoclave' is partially filled with a solution of 1 per cent sodium hydroxide in water, and the raw material in the form of pure crushed quartz crystals is placed in the bottom of the vessel. Carefully oriented slices of quartz acting as seed crystals are suspended from the top of the vessel which is then firmly sealed. The autoclave is then electrically heated from the base under careful thermostatic control. The temperature eventually reaches about 400°C and the saturated solution of silica rises till it reaches the upper regions where the seed plates are hanging. Here the temperature is 40° lower than at the base and the solution becomes supersaturated and crystallises on the seed plates. These are oriented for rapid growth and after about three weeks, crystals some six inches long and two inches thick have formed, having an attractive 'cobbled' top surface which represents the basal plane, not found in natural quartz crystals. Synthetic quartz coloured blue by cobalt, and green and yellow by traces of iron have been reaching the market during the past few years. These seem chiefly to come from Russia.

Modifications of this hydrothermal process have also been used in the preparation of emerald by the firm of Linde in the U.S.A. But the majority of synthetic emeralds have been manufactured by growth of the ingredients of beryl plus some chromium salts from solution in a suitable molten solvent such as lithium molybdate. In the first successful process by Espig and other workers in the giant German dyestuff firm of I. G. Farbenindustrie, growth was achieved by dissolving beryllium and aluminium oxides in lithium molybdate at about 800°C in a platinum crucible: floating on the melt were slabs of silica glass, and below these a platinum sieve on which small seed crystals of emerald rested. The beryllium and aluminium oxide reacted with the silica to form beryl, which with chromium to give it the required emerald-green, crystallised on the seed crystals provided. This was a long process, and the melt had to be replenished at intervals to keep the growth going.

The war intervened to prevent the marketing of these 'Igmeralds', which made an attractive exhibit in the International Exhibition held in Paris in 1937, where the Russian and the German pavilions challenged each other with their grandiose displays.

After the war the San Francisco chemist, Carroll F. Chatham, working virtually single-handed, succeeded in growing clusters of fine emerald crystals from which stones of increasing size began to reach the market and to cause considerable concern to the precious-stone trade, because the criteria they had come to associate with synthetic stones from the Verneuil furnaces were here entirely lacking. Chatham's emeralds had grown slowly *as crystals* under conditions not so very different from those pertaining in nature. Gemmologists, however, who had made a close study of the German 'Igmeralds' found the criteria in Chatham's stones (made by a secret but undoubtedly similar technique) to be closely comparable, and the distinction fairly simple. The density (2·65) was lower than for natural emeralds and exactly matched that of quartz, and the refractive indices and birefringence were also distinctively low (1·561–1·564), the appearance under the Chelsea filter was tremendously red, and the inclusions consisted of twisted veils of liquid droplets unlike any in natural emeralds. Similar criteria held true for emeralds prepared much later (1963) by Gilson in France, which however reached new heights in perfection of colour and freedom from inclusions. By this time the prices demanded for synthetic emeralds of fine quality were quite high—in the £50 per carat range, though still perhaps only one-fifth or one-tenth those asked for natural stones of like quality.

In 1960 came a new and ingenious idea from an Austrian scientist, J. Lechleitner, who succeeded in coating an already faceted beryl of poor colour with a thin layer of emerald which crystallised in continuity with the underlying beryl. The synthetic emerald coating was only a milli-metre or so thick, but of intense enough colour to impart a fair emerald colour to the whole stone. Only the upper facets were lightly polished after this treatment, the lower facets being allowed to retain their original crystalline finish in order not to weaken the colour unduly. This pro-vided the knowledgeable gemmologist and his lens with a ready means of recognition.

In 1964 Lechleitner manufactured completely synthetic emeralds by hydrothermal methods in an autoclave, and in the following year the firm of Linde also produced very beautiful emeralds by hydrothermal means. These have higher densities and refractive indices than the melt-grown stones, though still lower than most natural emeralds. Differences in fluorescence are helpful features, as are curious tapering inclusions with a phenakite crystal at their head, looking like very slender tin-tacks, which are often seen in profusion in the Linde stones. Colourless, squat phenakite crystals are in fact a most frequent feature in all synthetic emeralds, which is really hardly surprising as phenakite is a beryllium silicate, and would tend to form whenever beryllia was in slight excess in the emerald 'bath'. It is a useful consideration that the presence of any other 'foreign' mineral such as calcite, mica or actinolite in an emerald is a sure sign that it is natural.

While variety after variety of synthetic emerald has been entering the market so have natural emeralds from new localities. And as the gem-mologist depends on the differences in properties and the nature of the inclusions in each case, he has been kept exceedingly busy in staying abreast of all the latest developments.

Lastly in this already overlong chapter, I must say a few words on the synthesis of diamond.

To produce this masterpiece of nature in the laboratory was the dream of many a nineteenth-century chemist, and much ingenuity and heroic endeavour was spent in pursuing this aim. Amongst the few who honestly but mistakenly claimed success, and whose success was in fact accepted by many competent observers, were the French chemist Henri Moissan, and the Glasgow scientist, J. B. Hannay. Moissan's method (1896) was to dissolve carbon in molten iron in a carbon crucible, using his newly invented electric furnace for the job, and then to chill the mass suddenly, resulting in a solid iron crust holding the still liquid centre literally in a 'grip of iron', whereafter the carbon crystallised under what was thought to be very great pressure in the form of tiny 'diamonds'. In Hannay's experiments, carried out in 1878–80, mixtures of hydrocarbons were heated with lithium and other metals in partially filled, sealed wrought-iron tubes. Most of these burst in the furnace, but in the residues left in the few tubes which withstood the pressures produced, tiny hard fragments thought at the time (and later proved by stringent methods) to be diamond were found.

Modern knowledge of the extreme conditions of pressure and temperature needed for diamond to crystallise in preference to the stable form of graphite makes it certain that neither of these very able scientists had indeed manufactured diamond. Moissan's particles were probably hard carbides which would scratch sapphire (one of the supposedly infallible tests), while Hannay's diamond particles must have been the remnants of industrial diamond, either introduced by Hannay to act as 'seeds', or else introduced by an assistant without Hannay's knowledge, in the hope that his boss might be satisfied and ease up on these exceedingly dangerous experiments, which were damaging his health.

J. B. Hannay, after a brilliant start to a very unorthodox career, was bitterly disappointed at the refusal to accept his results, and turned peculiar in a religious way. He died in 1931 in a mental home. This means that I could have met and talked with him, which I should greatly have liked to do. The nearest approach I had to Moissan was to talk to Professor Hutton who in his youth had served as his assistant.

So much for history. The citadel of diamond did not in fact fall until more than half-way through the present century. The first announcement was made in February 1955 by a team of scientists working for the General Electric Company in America. They had enjoyed unlimited Government support for the project on account of the enormous strategic importance of industrial diamond in time of war—a supply of which in the case of the U.S.A. had to be imported from overseas. After the G.E.C. announcement the Atomic Energy Authority of Sweden claimed to have made diamond at least a year earlier.

In both cases success must have been largely due to a long series of researches into the production and physics of high pressures, which had been carried out by Professor P. W. Bridgman of Harvard University.

In the G.E.C. process it was found necessary not only to maintain pressures of up to 100,000 atmospheres, and temperatures of 1600°C to 2400°C, but to include some form of metal catalyst as well as the graphite raw material into the compressed capsule to enable the transformation from one form of carbon to the other to proceed at a reasonable speed.

The diamond particles as first produced had a dirty appearance rather like grit removed from an old bicycle chain, and were appreciably magnetic. Crystals viewed under the microscope were malformed and skeletal. But since then both the G.E.C. process and similar plants set up within a few years by De Beers in Johannesburg and Shannon have been so far perfected as to establish control over the shapes of the crystals produced, ranging from cubes at the lowest end of the temperature scale, through dodecahedra, to octahedra at the highest temperatures. This is not merely scientifically interesting but commercially important, as it enables the crystal to be tailor-made for various industrial purposes.

At the present time industrial diamond grit competes in quantity and in price with diamond grits derived from low-quality natural diamonds like those mined in the Congo—a fact which would have seemed quite incredible only thirty years ago.

On 28 May 1970, the General Electric Company in New York announced a further triumph for their technical mastery in diamond synthesis. They had in fact fulfilled the alchemist's dream and produced diamonds of gem quality in a size amply big enough to fit them for use in jewellery. The process involved using 'seed' diamond crystals of only 1/500 carat, together with diamond powder and a metal catalyst or solvent in a press which was capable of maintaining the enormous pressures and temperatures required not for a matter of minutes, but for periods as long as a week. In the course of this time a clear diamond crystal of 1 carat could be produced. To accomplish such a feat was extravagantly costly, and the cost would mount higher and higher if larger crystals were to be made. So far as can be foreseen, therefore, there is no threat to the supremacy of natural gem diamonds, except from the 'diagems', the 'diamonairs', and other small fry that yap continually around their heels.

I hope that my readers have not found this last chapter of the book too technical or too depressing. One can hardly speak other than technically about synthetic stones to any purpose. Unfortunately for the lover of natural gems they are with us to stay, and will inevitably improve and proliferate. I freely admit that these artefacts have their own interest, their own beauty and their own place in life. But alas, so often they don't know their place, and they and imitation gems of all kinds, are great temptations to fraud. Fortunately the science of gemmology has risen to the challenge. More and more jewellers are being trained in the necessary simple scientific skills to cope with most of their problems. News of each new type of synthetic, imitation or doublet is given prominence in the specialist journals which are now published in most industrialised countries. And behind the trade stand the gem-testing laboratories to protect the ancient and honourable profession of the jeweller from disrepute, and the public from being defrauded.

And let it not be thought that efficient gem-testing today must always depend upon sophisticated apparatus. A very important proportion of the work needs only two ingredients for its performance—a good gem-mologist and a 'ten times' lens.

GLOSSARY

———————— ◁◇▷ ————————

ABSORPTION SPECTRUM. A series of dark bands interrupting the continuous spectrum of white light after it has passed through a gemstone or other coloured substance.

AMORPHOUS. Literally, 'without form'. Used to describe non-crystalline substances which have no ordered internal structure and in consequence no characteristic external shape. The glasses and resins are the only truly amorphous solid substances (p. 224).

ÅNGSTROM UNIT. Convenient unit for the measurement of the wavelengths of visible light. 1 Ångstrom = 1 ten-millionth of a metre. See also NANOMETRE, MILLIMICRON.

ASTERISM. The 'starstone' effect. Seen when the sun or other single source of light is reflected from the surface of a *cabochon*-cut gemstone containing suitably oriented needle-like inclusions.

ATOM. The smallest particle of a chemical element, which remains unchanged during all chemical reactions. An atom is pictured as having a small dense nucleus consisting of protons and neutrons, the positive charge on which is neutralised by a surrounding cloud of electrons moving in definite orbits (p. 70).

ATOMIC WEIGHT. The weight of an atom compared with an atom of oxygen = 16·00.

BIAXIAL. Possessing two optic axes, i.e. two directions of single refraction in a doubly refracting crystal. All orthorhombic, monoclinic and triclinic crystals are biaxial.

BIREFRINGENCE. The degree of double refraction shown by a mineral.

BOULE. The usual pear- or carrot-shaped form assumed by a synthetic gemstone made by the Verneuil process (p. 315).

BRILLIANT. The most favoured form for cutting diamond. The standard brilliant has a round girdle, above which are the table and thirty-two other facets, while below are the culet and twenty-four other facets, making fifty-eight in all (p. 53).

CABOCHON. A form of cutting in which the upper surface forms a rounded dome. The base may be flat, convex or concave.

CARAT. The unit of weight for precious stones. The metric carat (now universally accepted) weighs 200 mg. There are 141·75 carats in 1 oz avoirdupois.

CHATOYANCY. The 'cat's-eye' effect. Shown by stones containing a series of fine inclusions parallel to one direction when *cabochon*-cut and viewed by reflected light from the sun or other single light-source.

CHELSEA COLOUR FILTER. A dichromatic filter transmitting only a narrow band of deep red light and another of yellow-green light. Useful for distinguishing between emeralds and other green stones and for detecting the presence of cobalt-blue in synthetic and imitation stones (p. 105).

CLEAVAGE. The tendency of a crystal to break or split along planes which are parallel to actual or possible crystal faces of that mineral, producing flat smooth surfaces. The octahedral cleavage of diamond and fluorspar and the basal cleavage of topaz are well-known examples amongst the gem minerals (p. 110).

COLLIMATOR. A device for producing a narrow beam of parallel light as used in spectroscopy. It consists of a tube, at one end of which is a narrow adjustable slit and at the other a lens, the focal length of which is equal to its distance from the slit.

COMPOSITE STONES. Stones consisting of two or more parts (doublets and triplets) cemented together to represent a stone of far greater value than that of the component parts. Usually constructed with intent to defraud (p. 312).

CRITICAL ANGLE. The largest angle (as measured from the normal to the surfaces of two media in contact) at which a ray of light can pass from the denser to the rarer medium without being totally reflected at the intersurface. The critical angle for light passing from a gemstone into air is smaller the higher the refractive index of the stone. Thus for diamond the critical angle is 24°, while for quartz it is 40°.

CROSSED FILTERS. A simple yet powerful technique for producing and viewing fluorescence in minerals in which the fluorescent glow is at the red end of the spectrum. In a darkened room a strong beam of light is passed through a flat-bottomed spherical flask containing a clear concentrated solution of copper sulphate and concentrated on to the specimen to be examined. Any fluorescent glow produced is viewed through a red gelatine filter through which the blue light from the copper sulphate cannot pass. Any light seen from the specimen must thus be due to fluorescence and, being seen against a black background, is very spectacular. Ruby and red spinel both show a strong red glow: garnets, red tourmaline or red pastes show none. Synthetic emeralds show a strong red glow, natural emeralds from Colombia show a weaker effect, other natural emeralds hardly react. Pink and yellow Brazilian topaz show a red glow, while citrine shows none. Alexandrite chrysoberyl shows a distinct red fluorescence. The effects mentioned are all due to the presence of traces of chromium in the gems concerned (p. 97).

CRYPTOCRYSTALLINE. Consisting of an assemblage of crystals which are too small to be distinguished as individuals. Chalcedony and turquoise are typical cryptocrystalline gemstones.

CRYSTAL. A substance in which the constituent atoms, ions or molecules are arranged in a definite pattern. When the circumstances are favourable this gives rise to a symmetrical external form bounded by flat faces which intersect at definite angles (p. 69).

CRYSTAL AXES. Imaginary lines passing through a crystal and intersecting at its centre. These are usually three in number and are chosen to act as a frame of reference for the position of the crystal faces and their relationship with one another (p. 72).

CRYSTAL SYSTEMS. The seven main symmetry groups into which all crystals can be classified. Their names are cubic, tetragonal, hexagonal, trigonal, orthorhombic, monoclinic and triclinic (p. 72).

DENSITY. The weight of a substance in grams per cubic centimetre. Numerically the same as specific gravity (p. 113).

DICHROISM. The variation in colour when a crystal is viewed in different optical directions. In general, each of the two polarised rays passing through a doubly refracting crystal is differently absorbed and is thus differently coloured. A *dichroscope* enables the colour of each of the rays to be examined side by side (p. 95).

DISPERSION. The difference in the refractive index of rays of different wavelengths (colours) when passing through a stone. The physical basis for the play of colour or fire as seen in diamond. In gemmology, figures for the dispersion of the various gems are taken to represent the difference in the refractive index of the stone for red and violet light as represented by the B (6870 Å) and G (4308 Å) lines of the solar spectrum. The dispersion figures for selected stones, multiplied by 1000, are as follow: rutile, 300; strontium titanate, 200; blende, 156; demantoid, 57; sphene, 51; diamond, 44; zircon, 38; YAG, 28; spinel, 20; corundum, 18; quartz and beryl, 14 (p. 90).

DOUBLE REFRACTION. When a ray of light enters a crystal belonging to any system other than cubic, it is split into two polarised rays vibrating in directions at right angles to each other, which travel at different speeds through the crystal and thus suffer a different degree of refraction. The maximum difference in refractive index of the rays is known as the birefringence or degree of double refraction of the stone and provides a figure which is sufficiently characteristic to be of great value in discriminating between stones of very similar index. In stones such as zircon (0·059); peridot (0·036); and tourmaline (0·020) the effect is large enough to show a 'doubling' of the edges of facets at the back of the stone when viewed through the front with a 10× lens (p. 95).

DOUBLETS. Composite stones consisting of two parts cemented together. One of these usually consists of a natural stone, though not always of the stone represented. Doublets most frequently seen are garnet-topped doublets with a base of coloured glass to represent ruby, sapphire, etc., and opal doublets in which a thin layer of precious opal is cemented to a base of potch opal or black onyx (p. 312).

The term doublet is also used in spectroscopy to describe two similar lines which are very close together, such as the deep red doublet in the absorption and fluorescence spectrum of ruby and the well-known yellow doublet in the emission spectrum of sodium (p. 93).

EXTINCTION. When a doubly refractive stone is rotated between crossed polarisers there are four positions of 'extinction' in a complete revolution of 360° where no light is transmitted through the stone. These positions mark the points (at 90° from each other) where the vibration directions of the polaroids coincide with those of the rays passing through the stone (p. 104).

EXTRAORDINARY RAY. In crystals belonging to the tetragonal, hexagonal and trigonal systems, one of the two rays in which light is divided in passing through the stone has a constant refractive index. This is the ordinary ray. The other varies in index according to its direction in the stone and is thus known as the extraordinary ray.

FIRE. The flashes of spectrum colour seen emerging from the crown facets of a diamond and certain other stones. The effect is due to dispersion (p. 90).

FLUORESCENCE. The visible light emitted by certain stones when exposed to rays of shorter wavelength, such as ultra-violet rays and X-rays (p. 96).

FRACTURE. The characteristic surface shown by a stone or by glass, etc., when it is broken in directions other than cleavage directions. Fibrous gems such as jade may show a splintery fracture, but for most gems, and particularly for glass, a conchoidal or shell-like fracture is the most commonly seen (p. 113).

FRAUNHOFER LINES. Dark absorption lines crossing the bright continuous spectrum of sunlight. Each line represents absorption of light by a particular element in the cooler vapour surrounding the incandescent surface of the sun. The principal lines designated by their discoverer, Fraunhofer, in 1814 have the following wavelengths in Ångstrom units: A, 7606; B, 6870; C, 6563; D, 5893; E, 5270; F, 4861; G, 4308 (p. 92).

FREQUENCY. The reciprocal of the wavelength of electromagnetic rays such as those of light.

GAUGE. In the trade frequent use is made of gauges to assist dealers and jewellers to assess the weight of mounted diamonds, as this has an important part to play in the difficult art of valuation. The simplest and least accurate type of gauges consist of circular holes stamped out of metal or plastic, and suitably marked. The most sophisticated and accurate is the Leveridge gauge, which is a spring-loaded millimetre gauge with specially designed jaws for insertion into open settings, etc. This is issued with elaborate tables for interpreting the measurements of width and depth of a brilliant- or emerald-cut diamond in terms of weight in carats. Differences in the thickness of the girdle are also allowed for.

To a fair approximation the weight of a brilliant-cut diamond is given by the formula $6\ td^2$, where t is the thickness and d the diameter expressed in centimetres.

GRAIN. In Troy weight there are 480 grains to the Troy ounce. This is quite different from the *pearl grain* which is one-quarter of a carat.

HABIT. The characteristic form assumed by a mineral when crystallised under favourable circumstances. This may vary considerably with locality, but is of great assistance in identifying the mineral. Simple examples are *octahedral habit,* diamond and spinel; *cubic habit,* fluorspar and pyrites; *rhombic dodecahedral habit,* garnet.

HARDNESS. Resistance of a mineral to abrasion. Usually referred to Mohs's scale of hardness (p. 107).

HEFT. This useful term, meaning heaviness or weightiness, is English in origin but is now chiefly used in the U.S.A. A zircon, for instance, when balanced in the hand should feel perceptibly heavier than a diamond, topaz heavier than yellow quartz, platinum heavier than white gold, etc. Judgement by heft is a skill worth practising (p. 114).

INCLUSIONS. Particles of other minerals, cavities, or droplets of mother-liquor may usually be found inside a gemstone if this is examined with a lens. The nature of such inclusions provides the most powerful means of distinguishing between natural and synthetic stones and also provides a clue to the locality from which the stone was mined. A few inclusions are not considered a blemish in coloured gems, but visible inclusions considerably downgrade the value of a diamond.

INTERFERENCE OF LIGHT. A beam of light falling upon a thin transparent film is partly reflected from the upper surface, partly from the lower surface and partly transmitted. The light-waves reflected from the lower surface of the film have in general become out of step (out of phase) with those reflected from the upper surface, and tend to 'interfere' with or destroy each other, while those rays which are in phase reinforce one another, giving gleams of pure spectrum colour. Such colours, known as 'interference colours', are seen in opal, labradorite feldspar, mother-of-pearl, etc., as well as in soap bubbles and films of oil on water (p. 98).

ION. An electrically charged atom, radical or molecule. In most crystals the constituent particles are positively and negatively charged ions which are held together by electrostatic forces.

IRIDESCENCE. If you have trouble in spelling this word, think of *iris,* which means a rainbow, and from which the word is derived. Iridescence is, in fact, the play of spectrum colours as seen in some opals, labradorite feldspar, or films of air trapped in incipient cleavage cracks, etc. (p. 98).

ISOMORPHOUS REPLACEMENT. The ions of one element forming part of a crystal can frequently be replaced to a greater or lesser extent by other ions of similar chemical nature and ionic radius without disturbing appreciably the crystal structure of the mineral. Where some 'isomorphous replacement' of this type happens extensively as in the garnets or spinels one gets an isomorphous group or family of minerals in which one subspecies tends to merge into another. The colour and the physical constants give a clue as to the extent of the replacement. Only where there is no such replacement possible, as in diamond and quartz, are the properties of a mineral virtually invariable.

ISOTROPIC. A term meaning the same in all directions. All crystals have a grained structure so that even cubic minerals vary in hardness with direction, exhibit cleavage, etc., and to that extent show directional properties. But they are *optically* isotropic and singly refracting in the same way as glass.

LASER. A convenient abbreviation of 'Light Amplification by Stimulated Emission of Radiation'. A device in which fluorescent light from a substance such as ruby can be stimulated and released in the form of an intensely powerful coherent beam of radiation capable of melting solids and of travelling immense distances without scattering.

LIGHT. A form of electromagnetic radiant energy which gives rise to the sensation of sight. Visible light varies in wavelength between 7000 Ångstroms for red light, and 4000 Å for violet light, merging at one extreme into invisible infra-red heat, and eventually radio-waves, and at the short-wave end into ultra-violet and eventually X-rays. All waves of this kind travel in space at a velocity of 186,285 miles per second (p. 87).

LUMINESCENCE. A general term covering the phenomena of fluorescence and phosphorescence (p. 96).

LUSTRE. The nature of the light reflected from the surface of a stone. In transparent substances those which are hard and have a high refractive index have the highest lustre, tending towards the so-called adamantine lustre typical of diamond. Most gemstones have a refractive index near that of glass and have a vitreous lustre. The terms resinous, waxy, pearly or silky lustre are sufficiently descriptive. In addition to metals such as gold or silver, some sulphide minerals (e.g. pyrites) or oxides (e.g. haematite) have a distinctly metallic lustre (p. 89).

MERCURY SPECTRUM. The emission spectrum of mercury vapour consists of a number of strong lines which make it a useful source of visible and of ultra-violet light. A knowledge of the wavelengths of these lines is useful to the gemmologist in calibrating spectroscopes, etc., and the lines themselves are readily observed through a spectroscope in any strip-lighting system. There are two lines in the red, (6907 Å) and orange (6234 Å), a strong doublet in the yellow at 5790 and 5769 Å, a line in the green (5460 Å), and two in the violet at 4358 and 4046 Å. A powerful line at 3650 Å in the ultra-violet acts as a strong stimulant to fluorescence and is used for this purpose in conjunction with a 'Wood's glass' filter which cuts out most of the visible light. A further line at 2536 Å when used with a suitable filter provides 'short-wave' ultra-violet light.

METAMICT. Certain minerals containing radioactive elements suffer internal bombardment with alpha-particles, and when of sufficient geological age (e.g. pre-Cambrian) may in consequence have lost their original crystal structure. Minerals in such a state are known as metamicts. Amongst gemstones 'low' zircon from Ceylon is the best-known metamict, another example being the newly discovered gem mineral, ekanite (p. 204).

METRIC CARAT. 200 mg—the standard weight for gemstones. See carat.

MICRON. One-thousandth part of a millimetre. Used as a unit for measuring the dimensions of fine diamond grit.

MILLIMICRON. One-thousandth of a micron, or ten Ångstrom units. The modern term for this is a nanometre, which is used as an alternative measure for the wavelength of light.

MINERAL SPECIES. A homogeneous substance produced by the processes of inorganic nature, having a chemical composition, crystal structure, and physical properties which are constant within narrow limits (p. 18).

MOHS'S SCALE. An order of hardness in minerals proposed by Friedrich Mohs 160 years ago and still in everyday use as a rough guide to hardness when this is defined as 'resistance to abrasion'. In order of increasing hardness the chosen standards are as follows: 1 talc, 2 gypsum, 3 calcite, 4 fluorspar, 5 apatite, 6 feldspar, 7 quartz, 8 topaz, 9 corundum and 10 diamond (p. 107).

MOLECULE. The smallest particle of an element or compound which is capable of an independent existence.

MONOCHROMATIC LIGHT. Light of one colour (wavelength) only. The standard monochromatic light used for optical measurements is the yellow light produced by glowing sodium vapour which consists of two lines of nearly identical wavelengths at 5896 and 5890 Å.

NANOMETRE. The now preferred unit for measuring the wavelength of visible light. From the Greek word *nanos,* a dwarf. It is one-millionth of a millimetre, or 10 Ångstrom units.

NICOL PRISM. The classic method for producing pure, colourless polarised light is by passing ordinary light through a calcite prism devised by the Scottish physicist, William Nicol, in which two pieces of clear calcite are cemented together with Canada balsam. Light entering the prism is split into two polarised rays. One of these, the ordinary ray, is totally reflected at the balsam layer, while the extraordinary ray is able to pass through the prism. In a petrological microscope two Nicol prisms were incorporated: one, the polariser, was placed below the stage, while the other, the analyser, was slotted into the body tube of the microscope. The high cost of Nicol prisms has led to the use of Polaroid sheets in their stead in most modern instruments (p. 268).

OPALESCENCE. The white milkiness seen in common opal, chalcedony, moonstone, etc. Some authors also use the term to include the play of colour shown in precious opal, but this is better described by the term iridescence (p. 98).

OPTIC AXIS. A direction of single refraction in a doubly refracting crystal. In hexagonal, trigonal and tetragonal crystals there is one optic axis parallel to the main crystal axis: these are termed uniaxial. Orthorhombic, monoclinic and triclinic crystals have two optic axes and are termed biaxial.

ORDINARY RAY. The ray which, in uniaxial stones, travels with constant velocity in any direction within the crystal. The vibration direction of the ordinary ray is always at right angles to the optic axis.

ORGANIC. Produced by vital processes. In chemistry, compounds of carbon are known as organic compounds, and their study as organic chemistry.

ORIENT. The characteristic lustre of a fine pearl, which includes the sheen due to layers of nacre in addition to slight iridescence caused by interference of light at the closely spaced serrated edges of the overlapping platelets.

PASTE. The common trade name for any glass imitation of a gemstone.

PHOSPHORESCENCE. The persistent luminous glow from a mineral *after* being stimulated by sunlight, ultra-violet light or X-rays. Fluorescence is a similar effect but is seen only while the exciting radiation is in action. Those diamonds which show a strong blue fluorescence under ultra-violet light invariably show a yellow-green phosphorescent afterglow of short duration. The two effects combined form a distinctive test for the mineral (p. 138).

PLASTICS. A useful general term for artificial resins which can be moulded under the influence of heat or pressure. Plastics are widely used for imitating amber, ivory, tortoise-shell, etc.

PLEOCHROISM. An effect whereby a gem or mineral appears differently coloured according to direction. It is due to polarisation, and the two differently coloured rays in a mineral can be seen separately side by side when it is viewed through a dichroscope.

POLARISED LIGHT. Light vibrating in one plane only. Polarised light can be produced by means of reflection from an unsilvered glass plate or a pile of such plates. More convenient is the use of a Nicol prism or a polaroid disc (p. 104).

POLAROID. Trade name of a plastic sheet containing strongly dichroic crystals which totally absorb one ray and transmit the other as completely polarised light. Much used in modern polarising microscopes replacing the expensive and cumbersome Nicol prisms previously necessary (p. 103).

RADIOACTIVITY. Several of the heaviest and most complex elements found amongst earth's minerals are unstable and are in process of 'breaking down' very slowly and in a series of stages. The process is accompanied by the emission of three kinds of radiation known as (a) alpha-particles or alpha-rays, which consist of charged atoms of helium (four times the weight of a hydrogen atom), which have a range of only a few centimetres in air, and less than a millimetre in a solid crystal; (b) beta-rays—high-speed electrons—which are only slightly more penetrating than alpha-particles; and (c) gamma-rays, which are electromagnetic rays of even shorter wavelength than X-rays, and thus even more penetrating. Radium, uranium and thorium are the best-known radioactive elements, and their presence in zircon and in ekanite have given rise to metamict forms of these minerals (p. 204).

RECONSTRUCTED STONES. Early forms of synthetic ruby were said to be reconstructed from small chips of natural ruby fused together under an oxy-hydrogen blowpipe flame. The only truly reconstructed stone at the present time is pressed amber.

REFLECTION. A ray of light meeting the surface of another medium is in part *reflected* at an angle equal to the angle of incidence.

REFRACTION. The change of direction suffered by rays of light when passing from one optical medium to another. On passing from air into a denser medium, rays of light are always refracted to follow a direction closer to the perpendicular between the two media.

REFRACTIVE INDEX. The most important optical constant of a gemstone, representing its refracting power. It can be defined as the ratio of the velocity of light in air to its velocity in the medium concerned, or as the ratio of the sine of the angle of incidence to the sine of the angle of refraction when light passes from air into the medium. Of gemstones in commercial use fluorspar has the lowest refractive index (1·434), and diamond the highest (2·417).

REFRACTOMETER. An instrument by which the refractive indices of gemstones and other substances can be conveniently and accurately measured. A small drop of highly refracting liquid is placed on the table of the refractometer to make optical contact between this and the table facet of the stone to be tested. A shadow edge (or two shadow edges) can be seen through the eyepiece of the instrument crossing a calibrated scale giving a direct reading of the refractive indices required.

SHEEN. The shimmering effect of light reflected not only at the surface but by layers parallel to the surface, as in moonstone or pearl.

SILK. Fine needle-like inclusions in a gemstone which show a silky effect by reflected light.

SPECIFIC GRAVITY. The weight of a substance compared with that of an equal volume of pure water at 4°C. The S.G. of a substance is numerically the same as its density.

SPECTROSCOPE. An instrument which resolves light into its component wavelengths either by refraction through prisms, or by diffraction in passing through a finely spaced grating.

SPECTRUM. A band of light in which the original source has been analysed into an orderly succession of wavelengths or colours.

Light from an incandescent solid produces a continuous spectrum representing an infinite number of contiguous images of the slit of the spectroscope. Light from a glowing vapour produces a line spectrum in which each narrow bright line represents some particular metallic element. The wavelengths of such bright lines are invariable and have been accurately measured and recorded providing a sensitive means of analysis. By means of suitable apparatus the spectra of infra-red and ultra-violet rays can be recorded and measured (p. 91).

STEP-CUT or TRAP-CUT. A style much used for faceting coloured stones in which a series of facets above and below the girdle have edges parallel to those of the rectangular table facet. In the emerald-cut the corners are truncated producing an octagonal outline. A modification of the emerald-cut, in which the angles of the facets are carefully controlled to produce maximum reflection of the light incident on the front of the stone, is used for diamond as an alternative to the brilliant-cut, but in general stones are step-cut to display the colour of the stone rather than its fire (p. 51).

SYMMETRY. In the study and classification of crystals three 'elements of symmetry' are recognised. These are planes of symmetry, axes of symmetry, and a centre of symmetry. On this basis, crystals can be divided into thirty-two classes of symmetry, which in turn can be grouped into seven crystal systems (p. 77).

SYNTHETIC STONES. Man-made stones having essentially the same composition, crystal structure and properties as the natural minerals they represent.

TRANSITION ELEMENTS. A group of eight metals which occupy consecutive places in the periodic classification of the elements, all of which are associated to some extent with the presence of colour in gemstones. Beginning with titanium, atomic number 22, we have vanadium, chromium, manganese, iron, cobalt, nickel and copper. Of these iron is the almost ubiquitous producer of colour in minerals, while chromium is well known as the main cause for the richest reds and greens amongst the gemstones.

TRANSPARENCY. The degree to which light is transmitted by a substance. In the majority of gemstones perfect transparency is of prime importance. But in stones such as cat's-eyes and star-stones, in opal and in jade, translucency is accepted as part and parcel of the special beauty of the stones. A transparent stone is one through which objects can be clearly seen as though through glass. Where a considerable amount of light is transmitted but outlines are blurred the term translucent is used; while where no light can pass the substance is known as opaque. Lapis lazuli and pyrites are examples of opaque stones.

TWIN CRYSTALS. Two crystals which have grown together in symmetrical fashion in such manner that the parts of the twin have some direction or plane in common, but others in reversed position.

ULTRA-VIOLET LIGHT. Light beyond the visible violet in the spectrum of electromagnetic waves. The approximate wavelength range of such rays is 4000–2000 Å. In practice it is conveniently divided into long-wave ultra-violet light typified by the powerful 3650 Å line in the spectrum of mercury vapour, and short-wave ultra-violet light exemplified in the 2537 Å mercury line. Long-wave U.V.L. produces showy fluorescent effects in many gem minerals, but fluorescence under short-wave U.V.L. is usually more diagnostic in distinguishing, for instance, between natural and synthetic rubies and sapphires.

UNIAXIAL. Minerals having one direction only of single refraction, i.e. one optic axis. Crystals belonging to the hexagonal, trigonal and tetragonal systems are uniaxial, the optic axis coinciding with the main axis of symmetry.

X-RAYS. Electromagnetic radiations having the same nature as visible light but of much shorter wavelength of the order of 1 Å, as compared with 5000. X-rays have only a short range but can penetrate matter which is opaque to ordinary light. X-rays are, however, unable to penetrate heavy atoms such as those of the metals. Diffraction of X-rays by crystal structures provides a powerful method for their identification, and X-rays are also an essential tool in the distinction between natural and cultured pearls. In honour of their discoverer, X-rays have often been described as Röntgen rays.

RECOMMENDED READING

———————— ◈ ————————

FOR THOSE who have become sufficiently interested in the subject of gemmology to feel the need of books which deal in detail with all aspects of the subject, there are two works available which can be thoroughly recommended.

Of these, *Gemstones* by Dr. G. F. Herbert Smith, was first published in 1912, and its fourteenth edition, extensively revised by Professor F. C. Phillips, was issued in 1972 by Chapman & Hall at a price of £7.50. There are 580 pages in this work, and it is well illustrated with plates in colour and black and white, and numerous line drawings. *Gemstones* has been recognised as the standard work on the subject for sixty years. It is well written, accurate and reliable, but is somewhat academic in tone and makes rather tough reading for those who have no scientific training.

An even more comprehensive book is *Gems* by Robert Webster, published in London by Butterworth. First published in 1962 in two volumes, a revised, single-volume edition appeared in 1970, followed in 1975 by the third edition, which has been further enlarged to a volume of 931 pages, costing £16. Two much smaller but useful works by Robert Webster are *Practical Gemmology*, representing a fairly elementary course in the subject (4th edition, 1966), and *The Gemmologist's Compendium* (4th edition, 1967) containing an extensive glossary and many tables of constants, etc., both published by the N.A.G. Press.

For those readers who would like to learn the theory and practice of testing gemstones there are two specialist books available, one British and one American: these are *Gem Testing* by B. W. Anderson, which when published in 1942 was the first work of its kind, and which has since been periodically enlarged and revised. The eighth edition was published in 1971 (Butterworth, £7). It contains 384 pages and is well illustrated. It is authentic, being based entirely on the personal experience of the author. The American counterpart to *Gem Testing,* though parallel in subject is surprisingly different in detail. This is the *Handbook of Gem Identification* by Richard T. Liddicoat, and is published by the Gemological Institute of America, Los Angeles. First published in 1946, the ninth edition appeared in 1972, and costs $11.75. Liddicoat is Director of the Gemological Institute of America: his book is well written, well illustrated, and can be thoroughly recommended.

There are growing numbers of hobbyists whose interest lies chiefly in polishing and cutting gem materials. The best books on amateur lapidary work have been published in America where the hobby has a very large following, and is linked with the collecting of gem materials from the many well-known localities in North America. Of several good books on lapidary work *Gem Cutting* by John Sinkankas is probably the soundest. The second edition of this work was published in New York by Van Nostrand Reinhold in 1963 and costs $12.95 (£3.95).

Any of these books can conveniently be obtained through the Gemmological Association of Great Britain, St. Dunstan's House, 2 Carey Lane, London, EC2 8AB. The Association also issues a quarterly *Journal of Gemmology* which enables readers to keep up with current progress in the science, and runs correspondence courses in gemmology in preparation for the Fellowship examination of the Association, successful candidates for which are awarded a Diploma entitling them to become Fellows of the Association. The distinction of becoming an F.G.A. is obtainable only through examination, and is a title coveted by gemmologists throughout the world.

An associated company, Gemmological Instruments Ltd., of the same address, can provide gem-testing instruments of all kinds, as well as specimens for those interested in making a collection. For mineral specimens and lapidary equipment two firms can be recommended: Gregory Bottley & Co., 30 Old Church Street, Chelsea, London SW3 and Gemrocks Ltd., 7 Brunswick Centre, Marchmont Street, London WC1, while Kenneth Parkinson, 11 Fitzroy Street, Hull, Yorkshire, is a reliable supplier of gemstones both rare and common for collectors.

ALPHABETICAL TABLE OF GEMSTONES GIVING THEIR MAIN CONSTANTS

———————— ◇ ————————

THE COMPILATION of a satisfactory table of constants for precious stones is no simple matter. In many cases the figures can vary appreciably according to the colour or the locality of the stone concerned. To indicate these variations would destroy the simplicity and usefulness of the table. For greater detail the text should always be consulted. The figures given here are those most usually met with. In doubly refracting stones the value given for R.I. is the arithmetic mean between the highest and lowest values in the same specimen. The actual figures can thus be obtained by splitting the values given for the double refraction evenly about this mean index. Taking tourmaline as an example, the mean index is 1·63 and the double refraction 0·020; hence the values for upper and lower indices are 1·620 and 1·640. Where the stone is singly refracting the word 'none' is entered in the D.R. column, while in cases where no clear reading of double refraction can be seen because the stone is a jumble of (doubly refracting) crystals, a dash is entered.*

Name	S.G.	Mean R.I.	D.R.	H.
Agate	2·6	1·54	0·004	7
Alexandrite	3·71	1·75	0·009	8½
Almandine	3·9–4·2	1·76–1·81	none	7½
Amazonite	2·56	1·53	0·008	6
Amber	1·08	1·54	none	2½
Amethyst	2·65	1·55	0·009	7
Andalusite	3·15	1·64	0·010	7½
Apatite	3·20	1·64	0·003	5

* S.G. is specific gravity, R.I. refractive index, D.R. double refraction, H. hardness.

Name	S.G.	Mean R.I.	D.R.	H.
Aquamarine	2·69	1·575	0·006	7½
Bakelite	1·26	1·65	none	3
Benitoite	3·67	1·78	0·047	6½
Beryl	2·7	1·58	0·006	7½
Blende	4·09	2·37	none	3½
Brazilianite	2·99	1·615	0·020	5½
Calcite	2·71	1·57	0·172	3
Californite	3·3	1·70	none	5½
Celluloid	1·38	1·49	none	2
Chalcedony	2·61	1·535	0·004	7
Chrysoberyl	3·71	1·75	0·009	8½
Chrysoprase	2·6	1·53	none	7
Conch pearl	2·84	—	—	4
Coral	2·68	—	—	4
Cornelian	2·64	1·53	0·004	7
Crocidolite	2·66	1·54	0·004	7
Danburite	3·00	1·633	0·006	7
Demantoid	3·85	1·89	none	6½
Diamond	3·515	2·418	none	10
Diopside	3·29	1·685	0·029	5
Ekanite	3·28	1·587	none	6
Emerald	2·71	1·58	0·006	7½
Enstatite	3·27	1·67	0·010	5½
Epidote	3·40	1·75	0·035	6½
Euclase	3·10	1·665	0·019	7½
Fibrolite	3·25	1·665	0·020	7½
Fluorspar	3·18	1·434	none	4
Grossular (pure)	3·594	1·734	none	7
Haematite	5·1	3·0	—	6½
Hessonite	3·63	1·745	none	7
Hiddenite	3·18	1·665	0·015	6½
Idocrase	3·40	1·708	0·005	6½
Iolite	2·63	1·548	0·010	7
Jadeite	3·33	1·65	—	7
Jet	1·33	1·66	none	2½
Kornerupine	3·32	1·67	0·013	6½
Kunzite	3·18	1·665	0·015	6½
Kyanite	3·68	1·725	0·017	5–7
Lapis lazuli	2·8	1·50	none	5½

Name	S.G.	Mean R.I.	D.R.	H.
Lithium niobate	4·64	2·25	0·090	5½
Malachite	3·8	1·78	—	4
Moldavite	2·35	1·49	none	5
Moonstone	2·57	1·52	0·005	6
Nephrite	2·96	1·62	—	6
Obsidian	2·35	1·49	none	5
Odontolite	3·1	1·6	—	5
Pearl	2·71	—	—	3
Peridot	3·34	1·67	0·036	6½
Phenakite	2·96	1·66	0·015	7½
Pyrites	4·9	—	none	6
Pyrope	3·7–3·9	1·73–1·76	none	7½
Quartz	2·65	1·55	0·009	7
Rhodochrosite	3·6	1·71	0·220	4
Rhodonite	3·6	1·73	0·014	6
Ruby	3·99	1·765	0·008	9
Rutile	4·25	2·75	0·287	6
Sapphire	3·99	1·765	0·008	9
Scapolite	2·70	1·555	0·020	6
Scheelite	6·1	1·926	0·017	5
Serpentine	2·6	1·56	—	5
Silica glass	2·21	1·46	none	6
Sinhalite	3·48	1·686	0·038	6½
Smithsonite	4·35	1·73	0·230	5½
Spessartine	4·16	1·80	none	7
Sphalerite	4·09	2·37	none	3½
Sphene	3·53	1·95	0·120	5
Spinel	3·60	1·715	none	8
Spodumene	3·18	1·665	0·015	6½
Strontium titanate	5·13	2·41	none	5½
Taaffeite	3·61	1·72	0·004	8
Topaz	3·53	1·63	0·008	8
Tortoise-shell	1·29	1·55	—	3
Tourmaline	3·06	1·63	0·020	7½
Turquoise	2·8	1·62	—	6
Yttrium aluminate	4·57	1·834	none	8
Zircon (high)	4·68	1·95	0·059	7½
Zircon (low)	4·0	1·79	—	6½
Zoisite	3·35	1·695	0·010	6½

NOMENCLATURE FOR GEMSTONES
AND PEARLS

———————— ⟨0⟩ ————————

RECOMMENDED BY the Gemmological Association of Great Britain.

In these rules, where the context permits, the singular includes the plural, and vice versa.

The nomenclature, arranged alphabetically, is not exhaustive and some of the rarer gemstones and gem minerals are not tabulated.

The constants given are typical but do not cover the whole possible range in each case.

Species	*Colours*	*Recommended trade name*

AMBER—Hardness 3–2½. S.G. 1·04–1·10. R.I. 1·539–1·545

AMBER	All colours	Amber, with or without appropriate colour description

ANDALUSITE—Hardness 7–7½. S.G. 3·1–3·2. R.I. 1·63–1·66

ANDALUSITE	Green, red, brown	Andalusite, with or without appropriate colour description

BERYL—Hardness 7½. S.G. 2·67–2·80. R.I. (Double) 1·57–1·58

EMERALD	Bright green[1]	Emerald
AQUAMARINE	Pale blue, pale greenish-blue	Aquamarine
BERYL	White	White beryl or Goshenite
	Green[2]	Green beryl

[1] Colour due to chromium.
[2] Colour not due to chromium.

Species	Colours	Recommended trade name
	Golden, yellow	Golden or yellow beryl
	Pink	Pink beryl, Morganite

CHRYSOBERYL—Hardness 8½. S.G. 3·70–3·74.
  R.I. (Double) 1·74–1·75

CHRYSOBERYL	Yellow, yellowish-green, yellowish-brown, brown	Chrysoberyl
CHATOYANT, CHRYSOBERYL	Translucent yellow to greenish or brownish —showing chatoyancy	Chrysoberyl cat's-eye
ALEXANDRITE	Green to greenish-brown by daylight, red to reddish-brown by artificial (tungsten) light	Alexandrite

CORAL—Hardness 4. S.G. 2·68

CORAL	Red, pink, white, sometimes black	Coral, with or without appropriate colour description

CORUNDUM—Hardness 9. S.G. 3·94–4·01.
  R.I. (Double) 1·76–1·77

RUBY	Red	Ruby
	Red, with star-effect	Star-ruby
SAPPHIRE	Blue	Sapphire
	Blue, grey, etc., with star-effect	Star-sapphire
	All colours other than the above	Yellow sapphire, green s., pink s., mauve s., etc.

DIAMOND—Hardness 10. S.G. 3·52. R.I. (Single) 2·42

DIAMOND	White, yellowish-white, yellow, brown, green, pink, red, mauve, blue, black	Diamond

FELDSPAR—Hardness 6. S.G. 2·55–2·71. R.I. (Double) 1·52–1·53

ORTHOCLASE	White	Adularia
	Yellow	Orthoclase

Species	*Colours*	*Recommended trade name*
MOONSTONE	Whitish with bluish shimmer of light	Moonstone
MICROCLINE, AMAZONITE	Opaque green	Amazonite or Amazon stone
OLIGOCLASE AND ORTHOCLASE *S.G.* 2·66	Whitish-red-brown —flecked with golden particles	Sunstone Aventurine feldspar
LABRADORITE *S.G.* 2·71 *R.I.* 1·55–1·56	Ashen-grey with bluish or reddish or yellowish or green gleams	Labradorite

FLUORITE, FLUORSPAR—Hardness 4. S.G. 3·18. R.I. 1·43

FLUORITE, FLUORSPAR	Green, yellow, red, blue, violet, etc. Banded blue and other colours	Fluorspar, Fluorite, with or without appropriate colour description Fluorspar or Blue John

GARNET—Hardness 7½–6½. S.G. 3·3–4·3. R.I. (Single) 1·7–1·9

GARNET	All colours	Garnet
ALMANDINE *Hard.* 7½ *S.G.* 3·8–4·2 *R.I.* 1·76–1·81	Violet-red	Almandine or almandine garnet
PYROPE *Hard.* 7½–7 *S.G.* 3·6–3·8 *R.I.* 1·74–1·76	Red to crimson Pale violet	Pyrope or pyrope garnet Rhodolite or rhodolite garnet
SPESSARTITE *Hard.* 7 *S.G.* 3·9–4·2 *R.I.* 1·80–1·81	Brownish-red, orange-red	Spessartite or spessartite garnet (or spessartine if preferred)
GROSSULARITE *Hard.* 7 *S.G.* 3·5–3·7 *R.I.* 1·74–1·79	Pale green and other colours (translucent) Orange—yellowish-red, Orange—reddish-brown	Grossularite, grossular garnet or massive grossular garnet Hessonite or hessonite garnet

Species	Colours	Recommended trade name
ANDRADITE *Hard.* 7–6½ *S.G.* 3·85 *R.I.* 1·89	Yellow	Andradite or andradite garnet
	Green, yellowish-green	Andradite or Demantoid or demantoid garnet
	Black	Melanite garnet (*R.I.* 1·8–2·0)
UVAROVITE *Hard.* 7 *S.G.* 3·42–3·5 *R.I.* 1·84	Emerald-green	Uvarovite or uvarovite garnet

IOLITE—Hardness 7½–7. S.G. 2·6. R.I. (Double) 1·54–1·55

IOLITE ⎱ CORDIERITE ⎰	Blue and dingy brown	Iolite or Cordierite

JADE (AMPHIBOLE)—Hardness 6½–6. S.G. 2·9–3·1.
R.I. (Double) 1·61–1·63

NEPHRITE	Green, white, single-coloured and flecked, opaque to translucent	Nephrite

JADE (PYROXENE)—Hardness 7–6½. S.G. 3·2–3·5.
R.I. (Double) 1·66–1·68

JADEITE	Green, whitish with emerald-green flecks, mauve, brown, orange, opaque to translucent	Jadeite, or Jade
CHLORO- MELANITE	Dark green or nearly black, with white flecks, opaque to translucent	Chloromelanite, or Jade

LAPIS LAZULI—Hardness 6–5½. S.G. 2·45–2·95. R.I. 1·5

LAPIS LAZULI	Blue (opaque) often with brassy specks of pyrite; opaque whitish-light blue	Lapis lazuli

MALACHITE—Hardness 5½. S.G. 2·3–2·4. R.I. 1·50

MALACHITE	Green-veined, banded	Malachite

Species	*Colours*	*Recommended trade name*

MARCASITE—See PYRITE

OPAL—Hardness 6½–5. S.G. 2·0–2·1. R.I. (Single) 1·44–1·46

OPAL	Milky with quickly shimmering rainbow-like play of colours	Opal or white opal
	The same on dark background	Opal or black opal
	Transparent straw-coloured or colour-less, iridescent	Opal or water opal
FIRE OPAL	Fiery red to browny-red	Opal or fire opal
MATRIX OPAL	Flecks of opal in matrix	Opal matrix

PEARL—Hardness 3½. S.G. 2·71

PEARL	All colours	Pearl, with or without appropriate colour description

PEARL (CONCH)—Hardness 3½. S.G. 2·84

CONCH PEARL	Pink, white (no pearly lustre)	Conch pearl, with or without appropriate colour description

PERIDOT, OLIVINE—Hardness 7–6½. S.G. 3·3–3·4.
R.I. (Double) 1·65–1·69

OLIVINE	Yellowish-green, olive-green, brown	Peridot

PYRITE AND MARCASITE—Hardness 6½–6. S.G. 4·9–5·1

PYRITE, MARCASITE	Brassy-grey with metallic sheen	Pyrite or Marcasite

QUARTZ—Hardness 7. S.G. 2·65. R.I. (Double) 1·54–1·55

ROCK-CRYSTAL	Colourless	Quartz or rock crystal
AMETHYST (*natural colour*)	Light to dark violet	Amethyst

Species	Colours	Recommended trade name
AMETHYST (*heat-treated*)	Yellowish, brownish-yellow	Citrine or golden or yellow quartz
	Reddish, reddish-brown, reddish-yellow	Quartz with or without appropriate colour description
	Green	Green quartz
CITRINE	Yellow, brownish-yellow	Citrine or golden or yellow quartz
SMOKY QUARTZ	Smoky or brownish-yellow to black— when brownish-yellow to brown or smoky brown	Smoky quartz Cairngorm, or brown quartz
ROSE-QUARTZ	Milky rose-pink	Rose-quartz

QUARTZ (with inclusions)

PRASE	Leek-green	Prase
CHATOYANT QUARTZ	Whitish-grey, greyish-green, greenish-yellow, blue, with shimmering streaks of light	Quartz cat's-eye
CROCIDOLITE (pseudo-morph)	Yellowish-brown, brownish-golden yellow with shimmering streaks of light	Tiger's-eye
CROCIDOLITE (pseudo-morph)	Like tiger's-eye but greyish-blue	Falcon's-eye
AVENTURINE QUARTZ	Yellowish-browny-red, yellow, brown, red, or green, with small flakes of mica	Aventurine quartz

QUARTZ (Cryptocrystalline) CHALCEDONY GROUP

CHALCEDONY (*translucent*)	Grey to bluish	Chalcedony
CHRYSOPRASE	Apple-green and light green	Chrysoprase

Species	*Colours*	*Recommended trade name*
CORNELIAN	Red in various shades	Cornelian
HELIOTROPE	Dark green with red spots	Bloodstone Heliotrope
JASPER	Whitish, yellow, red, green, brown, etc.	Jasper
PLASMA	Leek-green	Plasma
AGATE	Banded in various	Agate, onyx,
Hard. 7	colours, white, yellow,	sardonyx, etc., as
S.G. 2·59–2·67	grey, red, brown,	appropriate
R.I. 1·53–1·54	blue, black, etc.	
	Milky with green or rust-coloured moss-like inclusions	Moss-agate

SERPENTINE—Hardness 2½–5. S.G. 2·5–2·7. R.I. 1·57

SERPENTINE	Translucent green	Bowenite
	Emerald-green with black spots	Williamsite
	Green, grey-green, whitish and reddish-brown rock	Serpentine

SPHENE—Hardness 5–5½. S.G. 3·45–3·56. R.I. 1·8–2·05

SPHENE	Yellow, green, brown and grey	Sphene, with or without appropriate colour description

SPINEL—Hardness 8. S.G. 3·58–3·65. R.I. (Single) 1·72

SPINEL	All colours	Spinel; or red s., pink s., orange s., etc., respectively

SPODUMENE—Hardness 7–6½. S.G. 3·18.
R.I. (Double) 1·65–1·68

SPODUMENE	Yellowish-green, brownish-green, pale yellow	Spodumene
HIDDENITE	Bright green[1]	Hiddenite

[1] Colour due to chromium.

Species	*Colours*	*Recommended trade name*
KUNZITE	Rose-pink, lilac, violet	Kunzite

TOPAZ—Hardness 8. S.G. 3·50–3·56. R.I. (Double) 1·61–1·63

TOPAZ	All colours	Topaz; or white t., pink t., blue t., etc., respectively

TOURMALINE—Hardness 7½–7. S.G. 3·0–3·20.
   R.I. (Double) 1·62–1·64

TOURMALINE	All colours	Tourmaline; or red t., green t., particoloured t., etc., respectively

TURQUOISE—Hardness 6–5. S.G. 2·6–2·9.
   R.I. (Double) 1·60–1·65

TURQUOISE	Sky-blue, blue, bluish-green, greenish	Turquoise
TURQUOISE MATRIX	Flecks of turquoise in matrix	Turquoise matrix

ZIRCON—Hardness 7½. S.G. 3·90–4·70. R.I. (Double) 1·79–1·99

ZIRCON	All colours	Zircon; or blue z., red z., etc., respectively

USEFUL CONVERSION FACTORS

Centimetre — 0·394 inch
Foot   — 0·305 metre
Gram   — 0·353 ounce*
Inch   — 2·54 centimetres
Kilogram   — 2·205 pounds
Kilometre   — 0·621 mile
Litre   — 0·264 gallon
Metre   — 1·094 yards
Mile   — 1·609 kilometres
*Ounce   — 28·35 grams
*Pound   — 0·454 kilograms
Yard   — 0·914 metre

* Avoirdupois

INDEX

———— ◊ ————

The Glossary and two Tables on pages 328, 343 and 346 should be referred to separately

355